MANAGING QUALITY FADS

MANAGING QUALITY FADS

How American Business Learned
to Play the Quality Game

ROBERT E. COLE

ASQ

New York   Oxford
Oxford University Press
1999

Oxford University Press

Oxford   New York
Athens   Auckland   Bangkok   Bogotá   Buenos Aires   Calcutta
Cape Town   Chennai   Dar es Salaam   Delhi   Florence   Hong Kong   Istanbul
Karachi   Kuala Lumpur   Madrid   Melbourne   Mexico City   Mumbai
Nairobi   Paris   São Paulo   Singapore   Taipei   Tokyo   Toronto   Warsaw

and associated companies in
Berlin   Ibadan

Published by Oxford University Press, Inc.
198 Madison Avenue, New York, New York 10016

Library of Congress Cataloging-in-Publication Data
Cole, Robert E.
Managing quality fads : how American business learned to
play the quality game / Robert E. Cole.
    p.   cm.
Includes bibliographical references and index.
ISBN 0-19-512260-7
1. Quality circles.   2. Quality circles—United States—History.
3. Industrial management—United States—History.   4. Industrial
management—Japan—History.   I. Title.
HD66.C539   1998
658.5'62—dc21   98-5439

9 8 7 6 5 4 3 2 1

Printed in the United States of America
on acid-free paper

To Max Isaiah Cole,
Q is for Quality

The edges of everything are interesting.
—Ingrid L. Cole

Preface

The data for most books and the ideas that inform them are collected long before keyboards are exercised. When I began studying quality circles at Toyota Motor Co. in the late 1970s, I had no idea that this effort would culminate in a book about the American quality movement, which didn't even exist at the time. Fortune gave me a remarkable opportunity to be a firsthand witness to a remarkable upheaval in American industry as American manufacturing firms sought to cope with the Japanese quality challenge of the 1980s.

Even with my then modest knowledge of Japanese practices, I found myself in much demand by industry, and eventually that led to my work as a quality consultant to top management for two *Fortune* 500 companies. As an academic, these experiences gave me an extraordinary opportunity to witness managers groping toward the development of new ways of thinking about quality and quality performance. For someone whose scholarly life had been exclusively oriented toward writing for an academic audience, it was a remarkable experience. While I had earlier studied workers, suddenly I now also was traveling in management circles and felt like a voyeur or a fraud who would soon be found out. Notwithstanding, access to data is a critical starting point for researchers, and cumulative experiences of this nature gave me an entrée to observe behavior and collect data as a participant in the quality movement in ways that few scholars could match. This opportunity, however, also imposes the heavy burden of needing to make good use of these opportunities and experiences. My goal in this book is to convey to the reader the richness of the events I witnessed.

Consistent with this background, I am indebted to an unusually large number of individuals and organizations who made this research possible. I have tried to acknowledge as many of these as possible throughout the book. Beyond those who are acknowledged, there are the many managers and workers at Japanese auto companies I have talked with over the last 20 years, the managers from a white goods firm in Italy and auto companies in Sweden with whom I worked, and the thousands of American managers, organizational leaders, and consultants with whom I exchanged ideas.

The inspiration and time to actually sit down and write this book came with an invitation to spend a year at the Center for Advanced Studies in the Behavioral Sciences in Stanford, California, in 1995–1996. The center provided a most supportive environment, and numerous other fellows provided help with my efforts to integrate my real-world observations with social science theory. The book was finished despite Robert Scott's exhortations for "one more volleyball game." The center fellowship was made possible by the National Science Foundation Grant # SES-9022192. After I left the center, my research was sponsored by the Air Force Office of Scientific Research, Air Force Systems Command, USAF, under AFOSR Grant # F49620-95-I-0042. Gene Ulansky, a long-term friend, advisor, and would-be pitcher, provided excellent editorial advice.

Among those scholars to whom I am most indebted, I want to thank William Barnett, Sara Beckman, Glenn Carroll, Neil Fligstein, David Levine, David Mowery, John Myers, W. Richard Scott, David Stark, and Eleanor Westney. They provided comments on the working paper or selected chapters that eventually led to this book. Unfortunately, they are not responsible for the use I have made of their comments.

Writing a book is both an exhilarating and painful experience. Sure glad it's done, and so is my wife, Ingrid.

Berkeley, California   R. E. C.
June 1998

Contents

Tables and Figures

Tables

Figures

MANAGING QUALITY FADS

Introduction

The book deals with organizational learning in the context of the development of the American quality movement of the 1980s and 1990s. Paradoxically, this was also a period in which quality fads flourished. One of the major aims of this book will be to show, by studying the movement during these years, the conditions under which fads and organizational learning are compatible. The strong pejorative connotations associated with fads (and imitation) in American popular life are often quite misleading and indeed harmful to corporate competitive performance. To understand how this could be true, I begin with a brief historical perspective on our subject matter.

A new quality model developed in Japan in the period from 1955 to 1980. It arose out of a sense of crisis provoked by the devastation of World War II. Desperate to rebuild their nation's economy and restore its living standards, Japanese business leaders—especially former suppliers to the military, who were now forced to turn to civilian markets—saw the need to rebuild their manufacturing capability. They considered this a major requirement for their own as well as their national survival. In pursuing this goal, restoration and improvement of quality were major considerations, particularly in telecommunications. After Japan's defeat, many top executives were replaced. Their successors, as well as the chastened survivors, were very disposed to reexamine the premises of their prewar management practices (Nonaka, 1995: 548). They believed it was imperative that they make Japanese goods more competitive on world markets, which entailed removing the image of Japanese goods as cheap and shoddy. As Japan entered its domestic consumer revolution of the 1960s, the appeal of and commitment to quality as a competitive weapon intensified. Japanese firms that vigorously pursued the quality vision were extraordinarily successful. Not only did they eliminate poor quality as a disadvantage in international markets but they turned high quality into a strong competitive weapon. Eventually they found that consumers—particularly Americans, it would seem—were willing to pay a premium for quality goods.[1]

3

The question posed in this book is how did American manufacturing firms respond to this new competitive reality. Were American managers motivated to adopt that new quality model? The answer is more complicated than it appears. Was there a comparable sense of crisis that jolted management out of its traditional behavior? When did firms make these decisions? Did the timing vary by industry? Moreover, once firms made the decision to adopt, how did management go about choosing the right strategies and tactics for implementation? Where did they get good information? How did decisions get made, who made them, and when did they get made? Above all, what institutional arrangements shaped, mediated, and channeled those changes (cf. DiMaggio and Powell, 1991: 2)? What were the results of these efforts? In seeking to answer these basic questions, I expect to shed light on the phenomenon of organizational learning.

The Quality Challenge

The pressures to find a competitive response to the Japanese intensified across a broad array of large and medium-size American manufacturing firms from air-conditioning to autos, from consumer electronics to computers, from copiers to color TVs, from steel to semiconductor equipment, and from metal fabrication to machine tools (e.g., Dertouzos, Lester, and Solow, 1989). In almost all these cases, we can document a major quality gap between U.S. and Japanese companies (e.g., for sheet steel, see American Iron and Steel Institute, 1985: 57; for copiers, see Kearns and Nadler, 1992; for automobiles, see Abernathy, 1982; for semiconductors, see Okimoto, Sugano, and Weinstein, 1984: 51–62 and United States General Accounting [GAO] Office, 1992: 10, for color TVs, see Magaziner and Reich, 1982: 175–177 and Juran, 1978: 10–18; and for air conditioners, see Garvin, 1983). Typically, quality was not the only performance gap. Gradually American management came to recognize, however, that quality was a component of their performance deficit important enough to merit strong attention and response.

Common sense tells us, and evidence supports the proposition, that the adoption of the new quality model was closely linked with international competitive conditions. Lawler, Mohrman, and Ledford found in an early 1990s survey that companies facing foreign competition cover more employees with their total quality programs and use most of seven measured total quality management (TQM) practices with more of their employees (Lawler et al., 1992: 99). Some of these differences show up clearly in industry comparisons, where Lawler and associates found that firms in electronics, chemicals, and autos show the highest rate of adoption of seven measured TQM practices while utilities, transportation, and life insurance companies score among the lowest. Although the categories used in the survey do not cover the full range of quality activities, the data nevertheless suggest that internationally competitive situations stimulated TQM adoption.

However, domestic developments also pushed quality to the forefront across a broad range of industries. The rising tide of consumerism from the 1960s onward had left its mark in more numerous and costly product recalls and a growing flood of product liability suits. Companies became increasingly aware of the costs of poor quality. Between 1974 and 1981, product liability suits filed in federal district courts increased at an annual average rate of 28% (Garvin: 1988: 22–23).

A broader sweep of history suggests that the growing levels of education and affluence of the American public in the post–World War II period led consumers to be more critical and demanding regarding product and service quality. Strong cross-sectional evidence (suggestive but not conclusive) supports this proposition (American Society for Quality Control, 1988). People with higher education and income are more likely to say that they purchased items of exceptionally poor quality, to complain about inferior products, to see foreign products as superior in quality to U.S. products, and to be willing to pay more for high quality products.

Response to the Quality Challenge

All this appears quite consistent with the economists' efficiency models. The ability of the firm to generate profits, and indeed the survival of the firm in some cases, is challenged by shifting customer preferences, and firms respond defensively (eliminate the quality gap) to minimize or remove the competitive or legal/regulatory threat. Yet, in fact, relative to market pressures alone, the process by which firms came to acknowledge and act on the quality threat was quite slow; when executives faced evidence, their initial inclination was denial. Even when denial was no longer possible, confusion and ignorance reigned.

For those firms and industries facing the strongest pressures as a result of their inferior quality performance, the interesting question is why did adoption seem to take so long? Why did U.S. managers not quickly perceive the growing quality advantage of the Japanese, and why did they not rapidly move to erase the Japanese advantage? Why, after a decade and a half of exposure to the idea that a large deficit in quality is a key competitive factor, were most American manufacturing firms still struggling to improve quality? Even where enormous progress has been made such as in the automotive and semiconductor industries, why did that progress seem to take so long, and why are there still some gaps even today (see Rechtin, 1994: 8, 52)?

In the early 1980s, across a range of industries, a paralysis often gripped American firms as they sought to understand the new competitive forces. They did not understand the magnitude of the quality challenge; managers often dismissed the quality movement as just another fad or a Japanese public relations effort. They chose traditional solutions for their salvation: cost cutting, moving upscale to higher value-added products, and technological leapfrogging of the competition. Even as they came to acknowledge the seriousness of the quality challenge, they simply did not know what path to take—their own expertise lying in other areas—and often struck out in misguided directions. They searched for quick fixes destined to fail (cf. Juran, 1985: 18).

From a rational-actor perspective, it is hard to make sense of these events. Rapid imitation of the Japanese quality approaches would have stemmed market share losses, and hence profit losses, across a broad range of industries. That did not happen, and in the process hundred of thousands of jobs were lost and wealth transferred overseas. Firms, technologies (a great deal of the Dynamic Random Access Memory [DRAM] devices market), and even whole industries (color TV, videocassette recorders) were lost to the Japanese. To be sure, quality performance was hardly the only factor in the demise of these industries, firms, and jobs; uncompetitive costs, lack of capital investment in new process technology, adversarial relationships with too many suppliers, failure to ensure timely delivery of product, and slow product development, among others, were also critical.

Nevertheless, quality was a factor often interwoven with these others. For example, the successful Japanese assault on the market for the 64K RAM chip in the early 1980s resulted from a choice to "scale up" existing technology rather than adopt the more radical innovative design approach taken by many American firms. The Americans could not mass produce their new design in a timely fashion, and their product had serious reliability problems (Bylinsky, 1981b: 55).

The Japanese approach of continuous improvement of existing design, wherever possible, notable in the auto industry as well, contributes significantly to quality performance (Stalk and Hout, 1990). The Americans, with a strong tendency to push the technological frontier, often fail to use the less advanced processes and products that can be mass-produced reliably. The Japanese, by investing in volume production using more reliable technology, rose to dominance in the robotics industry, ironically, an industry pioneered by the Americans.

Why should we regard the 10–15 years to at least partially absorb the new Japanese quality model as excessively long? After all, from an historical perspective, this is a relatively short time. I argue that it was long from a rational-actor perspective precisely because of the loss of jobs, market share, and profits just mentioned. The slowness to emulate the Japanese did have real competitive consequences, which could have been mitigated by quick action.

Why believe that managers and firms could have adopted more effective quality improvement practices quicker? In every industry, some firms moved faster than others in recognizing the challenge and responding effectively to it. Motorola and Ford, for example, moved faster than their industry peers. But even their officials acknowledged that they missed many early signs.

To any claim that market forces were not strong enough to force a strong response, I answer: look at the loss of jobs, markets, and profits. From a market perspective managements' response was slow, but from an institutional perspective it was not slow at all. I will show that a variety of institutional factors that slowed managements' response were working against market forces. Following March (1991), one could even argue that learning more slowly through painful exploration practices can be more efficient in the end, at least for those who survive.

Rational Actors, Markets, and Learning

Why were firms not more adaptive? This question rests on the assumption that economic outcomes can be explained as a result of rational actors—in our case, managers, workers, and firms—making error-free choices that maximize their utility, given the constraints they face (cf. Nelson, 1994: 110). Certainly, as we shall see, a major problem for U.S. managers in adopting the new quality model was incomplete information, but neoclassical theory recognizes this constraint.

Yet other systematic errors flowed from "belief perseverance" in the face of contrary evidence, failure to respond to cognitive challenges, framing the problem in ways that inhibited learning, lack of management norms legitimating learning directly from the Japanese, errors of judgment in crises that led to intensification of existing approaches, and the confusion of distinctive and visible Japanese quality practices with invisible, critically important ones. These responses, in turn, were often mixed with heavy doses of hubris and arrogance reflecting American managers' incredulity about the new information on Japanese quality superiority.

I argue that requisite information for identifying the problem and solving it were available to the actors if they had only pursued "obvious" avenues of search and understanding. Of course, some rational choice advocates would argue that if managers did not perceive the obvious choices, then they were not so obvious. To argue in this fashion, however, runs the risk of tautology, which indeed, is a problem with some of the literature on rational choice. One can build more and more "ignorance" into the actor, thereby ensuring that, whatever the circumstances, he or she was acting rationally (cf. Tetlock, 1991: 26, 44). This logic however does not allow one to refute the hypothesis that actors behave rationally; yet refutability is the essence of science. Of course, it will always be easier in retrospect to identify courses of action managers should have taken; it is quite another thing to show that decision makers could, or should have been, or were aware of these courses of action at the time (cf. March, 1978).

Rational choice theory does not do well in situations where actors have little applicable experience and where there is a great deal of trial-and-error learning (Nelson, 1994: 11). Neoclassical economic theory would predict that efficient markets would price and allocate resources to rapidly eliminate the quality performance gap; barring that, efficient markets would eliminate slow-moving firms. Yet the former seems not to have happened and there are many exceptions to the latter effects as well. The fallback response to these observations is to take an evolutionary perspective: actors will learn to make correct decisions and learning plus competitive selection will eliminate inefficient firms.

Yet, as Tversky and Kahneman (1990) and Tetlock (1991: 35–36) point out, learning does not occur by magic. Effective learning occurs only under certain conditions. It requires accurate and immediate feedback about the relation between the existing situation and the appropriate response. Feedback is particularly necessary when we are interested in learning, which involves matching up means and end relationships in more efficient or effective ways. Managers often lack this kind of feedback because:

- outcomes are commonly delayed and not easily attributable to a particular action;
- variability in the environment degrades the reliability of the feedback;
- there is often no information about what the outcome would have been if another decision had been taken; and
- important decisions are often unique and therefore provide little opportunity for learning.

Tversky and Kahneman make this argument for individual learning, but they point out that the conditions are hardly better for organizational learning. In short, proponents of this learning view must be able to demonstrate that the conditions for effective learning are satisfied (Tversky and Kahneman, 1990: 85).

If all this is true for managers in general, it was true in extremis for learning about how to improve quality in the early 1980s. Initially, because the conditions for effective learning about the new quality model were not met, much time elapsed before an effective response to the Japanese quality challenge could be mounted. Applying Tversky and Kahneman's analysis to experience with the new quality model leads us to the following observations.

1. A consistent refrain among promoters of the new quality model is that it would take from 3 to 5 years before significant corporatewide results would appear. Dr. Deming stressed management's need for "constancy of purpose" precisely to deal with this problem. In short, there was an enormous delay in feedback time at the level of firm or even factory performance. As a result of the long time period, there was ample opportunity to attribute results (positive or negative) to a variety of other changes that coincided with adoption of quality practices. As Tversky and Kahneman suggest, this made effective learning very difficult. Without being able to show clear results attached to specific initiatives, management was reluctant to move forward. Only gradually were practices developed and institutional arrangements made to solve these problems.

2. Industry-and firm-level conditions in which the initial experiments with quality improvement in American firms were undertaken varied enormously. This compounded the problem of learning from individual experiences and applying that information more broadly. If an event happens infrequently under similar conditions, one cannot reliably predict the on-average performance. So the probability of misjudging results and making inappropriate policy responses sharply increases.

3. Consistent with Tversky's analysis, there was very little information about the potential outcome if firms either had taken a different approach to quality improvement or had bet on another set of competitive strategies. Selection is a stochastic process, and the winnowing out process involves large numbers of firms

and winning and losing strategies are not readily apparent (Carroll and Harrison, 1994: 746). Thus, as we shall see, firms hedged by adopting a broad range of alternative policies in their initial attempts to respond to the Japanese quality challenge.

4. Because of the discontinuity between knowledge required for the old and new quality model and the exogenous nature of the quality challenge, there was little evolutionary learning that prepared management for responding to the competitive quality challenge that burst on the scene in the early 1980s. That is to say, the quality challenge appeared to U.S. companies, for all practical purposes, as a one-time, never-before-seen event.

Furthermore, managers were also uncertain about what "quality" was (the goal) and about how efficient particular technologies (quality improvement methodologies) were in reaching those goals. Yet the rational actor model assumes the certainty of goals and the means to achieve them (March, 1978). As Philip Tetlock (1991: 26) puts it, "[I]t [the model] fails to address how decision makers cope with the causal ambiguity inherent in the complex historical flow of events." Abundant learning precedes effective responses. I am not talking about a simple additive learning process in which managers had only to acknowledge that more quality was better than less quality. Rather, we will see that the new model of quality challenged management's cognitive assumptions. It claimed black was white! Moreover, beyond the cognitive barriers, one had to actually figure out how to put the new model into operation. Indeed, sometimes the new practices preceded rather than followed the shift in cognitive understanding.

Joseph Juran (1995: 586), the noted student of the American quality movement, reports approvingly those observers who concluded that the basic lessons of the 1980s was that firms learned what *not* to do. Hyperbole aside, the point is that there was tremendous trial-and-error learning. It involved complex feedback processes wherein firms first pursued a limited number of avenues, learning often through painful experiences which avenues to pursue further, which directions needed to be abandoned, and which new directions were possible. There were many detours and dead ends. Some courses of action were "right" only when accompanied by some other course of action or in particular sequences.

For example, many companies invested heavily in problem-solving training for production employees only to discover that those new-found skills quickly atrophied without immediate enactment opportunities. As a consequence, in many cases, the initial large investments were lost and indeed became a negative factor, as the failure to follow up made workers more cynical. Some of the automobile companies, as well as other industries, faced this problem in the early 1980s (Juran, 1995: 585).

Not surprisingly, then, this is a book ultimately about organizational learning. It is also a book about performance on the competitive dimensions of quality. One should not equate learning and performance. I argue that we can obtain a deep understanding of the actual events and outcomes only when we weave institutional factors into the evolution of market forces. It is not that neoclassical theory is wrong or that market pressures are ineffective. Rather, an adequate explanation requires a melding of market forces and institutional factors. Following Williamson (1985), one can see the collective actions that emerged to facilitate the adoption of the new quality model as an efficient solution to problems of organizations in a competitive environment. Williamson shows organizations can approach—but not necessarily achieve—rationality by adopting organizational devices that deal with uncertainty (Stinchcombe, 1990: 2). At the same time, however, a variety of other institutional forces impeded the adoption of the new quality model. To be sure, the facilitating institutional forces eventually overcame, at least partially, those impediments. The delay, however, was real and had real economic consequences in the form of lost jobs, technologies, and industries.

The starting point of American management in the late 1970s dramatically affected the choices of both strategies and tactics for confronting the Japanese challenge in quality. The learning process of management was therefore path-dependent. The norms, values, beliefs, and prevailing practices (e.g., reward systems) that pervaded and reflected managerial thinking in particular had a powerful effect on the evolutionary response that American firms made to the Japanese quality challenge. By contrast, to take as a starting point what "rational actors" eventually learned would be to miss these kinds of dynamics and thereby provide an incomplete explanation (cf. Nelson, 1994:112). Moreover, because the imperatives imposed by the new quality model were strikingly different from those of the old, path dependency had the effect of slowing the American response to the Japanese quality challenge, especially in the early years. When change did come, it was often presented as radical change. But existing practices, values and norms could still be detected in the institutional mechanisms created to facilitate that change.

Media and Rhetoric

The media have played a major role first in highlighting quality as a competitive factor and later trumpeting the American quality movement's defects and failures. The *Wall Street Journal* in particular but also *Newsweek, The Economist*, and *Business Week*—not to speak of Dilbert cartoons—delight in pointing to the foibles (*many*) of American quality initiatives during the late 1980s and early 1990s (e.g., *The Economist*, 1992: 67–68; Fuchsberg, 1992: B1, B9; Mathews, 1992: 48–49; Naj, 1992: A1, A6). They seemed driven by the old newsroom adage, "If it burns or bleeds, lead with it." Commonly listed causes of failure for quality initiatives emphasized by the media include the faddishness of management commitments, conflicts with downsizing efforts, bureaucratization of quality activities, managements' program mentality, conflicts with traditional top-down management style, incompatibility with American values, and inflated expectations encouraged by quality zealots. While it would be wrong to dismiss these views, the causes of the slowness to adopt effective practices and the incompleteness of the American business response lie much deeper. I argue that they reflect the nature of the institutional fabric that weaves American corporate life together.

Considerable confusion arises from the rhetoric of the quality movement. Many confuse quality as a competitive issue with the particular name we assign to the efforts taken to achieve that end at any given time. In the course of the 1980s, the term *total quality management* became dominant. For some, TQM means simply doing quality control in an environment of good communication and teamwork. For others, it requires participative management with strong leadership from the top. Still others think of quality as doing things right the first time or conceive of it exclusively in terms of defect-free products. Many equate it with customer satisfaction. Still others see quality as a toolkit of quality methodologies. Finally, some see it as a management model. We might expect that *Quality Progress*, the journal of the major professional association promoting TQM, the American Society for Quality (ASQ, formerly the American Society for Quality Control), would push for a single definition of quality. Instead, the journal, deferring to its broad constituency, offers an array of definitions of TQM in its articles. That such different meanings exist is not surprising. Prior research suggests that the diffusion of "soft" innovations of this nature is characterized by substantial ambiguity of definition. Consequently, such innovations mutate as they get adopted and adapted in different environments, "leaving a puzzling trail of definitional issues for the analyst" (Winter, 1994: 101–102).

For the manager seeking to understand and adopt the innovation, this ambiguity is a two-edged sword. On one hand, the ambiguity introduces great uncertainty into the decision-making process. What should be our objectives? What is quality really about? What practices does it require and how should one go about implementing them? The lack of an agreed-upon definition of quality must be understood as one of the great barriers to managements' rapid adoption of practices that would improve quality. This consequence of ambiguity is hardly surprising. Less understood perhaps is the positive effects created by ambiguity. Because of the vagueness of the concept and its correlates, particularly in the early 1980s, firms and industries were free within a certain range to interpret it, position it, and adopt those practices that fit particular corporate traditions and industry imperatives.

Despite these ambiguities, among leading scholars and management practitioners in the course of the 1980s a generally agreed-upon conception of the content of the modern quality model emerged that differed from the old quality model. The new model constituted an "epochal shift" in how to think about quality and what was required to achieve it. These differences had dramatic implications for the strategies and tactics employed by American companies seeking to adopt the new approaches.

To add to the complexity, with management and media dynamics so close in America, almost as soon as such a term spreads widely, it becomes a symbol for everything that goes wrong under that rubric.[2] By the mid-1980s, predictably, articles began appearing with the inevitable title, "Beyond Quality." By the early 1990s the very name TQM was already stigmatized and increasingly out of favor. In the mid-1990s the Conference Board was considering changing the name of its Total Quality Management Center. Many of the high-level quality executives in its quality councils had come to believe that the name was a liability.

Whatever the particular labels in fashion, the important point to understand is that quality as a competitive factor is now well established in American economic life and the bar is continually being raised in industry after industry. Firms disregard this fact at their peril. *This is a book about quality as a competitive factor, not about TQM.* It is a book about the new quality model that evolved and was refined in large Japanese manufacturing export-oriented firms from 1955 through the 1980s and, with critical time lags, slowly spread through U.S. industry.

Imitation and Learning

One of the reasons why adoption is taking a long time from a market perspective is that, contrary to conventional views, imitation is often difficult (Nelson and Winter, 1982). It is often time-consuming and incomplete. To understand that, it is necessary to track the evolution of the modern American quality movement since its inception in the late 1970s. At the most elementary level, one cannot take for granted U.S. managements' perception of quality as a competitive issue; it took time for that awakening to occur. It is tempting to see this awakening as mere preamble to an analysis of the real issues: the tough behavioral change required to adopt the new quality model. I, however, agree with Hamel and Prahalad (1994: 270) that the competitive struggle, from a managerial perspective, is ultimately a fight against inertia, complacency, lethargy, convention, and myopia.

Once recognition of quality as a major competitive factor did occur, along with the recognition that success in this arena required dramatically different approaches, new roadblocks emerged, such as the lack of clarity about what the term quality meant and the lack of good information necessary for successful implementation. This suggests that some important market imperfections or even market failures were operative. Paradoxically, successful imitation requires adaptation to local conditions. American managers seeking to apply the Japanese model faced a whole new layer of obstacles and barriers.

In the early 1980s, many American managers had difficulty accepting that they could learn from the Japanese after a long era of American industrial success. Did they overcome this reluctance? If so, how long did it take, and how did they do it?

More broadly, many American managers and engineers did not accept the legitimacy of imitating competitors, foreign or otherwise. In American business culture, the term imitation developed strong negative connotations in the post–World War II period. Many American managers, and particularly product designers, came to condemn imitation as the work of unimaginative colleagues. Yet the strong creative aspects of the imitation process are seldom recognized. Successful imitation of even modest complexity contains significant creative challenges; Kikuchi (1983) describes this process in the development of the Japanese semiconductor industry. Moreover, the ability to imitate any aspect of electronics shows technical capabilities that go well beyond the negative connotations associated with imitation. Thus, a variety of capabilities are required for successful imitation. Many of these were not initially recognized and proved formidable barriers. The growing emphasis from the mid-1980s onward on conducting formal comparative analyses of practices of market leaders and then seeking to surpass them (benchmarking), a distinctive feature of the American quality movement, suggests that many of the inhibitions against imitation have been overcome.

If one thinks of successful competitive imitation as often involving creativity and innovation, in effect one interprets imitation as a learning process, an organizational and network learning process. Of course, imitation sometimes takes the form of a ritualistic copying process. Yet this also involves some learning processes, though of a different nature, and thus it may be the first step in an ongoing learning process.

Institutionalist have heavily studied the ritualistic aspects of imitation, especially in the nonprofit sector of the economy, most notably education (Abrahamson, 1996; DiMaggio and Powell, 1991; Meyer and Rowan, 1977). Ritualistic compliance can be undertaken for a variety of reasons and sustained for long periods. It can be coerced, or it can be undertaken voluntarily to build legitimacy in the eyes of customers, superiors, and other stakeholders. I examine these facets of imitation herein. In what specific industries and contexts do they appear? Can they be sustained in the for-profit manufacturing sector? Under some circumstances, ritualistic adoption is followed by the death of the practice, for its ineffectiveness becomes increasingly apparent over time, especially in competitive situations. Yet are there conditions under which ritually adopted practices are sustained by evolving to produce performance improvements? Some scholars think of institutional behavior as inconsistent with rational action. Yet is this consistent with what we observe in the quality movement?

Fligstein (1996: 664) has proposed social movement as a metaphor in describing the emergence of markets. Certainly, one does not often think of management's adoption of business practices such as quality improvement techniques as a social movement. Many scholars treat individual managers as atomistic agents, weighing all the evidence and then making rational decisions on behalf of their firms to improve or not to improve in the context of their specific environment. Yet, with the Japanese cast in the role of challengers in the early 1980s, the American incumbents banded together to mobilize resources and defend their markets. Managers developed networks to reduce knowledge barriers and to further adoption. Organizational action developed in response to a collective challenge, and these collectivities acted with common purpose, solidarity, and continuity to promote change in industry practices, often meeting strong resistance by those with vested interest in existing arrangements. Individual employees often saw quality as a kind of crusade and indeed were called quality zealots by their detractors. Thus, the very vocabulary suggests a social movement.

This U.S. collective action to pursue quality differed significantly from that used in Japan, but such action is nevertheless clearly identifiable in both countries. The U.S. infrastructure for diffusing new quality practices was composed of a decentralized network of collectivities, sometimes cooperating, sometimes competing, unlike the more centralized Japanese model. Contrary to popular images, the government was more involved in the development of this infrastructure in the United States than in Japan.

Learning networks from firm to firm, and between firms and infrastructural organizations helped managers slowly work out how to do quality improvement according to the principles of the new model. Moreover, the very content of the new quality model, as we shall see in the next chapter, is strongly associated with organizational learning. Thus, imitation and learning are effectively joined, especially in the context of absorbing the new quality model.

Fads and Crises

If imitation and learning are joined, can we not assume at least that fad and learning are incompatible concepts? Not necessarily. At first glance, fads do seem incompatible with the goal of building an enduring movement that successfully raises quality performance. Management fads appear inherently hostile to both effective imitative and learning activities. After all, the term *fad* connotes transiency. Webster's Third International Dictionary defines fad as "a pursuit or interest followed usually widely, but briefly and capriciously, with exaggerated zeal and devotion." The media delight in pointing to the rapid succession of fads, as manifested in the *Wall Street Journal* headline : "Many Companies Try Management Fads, Only to See Them Flop" (Bleakley, 1993: A1). Fads are seen as costly distractions that keep managers from concentrating on running the business, as panic responses to business crises. When a new approach does not yield the desired results, as is often the case, management acts capriciously, moving on to another seemingly more promising approach. Employees have learned through much experience to weather a succession of fads with a "this too will pass" philosophy. The expression "flavor of the month" is well ingrained in American corporate life and no doubt is, or should be, enshrined in a Dilbert cartoon.

Yet to leave the matter here is very unsatisfying. Although the previous commentary may suffice for conventional wisdom, there is another set of corporate experiences. Perhaps the important question is, how much survives from previous fads to be incorporated into, and serve as building blocks for, subsequent fads. This is my focus, which explains why "fad" appears in the book's title. The seeming succession of quality "minifads" (quality circles, statistical process control, quality function deployment, etc.) provides an opportunity to examine the relationships among these methodologies. In particular, the rise and fall of the business process reengineering movement in the early 1990s provides an opportune case for examining these matters. Have the quality minifads in the quality movement served as building blocks for the reengineering movement and, if so, how? Has the reengineering movement replaced quality initiatives, consistent with how its initial promoters positioned it, or have firms gradually modified it so that reengineering is now incorporated into their broader quality initiatives?

We have very few examples on the American business scene of long-term commitment to the new quality model without a concomitant, sustained strong sense of crisis.· Typically the crisis was created by the discovery of a huge quality gap between the American company and one or more of its Japanese competitors and the recognition that customers were choosing competitor products in large part because of this difference (cf. Winter, 1994: 102). With the downturn of the American automotive market in 1979 and rapid growth of the Japanese market share, for example, enormous gaps in costs, quality, and productivity became publicly apparent. This created a sense of crisis that was critical to mobilizing sustained efforts to eliminate these deficits. In industries not threatened by the Japanese, such as domestic airlines, pharmaceuticals, insurance, and food, quality in the modern sense, to be discussed in Chapter 1, did not emerge as a cutting edge competitive issue among firms.

Some firms without direct Japanese competition tried to adopt the new quality model as a preventive strategy. Typically, they were not as motivated as those firms and industries facing an immediate crisis, were less likely to take strong action to change past practices, and less able to sustain their innovative activities. Noriaki Kano, the noted scholar of the Japanese quality movement, built his "quality sweating" theory on similar observations about the Japanese quality movement (cf. Kano, 1995: 217–218). In short, a shock to an existing hidebound system seems critical to stimulating rethinking.

In principle, one might expect that once pioneers demonstrate the benefits, many followers would need a more gentle push. Yet success in adopting the new quality model requires large-scale employee involvement, commitment, and, in many cases, sacrifice; such motivated involvement is difficult to sustain without a sense of deep crisis (cf. Winter, 1994). Perhaps a constant stimulation of crisis is necessary if employees are to maintain their motivation, but such "manufacturing of crises," relatively speaking, has not been a strong point of American companies.

Although the sense of crisis was created in many cases by the Japanese competitive challenge, this was not always the case. Other kinds of crises motivated companies to see quality improvement as a solution to their problems. Florida Power and Light, for example, skillfully used the two oil shocks, rising electricity costs, increasingly unhappy customers, and an overall increasingly hostile financial and regulatory environment to build internal support for its quality initiative (cf. Hudiburg, 1991). A sense of crisis stimulated those firms adopting and sustaining a quality initiative, but not all firms experiencing such crises were quick to respond. Some paid the price in diminished market share and competitiveness, but others were able to delay the day of reckoning or moderate its effects and later rebound.

However large the obstacles placed before (and sometimes by) American management adopting the new quality model, many firms eventually did acquire the necessary information and skills to make the shift from the old model to the new model, operationalizing, at least partially, many of the new elements. The effort was time-consuming and often accomplished through a torturous trial-and-error learning process. Only then were these American firms able to stabilize their markets and, in some cases, win back significant market share. One needs to understand how that took place and what strategies and tactics worked. What institutional forces and inventions supported this initiative? Thus, in the end this is a book not about failures but about how obstacles to adoption were overcome. By the early 1990s American manufacturing reemerged as a remarkable, internationally competitive power. How does quality fit into that equation? Were firms succeeding in part because of their improved quality or despite of their poor quality?

Much of this book is about how institutional forces mediated market pressures. In the early 1980s, these institutional forces slowed firms' adaptive processes, but later in the decade new institutional arrangements arose that helped create and speed up the process by which firms successfully responded to market forces.

In this book, I use the experiences in the automotive and electronics/semiconductor industries to capture the American manufacturing response to the new quality model. My thesis is that despite many differences between the two industries in areas such as technology, management culture, unionization, and labor force characteristics, their experiences are parallel. Both industries were exposed to strong competitive challenges from the Japanese in the early and mid-1980s.

Semiconductor executives may find the parallels to the automotive industry surprising because many of them have tended to view it as an almost anachronistic twentieth century industry, with backward technology and outmoded management and personnel systems. Even so, I argue that the differences in approaches to quality improvement were more similar than dissimilar. Any differences flow from the sense of superiority that the semiconductor executives seemed to display, their narrow conception of technology, and the availability of alternative options. This combination of factors in fact delayed their response to the Japanese quality challenge relative to the automotive industry. Indeed, the automotive industry, as a major customer for semiconductor devices, replaced the military in the 1980s as one of the major drivers for quality improvement in the industry (Finan, 1990: 30–31).

In Chapter 1, I describe the nature of the new quality model and explore the extent to which adoption represented a discontinuous development. Has the status of quality changed in American manufacturing firms, or was quality a passing fancy? Chapter 2 deals with the initial responses of U.S. managers to the quality challenge as reflected in mounting market pressures. The recognition of quality as a major competitive issue was more problematic than one might think. Chapter 3 explores the learning strategies adopted by U.S. firms and in particular explores the degree to which American firms were willing to learn directly from their Japanese competitors. I also examine the cognitive barriers to learning at the time. In Chapter 4, I pursue some of the early manifestations of the quality movement as reflected in quality circles and the popularity of the teachings of Philip Crosby, the most influential of the early gurus. I use these cases to create a deeper understanding of the managerial decision-making processes then operative.

In the second part of the book, I begin my analysis of the institutional activities that led eventually to sustained quality improvement. Chapter 5 delineates the interfirm networks among original equipment manufacturers (OEMs) and suppliers that became critical for upgrading quality performance in the automotive and semiconductor industries. Of particular interest are the implications of the OEMs' pressuring suppliers to adopt quality improvement technologies. The automotive industry is my primary case. In Chapter 6, I describe the evolving institutional framework set up to further the adoption of quality improvement techniques and examine in detail the complicated networks among firms and these institutions. Chapters 7 and 8 explore the process by which Hewlett-Packard (HP), a pacesetter in quality improvement, absorbed new approaches from its Japanese subsidiary Yokogawa Hewlett-Packard (YHP). In the course of doing so, we have an opportunity to see how HP adapted these ideas to fit its organizational culture and also how this large, decentralized company dealt with the challenge of diffusing these new ideas across fiercely independent business units. Chapter 9 provides an occasion to bring together data on how quality performance in the automotive and semiconductor industries actually changed over time and what factors seem most responsible for the improvement. Was TQM responsible, or is that even the right question to ask? Finally, in the concluding chapter, I bring together our understandings about organizational learning in tracing the odyssey of the quality movement. I revisit the issue of the relationship between fads and learning and seek to crystallize the conditions most favorable to their harmonious development.

CHAPTER 1

The New Quality Model

Continuity or Discontinuity?

To begin, I explore these points: the definition of quality, the prevalence of quality improvement practices, and the nature of the differences between established approaches to quality and the new quality model. These are the tasks for this chapter. As I have already said, there was a great deal of confusion about the nature of this new competitive reality, for quality meant different things at different times in different industries. There was not a single American quality movement but many. These different approaches reflected the competitive circumstances of firms and industries, as well as their uncertainty about how to effectively respond to Japanese competitive pressures. We can describe various mini fads in the evolution of the American quality movement.

Chronology and Scope

Table 1.1 shows my chronology of these minifads as I observed them. They hit different industries at different times. The sequence characterized in rough fashion in Table 1.1 follows closely the fortunes of the automotive industry, which was hit hard by Japanese competition in the late 1970s. Industries such as home appliances, electronics, and the service sector have lagged behind these trends. One indicator of the auto industry's leading role is the extent to which firms in other industries benchmarked against their achievements. Saturn, Honda of America, Ford Motor Co., Toyota Motor Manufacturing USA, and Chrysler all report large numbers of other industrial and service firms visiting to examine their quality and production systems. Honda of America alone reports that since the mid-1980s at least 100 of the Fortune 500 companies have come to their Marysville plant for tours, seminars, and discussions (Heil, 1994: 19). Moreover, as we shall see, demands by auto industry customers were a major factor in stimulating quality improvement in the semiconductor industry.

Table 1.1. Quality Fads, Beginning Periods by Technique or Strategy

Late 1970s, Early 1980s

Quality control circles, EI
Statistical Process Control (SPC)
Senior management commitment and leadership
Competing gurus (Juran, Deming, Crosby)
Need to break down functional isolation in favor of cross-functional cooperation
 (especially in new product-development); teams (quality improvement teams);
 self-managing teams (both within and across functions)
QFD—concurrent engineering—Taguchi

Mid-1980s

Customer focus
Supplier collaboration
Continuous improvement (Kaizen): process-improvement focus for all business
 processes
Baldrige Prize (first awarded 1987)
Partnering with customers (co-design) and suppliers
Using Baldrige award protocol for company diagnostic 1990 customer satisfaction
 measurement
Benchmarking

Early 1990s

ISO 9000
System alignment (rewards aligned with desired outcomes, quality aligned with
 important business objectives)
Policy deployment (quality integrated with strategic business plan)
Deployment of annual objectives through all levels and employees
Business process reengineering

Late-arriving sectors, such as higher education and hospitals, tend to get exposed to the full accumulated weight of all the preceding developments. In principle, this allows a systematic quality movement linking all interrelated features logically. Yet each industry has its own set of dynamics that condition how the quality package is experienced and how it gets used. Moreover, the form of quality improvement practices adopted by firms tended to mutate as it diffused, thereby presenting late adopters with a variety of models to choose from.

Table 1.2 shows the peak number of articles on selected quality topics that appeared in the national quality journal, *Quality Progress*. It roughly corresponds to the observations reported in Table 1.1 with a lag effect. This is consistent both with the view that the auto industry responded relatively faster than many industries to the Japanese quality challenge and with the fact that formal publication is a lagging indicator of practice.

Table 1.2. Quality Minifads, Peak Number of Articles in *Quality Progress*

Early 1980s

Quality circles (3)
Supplier relations (14)
Management commitment and leadership (6)
Customer focus (4)

Mid-1980s

Process improvement (10)
Quality planning and strategy (16)
New product development (QFD) (12)
Benchmarking (5)
Rewards, motivation (5)
Process improvement (18)

Early 1990s

ISO 9000 (3)
Baldrige Prize and diagnostics (8)
Quality planning and strategy (17)

Notes: Numbers in parentheses show peak number of articles over a one-year period (calendar year). If two clear peaks are separated by four or more years, item is shown twice.

  Subjects associated with the new quality model were selected a priori by author based on knowledge of field.

Given this succession of minifads, I ask: How much has taken hold? If the answer is that enough took hold to make a significant difference in performance, are we better off thinking about these minifads as phases? Phases, unlike minifads, imply a continuity of elements in a large process. I will tackle this issue later in the book. Initially, I look at the evidence for simple adoption of something managers are willing to label TQM.

The strongest evidence for adoption per se comes from two surveys of *Fortune* 1000 companies carried out by Edward Lawler and Colleagues in 1990 and 1993 (Lawler, Mohrman, and Ledford, Jr., 1992; Lawler, Mohrman, and Ledford, Jr., 1995: 45–51, 75–76, 139). Seventy-three percent of the companies responding to the 1990 survey indicated that they had a TQM program or similar program, and the total rose to 76% in 1993. Eighty-one percent of the programs began after 1985 and 24% after 1991. Note that these totals include both service and manufacturing firms. Generally, adoption occurs later for the service sector firms.

These programs continue in approximately three quarters of the largest U.S. companies, a quite remarkable figure given that the initial burst of interest in quality took place in the early 1980s. If it is a fad in the conventional sense of that term, it is clearly a long-lasting one. Moreover, the use of TQM practices increased; companies reported that on average 50% of their employees were covered by TQM activities in 1993, compared to 41% in 1990. In 1993, 25% of the companies said all employees were covered, compared to 18% in 1990.

Finally, 83% of companies reported increased or greatly increased use of TQM over the three-year period. When asked about the future, 78% of the firms said that they anticipated increased or greatly increased use of TQM. This growth in coverage and expected growth fits well with the high satisfaction level that firms report about their TQM activities.

Eighty-three percent of the firms report that their experience with TQM has been positive or very positive (an additional 16% said it was neither negative nor positive). Large majorities report positive results measured by indicators in the two performance clusters: direct performance outcomes and profitability and competitiveness. Table 1.3 reports *perceived* impacts by respondents and therefore should not be treated as hard data. However, it is not unusual for researchers investigating perceived effectiveness of management programs to report negative results. Therefore, the results are quite suggestive. Much more convincing, however, are the findings of Easton and Jarrell (1998). Using a sophisticated analytic model, they examined the impact of TQM deployment on actual financial performance measured by stock market returns and accounting variables. They found a strong statistical association between deployment of TQM and improved financial performance in the three to five years following initial deployment. The results were particularly strong for those firms judged to have adopted the most advanced TQM practices.

Note that all the growth and positive perceptions are occurring in the early 1990s when TQM is taking a pounding in the media for failed initiatives, declining

Table 1.3. Perceived Impact of TQM by Mean Score and Percent Distribution

	Mean[a]	Very Negative	Negative	Neither	Positive	Very Positive	No Basis to Judge
Direct Performance Outcomes							
Productivity	4.0	0	1	11	66	14	9
Quality of product/services	4.2	0	0	3	69	20	7
Customer service	4.2	0	0	3	70	20	8
Speed of response	4.0	0	0	9	68	11	12
Profitability and Competitiveness							
Competitiveness	4.0	0	0	9	68	9	14
Profitability	3.9	0	0	19	53	10	17

Source: Adapted from Lawler, Mohrrman, and Ledford, 1995: 76.

  Note: All outcomes are measured on a 5-point scale where 5 = very positive and 1 = very negative. Data based on survey of 279 firms with a 28% response rate.

[a]Mean score calculated with "no basis to judge" response = missing.

applications for the Malcolm Baldrige National Quality Award (a *Wall Street Journal* favorite), and insignificant results compared to the highly touted benefits of business process reengineering. Moreover, Dogbert, that contemporary barometer of management's foibles, is being subjected to a barrage of new quality policies, each nuttier than the other.

It is reasonable to think that the adoption rate and breadth of TQM activities would be lower outside the *Fortune* 1000 firms. But how much lower? Is this a phenomenon limited only to large firms? In a 1992 national survey of for-profit American business establishments with over 50 employees, Osterman (1994: 177) found that 34% of the responding establishments reported adopting TQM (45% of all manufacturing firms). Twenty-five percent reported that 50% or more of their employees were covered by TQM activities (32% of the manufacturing firms). These results are quite consistent with those of Lawler and associates and show that this phenomenon goes well beyond large firms or even the manufacturing sector.

One last piece of evidence regarding the prevalence of TQM comes from the National Center on the Educational Quality of the Workforce (EQW), which conducted a comprehensive national survey of private sector firms in 1994; 37% of the responding firms reported a formal TQM program (National Center on the Educational Quality of the Workforce, 1995: 5).

It is important to understand that the exact phrasing of the questions influences the nature of these responses. Thus, respondents in the Osterman survey who requested clarification of what TQM meant were told that TQM meant a quality control approach emphasizing the importance of communications, feedback, and teamwork (Osterman, 1994: 187). This is a superficial definition of TQM that falls well short of incorporating the major elements of the new quality model. The net result would be an inflated estimate in the number of firms adopting the new quality model.[1] On the other side, the more a survey questionnaire relies on requiring *formal adoption* of a TQM program for inclusion, the lower the number of firms responding that they have adopted TQM. Lawler and associates adopt the most expansive language asking respondents about "total quality control, total quality management, or similar efforts." This definition, along with their concentration on large firms, explains their report of the widest level of diffusion. The EQW research adopts the narrowest wording, asking respondents "Has your establishment adopted a formal Total Quality Management program?" I expect this wording would elicit a lower number of firms moving toward the new quality model. Overall, the survey research results tend to overestimate the rate of adoption of TQM because of the superficiality of the questions and the optimism of the executives responding to them (see Easton and Jarrell, 1997a: 6–9).

All this focus on TQM, however, misses the important fact that the quality movement has had a powerful impact on many firms that did not choose to formally adopt a TQM program. Many companies, known well for their quality initiatives, have never used the term TQM to refer to these efforts. At companies like Hewlett-Packard (HP), TQM or TQC (C for Control) is used among the quality personnel and with outside customers but not in most divisions among ordinary personnel. Indeed, as one HP quality department manager said to me, "[T]hat's a name we 'quality geeks' use, but if you mention TQM to line personnel they are likely to say that 'that is something we tried and it didn't work.' " For them, the term TQC is associated with the "seven quality control tools." Yet HP is known for its leadership in adopting the new quality model. Still, other companies, not well known for their quality efforts but strongly committed to adopting quality improvement techniques and philosophies, never used the term TQM. Moreover, many companies make it a point of not thinking about TQM as a "program." Other companies such as Dupont, which initially adopted the term TQM, had overblown expectations followed by negative experiences in the course of which the term TQM was stigmatized. Nevertheless, many of the TQM quality methodologies, stripped of their label, have been introduced by "stealth," as one manager described the approach to me.

Intel's experience is not all that uncommon. Notwithstanding the 1994 Pentium chip disaster (from a public relations and quality reputation point of view), Intel has over the last 15 years, especially recently, instituted a whole range of practices designed to improve quality. Intel added quality to its list of three core values (results orientation, risk taking and discipline) in the early 1980s and later added customer orientation. The separate addition of customer orientation is revealing. In a company with near monopolistic position in many of its markets, those pursuing a quality focus have a strong tendency to turn inward. To counter that, a separate customer emphasis was added.

In addition, different process improvement activities have been undertaken, sometimes under the quality rubric. Intel also established more collaborative relations with its suppliers, developing a concurrent engineering process for product design that brings together customers, suppliers and manufacturing engineers. The firm also instituted rigorous process audits of suppliers to assess the process capability of their equipment (is it capable of producing the product reliably and in volume?) Prior to the quality revolution, such supplier audits were typically product audits. Teams are also heavily used. The use of quality tools, such as statistical process control, is highly institutionalized. Customers are regularly surveyed to get their views on Intel's product quality (Main, 1994: 181–185). Intel is also involved in a range of infrastructure organizations designed explicitly to improve quality; this includes some organizations aimed at semiconductor suppliers, whose quality improvement is critical to Intel's success.

In 1990, Intel made a commitment to apply for the Malcolm Baldrige National Quality Award and established a quality technology group to support that effort. This group had two charters: (1) to develop the tools that each division would use in implementing quality, and (2) to deploy the quality initiative within Intel (Clark, Walz, Turner, and Miszuk, 1994: 86). Typically, each division made an assessment based on the Baldrige award protocol and then identified where they came up short and worked to eliminate deficits in those areas. Of course, some divisions took these charges more seriously than others, but clearly quality improvement is a focus of management's activity and attention. The company also created an Intel Quality Award modeled after the Baldrige to provide internal recognition for the most successful divisions.

In short, for a company not "doing" TQM, Intel certainly has been allocating resources toward and accomplishing much that one associates with TQM; these activities are very consistent with the new quality model. Yet, if one mentions TQM to Intel managers, one often gets a very negative response. Intel is but one of many such companies.

At many high-tech companies, engineers in particular resist top-management mandates for TQM. They associate TQM with rigid standards and time-consuming, unwieldy bureaucracy. TQM is perceived as sapping the innovative energy that is the lifeblood of such firms (see Price and Chen, 1995). Cusumano and Selby (1995: 325, 340) note a similar situation at Microsoft, despite a growing emphasis on quality as a result of pressures from customers and competitors. Since 1990, it has succeeded in tightly integrating customer support and customer feedback with improving products and the development process (Cusumano and Selby, 1995: 360–361). These practices tap into the central principles of the new quality model without the term TQM ever crossing anyone's lips.

What do the data from high-tech industries tell us about the diffusion of TQM activities? Pittiglio Rabin Todd & McGrath (PRTM) surveyed electronics industry firms from 1988 to 1994 under contract with the American Electronics Association. Eighty-six percent of respondents reported having a TQC program (the term in use at the time) in 1988 (of that total 29% reported that they were just starting implementation).[2] In 1994, 73% reported that they had a TQM program (with 18% reporting that they were just starting). These figures exclude software firms, which were added to the survey for the first time in 1994 and generally have a lower rate of implementation (Pittiglio Rabin Todd & McGrath, 1995). The larger the firm, the more likely it is to report having implemented TQM programs. In part reflecting this fact, an impressive 87% of the 31 surveyed semiconductor firms reported some phase of implementing TQM (21% just starting) in 1994. Even though top executives label these activities as TQM in response to a survey, they may not use the term internally in the firm. Rather, executives become skillful at developing inside and outside languages to describe the same activities.

Whether these quality activities (labeled TQM or otherwise) produced the desired results is another matter. As judged by the data reported by the Lawler and colleagues survey, as shown in Table 1.3, many firms seem to think so. Organizational scholars and journalists alike, however, are by nature cynical about the impact of what they see as managerial fads and overblown management claims. Certainly, there is plenty of that. I will address the changing quality performance in the auto and semiconductor industries in Chapter 9. For now, I ask a slightly less broad question: has the quality movement been having a significant impact on organizational life? The answer, as seen from the results of the Lawler and associates, Osterman, EQW, and the PRTM data, is a resounding yes.

Of course, respondents may be giving socially acceptable rather than correct responses and thus may exaggerate their adoption of TQM practices. We should keep in mind, however, that by the early 1990s TQM already had a bad reputation in the media and in companies; consequently, it is not at all clear that the socially acceptable response would be to say one was involved in TQM. Osterman in his survey took great care to work with the most knowledgeable respondent available. He also notes that the subsequent statistical results show that adoption was related to explanatory variables in sensible ways, which suggests the validity of the data (1994: 176). The same can be said of the analyses by Lawler and associates and PRTM. Were one to redo these surveys today, would one get the same results? Probably not. No doubt there has been some falloff but not as much as the falloff in media coverage. Quality is a competitive reality today that firms cannot afford to ignore. They may emphasize somewhat different tools and approaches in the late 1990s, but quality improvement per se is increasingly part of "normal management."

Thus far, I have been talking about the old and new quality models as if their differences were apparent. It is time to map the changing landscape created by the new approach to quality. This is not the place for an extended historical treatment of the evolution of quality; for such treatments, see Garvin (1988) and Juran (1995). Rather, I aim to capture the analytic characteristics of the old and new quality models to provide a context for the discussion to follow. Inevitably, some history enters into the account.

Quality Models

Table 1.4 presents nine matching characteristics comparing the old with the new model. By creating this ideal type, I of course conflate a variety of historical and contemporary developments. My intent is not to suggest that every firm manifests one or the other of these two combinations of characteristics, only that each combination characterizes a model, the one of the old and the other of the new, as it crystallized in the early 1980s. Although many companies may approach quality through a tool kit of disparate techniques and principles, the view presented here is of an integrated set of principles that separate the old from the new quality model. Surely, a company can make substantial progress without fully manifesting all the characteristics set out here. Rather, I argue only that these most successful quality-oriented companies likely manifest the characteristics of the new quality model more fully.

With 1980 as a turning point, one can say that leading manufacturing companies in the United States at that time (e.g., General Motors [GM], Ford, Xerox, General Electric [GE], Boeing) practiced to a notable extent the characteristics associated with the old model, just as leading companies in Japan (e.g., Toyota,

Table 1.4. Characteristics of Old and New Quality Models

Old Quality Model	New Quality Model
1. Internal orientation stressing conformance to requirements (fitness to standard); reduction of internal costs is filter used to evaluate quality improvement proposals.	1. "Market-in" approach provides strong customer orientation; customer acceptability is initial filter used to evaluate quality improvement proposals.
2. Quality just one of many functional specialties.	2. Quality as umbrella theme for organizing work; used as common language throughout the firm.
3. Quality not seen as competitive element as long as you match your competitors.	3. Improved quality as strong competitive strategy.
4. Quality as specialized function carried out by small number of experts in quality department reporting to manufacturing.	4. All-employee, all-departmental involvement as pivotal strategy for improving quality of every business process; attention to incentives for all employees.
5. Downstream focus on inspection, defect detection, and "band-aid" solutions.	5. Upstream prevention activities key to quality improvement; built-in quality.
6. Quality improvement activities involve limited repetitive cycle of detect and repair, leading at best to stable equilibrium.	6. Well-defined problem-solving methodology and training activities tied to continuous quality improvement, aimed at improving key processes pivotal for business success.
7. Quality as stand-alone effort promoted by quality department, not well integrated into rest of organizational activities.	7. Integration of quality into control system of goals, plans, and actions.
8. Each functional specialty operating as independently as possible, maximizing their own functional goals, sometimes at expense of the firm.	8. Focus on cross-functional cooperation to achieve firm-level objectives.
9. See item 1.	9. Anticipation of customer need before customers are aware of these needs (fitness to latent requirements).

Note: These characteristics are drawn from the literature (Ishikawa, 1985; Mizuno, 1988; Scherkenbach, 1986; Shiba, Graham, and Walden, 1993) as well as from my own research on the subject in 1989. This research involved interviewing officials at 20 leading Japanese manufacturing firms noted for their quality achievements across a broad range of industries.

Komatsu, Matsushita, Ishikawajima Harima, NEC) were practitioners to a notable extent of the new model. It is *not* my argument that the new quality model is "right" in every respect or that its unconditional application will always yield optimum business results. To the contrary, other important competitive factors always contribute to outcomes. Finally, each of the items identified in both of the models is based on elaborate organizational mechanisms, so this simple listing should not obscure the complexity, cohesion, and sophistication of the two models.

Old Quality Model

I consider first the old model that rose in the course of American industrialization, reflecting some of the unique features of American industrial history, especially the rise of Taylorism (scientific management). It is a model that sees quality in terms of fitness to standard. Quality activities come into play primarily after the product design is settled and emphasize building the product so that it conforms to design specifications. This gives the quality focus a strong internal orientation and leads to a corresponding neglect of market considerations. It also means that quality efforts tend to concentrate primarily on the manufacturing department. If, in interviewing employees at a company, one finds that quality is deemed solely a manufacturing department responsibility, then the observer has a revealing clue that the old model is in force.

In the old model, the quality department has narrow jurisdictional rights over quality. It can make few claims on the attention and resources of other departments. Quality itself is seen as a narrow, specialized form of expertise.

Correspondingly, under the old model, managers do not think of quality as a major area for achieving competitive advantage and therefore do not invest substantial organizational resources in it. Rather, managers are aiming for scale economies, building brand consciousness, lowering unit costs, and the like—they see these as major arenas for building competitive advantage and allocate major resources to them.

Indeed, in the America of 1980, manufacturing itself was rather a neglected area of expertise. Finance and marketing prospered and increasingly became routes to the top over the course of the post–World War II period (Hayes, Wheelwright, and Clark, 1988: 35, 53–54). Ingrassia and White (1994: 155) document the powerful role of the finance department in GM in the early 1980s. In Chrysler and Ford, we find variations on the same theme. The bean counters really counted. If one wanted to work up to a position of corporate leadership, manufacturing was not the place to go, and certainly quality was not the place to be even if one's sights were limited just to working up to the top of manufacturing. In the auto industry, it was often said that quality managers were failed engineers or those close to retirement. One Motorola manager, commenting on the status of quality managers in the early 1980s, quipped, "Quality is like KP in the military" (cited in Main, 1994: 73). Despite some exaggeration, this negative image conveys a powerful message to all employees in the organization. In short, over the course of the post–World War II period, the quality manager in manufacturing was the low man on an increasingly lower totem pole.

In keeping with the heritage of scientific management, quality evolved as a specialized function carried out by a small number of experts in quality departments with reporting responsibilities to manufacturing. Under the old quality model, it is they who, by and large, had responsibility for quality results within the manufacturing operation. The growth of the aerospace and electronics industries in the 1950s and 1960s led to a still finer specialization with the rise of the field of reliability engineering (Garvin, 1988: 15–16). Interestingly while the knowledge associated with reliability engineering is well integrated in Japan, it is absent as an occupational specialty. The reliance on experts in America leads to an unfortunate abdication of quality responsibility by many engineering and assembly line personnel. These developments meant that learning about quality control tended to be limited to a small group of weak specialists.

Under the old model, the job of these quality experts is defect detection, which requires the monitoring of performance through inspection. Through inspection, the company aims to keep defective units from reaching customers. Inspectors constituted the rank-and-file members of the quality staff in American manufacturing corporations. Redundancy and a strong service organization are other common strategies designed to minimize the effects of quality failures on customers. If all else "fails," a strong after-sales service organization can mitigate the effects of poor quality. Even though inspection, redundancy, and a strong service organization can often accomplish many of the intended goals, they add considerable costs to production. Thus, under the old model, higher quality produces higher costs and hence higher prices.

In saying that the objective for the old model is quality control, I mean that the target is a quite limited one, to control quality problems, and to reduce variation from the designated standard. The implicit assumption, grounded in a very constrained cost-benefit equation, is that one reaches a limit beyond which it does not pay to improve quality. In practice, the consequence is that once modest quality objectives are achieved, attention can turn to higher priority objectives. More often than not, quality results would then deteriorate, thereby requiring renewed attention to quality problems and the imposition of the usual "firefighting fixes."

From an organizational learning perspective, the implications are profound. A rather limited repetitive cycle of detect and repair is set in motion, requiring only modest rotation of existing organizational routines as modest improvement is followed by regression. The amount of individual and organizational learning needed to sustain this cycle is limited indeed. Limited targets meant limited learning. The learning phase tends to end when performance is deemed satisfactory (cf. Winter, 1994: 103). As for the impact on consumers, an example will suffice. Anyone who bought a new American car from the post–World War II period through the mid-1980s often experienced the same problems in the new model identical to those in the previous year's model. That is to say, there was little organizational learning.

Implicit in the description of the old quality model thus far is that quality as an organizational objective and as a department is not well integrated into high-level corporate planning and goal setting. Under the old model, as with other departments, the quality department acts independently to achieve its objectives. Success in quality improvement, however, requires cooperation with other departments. Because the quality department is relatively weak, often reporting to the head of manufacturing rather than to divisional or corporate heads, achieving even quite limited objectives is difficult.

My description of the old quality model is now complete. However, there were in practice many variations of this model. Thus, in some industries, such as pharmaceuticals and chemicals, the consequences of quality failures for the public meant that, unlike in many other manufacturing sectors, quality was a high priority, as reflected in resource allocations. Nevertheless, even these sectors strongly manifest most of the attributes of the old model.

The New Quality Model

I turn now to a consideration of the new quality model and its constituent elements.[3] "Market-in" evolved in the post–World War II period as a major focus of Japanese quality improvement activities. This term, in common use in Japanese manufacturing companies, means deploying information on customer needs (current and potential customers) as widely as possible in the organization and defining those with a need to know as broadly as possible. It means bringing customer needs into every possible part of the organization. Customer acceptability becomes the lens through which employees learn to evaluate their improvement activities. Thus, a different set of management decisions emerges, unlike those guided by cost-reduction objectives alone. Cost-reduction targets, by contrast, typically lead managers to make decisions that are arbitrary or based on equity principles (across-the-board cuts) and that, more often than not, detract from quality as experienced by customers. In principle, every work process in every department becomes a link in an internal customer chain that extends to the most important customer, the end user. By infusing the organization with market considerations, managers introduce into the firm additional sources of uncertainty. Responding effectively to these pressures requires motivation, training, and flexibility through decentralized employee responsibility. Such training (shown in characteristic 6 of Table 1.4) and flexibility (shown in characteristic 4) ensures rapid changes in organizational routines. Both individual and organizational learning are intrinsically part of this process.

Quality improvement in Japan developed through the 1980s increasingly as an umbrella theme for organizing many work activities. A great many organizational objectives traditionally seen as cost-reduction and productivity-improvement initiatives are reoriented as quality-improvement objectives. This is not simply a matter of cosmetics. Of course, quality improvement is much more salable to employees and therefore more motivating and less threatening than traditional cost-reduction and productivity-improvement programs. Under a quality improvement focus, however, the criterion for creating targeted objectives is the ability to maintain or enhance customer satisfaction. Learning activities concentrate on the customer satisfaction axis.

With quality an umbrella theme, a common language of quality improvement develops through all functional specialties and organizational levels, thereby enhancing communication, understanding, and acceptance of common objectives and problem-solving methodologies. The significance of building a common language to bridge the inevitable differences among those in different functional specialities should not be underestimated. It has far-reaching ramifications. Individual and organizational learning capacities are enhanced. The quality movement developed a variety of tools to enhance organizational learning across often competing and somewhat self-contained functions. One such tool is quality function deployment (QFD), a structured methodology for problem solving in product development. QFD has power because it provides a common language and framework within which design engineers and marketers can fruitfully interact to identify customer needs and the design parameters that meet those needs (Wheelwright and Clark, 1992: 228–234).

A major characteristic of the modern quality model involves seeing improved quality as a strong competitive strategy. Firms learn to strategically target those specific dimensions of quality that customers highly value, and they gain advantage over competitors in so doing (Garvin, 1988). Effectively pursued, it means larger market share, lower costs (through reduced rework, scrap, etc.), and larger profits with potentially larger wages and employment security for employees. This element provides strong motivational incentives for individual learning and for individuals to embody their learning in new best-practice routines if pursued in an environment of growing markets.

All-employee, all-department involvement in quality improvement is one of the pivotal characteristics of the modern quality model. All employees, individually and in work teams, are expected to participate in improving the quality of their work processes so that they more efficiently and effectively serve internal and external customer needs. Managers lack the detailed knowledge to improve work routines, so they must delegate that responsibility to employees (Aoki, 1988). Management is cast in a supporting role. The implications for employee learning are profound. All employees are presumed to be learners (cf. Dore et al., 1989: 52). This assumption—combined with enhanced motivational incentives for employees to engage in learning, extensive training in problem solving, and opportunities to use that training—enable a strong organizational learning thrust.

A central theme of the new quality model is that solving problems at earlier "upstream" stages yields important savings for the firm. As one uncovers quality problems downstream, the costs multiply. This recognition directs quality improvement activities toward the design stage, where opportunities for prevention strategies can be most effectively applied and where "root causes" of problems are often located. Root-cause problem-solving activity increases the probability of organizational learning because of its greater potential to create opportunities for significant change in organizational routines.

Employees trained to use well-defined problem-solving methodologies characterize the modern quality model. By spreading well-defined routines for problem solving to a large number of employees at all levels of the firm, the firm increases the capacity for more individuals to engage in individual and organizational learning. Continuous quality improvement is the dynamic corporate principle, epitomized by a large banner I saw in 1988 over the assembly line at the Mazda Hiroshima transmission plant; it read, "Fear Established Concepts" (*kyofu kisei gainen*). The invitation to apply one's problem-solving skills to create better organizational routines is clear. Such mobilization is unthinkable under the old quality model.

Continuous quality improvement implicitly means that the traditional quality control practice of seeking conformance to specification limits (performance within a range of acceptable upper and lower limits) and then, once achieving it, seeking only to hold performance within that range is unacceptable. Rather, operating under the old model imposes great losses on customers and society because quality losses result from deviation from target. The firm must orient itself to continuous process improvement to meet optimum target values to satisfy customers (Gunter, 1987: 44–52).

Under the new model, the setting of corporate objectives is strongly influenced by the assessment of customers' current and latent needs. Once formulated, these quality improvement objectives are carefully cascaded down through the organization (what the Japanese call *hoshin kanri*, or policy management/deployment) and supported by top management.[4] When quality is integrated into the control system in this way, middle managers, as well as workers, become central components in the execution of quality improvement and get the message that what they are doing is important. There is a clear structure provided for individual and organizational learning associated with specified targets appropriate to one's level in the organization.

Management, through a structured control system applied to quality improvement, aims to provide the motivation, capacity, and opportunity for individual and organizational learning. In short, the new quality model involves a highly disciplined approach to improvement. Under the old model, financial objectives drive improvement activities. Under the new model, quality objectives focused on enhancing customer satisfaction share the focus with these financial objectives. This changes the character of the improvement effort. Moreover, the assumption is that quality improvement will enhance financial objectives.

Cross-functional cooperation is a hallmark of the modern quality model. It developed through the recognition that many quality and productivity failures occur at the boundaries between functional specialties—the white spaces in the organization chart—and result from employees in different functional specialties failing to fully cooperate with one another (Juran, 1989: 34; Rummler and Brache, 1990). Managers of departmental hierarchies are often rewarded for optimizing their functions (e.g., marketing, engineering) in ways that often lead to suboptimization for the whole organization. The modern approach to quality seeks to manage and improve work processes that span functional boundaries. It puts a premium on multiple groups sharing power and coordinating their activities and solving problems across horizontal as well as vertical boundaries (see Aoki, 1988). Cross-functional management is not just an ad hoc arrangement to solve pressing problems, but rather the normal mode of day-to-day management providing for integrated management of quality, cost, and delivery.

Finally, in the 1980s an approach to customers emerged that stressed it was not enough to meet customer expectations; the real rewards go to firms that can exceed customer expectations. The idea is to anticipate customer needs before the customers themselves were necessarily aware of these needs. The advantages of being first to market with products containing such features are great; during the period of monopoly, the firm can charge a premium for its products (see Shiba, Graham, and Walden, 1993: 11–12).

This completes my overview of the characteristics of the new quality model. It helps one understand the target for many of the American companies seeking to build their competence in continuous quality improvement in the early 1980s. However, this target was not immediately visible in 1980 rather, the scales were only gradually lifted from the eyes of American managers. Indeed, in many companies, problems of blurred vision remain to this day. In using the metaphor of scales, my intention is to convey the sense in which American managers experienced a shift in how they came to view quality. The new model contradicted the old model in fundamental ways and made existing ways of thinking obsolete. It said black was white. One CEO said to me, "My epiphany was when I realized the significance of the simple but profound observation that it is always cheaper to do things once than twice."

One additional observation about the characteristics of the new quality model needs to be made. A number of evolutionary developments not directly related to quality improvement were encouraging firms to adopt many of these practices. Productivity improvement efforts, demands for flexibility, shortened product development cycles pushed in many of the same directions. Employee participation was on the table as a management strategy in the United States independently (though evidence suggests that quality improvement initiatives gave it a strong shove forward) (Lawler, Mohrman, and Ledford, Jr., 1995: 52). In short, the old and new quality models do not exist in splendid isolation from their respective production systems.

Quality advocates have a strong tendency to talk about elements of the quality model as though they existed in a vacuum. Yet many of the most successful American adopters of the new quality model conceived and promoted their efforts as part of a broad manufacturing improvement initiative. If Toyota Motor Co. epitomizes many of the attributes of the new quality model, as surely it does, it is also the case that the approach to quality in Toyota is carefully integrated into the overall Toyota production systems with its many different elements and imperatives. Similarly, the old quality model was well integrated into the traditional post–World War II production systems of large American manufacturing firms.

Thus far, I have described in this chapter the process characteristics of the old and new quality models. I have also clarified many of the characteristics expected in manufactured products according to the two conceptions. Conformance to requirements under the old model versus a customer-driven orientation under the new model captures the heart of the differences. The new quality model requires the integration of customer needs into all phases of the business and in all functions and among all employees. Although the control element of the old quality model clearly continues to be important, to operate effectively it is carefully balanced with a thrust for innovation and creativity in the service of customer satisfaction.

The characteristics of the new quality model have continued to evolve through the late 1990s with the arrival of ISO 9000 and as the perceived need to integrate quality more effectively with strategic business objectives strengthens. My examination of the transformation of quality at HP in Chapters 7 and 8 will capture many aspects of this ongoing evolution.

I round out this discussion by clarifying the quality dimensions around which firms can and do actually compete. David Garvin (1988) provides this framework by identifying eight categories of quality: performance, features, reliability, conformance, durability, serviceability, aesthetics, and perceived quality. Obviously, the old model emphasized conformance. The essence of the new competitive reality is that firms need to think strategically about all these categories, evaluating what competitors emphasize and what customers want, targeting dimensions that promise large competitive advantage. It is fair to say that the Japanese discovered in the early 1980s that Western manufacturing firms had underplayed the importance of reliability to customers; thus, many Japanese manufacturers targeted their improvement activities and market entry to this dimension. The Japanese manufacturers were thinking more strategically about quality in general. This strategic orientation toward quality was still another hurdle that the American manufacturers needed to jump to be competitive.

An Epochal Shift?

In thinking about the differences between the old and new quality models, one infers, from the preceding discussion, that the new model directly contradicted and made obsolete much of the expertise required by the old model. Behavior rewarded under the old model, like heroic acts of John Wayne firefighting to deal with major failures are indicators of failed systems under the new model. It is a waste of resources that should not happen in a regime based on upstream prevention. Supervisory skills designed to monitor workers to minimize variation are replaced by employee self-monitoring, correction, and improvement of work processes. Instead of minimizing incentives for individual and organizational learning as under the old model, continuous improvement contains a strong model of learning applicable to all employees and requires a management mode that supports these efforts.

We have here a version of what Tushman and Anderson (1986: 439–465) label "competence-destroying" rather than "competence-enhancing" technological advances. They particularly refer to *technological* discontinuities, and the new quality model can be understood as a set of specific process technologies. Much discontinuity and disruption of established routines arrived with the introduction of the new quality model. The skills and knowledge required to implement the new quality model were fundamentally different from those required under the old quality model. Because, under such conditions, established firms are often slow to acquire the new competencies, new competitors, better able to exploit these new technologies, acquire greater market share and power. During the 1980s this trend clearly emerged in many key manufacturing sectors. In the case of the auto and much of the electronics industry, the Japanese gain in market share throughout most of the 1980s was strong. Of course, their success was not solely attributable to quality differences, but persistent quality differences do clearly contribute. The new quality model required major changes in skills, distinctive competencies, and the organization of production processes. Changes of this scope and magnitude are typically associated with major changes in the distribution of power and control within firms and industries (Tushman and Anderson, 1986: 442).

In short, I believe the new quality model was associated with competence-destroying discontinuities that disrupted existing patterns of dominance in industry structures. A subset of skills used by product class leaders was rendered largely obsolete. Many of the existing large American manufacturing organizations bound by tradition, costs sunk in existing routines, internal political constraints, and skepticism of the new technology lost market share to the bearers of this new technology.

In stressing the competence-destroying rather than competence-enhancing mechanisms associated with the shift to the new quality model, I take issue with David Garvin (1988: 36–38), who argues for an evolutionary perspective whereby quality moves through the following historical stages: inspection orientation, statistical quality control, quality assurance, and strategic quality management. According to this view, strategic quality management is simply the capstone of a trend initiated more than a century ago. While there is merit to this view from an analytic perspective, I believe this view dramatically underestimates the shock to the existing management systems posed by the Japanese quality challenges in the early 1980s. A practitioner consultant, Richard Schonberger, who had considerable influence in introducing the new manufacturing model to American management in the mid-1980s, makes the following observations: "Before the ferment of the 1980s, quality in Western industry had gone through thirty-five years of stagnation. Yes, we did change the name of the quality function: quality assurance department instead of quality control department. Slogans like 'quality is everybody's business' appeared, too. It was talk without action" (1986: 123).

Evidence for Discontinuity?

Garvin (1988) sees the recent developments in quality as part of a long evolutionary development. Viewed from this perspective, my contrast between the old and new quality models seems to greatly exaggerate differences in practices. Have I created a straw man? I emphasized the discontinuity between the old and new quality models. From my perspective, an evolutionary take on the matter misses the shock, the disbelief, and total lack of preparedness for the new quality competition contained in the American response to the Japanese manufacturing challenge. This discontinuity is critical to understanding managements' delayed response to the quality challenge. Is there a way to structure these competing views of the shift from the old to new quality model (discontinuity versus continuity), to bring evidence to bear on the matter? I think so.

I first examine the continuity of skills required under the old and new models. A corollary of this discontinuous view is that the skills and talents required to be successful under the old model would not be helpful in implementing the new model. I argue that the new required skills, by and large, were competence-destroying rather than competence-enhancing. One way to get at this matter is to examine the role and careers of leading quality executives over time.

I begin with the results of a survey conducted by the Conference Board in conjunction with the American Society for Quality Control (Conference Board, 1994). The study, conducted in 1992, surveyed the top quality executives in *Fortune* 1000 companies actively engaged in improving their quality processes. The sample was composed of 154 manufacturing firms and 98 service firms. The response rate was 36% for manufacturing firms and 22% for service firms, the difference reflecting perhaps the longer and deeper experience with quality as a focused activity in manufacturing.[5]

The survey data reveal the degree of career continuity of top quality executives through an examination of the diversity of their skills and experiences. A traditional quality control or quality assurance career took place mostly in the manufacturing department of a manufacturing firm often in the following trajectory: inspector, in-process inspector, quality technician, quality supervisor, and quality assurance manager. Or, as Juran (1988: 11, 32–33) notes, one might progress through a set of inspector grades and then, with more education, progress through engineering work with greater and greater management responsibilities as quality control engineer, chief of quality control engineering, and quality manager.[6]

If quality were a competence-enhancing technological change, one would expect management to add to this chain of jobs a position of senior quality manager to carry out the expanded activities necessary under the new quality model. In short, an evolutionary perspective would lead one to expect a strong continuity of experience and skills reflected in the careers of those spearheading the new quality initiatives. One would expect those leading the effort to be the most knowledgeable about quality and able to build on their prior experiences in the quality field. If, on the other hand, quality were a competence-destroying technological change, one would expect that the new leaders of this drive for change would come from other fields and would not benefit from a strong quality background.

The Conference Board study reports the top quality executives' fields of expertise and duties in previous jobs. The first set of data examine the extent to which the top quality executives have job responsibilities in other functions. The results show that, in addition to quality, 53% of respondents are responsible for areas other than quality that cover a broad range of functional activities. The leading operations for which these quality executives have responsibility, in order of listing, are human relations (23%) and manufacturing (18%).[7] In short, the results suggest considerable diversity of skills and experiences in the background of these quality executives. Many firms have drafted individuals with expertise outside the traditional quality field and put them in charge of leading the quality initiative along with their other responsibilities.

The second set of data is even more telling. It reports prior jobs within the current firm of these leading quality executives. Only 26% had a previous job in the quality area. The rest came to their current job from quite diverse functions. Even more revealing is that if we go back to the second previous job, only 15% had quality responsibilities, and in the third previous job, only 9% did. Thus, these senior quality executives have quite modest experience in traditional quality control/quality assurance.

By studying Harley-Davidson, one can capture the thinking of top management in choosing new quality leadership from outside the ranks of existing quality personnel. Harley's top management became aware of severe quality deficits vis-à-vis their Japanese competitors in the early 1980s.

> Harley's top management realized that quality had to improve sharply and that the person in charge of quality assurance would have to be oriented toward making the kind of drastic change that was demanded. Their choice was Ron Hutchinson. Hutchinson had been with Harley-Davidson since 1975 in a variety of engineering and program-management positions, but he had never been directly involved in quality assurance. This was actually a plus, because Harley's leaders were looking more for a fresh viewpoint than for experience. They wanted someone free from restrictive preconceived notions about quality that could impede the radical changes that had to be made (Reid, 1990: 72).

We see here in microcosm the kind of discontinuity between the old and new quality models as reflected in the thinking of top management.

The discontinuity described here was not limited to the corporate leaders directing the quality improvement initiative. Consider the experiences of HP, a company known as a pacesetter for its early and successful adoption of the new quality model (Main, 1994: 164–168). Craig Walter took over as the chief corporate quality officer at HP in 1983, having had prior work experience at HP in the research and development (R&D), manufacturing and marketing areas; he began working in the quality area in 1974 in HP's Loveland, Colorado, operations. One of the first problems he faced as chief corporate quality officer was that roughly half of the quality managers at the division level were perceived as incapable of practicing the new quality model. Most were glorified inspectors with their jobs containing a small reliability and engineering component. "They were doing 'old line' reactive QA."[8] To deal with the problem, the quality manager's job was redesigned and split into two new jobs from 1984 to 1985. The first job was consistent with the existing job duties of quality managers and involved running inspection and electronic maintenance and quality services. The second job was to work as staff for the general manager by designing a TQC program (modeled to a large extent on the Japanese TQC efforts practiced at Yokogawa HP), in addition to taking responsibility for reliability improvement and product testing. To send the right signal, the second job was rewarded at a higher level than the first. Indeed, the signal was so clear that no one ever tried to qualify for the first job. All the general managers who were interested searched for occupants for the second job.

At this time there were about 60 quality managers in HP at the division level. Almost all of the existing quality managers had qualifications for the first job and almost none had qualifications for second. The first job gradually disappeared over the next two to three years. Roughly half of the existing quality managers were identified as able to adjust to the new job description. They underwent informal training over the next few years with the annual companywide quality council meeting for all quality managers being one important avenue for socializing them into their new job requirements. Some of those who could not make the transition took early retirement. According to Craig Walter, "It was real hard to find new jobs for the others." In those days, the quality department still had a reputation as a haven for those who could not "cut it" in manufacturing. Whereas in the past, the old quality manager job had recruited almost entirely from manufacturing, the new job began to recruit from a broader base, drawing from functions such as sales, marketing, and R & D.

This description of HP experiences suggests considerable discontinuity in quality job functions at the divisional level. The transition to implementing the new quality model had important new career consequences for the old as well as the new quality manager job occupants.

Let's return to the Conference Board survey in which respondents were asked which characteristics made them eligible for their current position. Despite provision for multiple responses, only 25% of respondents listed their experience with quality as a major criterion. Those responses receiving a higher rank included other work experiences (56%), educational background (38%), and other personal qualities (28%). By other personal qualities, respondents referred to facilitation and leadership skills, high achiever, and good planner. In short, on-the-job experiences in other functions, disciplines, and areas were judged to be more useful than a quality background in leading the quality initiative. Finally, the study found that senior quality executives divided on the issue of whether quality constituted a profession and a career. Forty-nine percent agreed and 51% disagreed. If there had been a strong career line based on a continuity of skills leading to the top quality position, one would have expected much stronger support for quality as a profession.

In summary, it seems abundantly clear that those leading quality initiatives at these *Fortune* 1000 firms did not come from a background in quality assurance and did not judge quality experiences to be critical to their job performance. Why would this be true? Only one explanation seems plausible. Management concluded that those with a quality background in the firm were not suited to lead this new effort because their skills and knowledge were fundamentally different from those required for the new positions. What were some of the new skills required? The major job responsibilities of the quality leaders responding to the Conference Board survey were to deploy and lead quality and to develop processes and plans to do that. These are not the kinds of tasks that predominated under the old quality model, wherein specialist expertise was expected to solve problems, and minimize variation and where mass mobilization of employees was not an issue.

Recall that Tushman and Anderson argue that competence-destroying technological advances are often associated with major changes in the distribution of power and control within firms and industries. One way to examine this condition is to look at the changing status and job characteristics of high-ranking quality officials over time. If the quality movement meets this condition, then one would expect to see some major changes in the position and responsibilities of top quality executives in the period under investigation (roughly 1980 through 1995). A sharp shift reinforces my argument that the new quality model represented a major discontinuity in practice.

I have chosen to operationalize this task by collecting data on the number of vice presidents for quality in the *Fortune* 500 manufacturing firms over a 14-year interval beginning in 1980 and using 1987 and 1994 as additional sampling points. In each of these three years, I have sought to document the number of firms by industry with vice presidents for quality. Using electronic databases, I examined all *Fortune* 500 firms in each of the three years and supplemented this methodology with a variety of other approaches, including comparing the findings to data from the Conference Board study (which they kindly made available) and calling companies to verify any differences.[9]

Table 1.5 reports my findings. It shows that the total number of quality vice presidents at the corporate level among the *Fortune* 500 totaled 22 (4.5%) in 1980, 45 (9%) in 1987 and 108 (21.6%) in 1994. This constitutes a striking increase in the number of quality vice presidents in the 14-year span. Is this change accounted for by shifts in industry composition of the *Fortune* 500 over time, or have the

Table 1.5. *Fortune* 500 by Industry, Number of Firms in Industry, and Firms with Corporate-Quality Vice Presidents

Industry	SIC Code	No. of Firms in Industry				No. of Firms with Quality VPs			
		1980	1987	1994	Change, 1980–1994	1980	1987	1994	Change, 1980–1994
Aerospace	37	12	18	16	4	0	4	10	10
Apparel	23	9	10	9	0	0	0	0	0
Beverage	20	12	8	10	-2	2	1	1	-1
Building materials	32	15	18	8	-7	0	2	2	2
Chemicals	28	37	44	46	9	0	0	6	6
Computers, office equipment	35	13	23	27	14	1	8	11	10
Electronics	36	35	47	44	9	1	4	17	16
Food	20	54	53	49	-5	4	2	9	5
Forest and paper products	26	29	33	34	5	0	4	5	5
Furniture	25	2	5	7	5	0	0	3	3
Industry and farm equipment	35	43	33	32	-11	2	2	6	4
Metal products	34	29	21	16	-13	1	2	3	2
Metals	33	41	22	26	-15	1	2	6	5
Mining, crude-oil production	10	14	12	12	-2	0	0	0	0
Motor vehicle and parts	37	21	18	22	1	4	3	2	-2
Petroleum refining	29	36	32	32	-4	1	1	2	1
Pharmaceuticals	28	17	16	16	-1	2	1	7	5
Publishing/printing	27	12	19	20	8	0	0	2	2
Rubber products	30	7	15	12	5	1	1	3	2
Scientific and photo equipment	38	17	17	22	5	1	7	8	7
Soaps, cosmetics	28	8	10	12	4	0	0	1	1
Textiles	22	11	11	13	2	1	0	2	1
Tobacco	21	7	4	6	-1	0	1	1	1
Toys, sporting goods	39	4	5	3	-1	0	0	0	0
Transportation equipment	37	7	4	5	-2	0	0	1	1
Total		492	498	499		22	45	108	

Note: The total firms do not add to 500 because the broadcasting industry, the motion picture production and distribution industry, the jewelry and silverware industry, and the leather industry were excluded from this table. Broadcasting was deleted because it was dropped from the *Fortune* 500 after 1981, and jewelry and leather because the small number of firms in the *Fortune* 500 makes the findings too unreliable.

changes been produced by only a few industries, thereby giving a misleading impression?

The left-hand column of Table 1.6 provides clear answers to these questions. In examining the shift from 1980 to 1994, one sees that 20 of the 25 industries recorded gains in the percentage of quality vice president executives; three started at 0 and ended at 0 and two (motor vehicles and beverages) suffered a loss in the percentage of quality vice presidents. Thus, there is a strong trend across manufacturing sectors over this 14-year period for firms to appoint corporate vice presidents for quality. Shifting industry composition does not account for these broad and deep changes, nor do a few high-profile industries.

We cannot draw the conclusion that firms which did not create quality vice president positions at the corporate level did not develop a growing commitment to quality. Many firms with strong divisionalized operations chose to create vice president positions at the divisional rather than corporate level. This was the case with many of the auto companies. Thus, GM has a vice president of quality for North American operations, one of its major divisions, but not at the corporate level. While I have no conclusive data, I do have suggestive data to indicate that, over the 14-year time span, the urge to create quality vice presidents at the divisional level was even stronger than for the corporate level. It turns out that the Conference Board's 1992 study included in its sample 38 manufacturing firms that were either divisions or subsidiaries of a Fortune 500 parent. I found that the percentage of these firms with vice presidents (28.3%) was even higher than the comparable figure for *Fortune* 500 companies (21.9%).

An examination of Table 1.6 reveals a clear pattern. The durable goods sector firms (shown in Table 1.6 by the two-digit Standard Industrial Classification (SIC) code beginning with 3) dominate the top rankings in terms of both amount of change from 1980 to 1994 (left columns) and in terms of the absolute ranking of firms with quality vice presidents in 1994 (right columns). By contrast, the non-durable goods sector firms (shown in Table 1.6 by the two-digit (SIC) code beginning with 2) dominate the lowest rankings.[10] It is also clear that the heaviest Japanese competition in quality in the 1980s and early 1990s was in the durable goods sector.

In accounting for the different industry positions in terms of amount of change between 1980 and 1994 and the absolute rank in 1994, one should note a number of factors. Eight of the 22 quality vice presidents in 1980 shown in Table 1.5 were in industries with long-standing concerns about quality as they related to public safety (food, beverage, and pharmaceuticals). At that time, quality vice presidents were the products of the traditional quality discipline of quality control and quality assurance. Corporate vice presidents in these industries provided legitimacy to the firm by assuring the public they were taking quality seriously, though this did not preclude them from having strong functional roles as well. A number of the companies in these areas, included in the Conference Board study, reported that they had adopted new TQM-like approaches to quality in the late 1980s.

Table 1.6. *Fortune* 500 by Industry and Percentage of Quality Vice Presidents

SIC Code	Industry	Percentage of Quality VPS: Change, 1980–1994	SIC Code	Industry	Percentage of Quality VPS: 1994
37	Aerospace	62.5	37	Aerospace	62.5
25	Furniture	42.9	28	Pharmaceuticals	43.8
36	Electronics	35.8	25	Furniture	42.9
35	Computers, office equipment	33.0	35	Computers, office equipment	40.7
28	Pharmaceuticals	32.0	36	Electronics	38.6
38	Scientific and photo equipment	30.5	38	Scientific and photo equipment	36.4
32	Building materials	25.0	32	Building materials	25.0
33	Metals	20.6	30	Rubber products	25.0
37	Transportation equipment	20.0	33	Metals	23.1
21	Tobacco	16.7	37	Transportation equipment	20.0
34	Metal products	15.3	35	Industry and farm equipment	18.8
26	Forest and paper products	14.7	34	Metal products	18.8
35	Industry and farm equipment	14.1	20	Food	18.4
28	Chemicals	13.0	21	Tobacco	16.7
20	Food	11.0	22	Textiles	15.4
30	Rubber products	10.7	26	Forest and paper products	14.7
27	Publishing/printing	10.0	28	Chemicals	13.0
28	Soaps, cosmetics	8.3	20	Beverage	10.0
22	Textiles	6.3	27	Publishing/printing	10.0
29	Petroleum refining	3.5	37	Motor vehicle and parts	9.1
23	Apparel	0.0	28	Soaps, cosmetics	8.3
10	Mining, crude-oil production	0.0	29	Petroleum refining	6.3
39	Toys, sporting goods	0.0	23	Apparel	0.0
20	Beverage	−6.7	10	Mining, crude-oil production	0.0
37	Motor vehicle and parts	−10.0	39	Toys, sporting goods	0.0

Source: Derived from Table 1.5.

Over time, the selection of vice presidents for quality involved a transition from traditional quality assurance types to the quality vice presidents whose duty was to promote the more comprehensive activities associated with the new quality model. By including vice presidents with the term "customer" in their title in my sample, however, I have included many whose responsibilities are in providing equipment service for their customers. Such roles are particularly prominent in the computer/equipment industries. Furthermore, these and other companies sometimes create a vice president position responsible for following customer orders from sale through production and delivery. Such individuals do not have broad responsibilities for quality improvement activities in the company.

Thus, LSI Logic Corporation in 1994 had a vice president for customer service and logistics whose job included customer service responsibilities for tracing customer orders from sales through production. There was no quality vice president with broad quality improvement responsibilities (some companies have both). Including such individuals inflates the total of quality vice presidents and encompasses job duties very different from the promoter of quality improvement, as described in the data from the Conference Board study. Manufacturing sector totals strongly affected by these practices include computers, office equipment, and electronics. A former copier industry quality executive examined our list and estimated that perhaps 10 of the 108 listings in 1994 were for companies in which the position was filled by a customer service person (these were companies with no additional vice president for quality with broader responsibilities). So why include only companies that had individuals with such titles in our sample? These positions are also a measure of the changing times; such positions did not exist in 1980 and thus legitimately can be included as one of the new features produced by the modern quality movement, though the role is quite different from a promoter of corporatewide quality improvement.

Finally, in what way are the roles of the vice presidents I have identified important? Are they operationally significant? Are they primarily ceremonial to assure the public that a company is paying attention to quality, or are these companies simply imitating other successful companies? These three functions are not necessarily mutually exclusive. I do not have data from my survey that directly bears on this issue, but the Conference Board study is suggestive. When asked to compare their ability to influence decisions with that of other executives, 46% of respondents said that it was about the same (28% said it was more than others and 26% said it was less than others).

Furthermore, respondents to the Conference Board study compared favorably with top executives in marketing, information technology, and human resources in terms of whether they report directly to senior management. Fifty-five percent of the senior quality executives identified in the Conference Board study (which includes those at and below the vice president level) reported directly to top management; this compared to 50% for chief marketing executives, 29% for chief human resource executives, and 8% for chief information officers. The data for the other functions come from other studies using different methodologies, so the results, while impressive, are only suggestive.

One would expect that if the employee reports directly to senior management, he or she is less likely to occupy a purely ceremonial position. Similarly, the job duties described by respondents to the Conference Board study point to individuals with responsibilities to promote a broad range of quality improvement activities throughout the firm.

These interpretations are consistent with the competitive uncertainties firms faced in responding to the Japanese quality challenge at the time many of these positions were created. Establishing small corporate offices headed by vice presidents of quality was a means for the organization to capture information about the central uncertainties firms faced in these areas (cf. Stinchcombe, 1990: 19). Typically these new quality executives monitored progress toward implementation of effective quality practices in other firms; many participated in networks of comparable executives. I describe these activities in more detail in Chapter 6. Although there is no systematic evidence, apparently many of these individuals were selected because of top management's trust in them and their reputation as individuals who knew how to get things done. All this suggests that appointing vice presidents for quality was not simply an imitative or token appointment to establish legitimacy.

The data allow one additional test of my interpretations. The information from Fortune 500 manufacturing firms that had positions of vice presidents for quality in the three years sampled allowed us to identify 174 vice presidents for quality from 176 companies.[11] These names allow us to return to the functional specialty in prior jobs. Recall that a relatively low proportion of those quality leaders had a background in quality.

With these new data from *Fortune* 500 firms derived from a different source, one can address this same issue from a slightly different angle. The major source of information for the quality control professional has traditionally been the American Society for Quality (ASQ).[12] It is the association for quality professionals and has had a virtual monopoly on the distribution of information about the progress and development of the quality discipline. ASQ has been dedicated to improving the career status and prospects of quality practitioners.

With the cooperation of ASQ, I examined how many of these 174 individuals whom we identified had ever been members of the organization.[13] ASQ membership serves as a reasonable proxy for measuring the proportion of these quality vice presidents who had a career in traditional quality control prior to assuming their position as vice president. I found that 49 (28%) of the 174 vice presidents had been members of ASQ at one time, well below a majority. Even this number, however, exaggerates their quality background; anecdotal evidence suggests that it is not all that unusual for individuals to join ASQ on promotion to the position of vice president for quality.[14] Thus, one needs information on year of initial membership in ASQ to determine correlation between members' early positions and their new leadership roles.

I examined how many of these 49 individuals' initial membership in ASQ preceded their vice presidential status, by at least 10 years. It takes time to build a career; one typically does not become a vice president in a *Fortune* 500 company in one's twenties and thirties. Thus, a 10-year frame seemed a reasonable condition for measuring career commitment to quality.

I found that only 15 of these 49 vice presidents who had been members of ASQ had 10 or more years of membership experience with ASQ before the year of their vice presidential role. If one uses this as a measure of career commitment to quality, instead of 28% of our 174 executives qualifying, the percentage falls to less than 9% (15/174). In short, as measured by ASQ membership, the overwhelming majority of the 174 vice presidents for quality did not have a career in quality prior to assuming their vice presidential role. These data, while not conclusive, are remarkably consistent with the Conference Board findings, in which, of the *Fortune* 500 quality leaders surveyed, only 9% had quality responsibilities in their third previous job. In summary, as measured by career trajectory and longevity, one can hardly argue that the experience over the last decade with quality represents an evolutionary change in which the new approaches to quality built on past technological expertise. Rather, the multiple sources of evidence show sharp discontinuity.

In summary, the picture I have drawn in this chapter shows the leading quality executives' growth in status. The number of quality vice presidents rose, but they had few skills congruent with traditional quality control. Seemingly, their power grew during the 1980s and early 1990s, as reflected in their decision-making, information-gathering, and reporting relationships. These data are consistent with Tushman and Anderson's characterization of competence-destroying technological advances causing major changes in the distribution of power and control within firms and industries. In short, adoption of the new quality model appeared to be associated with a major discontinuity in practice.

Will we see a maintenance of the current level or further growth in the number, status, and power of vice presidents for quality in U.S. corporations? Anecdotal evidence suggests the peak has arrived. In 1997, American Express decided to close its corporate quality office, merging some functions with human resources and leaving the business units to manage quality. In a number of companies, retiring vice presidents for quality have not been replaced. Such was the case at Corning (though a corporate-level quality entity was maintained) in 1994 when the incumbent, David Luther, retired. Since Luther had recently served as the president of the American Society for Quality, it was a quite visible decision. The top-management view was that quality should now be built into every department and division and that the firm no longer needed an overall czar. The initial quality challenge required huge changes and a centrally directed rapid management response involving large-scale corporate mobilization. Now that the challenge had more or less been successfully met, the need for such a central solution was less compelling. Should the perspective represented by Corning become more pervasive, as it likely will, at one level the new quality model will be institutionalized as part of everyday corporate management. Surely some downgrading and dilution of the concentration on quality will result, but the institutionalization of quality improvement practices at the divisional level and the importance of quality as a competitive issue ensures that pre-1980s status will not return.

It is now time to turn to the initial responses of American management to the Japanese quality challenge. The thrust of this chapter suggests that the challenge was quite formidable, given the high degree of discontinuity. Management had to cast aside some ingrained ways and move on to adopt a very different mindset and a different set of practices.

CHAPTER 2

Market Pressures and Quality Consciousness

How are we to understand the rise of the American quality movement in the 1980s? Was it a simple response to market pressures or did more complicated institutional factors shape how and when the movement developed? Quality does not at first glance appear to be an issue like those noted by March and Olsen (1976) in which top management discovers motives only through adopting new approaches. After all, in the early 1980s, the objective became clear in one manufacturing sector after another: meet the Japanese quality challenge. Seems straightforward enough.

Barriers to Recognition

If one wants to understand the slow adoption of the new quality paradigm, one should start at the beginning. Only in the late 1970s and early 1980s did a general understanding grow among managers that a quality deficit was a major factor in their competitive problems. Late recognition, despite ample signs, resulted from a mindset that dismissed quality as a major competitive factor in mass markets. These men (by and large) were accustomed to thinking in terms of competing over lower unit costs, new products, shifts in resource allocations from low return inputs to high return inputs, expanding markets, building better sales networks, achieving economies of scale and scope, increased output per worker, technology, brand names, product differentiation, and creation of strong top management teams (cf. Chandler, 1962: 393–396; 1990: 497–498).[1] They had made their careers in functional departments such as marketing and finance, and they were dedicated to realizing corporate objectives through applying the principles learned in these departments. They had accepted Alfred Sloan's dictum, laid down in the 1920s, that superior competitive quality was not necessary to gain market share against a competitor. Higher quality mattered mostly in terms of adding product attributes. Product differentiation and increased volume at reduced costs were the keys to success

(Sloan, 1963: 66). Thus, they aimed for acceptable quality levels (AQLs) in line with those of other domestic competitors.

Within the firm, AQL can be defined as an acceptance sampling procedure whereby the customer agrees to accept a product from its suppliers as long as it does not exceed a known and specified quality level (such as x defects per hundred units). Once fixed in practice, these levels tended to be static; there is no everyday need of continuous quality improvement. In effect, AQL came to mean that "there *was* an acceptable level of bad quality" (Hayes, Wheelwright, and Clark, 1988: 17 italics in original). "Off spec" quality was covered by establishing repair facilities and selling service warranties, viewed as profit centers. With hindsight, one cannot help being struck by the hubris of companies profiting from their own failures by asking customers to bear the costs. Historically AQLs developed through the Military Standard specification (MIL-STD-105D) first issued in 1950; the civilian sector later formally adopted a parallel version (ANSI/ASQC Z1.4) in 1981 (Juran, 1988: 25–44). As long as everyone in an industry played the same AQL game, there was no problem. It was like agreeing to give an industrywide wage contract to all employees, thereby taking employee compensation out of the competitive game. Only, in this case, quality was eliminated as a competitive factor in mass markets. That is, it was eliminated until Japanese competitors entered the game.

Not surprisingly in this environment, top manufacturing managers were accustomed to thinking about quality as a low-level function involving inspection, which in fact it typically was. Their inclination to ignore or deny quality as a competitive factor is therefore quite predictable. Moreover, if, by chance, top management consulted their quality experts about how to respond to an emergent challenge in quality, they were not likely to get much guidance, since most were still committed to the traditional quality model.

Those at the top of organizational hierarchies usually have expertise related to older and more stable job routines based on the past competencies of the firm; they are prone therefore to interpret events in these terms, and they promote employees and favor strategies that will keep these tasks central (Burgelman and Grove, 1996: 14; Starbuck and Milliken, 1988: 53). They participate in information structures associated with their accumulated functional expertise and tend to be isolated from new ideas and methodologies (cf. March, 1994: 236). In effect these leaders had what Thorsten Veblen, that remarkable twentieth century institutionalist, called a "trained incapacity," or what the French call *déformation professionelle*. Robert Merton (1968: 252) later interpreted trained incapacity as that historical situation in which one's abilities turn into inadequacies or blind spots. Actions based upon training and skills that have been successfully applied in the past result in inappropriate responses under changed conditions. The new conditions are not recognized as sufficiently different, so all that past experience and training, and the rewards associated with them, lead the individual to adopt familiar, but wrong, solutions.

The inertia at the individual level resulting from trained incapacity parallels a system of power at the organizational level that benefits the existing organizational leadership (Fligstein, 1991: 316), who, understandably, tend to be suspicious of changes that would challenge their base of power and expertise.

Were American managers simply slow-witted? No. Bad results and mistaken actions and thinking always show up in retrospective analysis (Starbuck and Milliken, 1988: 38). Managers had been rewarded in the past for certain behaviors, and they had no reason to think that different responses were required this time. This response is quite rational; it would not be rational to respond to each new challenge with an assumption that "this time things are different and I need a very different way of thinking" (Ross and Lepper, 1980). Nevertheless, in the case of the quality challenge, their rational response based on past experiences was not rational from a market perspective. Unfortunately, it was inappropriate, given the new circumstances their companies faced.

American managers' extended economic success during much of the post–World War II period gave them precious little preparation for thinking about quality as a new basis of competition. Success gives individual managers and organizations an overconfidence that insulates them from changes in their environment (Starbuck and Milliken, 1988: 49). Managers came from around the world to study at U.S. managers' feet, not the other way around. Hubris and arrogance resulted. Yet Japanese managers were not immune to similar behavior at the height of their competitive success in America in the late 1980s.

In the early 1980s, the standard information reporting systems did not routinely bring quality performance to the attention of top management. Top executives lacked information on customer satisfaction, competitor comparisons of quality performance, customer perceived needs, and the costs of poor quality performance (cf. Juran, 1995: 583). Nor was it a matter of getting the right reports channeled to top executives. In many cases, the data simply were not collected and the reports not written. The case had not yet been made and the mental framework not yet created for collecting and analyzing comprehensive kinds of quality data. When companies did collect quality-related data, it was typically information on complaints, not a comprehensive data-gathering effort that involved the reactions of all customers. Indeed, the most pervasive kind of quality data used by American manufacturing firms in the early 1980s was field failure data, ideal for performance under the old quality model because it was all about detection and not prevention. Moreover, even when companies collected this limited slice of quality data, it often sat unanalyzed and unused.

The reports management did receive at this time consisted mainly of financial information. Not surprisingly, as Juran (1995: 583) observed, management came to believe that Japanese competition was primarily price competition based on cost advantages (access to cheap capital and low labor costs) rather than quality competition. The former masked the latter. Yet quality competition increasingly supplemented price competition during and after the late 1970s. The managerial misperceptions seen here are less a matter of information-processing errors than an unconscious filtering of information based on established work routines that confirmed their existing definitions of the situation (cf. Starbuck and Milliken, 1988).

Even those well-traveled business school professors at the elite institutions did not recognize quality as a major competitive factor until the late 1980s and many not even then. Their specialties, not surprisingly, paralleled those in the business world. That quality was a new competitive reality escaped almost all of them. In short, academics were of little use to managers as they sought to understand the new competitive reality.

Denial took two forms in the late 1970s and early 1980s. First, managers denied quality as a major competitive factor or they denied Japanese superiority. To deny strong evidence, individuals typically require a cognitive mechanism that allows them to accomplish that goal (Ross and Lepper, 1980: 24). That is, they had to have a plausible account that would explain events in a different fashion, blaming competitive problems with the Japanese on a variety of others factors. Cost competition based on low wages, access to cheap capital, exploitation of suppliers, unfair government support, and manipulation of currency rates were all prominent parts of this alternative explanation. Singly or in combination, these accounts provided the cognitive grounds that protected existing beliefs from the impact of logical and empirical attacks asserting the primacy of Japanese quality. These accounts allowed managers to resist the otherwise irresistible, at least for a while.

Early Warnings

From this broad perspective, it is plausible that managers would not even notice some of the early cues that pointed to quality as a major competitive issue. Yet, as Starbuck and Milliken also point out, if you do not notice important cues, they are not even available for "sensemaking" (Starbuck and Milliken, 1988: 45; see also Weick, 1995). Instead of learning from the experience of industries such as sewing machines, cameras, watches, and color TVs (see Tsuru, 1993: 82) and from the early inroads on their own markets, managers found it much easier to attribute the failure of these industries to unique industry factors, normal product cycle developments, and unfair competition from the Japanese. Managers argued that their industry or division or plant or technology was different, and therefore the lessons learned elsewhere did not apply. The ability to hide from an emergent reality in this fashion should not be underestimated.

Consider the color TV industry. Here, unfair competition was seen as flowing from low wages and Japanese government subsidies and protected domestic markets.

Japanese consumers could be charged higher prices with the resultant profits used to target export markets. Emblematic of this view was the long-running dispute, starting in the early 1970s with Zenith Radio Corporation's dumping petition against the Japanese TV industry. Whatever the validity of the grievances of the domestic producers, they were not inconsistent with quality becoming an increasingly important competitive factor.

Economists and U.S. policy makers explained the decline of U.S. TV production in terms of comparative factor cost differentials favoring Japan. Product cycle theory was much in vogue and provided a rationalization for the loss of these industries. Once production becomes standardized, according to this view, production moves to countries that have a comparative advantage, usually deriving from low labor costs. The relatively high cost of labor in the United States became the villain, and moving the industry offshore, or giving up on it, became the solution. From 1973 to 1976 alone, more than 33% of those Americans employed in television assembly lost their jobs (from 35,711 in 1973 to 23,713 in 1976), and most of that loss could be attributed to the increased use of foreign components and products. Within only a few years after color TVs became available, foreign imports (mostly from Japan) captured 17% of the domestic market (1970). Six years later, foreign imports (including those from American plants that had been relocated abroad) accounted for 36% of the market.

Not only was product cycle theory in vogue but also the view that the country was rapidly moving from an industrial to a postindustrial service economy. Promoted by relentless media hype and by reports from influential players, the view that a strong manufacturing sector was not required for a prosperous economy took hold (advocates often confused the inevitable decline of employment in manufacturing with manufacturing's contribution to national economic output through increased productivity and its support of service industry growth). These analyses led to policy prescriptions focused on strengthening the service economy and leaving manufacturing to its inevitable decline (New York Stock Exchange, 1984: 32; Cook, 1983: 142–149).

Yet other lessons were inherent in the decline of industries like TV. In the case of TV, the Japanese producers invested heavily in developing solid-state technology for application in monochrome and color television sets, succeeding far more rapidly than the American producers. Solid-state technology had the advantage of increased product safety and product reliability and reduced costs in process technology. The Japanese TV producers excelled at the kind of lean manufacturing processes that yielded minimum defects, carefully crafted products, and cost reductions (Juran, 1978: 10–18). In the mid-1970s, Western color TV sets were failing in service at a rate of about five times that for Japanese sets. Although American firms initially held a lead in picture quality and product appeal (two important quality dimensions), their woefully uncompetitive performance on reliability, the measure that seemed to matter most to customers, shrunk the lead (Juran, 1978: 10–11).

American scholars and managers typically interpreted product cycle theory to emphasize the reduction of wage costs as the only means of reducing labor costs because product and process technologies were considered too fixed to provide much short-term opportunity for cost reduction. In practice, this meant moving production facilities abroad or ceding market share. In contrast, the Japanese minimized increases in their labor costs while raising wages through the savings achieved from the progressive improvement of their manufacturing processes and improved market share. Ironically, as the American producers were losing market share and moving production bases abroad, the Japanese were increasingly locating their production facilities in the United States to counter U.S. protectionist measures. By 1979, Japanese production of color TVs in the United States exceeded their total of TV exports to the United States (Tsuru, 1993: 198). Journalists and researchers began circulating information on the major improvement in quality as the Japanese took over U.S. production facilities. The Matsushita takeover of the Motorola Quasar plant in Chicago received a great deal of publicity (Juran, 1978: 17).

Just as they later did in the auto and semiconductor industries, the Japanese producers attacked the low-price end of the market that American producers often disdained for their low profit margins. Small, highly reliable Japanese color TVs became preferred consumer products and allowed the Japanese to build and take advantage of scale economies. By the mid-1970s they gained outlets through the private label domestic retailers. Sears, Montgomery Ward, and Kmart all began to purchase color TV sets from foreign suppliers between 1975 and 1976. In short, the lessons for other industries were there to see, for those who wanted to see.[2] Juran remarked that while some of the forces producing the outcome in color TVs were unique to the industry, most of them were applicable to all industries (1978: 11). Again, hardly any one was listening.

The Semiconductor and Auto Industry Responses

The initial managerial response to claims showing sharp quality differences was often denial and attempts to explain away the differences. Okimoto, Sugano, and Weinstein (1984) document the experience with semiconductors. In March 1980, a senior executive of HP at the Data Systems Division announced the results of a company study that involved testing 300,000 16K DRAM chips from three American and three Japanese firms. Japanese-made chips had consistently higher reliability. At incoming inspection, Japanese chips had a failure rate of zero versus the U.S. chips rate of 0.11% to 0.19%. After 1,000 hours of use, the simulated field failure rate of the Japanese chips was between 0.010% and 0.019%; the comparable failure rate for the U.S. chips ranged between 0.059% and 0.267% (see also Garvin, 1988: 22). In short, the best Japanese performers' defect rate was almost six times lower than that for the best American companies, and the Japanese worst performers had over 14 times better performance than the worst American companies.

By 1983, HP data show that the gap in failure rates for 16K DRAMs had been eliminated, and indeed U.S. vendors had a slight advantage (Finan and LaMond, 1985: 168). The results, however, were achieved in large part by tighter inspection standards, and that signaled the old model (higher quality at added cost). Moreover, reliability gaps developed in other more advanced chips at a later date, the Japanese continuing their advantage. As chip memory capacity increased from 16K to 64K, the difficulty of achieving high quality performance increased exponentially (Bylinsky, 1981a: 118).

Although this discussion focuses on reliability measures, many other dimensions to quality impinge on competition. One of the most important in the semiconductor industry is yield. Yield is the percentage of initial product set in production that survives after the last step of the production process is completed. Historically, yields in the semiconductor industry have been quite low because of the complexity of the manufacturing process. Yield in the semiconductor industry is a critical indicator of both productivity and quality, and here the Japanese developed a large advantage over the Americans with powerful cost implications. In the mid-1980s one research team reported that the cumulative yield for 64K chips was 23% for American producers and 38% for Japanese producers (Finan and LaMond, 1985: 156).

Data on comparisons between American and Japanese producers in probe yield from VLSI Research shed further light on the matter. Probe yield is the last electrical test for functionality before semiconductor chips are cut from the wafer, packaged, and assembled. According to the data, the American chip producers had a probe yield advantage of 10% in 1981, but by 1986, the Japanese held an advantage of 15% and by 1987 19% (U.S. General Accounting Office, 1992: 10). In short, the Japanese quality advantage, as shown by various measures of yield, actually grew for much of the 1980s.

There were a great many industry naysayers to the initial HP announcement about chip reliability. The extent of the reported differences shocked industry leaders, many of whom did not believe it. Executives at a number of semiconductor producers said that their industry customers had found no difference in field failure rates between U.S. and Japanese memory chips. They questioned the validity of HP's data and even suggested the company had used improper screening procedures or used a particular test that favored the Japanese companies. Others accepted the HP data but argued that the Japanese had engaged in selective shipping so that their best quality products were sent to U.S. customers (Bylinsky, 1981: 116). Still others argued that the Japanese were engaged in "quality dumping," whereby the high prices in their protected domestic market made the funds available to produce the higher quality chips exported to the United States. Note the continuing assumption here that if they did have higher quality in their U.S. exports, they must have been spending more money to get it (see Okimoto, Sugano, and Weinstein, 1984: 54–55, for a summary of the arguments listed above).

More broadly speaking, quality was not on the minds of semiconductor industry leaders for different reasons. This was an industry driven almost entirely by technology. Leadership of the industry in the 1970s and 1980s was very much in the hands of electrical engineers and applied physicists. Electrical engineers had a tendency to feel superior to other engineers and nonengineers, not the best approach for building cooperative activities across functions and levels necessary for high quality and manufacturing performance. Many electrical engineers arrogantly believed, "We created the industry from nothing." For them, the winner is he who initiates new technology.

The problem was not that the leadership focused on technology per se but rather their conception of technology. Their preferences and priorities, reinforced through past successes, led them to a very narrow conception of technology aimed exclusively at the cutting edge of research and development. The highest priority goes to projects that promise to build proprietary products. What is needed for improving quality and productivity performance, however, is a broad conception of technology, tightly linking R & D to the manufacturing process (cf., Angel, 1994: 3). Thus, it was very hard for industry leaders to take quality and productivity competition from the Japanese seriously or to learn from other seemingly more "backward" industries.[3]

Despite dramatically different management cultures, the auto industry provides a remarkably parallel case. The coordination between product design and manufacturing was extremely poor. Incremental improvements to product design were seen as central to corporate success; process improvement was a relatively low-status function. Early warnings, however, were available in the auto industry as well. Thus, Louis Latiaf, a Ford vice president in the mid-1980s, observed that individual buyers in the 1970s were saying they did not like the products, but the organization did not hear them until losses were running in the billions of dollars (Easterbrook, 1992: 319).

In a November 1978 interview with the *Detroit Free Press*, Ford chairman and CEO Philip Caldwell, in response to criticism of U.S. auto quality, said that Ford owners were happier with the quality of their cars than with that of any other domestic producer. He conveniently chose not to address the quality of Japanese competitors nor other data that showed Ford had the worst quality of the Big Three (Petersen and Hillkirk, 1991: 5). In 1980, John Manoogian, Ford's newly appointed executive director for product assurance, conceded that "the Japanese had a slight edge in quality delivered to the dealer." Later that year Ford vice president Bidwell told the *Detroit Free Press* that "the high quality of Japanese cars is to some extent real and to some extent perceived."

Some of these public utterances are likely damage control statements. After all, it would not make sense to publicly acknowledge your competitors' superiority. Yet similar statements were also made to internal audiences. In a November 1980 issue of GM's *Tech Center News* (an internal organ designed to reach GM employees), GM's president-elect James McDonald first extolled GM quality and then remarked: "[W]e think we have not always given enough attention to some appearance items. And to our potential customers, quality is often determined by the first impression of these fit and finish items" (Cole, 1990: 71).

Standard industry responses in the late 1970s and early 1980s stressed that any differences between U.S. and Japanese cars were only superficial fit and finish differences and therefore "perception" problems created by uneducated consumers.

Professor David Cole, a well-known and respected commentator on the state of the U.S. auto industry, defended the domestic industry on the quality issue in a 1981 University of Michigan conference address to a large industry audience (Cole, 1981: 99–122). He argued that, with the exception of fit and finish quality, U.S. vehicles were at least as good as and often better than Japanese products. The problem was how to convey the importance and existence of hidden quality to technically untrained consumers. But this argument misses the point. Even if the Japanese were better only in one area and the Americans were ahead overall, the customers had their own method of prioritizing and seemed to be voting with their wallets and purses for Japanese autos in this period. Perception is reality. Moreover, industry leaders were later to find out that the problems went far beyond fit and finish.

To be sure, there were middle-and even top-management officials who realized the significance of quality as a competitive issue at a much earlier date. Juran, for example, reports such conversations with upper-level U.S. auto managers in 1978 (Juran, 1978: 16). It took time for these individuals to build their case with their peers. Afterward, they faced the even more daunting task of changing the views and behaviors of the large core of middle managers and workers.

Yet, by 1980, increasingly reports and studies circulated in these companies that their products, as compared with Japanese products, were suffering massive deficits in quality measured by reliability performance. In the early 1980s, I witnessed a presentation of an internal study to Ford managers that found a 6 to 1 ratio of trouble frequency for Ford vehicles to Japanese vehicles. But managers at all levels of each company could not quickly accept the validity of these reports.

Karl Weick (1995: 2) captures the psychological and social components of this resistance. Citing Westrum (1982), he points to the concept of the "fallacy of centrality." The concept refers to individuals who deny the existence of a fact or event (the Japanese have higher quality than we do), believing that "because I don't know about this fact or event, it must not be going on." This view is damaging because it not only discourages the believer's curiosity but often creates in him or her an antagonistic stance toward the events in question. American managers' strong denials that the Japanese had a quality advantage in the late 1970s and early 1980s are a case in point. These denials are not surprising because the claim of a quality advantage for the Japanese called into question America's senior manufacturing managers' very competence as managers. After all, if they were competent, they would have known about the problem much earlier, the gap would not now be so large, they would know what to do about it, and they would have done it.

Faced with these kinds of evaluations, both manifest and latent, it is easy to understand how managers sought to avoid facing up to the problem. It is also easy to see how networks of managers "conspired" to reinforce these denials. In the case of automobiles, the closed world of Detroit executives in the late 1970s has been well documented. The housing locations, the kinds of leisure pursuits, the reading materials, and the topics of conversation all created an insular and conformist world slow to see change in consumer behavior and quick to condemn auto industry critics (Yates, 1983: 77–109).

With their competence at issue, many managers responded to this major challenge by assuring constituencies (workers, shareholders, customers) that they had everything under control and that there was no need to worry. This response was almost reflexive since management success in the traditional system emphasized the importance of executing management control through the enforcement of rules and orders. Thus, president McDonald's statement in the GM *Tech Center News* mentioned before is quite understandable.

There may well be a cultural component here. Various authors have noted that Japanese companies tend to magnify even small challenges as a strategy to mobilize all employees on behalf of aggressive new corporatewide goals (Turner, unpublished manuscript; Fruin, 1992, 174–175; Cole, 1979, 207–208). The American management tendency, by contrast, often was to contain and minimize the challenge or to rely on a small core of experts to deal with it. Extending the ideas of Shiba, Graham, and Walden (1993: 76–78), one can suggest that large growth-oriented Japanese manufacturing firms throughout most of the post–World War II period have been characterized by a weakness orientation, which is designed to reveal problems in current performance to a broad range of employees. By contrast, comparable American firms throughout much of the postwar period were characterized more by a strength orientation.

Continuing Market and Media Pressures

Notwithstanding attempts to ignore or deny the problem, the relentless pressure of the market pushed for recognition of quality as a competitive issue. The media, less accepting of a belief in managerial competence and with more of an incentive to challenge the conventional wisdom, played a large role in bringing the quality gap to the attention of a wider public. Articles in popular and business journals such as *Consumer Reports, Business Week,* and *Fortune* contributed to reconfiguring managerial understanding of their competitive situation (for semiconductors, see Bylinsky, 1981a,b).

There were some dramatic "public" events that crystallized the new understanding that "it's the quality gap, stupid." Notable was HP's previously mentioned March 1980 public announcement. Coming from a recognized market leader, these statements were more difficult to dismiss as the ravings of ignorant or duplicitous media personnel. T. J. Rodgers, president and CEO of Cypress Semiconductor, recalls thinking the day of the announcement: "If I don't do something about quality, I'm going to die" (cited in Siegmann, 1993: B3). There was also the powerful June 1980 NBC documentary *If Japan Can, Why Can't We,* which had an absolutely galvanizing effect on American managers. It was one of the most successful business documentaries ever produced in the United States and was widely shown to large numbers of employees in American corporations over the next few years (Bowles and Hammond, 1991: 43). The sole legal distributor, Films Inc., estimates that it sold some 30,000 units. This documentary introduced Dr. Deming to America.[4]

Widely publicized popular surveys in the early 1980s similarly confirmed that a growing majority of American consumers were coming to believe in the superiority of the quality of Japanese products and were acting on this knowledge (see Garvin, 1988: 251). Automobiles were the most dramatic example where the Japanese reputation for quality rose rapidly and consumers raised quality considerations from a low ranking to the number one or two factor (depending on the survey) in car purchase decisions. The Institute of Social Research at the University of Michigan reported that public concern about auto quality doubled between 1968 and 1975 (Cole, 1981: 29). Here was a clear early warning signal for American auto executives, if they had chosen to notice, interpret, and act on it.

The data began to pile up in industry after industry, and eventually denial was no longer plausible. The once-dismissed anomalies or misinterpretations of the data appeared more credible. Here the social aspects of the reconstruction of understanding takes precedence. Networks of managers within and between companies slowly came to terms with the implications of these "suddenly" visible new patterns.

We can see these reformulations developing through the experiences of Ford Motor Company. Donald Petersen, who became president and chief operating officer of Ford Motor Co., watching TV at home, saw the 1980 NBC documentary on quality. He was so impressed that he arranged for W. Edwards Deming, who was featured in the program, to be hired as a consultant at Ford. He became the first major auto executive to embrace Deming's ideas (Ingrassia and White, 1994: 140). He personally met with Dr. Deming about once a month (Petersen and Hillkirk, 1991: 7). Petersen's acts gave visible credence to the newly crystallizing reality that quality as a competitive issue demands a strategic response. At the same time Deming's ideas provided a framework for understanding the new competitive realities. The development of a sensemaking framework is critical for facilitating the rethinking of the importance of practices and outcomes and the nature of causal sequences; in other words, a new sensemaking framework is essential to creating new understandings (Starbuck and Milliken, 1988: 51).

Petersen's statements and actions encouraged other executives in the company and industry to reconsider their own past understandings. A clear message was sent throughout Ford in the early 1980s with the corporate decision to close the newer and larger Mahwah, New Jersey, assembly plant, which had poor quality, instead of the older Norfolk, Virginia, plant, which had a strong quality record and good employee relationships. In the mid-1980s the word went out that promotion was unlikely if the units one was responsible for had a poor quality record. Late in the 1980s the decision to delay initiating production on new projects like the Ford Escort also sent the same message. Top management established the practice of beginning with quality as the first item on the agenda at all major meetings (Petersen and Hillkirk, 1991: 23).

Gradually, the message got out that top management appeared serious about improving quality. Programs were announced like the Q1 (Quality is First) Award for suppliers in 1983. Lower-level managers sensed a change in the wind and made themselves available to support emergent initiatives, seeing an opportunity to ride the new wave. Programs were enacted and experience gained. A large number of randomly selected Ford employees were consulted in the drafting of a corporate mission statement, a set of company values and guiding principles. Quality was prominently featured with the list of guiding principles beginning with "Quality comes first." These statements were officially adopted in 1984 but in use informally much earlier (Petersen and Hillkirk, 1991: 12).

A convergence of ideas among managers within the firm as to the importance of quality started to form through a combination of enactment and imitation (see Weick, 1995: 80). New corporatewide practices served as a model for local plant and divisional initiatives. These understandings were also in their embryonic stage in other domestic auto firms. The social interaction among auto executives across firms, based on a variety of personal-and work-related networks in the Detroit metropolitan area, furthered this process of enactment and imitation. Local media coverage of the various initiatives also furthered the imitation process. In this sense, management did indeed come to understand its motive—to create a strategic response to the Japanese quality threat—in part through the act of adopting new approaches.

Even so, this slow awakening had its costs. In Figure 2.1 we see Joe Juran's educated estimate of the automotive quality gap, indicating that it actually grew in the first half of the 1980s (Juran: 1995: 582). Note that contrary to conventional wisdom, Figure 2.1 indicates that American quality did not decline in the 1970s; rather, it remained constant. One can also see in this figure that, as with semiconductors, the Japanese auto producers' improving quality performance presented their American competitors with a moving target throughout the 1980s.

Alternative Courses of Action

Once the competitive threat was recognized (whether from quality or price competition), protectionism arose. The political process was used to insulate firms from market pressures. It is estimated that the total value of trade covered by protectionist measures nearly doubled during the first half or the 1980s (Bowles and Hammond, 1991: 11). The steel industry delayed the day of reckoning through protectionist action, but, in the end, all of the old line integrated steel producers accepted large Japanese equity shares and often even management control (except Bethlehem Steel).

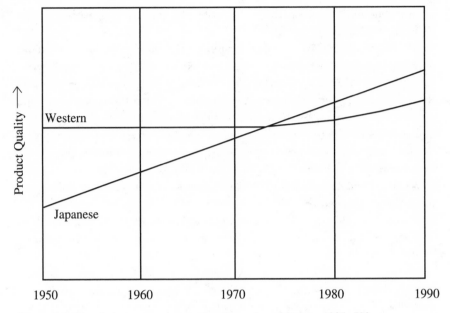

Figure 2.1. Trends in automotive quality. *Source:* Joseph Juran, 1995: 582.

Similarly, the U.S. auto industry, suffering heavily, used the threat of quotas to get the Japanese producers to agree in spring 1981 to a self-imposed annual ceiling of 1.68 million cars exported to America. This temporarily took some of the market pressure off the American producers to improve both costs and quality, although the uncertainty of the duration of the quotas acted as a continued spur to improvement. More importantly, the growth of Japanese auto production in the United States, beginning with the Honda plant in Marysville, Ohio, in late 1982, followed by similar decisions of the other Japanese producers, acted over time to negate the impact of the quotas.

U.S. semiconductor producers also sought political help in stemming the tide of Japanese products into the United States, claiming that the Japanese were "dumping." These claims and counter claims led to a ruling against the Japanese by the International Trade Commission in 1984 and eventually culminated in the 1986 U.S.-Japan semiconductor trade agreement. At best, as in the auto industry, the agreement may have bought the semiconductor manufacturers more time to address their manufacturing problems with yield and reliability (see Angel, 1994: 82–83). Yet, as in auto, the argument can be made that the producers did not use this breathing space very well.

An alternative strategy to the political solution was for firms simply to exit markets so as not to engage in head-to-head competition with the Japanese (Dertouzos, Lester, and Solow, 1989: 229). Thus, U.S. auto manufacturers all but abandoned the compact car market in the early 1980s and invested more heavily in the more profitable midsize market. Still, they could not escape growing Japanese dominance in the automotive industry. Eventually, in the 1990s, they did move into light trucks, including sports utilities and vans, where the Japanese had less experience and faced some tariff barriers.

Similarly, in the mid-1980s, U.S. semiconductor firms all but abandoned the volume DRAM market and focused their investment in more proprietary technologies. Indeed, for much of the 1980s, top management's time and resources were devoted to redeploying resources away from DRAMs and other commodity devices to more design-intensive product markets, such as microprocessors, mixed signal devices, very fast logic devices, and application-specific integrated circuits. There was a search for markets in which the American capability in design could yield high profit margins and offset the Japanese advantage in manufacturing (Angel, 1994: 81).

While automotive managers partially deployed some assets, they had basically no place to go and thus were forced to address more actively and immediately the Japanese challenge in quality. The slowness of semiconductor managers in addressing quality problems stemmed not simply from their trained incapacity but also in large part from their decision to pursue alternatives, involving the radical restructuring of the American semiconductor industry.

Quality improvement or restructuring to avoid quality improvement was not the only alternative in the 1980s. A variety of corporate strategies designed to cope with the changing environment unfolded. The merger movement gathered force, leveraged buyouts were in vogue, with the premise that debt was a virtue. There was a growing focus on getting back to basics by concentrating on one's core businesses; there was the contrary move toward diversification. Decentralization and centralization were again in vogue, and maximizing shareholder value came to the fore in the late 1980s as a corporate rallying cry. Some of these practices were compatible with a quality focus, but others greatly damaged quality efforts. Much depended on how a particular company handled the approach and its competitive situation. A brief comparison of GM's efforts compared to Harley-Davidson's, Intel's, and IBM's show a broad range of possible actions and outcomes.

General Motors was the slowest of the Big Three to respond to the Japanese quality threat. Its commanding market share, stronger balance sheet, and corporate arrogance insulated it from the pressure to respond. With declining market share and pressure on profits, however, GM too eventually had to respond. Roger Smith took over as chairman in 1981 and left in 1989. Roughly paralleling that time period, GM's market share in passenger vehicles went from 46% in 1980 to 35% in 1989. In 1979 figures, that was more than the equivalent of the disappearance of Chrysler Motor Co. Clearly, the market pressure to improve quality remained powerful.

Apart from a plummeting market share, Roger Smith's legacy was in large part splashy high-technology acquisitions (EDS and Hughes Electronics Corp.), a massive and disastrous 1984 reorganization, and staggering expenditures in new technology totaling 42 billion dollars between 1980 and 1985 (Ingrassia and White, 1994: 70–78).

The 1984 reorganization was aimed at reducing costs, improving quality, and improving cooperation across functions through creating two large car divisions and a third one for trucks. It broke down the centralized role of GM's Assembly Division and Fisher Body with each of three new groups getting its own combined engineering, manufacturing, and marketing functions. In many ways, this "new" approach represented a pendulum swing of traditional corporate strategies. If one is centralized and having competitive problems one decentralizes. And if one is decentralized and having competitive problems, one centralizes. By all accounts, GM's reorganization was a disaster; it led to chaos and massive morale problems, and as one set of close observers put it, a "corporate nervous breakdown" (Ingrassia and White, 1996: 96–98). The quality of GM cars in the mid-1980s now was not only inferior to the Japanese but had also become inferior to that of its major domestic competitors. The moderation of market pressure for improved quality that resulted from the imposition of quotas by the Japanese was diminished by the growing pressure from domestic competitors.

General Motor's other foray was into advanced technology. Top management officers operated as if what they needed was a one-time technological breakthrough that would restore their falling position in the market. Huge investments in technology did not translate into significant operational improvements in quality or productivity. From a quality perspective, combining the automation of processes with higher levels of technology (neither of which is fully understood) results in producing more defects faster.

At the same time, the NUMMI joint venture between GM and Toyota, managed by Toyota, was recording high productivity and the highest quality ratings in the GM accounting system. All this was taking place in a relatively nonautomated setting with American workers, a significant number of whom were minorities. The lessons were not lost on subsequent GM leaders; it was not until the late 1980s, however, that GM overall would make sustained improvement in quality.

Developments at GM in the early and mid-1980s can easily be held up to show the disastrous consequences of pursuing alternative strategies (cutting-edge technology and acquisitions) rather than focusing on quality and manufacturing improvement. Yet the cases of Harley-Davidson, Intel, and IBM demonstrate a different set of dynamics.

Harley-Davidson, the motorcycle manufacturer, went through some very hard times in the early 1980s. Their high costs and low quality put them in a very weak position vis-á-vis aggressive Japanese competitors. This situation culminated in a leveraged buyout. To generate the cash flow that would allow them to pay down their debt, the new owner-managers embarked on a massive manufacturing/quality improvement program that led to dramatically improved quality and reduced costs (Reid, 1990: 66).

Intel's pursuit of an alternative product to DRAMs was driven by a different dynamic. Its internal resource allocation rule allocated scarce manufacturing capacity based on margin-per-wafer-start. This favored products with greater profitability and competitive potential than DRAMs (Burgelman and Grove, 1996: 17). Top management ultimately gave its seal of approval to the emergent strategy of making Intel a microprocessor company. It proved to be a remarkably successful decision. It also bought the company the time it needed to eventually address its manufacturing problems.

For one last example, IBM developed a strong quality initiative in the mid-1980s, but it could not really bear fruit until chairman Louis Gerstner, Jr., took office in 1992 and put in place a new strategy that slashed the workforce, sold off peripheral businesses, and focused resources and energies on the core businesses.

In all three cases, and unlike that of GM, one sees that the alternative scenarios ended up being quite compatible with pursuing the new quality model. Indeed in all three cases, corporate survival required both. For that matter, even GM, while wasting an awful lot of resources, eventually got on the right track for improving quality, but the time it took certainly cost a great deal in market share and profits.

In industries where competition over quality was not paramount, perhaps because of the lack of foreign competition or the commodity nature of the business, traditional bases of competition dominated. In the airline business traditional bases were supplemented by new refinements such as merges and acquisitions, alliances hub-spoke logistics, strategic use of Chapter 11 status, and two-tiered wage structures.

Economic models grounded in neoclassical theory with their emphasis on the "discipline of the market" would lead us to expect that failure to respond to a strong competitive challenge in a timely fashion would result in certain and instantaneous retribution (Fligstein and Dauber, 1989: 82). In fact, although the responses of many firms to the quality challenge were slow and included many false starts, a remarkable number of such firms survived into the 1990s and indeed in some cases (Chrysler and Intel) rebounded quite nicely. Often an almost invisible safety net protected firms from the extinction that economic models of efficiency would predict. This safety net included some combination of market power, control over resources, patent protection (especially intellectual property law), diversification strategies, proprietary knowledge, political leverage, expanding overall demand, and customer loyalty (cf. Fligstein and Dauber, 1989: 82–83).

Conclusion

In summary, it is hard to exaggerate the impact of the Japanese quality challenge upon American management. The Americans were truly blindsided by the strong Japanese attack on their prevailing understanding of competitive activity. Whole industries, like color TVs, were lost before U.S. managers even comprehended the major factors contributing to these outcomes. At the very beginning, they simply denied quality as a competitive issue and denied the possibility that the Japanese had bested them in those dimensions of quality that mattered most to consumers.

We see how managers over the course of a decade and more constructed new social meanings and made sense of their new environment as they slowly came to grips with the content of the new Japanese quality paradigm. Only after managers recognized the quality gap as a major competitive factor, could they take action to address this deficit. Only after publicly acknowledging it to their own employees could they hope to enlist their employees' support in addressing the problem—an essential element in improving quality. Only after they stopped blaming their own employees for the problem could they begin to address their own responsibilities. Meanwhile, with little Western knowledge of their growing success using quality, and consequently with little effort on the part of the Americans to master the new quality model, the Japanese had the luxury throughout the 1970s and first half of the 1980s of refining and deepening their production model and collecting monopoly rents from their successive refinements. Collectively, the large Japanese export-oriented manufacturing firms had a strong first-mover advantage and they continued in the 1980s to move rapidly down the learning curve.

One might presume that once American managers recognized the threat for what it was, they could proceed rapidly to erase it. As I show in subsequent chapters, however, other roadblocks ahead interacted with the factors described in this chapter and lead to some dead ends, as well as to some rather circuitous routes. All that took time, lots of time.

CHAPTER 3

How Much Did You Know and When Did You Know It?

After U.S. managers accepted that quality was a major competitive issue, that the Japanese really were doing better, and that they lacked information on how the Japanese did it, the next logical issue for them was how to go about acquiring that information. Would these firms choose to learn directly from the Japanese? This expectation is rooted in an understanding of the critical role of information in organizational life. Stinchcombe (1990: 2) focuses on organizations using the "earliest available information" to resolve actor uncertainty. Earliest information shows actors the competitively successful direction. An organization must "be where the news breaks, whenever it breaks" (Stinchcombe, 1990: 3). Not only do firms want the earliest information available, they also want knowledge about their specific problems from real-world "how to" practitioners to reduce the costs associated with customization.

In the light of these observations, one might expect managers to have been willing to engage in systematic learning from their Japanese counterparts. Such was not the case. Easton and Jarrell (1997b: 18–20) studied intensively 44 companies with the most advanced TQM systems they could find. These firms were part of a larger sample identified in a comprehensive search for firms active in TQM activities in the 1980s and early 1990s. The authors explored the factors associated with the initial deployment of quality improvement efforts. Only 2 of the 44 reported a significant Japanese influence. Based on various company accounts in the literature, ostensibly this appears to be a reasonably representative situation; in small and medium firms, one would expect the direct Japanese influence to be even lower.

Three nonmutually exclusive explanations seem responsible for managements' reluctance to learn from the Japanese: the uncertainty that Japanese practices would work in the United States, the high costs of learning from the Japanese, and the lack of management norms legitimizing learning from the Japanese. Institutional theory involves examining the forces and agents that create patterns and directions of learning activity in given organizational fields (cf. Westney, 1997). Factors affecting willingness to learn in a particular organizational field are among the most fundamental of such forces. Therefore, this subject bears closer study.

Uncertainty that Japanese practices would work in the United States constituted the first set of barriers for learning directly from the Japanese. In the early 1980s, many thought that Japanese quality achievements represented Japanese culture. Books on the mystical historical elements of Japanese strategy, such as *A Book of Five Rings* by Miyamoto Musashi (1982), were in vogue. In particular, the notion that high quality was due primarily to committed workers dominated management thinking. The idea that it was more the result of the effectiveness of management systems did not take hold until the late 1980s.

Japan was seen as a nation of culturally induced workaholics, while the United States was described by many popular writers as a nation that had lost its work ethic. Managers saw it as risky to import practices that might not work in the United States. Not until the late 1980s did the operation of Japanese subsidiaries in the United States (e.g., Honda and NUMMI) make it clear that these practices would be effective in the United States with U.S. workers. Thus, much time transpired before this uncertainty dissipated.

Ultimately the uncertainties of the early 1980s arose from two sources. First, there was the sharp discontinuity between existing practices and the behaviors required by the new quality model. Ongoing monitoring of Japanese practices in the 1970s would have lessened this problem. Second, there was no existing information market between Japanese and American industry regarding quality improvement strategies and tactics for American firms to draw upon in the early 1980s. But before that exchange could happen, two other barriers needed to be overcome.

In the early 1980s, learning from the Japanese constituted a formidable challenge because of the high costs associated with overcoming language and cultural barriers, mastering the difficult logistics of learning from faraway facilities, unearthing the tacit knowledge upon which many Japanese practices were based, and separating out the universal elements of the Japanese quality experience from its more particular elements. With hindsight, one sees these costs were worth bearing, but in the early 1980s most companies underestimated the challenge of mastering the new quality model. They did not understand its full scope and often thought they could make the problem go away with simple solutions such as quality circles.

The third barrier to learning directly from the Japanese present in many management circles was simply the lack of legitimacy for such efforts. To be sure, in the early 1980s, there was a brief but superficial "contagion of legitimacy," to use the language of Lynn Zucker (1983), as firms, one after another, sent teams of managers and even workers and union officials to Japan on study visits to learn about Japanese approaches to quality. Activities that directly drew on these experiences in Japan, however, seldom became the basis for sustained learning exchanges between Japanese and American firms. Moreover, after the early infatuation of learning from the Japanese in the early 1980s, a backlash set in during the mid- and late-1980s in many firms and industries (Sethi, Namiki, and Swanson,

1984), especially so in the industrial heartland, where many managers and employees had tired of hearing how the Japanese "seemed to do everything better."

From an institutional perspective, legitimacy means a taken-for-granted quality that requires no explanation or justification. Shared cognitions define meanings and actions (Zucker, 1983: 2). Efficiency arguments suggest that learning from the Japanese about quality became an imperative for many industries by the 1970s and 1980s. Yet legitimacy for such efforts remained elusive. The lack of legitimacy for these efforts is one piece of the puzzle that requires further explanation.

Consider the context. As the most successful industrial agents in the world, American managers basked in a glory that they could superstitiously ascribe to their own competency and professional skills (Ouchi, 1981: 221). The idea of learning from abroad, much less from the Japanese, about quality was literally incomprehensible for managers throughout much of the post–World War II period. After all, this generation of managers had been brought up seeing Japan as a country producing cheap, shoddy products. Managers could acknowledge selected technical areas that one might learn abroad, especially from Western European firms, but the idea that they could learn basic management practices from Japan was hard to countenance. From a rational perspective, this makes little sense. After all, by 1970, Japan was the world's third largest economy.

Perhaps readers have trouble accepting the validity of these assertions. Here is a revealing anecdote about the problematic nature of legitimacy in the learning process. In 1990, I suggested to German managers of a multinational corporation that they could improve their product design process by learning from the cross-functional cooperation practiced at their company's Italian plant. One can hardly capture in words the incredulity that greeted this suggestion. I was seen as either incredibly naive or incredibly stupid. It simply was not legitimate, not a remotely acceptable pattern of thinking, much less acting, for German managers to learn from the Italians and especially to learn about, of all things, quality. The German managers were simply unable to get past the idea of learning from the Italians to actually consider the content of my suggestion. Here is the mindset of many U.S. managers in the early 1980s in response to the idea that they could learn basic management practices from the Japanese.

Leaders in major American corporations in 1980 were generally white men older than 55, who had either personally experienced World War II or were strongly affected by it. In the case of the auto industry, in particular, there was very little place for minorities of any type in the top leadership of the industry (Yates, 1983: 81–82). For many, there were strong negative connotations associated with the idea that they could learn from the vanquished Japanese; sometimes rejection was tinged with racist sentiments (hard to learn from people you call "Japs"). In short, existing management norms did not support learning from the Japanese.

Tversky and Kahneman (1990) provide further insight. They show that how an issue is framed determines choice and preferences. In other words, managers do not choose tactics and objectives; they choose descriptions of tactics and descriptions of objectives.[1] When making decisions, individuals tend to assimilate the content suggested by the label for given activities or ideas. That is to say, packaging is critical. A simple example suffices. Tversky points out that if one labels the prisoner's game dilemma as a community game, then the subjects play it differently than if one labels it as Wall Street game. By labeling quality practices in Japan as Japanese rather than universal, U.S. managers made it an unattractive object to borrow to solve their quality problems. They weighed it down with potentially negative cultural content. Yet they would later try to adopt these very same ideas when they were "unpacked" and became available in an American environment. By waiting until these models became available, however, they lost valuable time.

Tversky and Kahneman also note that if the only major difference between choices is how they are framed, then it is hard to assume respondents chose rationally in preferring one over the other. They also observe that one way to protect the assumption of rationality put forward by rational choice theorists is to show that any violation of the rational choice model can be dismissed as an insignificant choice problem. With the developments surrounding adopting new quality practices in the early 1980s, however, we have a real-world situation with important economic outcomes depending on choices. Thus, one cannot wish away managers' violations of rational choice when they incorrectly framed quality problems and solutions.

We can gain further leverage on this matter by examining the exceptional case of Florida Power and Light (FPL). FPL begins its quality improvement activities in 1981. In 1985, it became the first large American company (15,000 employees) that threw itself wholeheartedly into comprehensively and systematically learning directly from the Japanese. It entered into a deep exchange relationship with Kansai Electric and other Deming Prize–winning Japanese companies and worked closely with Japanese professors who served as "counselors" to their quality initiative. I asked a number of the FPL managers how they could account for this willingness to work with the Japanese at a time when no other large company seemed to be making a similar decision. The following composite answer reflects both intended and unintended developments.

Flordia Power and Light anticipated serious problems that required change, but they were not in direct competition with their Japanese counterpart. "We were in the same business and had the same problems and we could learn from them without worrying about being in competition with them." In particular, both had much the same equipment, including similar Westinghouse-designed nuclear plants. The Mihama facility, however, reported roughly 10% of the quality problems reported by FPL's Turkey Point facility. This provided an ideal opportunity to identify practices responsible for differences. It made it hard to ascribe these differences to mystical cultural differences or technology and easier to identify the specific management practices producing the differential outcomes.[2] In addition, an extensive visitation program was instituted with the teaming of counterpart personnel in FPL and Kansai Electric. This led to strong personal relationships and contributed to demystification of Japanese TQC.[3]

The openness of Kansai Electric meant that American employees could hardly voice sentiments about Japanese sneakiness or duplicity. It simply was not acceptable at FPL to be publicly anti-Japanese. Crucially, the rhetoric of FPL's quality initiative was not "How can we copy the Japanese?" but what practices constitute the world-class standard and how can we get there? The idea was to mitigate any reluctance employees might have felt about acknowledging Japanese superiority and to make the task of learning from the Japanese easier. It just happened that most of the best quality practices identified and adopted were Japanese. Finally, the Japanese, and Kansai Electric in particular, proved remarkably open in sharing the sources of their success. The respective chief executive officers (CEOs) established a strong personal rapport. A formal technology-sharing agreement to make available to FPL relevant company documents cemented these relationships. One official captured the openness of Kansai Electric with the following observation: "If we asked for their help in solving a problem, next thing we knew someone would show up on our doorstep from Japan to help us work the problem. I got the feeling that if we asked them what color their underwear was, they would have told us that too."

The views expressed in this composite response must be seen against a backdrop in which the Japanese were proud of their accomplishments and flattered by American willingness to learn from them. In addition, Japanese companies were obsessed at this time with becoming "international," exposing their employees to their American counterparts was seen as a good way to begin that process. The Japanese counselors (Japanese academics serving as company advisers) were quite idealistic and internationally minded; they saw it as their mission to spread the benefits of Japanese TQC to the world. They selected FPL to be the first non-Japanese company to be encouraged to apply for and win the Deming Prize (awarded in 1989); FPL was their chosen vehicle for showing how Japanese TQC could work in the West.[4] Indeed, the exhaustive 290-page examiners' report for their Deming Prize examination concludes that "FPL has succeeded in introducing the Japanese style quality control" (Florida Power and Light, 1989: 2). This evaluation was based on examination of company documents and 10 days of intensive site visits by the Deming examiners to its various facilities. John Hudiburg, the chairman and CEO at the time, said in his address at the Deming Award presentation, "It has been, since 1985, our desire to install a *Japanese* style quality management system" (Hudiburg, 1991: 188, italics in original).

On a more subtle level, Dr. Asaka, the lead Japanese counselor at FPL, was also the lead counselor at Kansai Electric at this time. Kansai Electric personnel from the quality improvement department, as a matter of pride, were determined to see that Dr. Asaka's reputation would remain untarnished by doing whatever it took to help ensure FPL was ready for the Deming Prize Challenge. They worked tirelessly and relentlessly (and not without some friction with FPL personnel) to prepare FPL personnel. In the context of the relatively hierarchical environment of FPL, the Kansai Electric staff were able to transmit many of their ideas through FPL and turn them into practice.

The extraordinary confluence of events, implementation strategy, structural conditions, competitive circumstances, and personal relationships at FPL and Kansai Electric help one understand why most American firms failed to make the decision to comprehensively learn and introduce TQC directly from the Japanese at this time. Few could duplicate FPL's conditions.

Many, however, were to benefit from FPL's decisions; by late 1985, managers from around the country started flocking to what was to become FPL's once-a-month visitor orientations to learn the secrets of quality improvement. Between 1985 and 1988 roughly 2,000–3,000 managers a year attended these seminars with the numbers increasing in 1989 and 1990 (after FPL won the Deming Prize). The company estimates that between 1986 and 1990, roughly 90% of the *Fortune* 1000 companies sent personnel to participate in monthly orientations. Large companies that brought their top-ranking managers, like Alcoa, Procter and Gamble (P&G), and General Dynamics, often received their own briefings. The FPL group set up a separate for-profit consultant subsidiary, Qualtec, in 1986, which worked with a large number of the visiting companies to implement quality improvement practices (Brecka and Rubach, 1995: 29). In the late 1980s, despite growing rapidly, Qualtec was unable to keep pace with and respond to the many prospects it had among those companies participating in the monthly orientations. In 1995, it reported that it was training about 11,000 people annually and had a full-time staff of 63 with 25 contracted instructors and consultants. Qualtec was bought by the Marshall Group in 1995.

Ironically, FPL can also be termed the company that learned too much from the Japanese. In the early 1990s, a backlash developed in the company, led by the new CEO, James Broadhead, against what was seen as the overly rigid Japanese formula for producing quality improvement. The quality department staff was dramatically reduced from 46 to 6. Some left the company and the rest were dispersed into operational units. The new quality department became responsible for further integration of quality into the organization, especially its integration with overall business planning. Enormous documentation demands had been built up in the quest for the Deming Prize. It was hard to separate out what was required for winning the prize from what added value to the quality improvement efforts. Japanese companies that have won the Deming Prize have voiced similar complaints. These documentation demands had placed a heavy burden on FPL employees and were seen by many as interfering with their ability to do their jobs. Thus, Broadhead acted to drastically slash these requirements. For some outside managers, this experience became proof that TQM was a fad and learning from the Japanese a useless effort. Others saw a new CEO anxious to put his own mark on the company. For still others, the FPL experience showed that valuable Japanese ideas about quality needed to be more fully adapted to create a truly American approach that fostered creativity and innovation without excessive bureaucratic documentation and discipline. Nevertheless, for the mainstream business media, in the short period between 1984 and 1994, FPL moved from being a positive to a negative role model.

In a largely unnoticed (especially by the business media) chapter in its unfolding history, FPL recognized earlier than most American companies that there were limits to pursuing quality improvement independent of other business objectives. The new CEO continued to support quality, but quality characterized by cost-effective improvement more firmly integrated into overall corporate objectives. He also further developed the company's Japanese ties, including making the decision to seek a post–Deming Prize review in 1994. The company launched a variety of new initiatives in the early and mid-1990s aimed at this more strategic business-oriented approach to quality improvement (Broadhead, 1996: 11–17). These changes included the introduction of extensive benchmarking, an emphasis on self-managing teams, a greater stress on accountability, business process reengineering, and increased emphasis on giving employees more opportunities to be creative and flexible. A variety of key measures showed continued quality improvement over the performance achieved when FPL received the Deming Prize (e.g., further reduction in number of unplanned outages and dramatic improvement in quality performance of the Turkey Point nuclear plant). In short, rumors of the death of the quality initiative at FPL were greatly exaggerated, but certainly it has been a very bumpy road.

Regardless of this uneven trajectory, FPL had an enormous impact on the efforts of American companies trying to implement the new quality model. To take one well-documented example, the nine or so top managers at Alcoa visited FPL three times in 1988, each for roughly a day. Well before the rebellion against the over-Japanized version of quality improvement at FPL took place, Alcoa managers were put off by what they saw as the "rather slavish adoption of Japanese total quality control techniques," the "quasi-military management style" at FPL, and what they perceived as the too heavy focus on wining the Deming Prize rather than improving quality. One participant in these meetings recalled how it took a team using the prescribed problem-solving methodology nine months to move a telephone from one side of the street to the other (Kolesar, 1995: 185–189). Presenters at FPL had intended the session to be about learning the problem-solving process, tools, and team dynamics, but that is not what the Aloca people took away from it.

At the same time, Alcoa executives reported that the visits to FPL, along with those to Xerox, were the most influential of the six visits to outside companies. Alcoa mangers were impressed with the Japanese style of policy deployment as a means to focus and give accountability to the quality effort; they also adopted (indeed licensed) the FPL quality improvement storyboard method of running improvement teams. In short, Alcoa management showed an ability to sift through the FPL quality initiative and select and adopt features that seemed workable in a

U.S. environment. Yet this is exactly what many American manufacturing companies had the opportunity to do much earlier by learning directly from the Japanese but chose not to.

This discussion suggests that learning was typically a two-step process; in the early and mid-1980s only a few companies like FPL were willing to invest directly in sustained learning from the Japanese. The other companies that did so typically had joint venture or subsidiary operations in Japan with whom the American parent worked to learn Japanese quality practices. But none I have been able to identify was even remotely as intense as the FPL-Kansai Electric relationship. Most companies waited until successful American models were developed that seemed to have assimilated Japanese approaches to American conditions, and then they sought to learn from them.

This two-step flow model has a classic place in the literature on diffusion. Lazarsfeld and colleagues (1944) found that individuals were influenced not directly by the mass media but through opinion leaders who were so influenced. Many subsequent studies in different areas showed variations of this phenomenon (Rogers, 1995: 285–286). In the language of this model, the Japanese created the innovation (the new quality model), but for many U.S. firms the persuasion, the decision to adopt, how and what to adopt, and the confirmation of these decisions were more affected by learning from FPL (as well as other U.S. adopters including Japanese subsidiaries in the United States). All this, however, took lots of time.

As stated, FPL initially choose to replicate as faithfully as it could the Japanese model and it was certified as having done so in the Deming Prize evaluation. Substantively, American firms would have learned relatively similar things from working directly with Japanese firms or from FPL. They presented quite similar models.

Timing and framing are the differences. Unpacking the Japanese experience in America did not change its fundamental contents. Many U.S. companies chose to wait, however, because they framed Japanese company quality practices as Japanese and therefore not accessible. It is hard to see their decision to wait as an act of rational decision making. They could have found companies (e.g., suppliers) with whom they had a noncompetitive association and with whom they could have established a learning relationship.

Of course, most large U.S. manufacturing firms were not just sitting idle in those years. They were making efforts to learn how to do quality improvement, but those trial-and-error efforts, as I show in the next chapter, often led down blind alleys, alleys that could have been avoided with better information. Clearly, they underestimated the difficulties of absorbing the new quality model; indeed, they underestimated the difficulties of even understanding the new quality model. At the same time, in 1980 no one knew that an American model like FPL would emerge, adding reasons why trying to learn directly from the Japanese might have been a good idea.

By waiting and learning from U.S. companies, many potential adopters reduced the transaction costs that would have resulted from efforts to learn directly from the Japanese (costs flowing from language and cultural barriers, the logistics of long-distance learning, efforts to unearth tacit knowledge, and separating out universal from peculiarly Japanese features). Great effort and expense were required to overcome these problems. Instead of incurring these costs, most U.S. companies chose to be late adopters taking advantage of the efforts of those like FPL who did learn directly from the Japanese. In so doing, however, they lost much time, and for many, there were large costs associated with their slow response time: declining market share, continued negative reputational effects for their poor quality, and lost jobs and profits. These were the costs of not systematically going after the earliest available information.

These costs were especially high in industries in which the quality bar was continually being raised (e.g. automotive and semiconductor industries) and where quality came to figure more and more in customer purchase decisions. For these industries, the decision *not* to learn directly from the Japanese in a systematic fashion is the most difficult to equate with rational decision making. General Motors and Chrysler evinced modest efforts to learn about quality directly from the Japanese in the early 1980s. General Motors' joint venture with Toyota, NUMMI, which opened under Toyota management in December 1984, was intended to be a learning instrument for GM. It is widely evaluated, however, as having failed in that effort, at least for the 1980s, in large part because of the lack of support from GM's top management (Ingrassia and White, 1995: 56–59).

Chrysler's leaders seemed more comfortable with Japan-bashing than with learning how to achieve quality from the Japanese. It was not until 1987 that Chrysler set up a systematic study of the Japanese producers, using Honda as their target. The intent of the study was to assess Honda's company organization, particularly its product development process, to see what information might be useful in changing Chrysler's practices. In early 1988, the study group issued two major recommendations: the first was to greatly strengthen the emphasis on quality and customer satisfaction, and the second was to use cross-functional teams in the operational management of the firm, especially in product development (Levin, 1995: 202–208). These conclusions could have been made much earlier.

General Motors was profitable in 1981 and 1982, had a large cash reserve, and was thus somewhat less threatened by Japan's quality challenge. In contrast, Ford and Chrysler were both hemorrhaging red ink in the early 1980s, but Ford responded more positively to the quality challenge. Chrysler focused on gaining government support to save itself, using Japan as the bogeyman. With leadership in the personage of Mr. Iacocca, managers were unable to get authorization to prioritize the quality initiative. Ford, with its ties to Mazda, not quite on the ropes like Chrysler, and with executives who appreciated the seriousness of the quality challenge, was better positioned to respond (see Main, 1994: 29). One form their response took was to learn from the Japanese through their Mazda ties. In the early 1980s Ford also very actively encouraged its suppliers to take study trips to Japan. The American Supplier Institute (ASI), a spin-off of Ford's training efforts, played a major role in bringing Japanese practices to the attention of Ford managers and in training Ford employees. Indeed, ASI played an important role in teaching quality technologies to managers in other industries as well, especially in the late 1980s.

In the semiconductor industry, even Motorola, widely acknowledged as the leader in responding to the Japanese quality challenge, took quite a while before accept direct lessons from the Japanese. One author characterizes Motorola's willingness to adopt Japanese-style production techniques as evolving from "first ignore 'em, then sue 'em, and finally learn from 'em" (Henkoff, 1989: 157). When the quality drive caught fire in Motorola in the early 1980s, the company found it deceptively easy to improve quality; this was true at Ford as well. It was not difficult to make improvements just by focusing employee attention on quality. But to get past a plateauing effect in the mid-1980s and to develop and sustain breakthrough improvements, more fundamental change had to take place. Learning directly from the Japanese proved to be very important at both Ford and Motorola (for Motorola, see Henkoff, 1989: 157, 160, 164, 168).[5]

In another set of industries, however, the Japanese competitive challenge was marginal throughout the 1980s, and thus the costs were minimal for waiting to imitate slowly evolving American models. Here, waiting to learn American models can be see as a rational decision as long as a domestic competitor did not adopt first. As an example, the home appliance industry, one of the late adopters of the new quality model, apparently did not suffer from that delay.[6]

Waiting to adopt from an American firm did not make a lot of sense in industries in which quality was a highly competitive issue. Yet that decision should not be seen as surprising. All things being equal, diffusion of practices occurs more rapidly when the potential adopters perceive themselves and their immediate conditions as similar to those from whom the practices are borrowed (Strang and Meyer, 1993).

The Deming Effect

An objection might be raised to my analysis. In the early 1980s, and even today for that matter, many managers believed that the new quality model was composed of basically homegrown ideas and that the Japanese were only following Dr. Deming's lead (Walton, 1986). In this context, it would seem that borrowing from the Japanese was simply a matter of learning good old American ideas. Learning from the Japanese should have been seen as legitimate. Indeed, the American Society for Quality's journal, *Quality Progress*, can be seen as promoting just this view, displaying ads showing an apple pie and claiming that "quality was as American as apple pie." To understand why this perspective was insufficient to encourage U.S.

manufacturing firms to learn directly from the Japanese, we need to pursue W. Edwards Deming's role in all these developments.

Dr. Deming, a little-known statistician, was introduced to American business through the very successful NBC special, *If Japan Can, Why Can't We*, in 1980. Dr. Deming became an instant celebrity. The special implied that early in the postwar period American industrial leaders rejected Dr. Deming's teachings and then he had gone off to Japan, where he was eagerly embraced. This theme became progressively embroidered by his adoring disciples and the media. Deming, the man, increasingly took on godlike characteristics among these followers. Great Man theories of history, however entertaining to the reader and appealing to the journalist and television producer, leave much to be desired as causal explanations.

It did not matter that much of this history was myth and that the Japanese, using Dr. Deming's ideas, as well as those of Dr. Juran and Feigenbaum, created a management system that went far beyond Deming's ideas of statistical control. One common objection to this view is that Japanese leaders would not have created a prize in Dr. Deming's honor if he had not been the "father" of the Japanese quality movement. Yet the history of the Deming Prizes lies in Dr. Deming's refusing payment for his 1950 lectures and offering the proceeds from reprints to the Japanese quality control organization, the Japanese Union of Science and Engineers (JUSE), which used these funds to create two national quality prizes and named them in his honor. Surely they did this out of appreciation for his efforts, but it hardly means that the bulk of their subsequent efforts were mere implementations and extensions of Deming's ideas. Off the record, Japanese quality leaders are quite frank on this matter. We probably would be talking about the Juran prizes today if Juran had made these donations. But Juran was not the father of the Japanese quality movement any more than Dr. Deming was.

Kolesar (1994: 9–24) shows that the content of Dr. Deming's famous weeklong lecture series in 1950 primarily involved statistical methods (seven of the eight days). If one focuses on Kolesar's summary of the first day, in which Dr. Deming gave the broad overview of quality, one can see that, despite the emphasis on customers and on quality as a strong competitive strategy, most elements of the new quality model as described in Chapter 1 were missing. Furthermore, contrary to the conventional views, he did not teach the Japanese the importance of top-management involvement in quality; much in their own immediate postwar experience lead them to this view (Cole, 1987: 49–51; Bowles and Hammond, 1991: 36–43). Some of the confusion results from the fact that Dr. Deming, to his credit, incorporated much of what he learned from watching the Japanese into his later writings, though in a rather disjointed fashion. Even here, the message is confused. Deming's 14 points include drive out fear, eliminate work standards, eliminate merit ratings, eliminate numerical goals, and eliminate slogans. If these were indeed absolutely essential elements in successful quality improvement, then the Japanese would not have made their remarkable progress over the last 50 years.

The significance of Dr. Deming in large part is that Deming the man and his teachings were used first as a wake-up call to American management and second to legitimate the new quality model. A Ford Motor Co. manager who was a Deming disciple and had major responsibilities for Ford's quality initiative in the early 1980s said to me it was not a matter anymore of learning something new from Dr. Deming during his visits to the company, but rather that he served as a rallying point for company efforts to upgrade quality performance. This included reaching a wider audience in the company than those in the quality department were capable to influencing. In this sense, Dr. Deming served as a kind of battering ram within each company he worked in. James Bakken, vice president of North American operations at Ford in the early 1980s, said in a public statement, Deming functioned for the company as "our mentor, a catalyst, our conscience and on occasion a burr under our saddle" (Cole, 1987: 51).

On the negative side, those who saw Deming's ideas as the embodiment of a modern approach to quality were led to dismiss Japanese quality practices for they could just try to follow Deming's ideas. This was especially the case in industries such as health care and education with no directly comparable Japanese models to follow, but the idea was widespread among many manufacturing firms as well. Dr. Deming's ideas, however, often sent conflicting messages and were a poor substitute for observing the actual practice of quality improvement. Follower firms that successfully grasp information about improvements are often in direct contact with the initial innovators (cf. Stinchcombe, 1990: 152–193). Thus, the decision to rely on homegrown experts like Deming and Crosby can be seen as having slowed the progress of the implementation of the new quality model.

The two-step learning process that I described, whereby companies waited to learn from American leaders in adopting the new quality model, had some interesting consequences apart from the loss of time. As the 1980s wore on, consultants and managers increasingly presented the key ideas of the new quality model with no mention of the Japanese. Ideas such as continuous process improvement, close supplier cooperation, and cross-functional management (especially in new product design) came to be seen as American ideas. The late 1980s saw an increasing number of American "success stories" that provided templates for what needed to be done.

In summary, American managers gradually presented the new quality model in ways that built on American firms' adoption and adaption of Japanese practices without mentioning the Japanese. I make this observation not to deplore it; indeed, it would seem a necessary part of the adoption process in the context of American organizational culture.[7] As Rosabeth Kanter (1983), observed, part of the adoption process for new ideas often involves relinquishing ownership of early sources of inspiration to new sources so that the new champions develop a sense of ownership. This transfer strengthens the commitment to move forward. However essential the two-step learning process may have been, initially it slowed the absorption of the new quality model.

Cognitive Barriers

In the preceding chapter, I discussed a set of denials that delayed managements' response. These involved top managements' unwillingness to accept quality as a competitive threat and a reluctance to see Japanese quality as superior. Once these denials were gradually laid to rest, a second layer of denials came to the fore as top-and middle-level managers began to grapple with addressing the problem.

Compounding the problem, managers had strong cognitive defenses that served as additional barriers to adopting specific elements of the new quality model. David Nadler (1992) has characterized quality-hostile assumptions that have limited the success of American corporate initiatives in quality improvement. An adapted version appears in Table 3.1. Together, these assumptions capture a broad set of problems that underlie many of the barriers to adoption. How serious a barrier these assumptions were is open to question. If one subscribes to Professor Kaoru Ishikawa's view that the new quality model requires a "thought revolution," then they were serious barriers indeed (Ishikawa, 1985).

Institutionalized behavior, as we have seen, has a large taken-for-granted character. It is hard to change what we take for granted because we do not even recognize how our taken-for-granted assumptions underlie our existing behavior. Although the Nadler list was published in the early 1990s, many of the illustrative assumptions apply with even greater force in the early and mid-1980s. By the 1990s, a number of them had been attacked explicitly and were no longer seen as automatically acceptable behavior (e.g., if it ain't broke, don't fix it). Nevertheless, for the early 1980s we can think of these assembled assumptions as providing an integrated cognitive structure for many managers to order social interaction.

Each element in this cognitive map is consistent with the old quality model and the low status of quality in the organizations that practiced the old model. These elements also flow from the dominance of finance and marketing personnel and their trained incapacity described in Chapter 2. My discussion of Table 3.1 deals only with the first two performance assumptions: (1) it costs more to provide a quality product or service and we will not recover the added cost, and (2) the law of diminishing returns makes continuous improvement unworkable.

The contrary assumptions that higher quality can lead to lower costs and that continuous improvement should be the centerpiece of corporate improvement efforts, are both counterintuitive to persons wedded to the old model. Together, they constituted perhaps the primary cognitive roadblocks to the implementation of the new model in the early and mid-1980s. While many top-management leaders jumped aboard the quality bandwagon in the early 1980s, the critical layers of management below them, who were responsible for actually doing something, voiced strong reservations reflected in these first two performance assumptions. Both concerned the relation between costs and quality improvement and therefore touched some of the core beliefs about the centrality of financial management of the firm.

Table 3.1. Clusters of Quality-Hostile Assumptions

Corporate Purpose

Our primary and overriding purpose is to make money—to produce near-term shareholder return.

Our key audience is the financial markets and, in particular, the analysts.

Customers

We are smarter than our customers; we know what they really need.

Quality is not a major factor in customers' decisions; they cannot tell the difference.

Performance

It costs more to provide a quality product or service, and we will not recover the added cost.

The law of diminishing returns makes continuous improvement unworkable.

Strategic success comes from large, one-time innovative leaps rather than from continuous improvement.

The way to influence corporate performance is portfolio management and creative accounting.

We will never be able to manufacture competitively at the low end.

People

Managers are paid to make decisions; workers are paid to do, not to think.

We do not trust our people.

The job of senior management is strategy, not operations or implementation.

The key disciplines from which to draw senior management are finance and marketing.

Problem Solving and Improvement

To err is human; perfection is an unattainable and unrealistic goal.

Quality improvement can be delegated; it is something the top can tell the middle to do to the bottom.

Celebrate success and shun failure; there is not much to learn by dwelling on our mistakes.

If it ain't broke, don't fix it.

Organization

Functional loyalties take precedence over other loyalties.

An emphasis on system inevitably leads to deadly bureaucracy.

Source: Adapted from Nadler et al., 1992: 151.

The first, the idea that high quality and low cost went together, was simply not on the mental horizons of top American managers in the early 1980s (Robinson, 1980: 585). There was literally a cognitive gap that did not allow U.S. managers to conceive of the possibility of a unity between low cost and high quality. In the traditional model, higher quality meant more product attributes, and that logically meant higher costs. Quality was thus seen in a trade-off relationship with higher costs. One could add only so much in the way of costs associated with additional attributes before consumer demand would fall off.[8]

Managers challenged the logical possibilities that low cost and high quality could go together, based on their understanding of the traditional model. Yet this unity was at the heart of corporate Japan's approach; by eliminating waste and rework in business processes, one could achieve both higher quality and lowered costs. The Japanese were using a process rather than product definition of quality improvement. In short, the existing narrowly constrained definition of quality blocked conceptual clarification.

In my interviews with Japanese managers in leading firms, I asked about their meetings with U.S. managers in the early and mid-1980s. The Japanese often cited the difficulty that many U.S. managers had in grasping their approach on these issues. The head of quality at Fuji Xerox Co. Ltd. described to me a meeting in the mid-1980s with John Smale, chairman of the board of P&G:

> I think it is difficult for Americans to understand why cost is not our first concern. Mr. Smale spoke of lowering cost and improving quality simultaneously. However, Japanese companies which have firmly pursued TQC focus on building quality in first with the cost reductions flowing from that. We had a long discussion about this and he clearly had trouble accepting our position. Of course, we went through this same process. Originally we also thought we should pursue these goals simultaneously.[9]

By the late 1980s many U.S. managers accepted the counterintuitive claims that high quality and low cost went together and that continuous improvement was financially rewarding. Yet the new slogans were initially often recited as mantras and used as litmus tests by lower-level employees to test management's new-found commitment to quality. Many managers and lower-level employees still did not understand the mechanics that produced the desired results. Predictably, this lack of understanding would delay the production of the desired outcome, improved quality.

The second counterintuitive assumption of the new quality model was that continual improvement could be cost-effective. The old model stressed that the law of diminishing returns would set in, and thus the cost of additional quality increments would eventually exceed the benefits. The costing out of the benefits of improvement and the setting of minimum thresholds for instituting improvements were deeply ingrained in the culture of American manufacturing firms and reflected a primary means by which the finance department exerted control over manufacturing.

Skeptics of continuous improvement mistook the real dangers and excessive costs of perfectionism for the careful targeting of improvement targets. First, under the new quality model, not just any quality improvement path is taken. In my own investigation of quality practices among leading Japanese companies in 1989, it became clear that costly quality improvement paths were rejected on the shop floor with strong organizational pressure exerted on behalf of the least costly improvement measures. In short, the costs of improvement can be minimized. Put differently, optimum quality costs (a sum of prevention, appraisal, and failure costs) can lie very near or at zero defects if the incremental costs of approaching zero defects are less than the incremental return from the resulting improvement. Schneiderman (1986) demonstrates a variety of circumstances under which this could be true. Fine (1986) observes that learning benefits accrue to high-quality performers with a reduction in cost for increased conformance.

Second, skeptics ignored the possibility of disrupting the quality-cost trade-off through breakthrough practices (Kondo, 1979; 1990). For example, if a manager could not cost-justify the improved quality that would result from, say, buying a new machine for a given process, one might instead thoroughly reinvent the process, thereby improving quality. Third, the benefits of improved quality and the costs of poor quality are often insufficiently measured. In 1989, I interviewed the head of the quality department at Toyota Motor Co. and specifically asked if there was merit in continuous improvement. He responded:

> This has always been a problem because to research a 20 yen problem you may have to spend 100 yen. However, we have stopped arguing about whether the research compensates for the loss in money. We stopped it 20 years ago. This is because failure cost is really only a small part of the total cost. For example, with our warranty system, a customer will bring a faulty automobile which we fix for free. So, it takes a certain amount of money on our side for repairs. But, the customer must pay for gasoline to bring the car to the shop, and he must find a way to get home, plus he will not be able to use the car for a certain period. And since the car is not being used, this is a minus for the national economy. Therefore, we are not covering all of these losses with the money we use at the factory to repair the car. In short, the losses far exceed the costs we incurred fixing the problem.

Critical here is the implicit assumption that the unmeasured customer-and society-incurred costs will become company costs (through negative reputational effects), if not addressed, and that reducing these costs, even if we cannot measure them precisely, is well worth the investment. No top-management team in the American automotive industry was even remotely thinking in these terms in the early and mid-1980s.

Even though continuous improvement can be economically feasible, employees may occasionally face practical options that are more costly than the likely benefits in quality improvement. Such a reality does not eliminate the organizational benefits (motivational in particular) of having a continuous improvement philosophy. Even in the case just described, when a lower-cost improvement opportunity resulted eventually from dynamic changes in the workplace, employees are more likely to identify and act on it if a continuous improvement mindset has been internalized.

Where's the Evidence?

For both these assumptions, management demanded hard evidence to support these counterintuitive claims. It is a social psychology truism that individuals are willing to make inferences and take action without evidence when the inferences are consistent with their prior beliefs. However, when the inferences challenge existing beliefs, individuals want evidence before taking action (see Ross and Lepper, 1980). The more problematic the nature of a claim, the more social actors want standard scientific evidence to support that claim before they invest in its purported solution (Stinchcombe, 1990: 176–179). Faced with great uncertainty as to the nature of the new quality model and how to go about implementing it, management responded with calls for evidence.

Managers wanted evidence, but the evidence was hard to come by. Even where it existed, they did not know the right questions to ask or where to look for it. Moreover, they often rejected what evidence there was. Experience with applying the new quality model was still modest in the United States. Accumulating creditable data would take time. Nor was this a subject attracting the attention of American academics. As late as 1990, a leading business scholar, Michael Porter, was writing in his influential book, *The Competitive Advantage of Nations*, that "providing unique performance, quality or service is inherently more costly in most instances to seeking only to be comparable to competitors on such attributes" (1990: 38). Garvin (1988: 69–92) published one of the first serious efforts to determine the correlates of quality in 1988, but his results were "tentative and inconsistent."

Even though the Japanese experience presumably offered a stock of experience, it was often seen as inaccessible. More important, the Japanese seemed to have a much more relaxed approach to measurement in many areas than did the Americans. When American management officials toured Japanese plants in the 1980s, they often asked for evidence of the benefits of quality control circles in financial terms; the Japanese mangers typically had no data to offer.

Indeed, the Japanese were often puzzled by these requests and would scratch their heads and say, "Well, let's go down to the shop floor." Then they would point out all the improvements to equipments and processes made by the employee suggestions coming out of quality control circles; clearly they considered that sufficient evidence. The also argued that the improved morale resulting from employees solving work shop problems translated into improved productivity and quality in many intangible ways. For the American managers, however, steeped in measurable cost-benefit calculations, this was hardly evidence. They wanted systematic evidence, but they needed salient, well-developed, concrete examples. Compounding the problem were the American quality zealots, who made many extravagant claims for the benefits of quality improvement, thereby alienating many intelligent and experienced managers. This muddied the water regarding the benefits of a strong quality improvement focus and made many managers reluctant to proceed.

Finally, all evidence is not equal. Even when an empirically based and logically sound presentation could be made advocating the benefits of quality improvement, if it attacked strongly held predispositions, it was likely to be rejected. This is entirely consistent with social psychological research; indeed, such attacks sometimes have the effect of strengthening existing predispositions (Ross and Lepper, 1980). Rejection took the form of managers questioning the applicability of results or suggesting other possible explanation for the data. Information that is concrete, directly comparable, and based on firsthand experience is more likely to overcome prior beliefs (Ross and Lepper, 1980: 30).

Alex Mair, GM vice president, was well known within GM for his convincing demonstrations in 1986 in which he would hold up and compare two connecting rods from GM and Honda engines. Point by point, he would show how GM's mode of production was less efficient and its technology deficient, and how this translated into poorer quality and higher costs from a customer perspective (Ingrassia and White, 1994: 88–93). Parenthetically, note here that this was 1986 and GM was still struggling through the awareness stage. If it took that long to make the case for hard, concrete technologies, it is not surprising that Flynn and Andrea (1994) concluded that American auto firms found it hard to accept the superiority of Japanese soft/linking technologies (organizational practices that cross departments and functions).

The General Accounting Office (GAO) issued a report in May 1991 evaluating the effects of quality practices among Baldrige Award finalists. The evaluation was generally positive. Testifying to the managerial thirst for evidence, more copies of that report were distributed by September that year than any other GAO report ever issued (Winter, 1994: 107). Despite the positive results the report attributed to quality improvement efforts, it could easily be attacked on methodological grounds for its nonrepresentative sample and selective choice of practices. Clearly, evidence as a factor in changing management's working assumptions is much overrated. Overcoming deeply held core beliefs is difficult. Yet a strong belief in the power of evidence is exactly what underlies the rational actor model.

Given the accumulated weight of all these quality-hostile assumptions, it is not surprising that managerial response to pressures for change was slow to develop.

These assumptions represented, on balance, a strong reinforcing cultural system regulating behavior. In the language of Bourdieu (1981), members of each level (department, function, and job), share common histories and a similar "habitus," creating regularities in thought, aspirations, dispositions, patterns of appreciation, and, most of all, practices linked to their particular positions in the organizational structure. Change at a deeper level is problematic in this environment.

CHAPTER 4

It Ain't Rocket Science, But . . .

If the last chapter was mostly about what American management did not do, this chapter describes and interprets American managers' actual early responses to the quality challenge. Joseph Juran, that keen observer of the American quality movement, concluded in the mid-1990s that in retrospect the results of the quality initiatives of the 1980s were deeply disappointing (1995: 586). Surely, there were some real success stories, he argued, but, by and large, corporate efforts did not yield rapid improvements across a broad range of firms and industries. Improvements at leading companies like Ford and HP in the early 1980s were the exceptions, not the rule.

How could that be? Why was adoption of the new quality model so difficult? Juran points to a poor choice of strategies and to poor execution of valid strategies, and he traces these in turn to the failure of top management to provide the necessary leadership because they lacked training and experience in managing for quality. Alternatively, Deming argued that managers could not make progress until they learned to understand statistical concepts of controlling variation in an economical fashion. Yet, once they recognized the importance of quality, would they rapidly acquire the necessary information and expertise necessary to identify the proper strategies and to execute them effectively? That is what we anticipate in a world free of institutional constraints.

After all, as many executives liked to say during this period, "Quality improvement is not rocket science." Would not an efficient functioning market assign a proper price for the necessary information and expeditiously deliver it to those willing to pay the price? If the information was not readily available, would not a variety of entrepreneurs—consultants, for example—arise to seek out that information and then make it available to potential users? Certainly the number of consultants offering information and implementation advice in the quality arena in the 1980s dramatically increased. Without direct continuous access to Japanese practices, however, their sources of good information were modest and their value limited. Without good information, the outlines of the new quality model, or for that matter, whether there even was one, were none too clear to managers. In short, it took a lot of time to learn what broad directions to pursue, and even then rapidly improving quality performance did not follow at once. Learning broadly what to do was followed by many trial-and-error initiatives in the course of implementation, and that took time as well. In each set of decisions managers had an opportunity to follow the wrong path, and they often did.

To recreate the environment in which managers took their first tentative steps to address the quality problem, we can think of the first half of the 1980s as a period of the "competing quality gurus" (for the Xerox experience, see Kearns and Nadler, 1992: 162–165). Because managers were not going to rely on systematically learning directly from the Japanese, they turned to their homegrown experts. Philip Crosby, W. Edwards Deming, Armand V. Feigenbaum, and Joseph M. Juran were the leading quality figures of the time. However, they had different focuses and often made deprecating remarks about the others' contributions or lack thereof.

Philip Crosby was associated with the importance of conformance to requirements and measuring the costs of nonconformance; Deming with statistical quality control, understanding and reducing the sources of variation, and developing an ongoing cycle of continuous quality improvement; Feigenbaum with his general systems approach that included new design control, incoming material control, product control, and special process studies; and Juran with applying principles of financial planning, budgeting, and control and using a project approach to quality improvement (cf. Bowles and Hammond, 1991: 201–208). The early 1980s through the early 1990s saw an seemingly endless stream of articles analyzing the respective contributions of the various quality gurus, trying to show differences and similarities (e.g., Oberle, 1990). Despite some real differences, these articles typically ended with platitudes about the fundamental similarity in approaches. Needless to say, management confusion was great. Many large manufacturing companies tended to develop loyalties to one or the other. At some companies, there were divided loyalties and factional conflicts.

Many leaders, however, sent representatives to the seminars, studied the materials of all the quality gurus, and developed their own amalgamated approach (Main, 1994: 164). These consolidated approaches, however, did not develop until the late 1980s. The early 1980s was a time of great confusion for top management seeking the keys to quality improvement. They did not know where to turn or on whom to rely, which ideas complemented one another and which did not. To many managers, it seemed the quality gurus knew a lot about quality but not that much about management, specifically the organizational transformation necessary to get to the promised land (see Kearns and Nadler, 1992: 164–165).

In short, managers could not separate the bad information from the good information. Not surprisingly, the sorting-out process was time-consuming, with many false steps and wasted investments. In addition to the well-known quality gurus, consultants emerged to guide the quality improvement process and quickly created their own versions. Like the clients they served, successful consulting firms learned that product differentiation and mass distribution of their standardized products was the key to a successful consultancy. While a specific consultant's approach could be helpful to an individual company, this fragmented market for information meant that firms were not in the best position to build on and learn from others' successes.

In the early 1980s, the consultant industry pursuing quality was still modest and fragmented. Unlike other consultant-driven efforts (e.g., portfolio management and business process reengineering), (cf. Micklethwait and Wooldridge, 1996) the quality initiative had its origins in Japanese manufacturing practices; it evolved through the imitation and adaptation of these practices by U.S. business firms. In this context, it is understandable that the U.S. consultants were mostly playing catch-up.

Many of the quality consultancies in the early 1980s were old-line quality assurance firms, human resource consultancies that latched onto quality as a theme, and firms started by quality managers who, after one or two years of applying new approaches like quality circles and statistical process control (SPC), decided to quit their firm and set up their own consultancy. A case in point was Wayne Rieker, a manufacturing manager at the Missiles System Division of Lockheed Missiles & Space Company. Rieker led its quality circle initiative, subsequently retired, and then started his own quality circle consultancy. His firm was spectacularly successful in the first half of the 1980s. With limited good information, however, many of these firms were often only one step ahead of their clients, if that, in their knowledge about quality improvement; the blind lead the blind. Over time, of course, those consultancy firms that survived acquired additional expertise and understanding, and the number of new entries grew rapidly. By 1991, *Business Week*'s special issue on quality reported a Boston Consulting Group study that concluded American companies were paying out $750 million a year to 1,500 third-party providers of advice and materials on quality improvement (Byrne, 1991: 35). Clearly, this was a boom of extraordinary proportions, which was extended through much of the 1990s by the demand for help with certification in the International Standards Organization (ISO) 9000 series.

Doing What We Know Best

Even though each element of the new quality model did not require rocket science expertise, the required integration of all the key elements involved a degree of organizational transformation for which few companies were prepared. The Japanese quality challenge was exogenous. There were no strong internal contradictions that gave rise to the pressure for change among managers. Rather, the process is similar to Neil Fligstein's (1991) description of the growth of diversification among American businesses in response to the exogenous shock of the Great Depression.

Initially people are confused, response is slow, and management relies on tools in their existing repertoire. When hit with an unforeseen crisis, the magnitude and character of which were not well understood, naturally individual actors choose familiar behaviors and policies. One can understand their initially reasoning: "We are in this problem because are not performing our existing work routines very efficiently. Consequently, we need to execute much better what we are already doing." More broadly, they continue to rely on actions that produced the stable order among existing competitors from which they have long been deriving benefits (Fligstein, 1996: 667).

Phillip Tetlock's (1991: 28–32) analysis of learning in U.S. and Soviet foreign policy captures a variant of this perspective. Applying his model to this analysis, one sees management belief systems hierarchically organized with fundamental assumptions and policy objectives at the apex of a system, strategic policy beliefs and preferences at an intermediate level, and tactical beliefs, preferences, and practices at the base. The initial response of actors to new evidence and arguments is to accommodate them by minimizing the number of related cognitions, preferences, and practices that must be changed in the process of incorporating the new evidence into the belief system. Thus, a typical response would be to try new tactics before considering any changes in strategic policy beliefs, preferences, or practices that derive from them. Management begins to question strategy and fundamental goals only after repeated failures to find solutions. This model fits surprisingly well with the actions management initially took in response to the quality challenge. That response was dominated by tactics.

Thus, it is perhaps not surprising that the most common early response of top management to the quality challenge in the early 1980s was "quality by exhortation" (cf. Juran, 1995: 584–585). Many managers thought that by raising quality awareness through speeches to employees, they could motivate employees to improve quality. At a time when many managers thought quality problems were located at the individual level, this approach seemed quite reasonable. It also gave managers a sense that they were addressing the problem. Employees were urged to do quality work and assured of career success if they just worked harder to build quality priorities into their thinking. At the time, in many companies this was the extent of top-management leadership for quality improvement. Such exhortations are in the great American tradition of "positive thinking" in which individual effort overcomes institutional barriers. Of course, there is little evidence that such exhortations had much effect.

On a par with quality exhortation was quality awareness training. It was all the rage in the early 1980s to devote full-day sessions to quality awareness presentations in which layers of managers, and sometimes lower-ranking employees as well, were successively exposed to a range of presentations on quality improvement. Usually, this included some data on how poorly the company was doing on quality, comparing its performance with that of selected competitors. Exhortations to do better were standard fare as well. Over time, companies increasingly came to understand that awareness meetings and simple motivational exhortations to produce better quality simply did not work.

A major figure in the early 1980s was Philip Crosby, a former corporate vice president for quality at ITT. His appeal to American managers in this early period confirms managers' strong tendency to turn to their existing toolkit for effective responses to a crisis they did not anticipate or understand. In 1979, Philip Crosby published *Quality is Free*, widely acknowledged as the first and probably only book on quality that American top management had read up to that time (Groocock, 1986: 22). It is said to have sold two million copies in several languages. In the early 1980s many manufacturing firms purchased the book in bulk and distributed it to all their managers. Unlike Juran and Deming, Crosby was "untainted" by any foreign, read that Japanese, influence. Japanese company practices were notably absent in his books and training materials; for those looking for an American solution to quality problems, Crosby seemed to offer a new direction. Moreover, his homegrown analysis played to the importance of two tried and true emphases to which American managers could relate: leadership and motivation.

Quality is Free probably did more to raise top managers' awareness of quality as a major issue linked to the financial performance of the firm than any other event or publication during the early 1980s. The title was a marketing stroke of genius. Moreover, Crosby was clear about management's responsibility for improving quality. Above all, the book contributed greatly to managerial awareness of the cost of quality (costs of poor quality) and its impact on the bottom line through encouraging firms to measure the "price of nonconformance." Borrowing from Armand Feigenbaum, he focused on being able to show top management how much it cost to produce poor quality. In fact, this was a slippery concept to measure, but it captured top management's attention and motivated their action.

Crosby stressed what he called the four basic absolutes of quality management: the definition of quality is conformance to requirements, the system causing quality is prevention, the performance standard for quality is zero defects, and the measurement of quality is the price of nonconformance. He describes a 14-point program for implementing his approach:

1. Management Commitment
2. Quality Improvement Team
3. Measurement
4. Cost of Quality
5. Awareness
6. Corrective Action
7. Zero Defects Planning
8. Employee Education
9. Zero Defects Day
10. Goal Setting
11. Error Cause Removal
12. Recognition
13. Quality Councils
14. Do It All Again

One can begin to see how the Crosby program reinforced a "more of the same but do it better" mentality by comparing its core elements to the characteristics of the old and new quality models introduced in Chapter 1. In terms of the characteristics of the new quality model, Crosby's teachings in the early 1980s are consistent with using quality as a strong competitive strategy and a prevention focus; integrating quality into the control system of goals, plans, and actions; and a focusing on cross-functional cooperation to achieve firm-level objectives. It was most at variance with the new quality model in terms of its almost total absence of focus on customers (final users), the central organizing element of the new quality model, and in its neglect of a concrete strategy to involve all employees in a well-defined problem-solving methodology. Crosby eschewed statistical methods. He did not see the significance of statistics in characterizing a process or in prevention. While he included some cosmetic references to employee involvement and problem solving, they were clearly tertiary themes with no operational implications. Certainly, the training materials were rich in the vocabulary of customers, but the focus was overwhelmingly on describing each employee as a consumer and customer of internal services; paradoxically there were few references to the customer as purchaser and final user. The final user was mentioned in terms of asking marketing what the customer wanted.

Crosby's idea of employee involvement was telling workers to write up any problems that kept them from performing error-free work and to turn that over to their superiors. He was at pains to say that this was not a suggestion system. "All they [the workers] have to do is to list the problem" and to turn their ideas over to the industrial engineering group (Crosby, 1979: 117). A high-level manager of a large manufacturing firm that stayed committed to Crosby for much of the 1980s explained to me in 1996 that the "Crosbian view of empowerment was to task multifunctional teams of middle mangers to take responsibility for quality (a new responsibility for them). This appealed to 'top-down' control-oriented top management who weren't prepared for the full implications of a decentralized approach to problem solving." Even many of the seeming similarities between Crosby's ideas and the new quality model are deceptive. While Crosby did stress the importance of prevention, he focused on individual attitude change, not on upstream prevention devoted to developing tools and systems for defect-free processes in the design stage. Similarly, Crosby talked about cross-functional cooperation and integration of quality into the corporate control system, but it was more a matter of labeling an area rather than doing the hard work of developing a structured approach to achieving these ends. As one CEO who used Crosby put it to me, "Crosby was no help in navigating the corporate hierarchy to make quality happen."

A different story emerges when we compare the old quality model and its fit with the Crosby model. Surely, Crosby would reject many of its elements, such as quality as a stand-alone effort and quality as a specialized function carried out by quality experts. His model, however, affirms the old model's defining theme, which is its inward-looking orientation with an overriding emphasis on conformance to requirements. Indeed, by stressing conformance to requirements rather than conformance to specifications, he in effect broadened the scope of the internal application. It now not only included technical specifications (Crosby estimated that only some 10% of the requirements for an automobile are technical specifications) but also the broad range of management-imposed rules. Moreover, in keeping with the old quality model, Crosby maintained the emphasis on the quality manager as policeman, whose role was to monitor operations personnel to ensure they were producing quality products and services. In summary, Crosby's ideas in the early 1980s made only a modest departure from the old quality model.

The appeal of Crosby in the early 1980s was based on his personal skills at motivating top management and the sense that, unlike others, he had a method. The CEO of a large integrated circuit maker explained his adoption of the Crosby package in 1980 as follows: "No one else at the time seemed to have a method. We hadn't yet heard of Deming and Juran was a guy whose lectures seemed to put people to sleep. Crosby talked the language of management." Note that this statement implicitly assumes that the Japanese are not available as a reliable source of information on quality. In a similar vein, a high-level official at Atlantic Richfield Company (ARCO) explained the relatively durable appeal of Crosby at his company in the 1980s by noting that Crosby had an especially strong appeal to engineers, who liked his "formula" and "deliverables."

All these observations are consistent with the findings of Easton and Jarrell (1997b) that Crosby was overwhelmingly the most influential of the quality gurus in giving companies a new start with quality—even if these efforts stalled after a few years. By seeming to provide a coherent managerial system, as deficient as it turned out to be, Crosby proved to be the only game in town. In the rapidly deteriorating competitive environment of the early 1980s, the pressure to do something, almost anything that showed promise, had especially strong appeal. It is not surprising that without serious competitors, this bias for action might lead managers to Crosby. As for the Japanese, their game was "in another town" and judged irrelevant.

In 1979, Crosby left ITT and set up Philip Crosby Associates in Winter Park, Florida, as a residential training center. By 1985, the firm was grossing $20 million a year in revenues and by 1990, 20,000 managers were passing through its classrooms, paying a total of $84 million for the company's services (Byrne, 1991: 35, 38). Crosby developed a 2 ½ day seminar for senior managers and a week-long one for middle managers at his "executive college." The firm also did in-house training and set up other training centers; the firm went on from training for IBM to teach managers from an estimated 1,500 companies by 1990 (Dobyns and Crawford-Mason, 1991: 68). Signetics, the sixth largest integrated circuit maker at the time, looked to Crosby for a solution to its quality problems. General Motors and Chrysler were also major customers of the firm in the early and mid-1980s, and GM went so far as to buy 10% of the firm for $4 million. In 1985, the firm went public and in 1989, Crosby sold off his interest in the firm. By December 1986, GM had sent 4,000 employees, mostly executives, to the GM Quality Institute, which was licensed to teach Crosby materials (Cole, 1989a: 253). Numerous other GM executives attended the Crosby program at his Winter Park facility. General Motors stayed committed to Crosby's approaches long after many others had moved on.

Not until the 1987 hiring of William Scherkenbach, a Deming disciple who worked at Ford did GM signal a strong shift away from Crosby's approaches. Scherkenbach's hiring coincided roughly with the departure of President James McDonald, one of Crosby's strongest supporters at GM throughout the early and mid-1980s. One keen observer of the industry, Mary Ann Keller, describes McDonald's view of quality as follows:

> McDonald subscribed to a simple, old-fashioned view that quality attainment was easy—you just look in a mirror and say, like a mantra, "It's up to me." He shunned what he thought were "fancy techniques": gurus like Deming angered him—they just seemed to cloud the issue. Once McDonald even passed out little blue plastic mirrors to managers at a quality conference and told everyone to look in the mirror and "just zap out that poor quality." (Keller, 1989: 238)

Managers with these kinds of views seemed particularly attracted to Phil Crosby's approach in the early and mid-1980s. Individual attitude change is seen as the critical variable. There is a striking similarity to McDonald's views and what Crosby is said to have told Xerox managers in the early 1980s: "If you want people to act in a different way, all you have to do is tell them. You tell them and they do it" (Kearns and Nadler, 1992: 162).

Given the enormous quality challenge facing many manufacturing firms during the early 1980s and the sense of crisis, it is of no small importance to understand how managers looking for radical solutions to their problems would end up implementing very conservative ones. Crosby's training stressed that managers experiencing it would never be the same again; they would be transformed as managers, able to act with fresh insight. Yet, once managers returned to the workplace, they often ended up reinforcing the old approaches (doing more of the same). How can we reconcile these two seemingly contradictory observations, given the assumption that these managers were intelligent individuals selected for their talent, capabilities, and analytic skills?[1]

The understandings arrived at by middle managers at a week-long training in an isolated residential facility is one thing. Returning to apply these ideas in the workplace is another. We know enough about the ability of leaders to construct new realities among participants in isolated settings to believe that managers could undergo a kind of transformation that would make them true believers. Crosby's approach contains some central characteristics that are strikingly similar to those Ernest Gellner (1979: 118–121), the philosopher, identifies with ideology. Crosby's package contains bait, a unifying idea, and an organizing concept with explanatory power; it illustrates what was previously seen as obscure; and it contains both promise to the believer and fear to those who do not believe, thereby separating believers from skeptics.

The bait is zero defects, a promise of perfection. The unifying idea is conformance to requirements, a concept with putative explanatory power. Its absence explains why we are doing so badly and its presence is the precondition for success. Conformance to requirements illuminates what has previously been obscure in exquisitely simple terms. Above all, it promises salvation—zero defects leading to competitive success. In so doing, it raises the stakes, suggesting hope for those who believe and fear for those who do not. Taken in its entirety, it provides a way of looking at the world that separates the believer from the skeptic. What comes through here is the power of Crosby's ideas as a logically consistent, marketable package, presented in an isolated setting conducive to its acceptance.

The inability of participants to verify empirically the assertions made in isolated settings lends great power to the leaders seeking such a transformation. Crosby and the other teachers' style was to lecture to the students, who were not encouraged to think and work through problems and arrive at solutions themselves. There were no cases. Rather, students were receptacles for the new understandings imparted lecture-style by the instructors. Not surprisingly this put the participants in a weak position to evaluate their experiences critically.

Yet, once back in the workplace, the seminar participants were surrounded by peers, subordinates, and even superiors who did not share their assumptions. Paradoxically, in the short term, this often had the effect of strengthening their beliefs by making those managers who had been through the Crosby training realize just how far they had come relative to their co-workers. The presence of uninformed co-workers highlights the shining virtue of those who have attained truth (Gellner, 1979: 138). In the long run, however, they were forced to trim their radical initiatives in profoundly conservative ways.

At the training sessions and in written publications, the language used was clear and straightforward; trainers talked about how simple quality improvement was, if you just understand the aforementioned four basic principles. The stress was on implementing Crosby's clear 14-point program in ways that would yield change. Because it was easy to show managers that the cost of quality (cost of nonconformance) at major manufacturing firms typically was 20% or more of their total costs, it seemed only logical to conclude that conformance to requirements was the right direction to pursue solutions. Saving some 20% would go right to the bottom line and one would get high quality to boot. This was a heady brew, hard for managers to resist. This logic, however, ignored the fundamental problem that one could have a perfectly conforming product in which customers had little interest because it was the wrong product, or had the wrong price or the wrong features, or it performed badly on some other quality dimension important to customers. Crosby also had weak problem-solving tools for ensuring conformance to requirements.

The rhetoric of the training was about making business processes transparent so that proper requirements could be set. This in turn would lead to new requirements, hence, change. Participants were told that failure to follow set requirements had been a persistent source of quality problems, something they could all agree upon and recognize. So getting employees to follow the agreed-upon requirements in itself could be seen as a revolutionary act.

Moreover, even though Crosby claimed that his program was not motivational (a matter about which Juran [1966] had scathingly criticized him in the past), he stressed the importance of getting every individual employee to adopt a zero defect mentality (recall the McDonald quotation). Employees were asked to sign declarations promising not to make any errors on a given day or for the next 30 days. We see again managements' tendency in those days to see quality improvement as simply the aggregate of individual commitments to a high quality standard. This, after all, was the period of management by exhortation. At the same time, instead of providing any real engine for change, managers were taught to strengthen the motivational focus though a reliance on "trinket awards," zero defect hats and T-shirts, Zero Defect Day, and so forth.

What happened when these initiates returned to the workplace? They are supposed to be leaders. Crosby typically gave all graduates a baton to symbolize their role as transformational leaders. Yet the methodologies for how to set the new requirements were abstract and often led to boiler plate specification of the requirements necessary to make the process work from the point of view of the person in charge (e.g., number of employees required, who had to be where at what time, etc.).

The pronoun used in many of the training materials was "you," as if there were a universal *you*. Thus, there was no specification of a social process in which individuals collectively identified these requirements. Nor was there a collective problem-solving methodology that provided an engine for change. The image is of an organization in which all employees need to be programmed with the same imperatives to identify the requirements of the process for which they are responsible and to aim for zero defects. There is little social structure in this abstracted firm. The "one size fits all" training materials that flow from this model were appealing to managers because the lessons taught seemed to apply to everyone. From the consultant's point of view, it is ideal because it enables the delivery of a standard product without the extra cost of customizing it to a given firm, industry, or type of employee. Employees in the workplace, however, when subjected to the new regime, tended to perceive it as too abstract to provide much guidance in their daily work.

Employees ultimately tired of the hoopla of Zero Defect Day and the plastering of the workplace with quality slogans. In the face of disaffection and the lack of concrete courses of action, managers tended to fall back on the idea that change is about getting employees to follow agreed-upon requirements. Since there were no operational mechanisms for creating the new and improved processes, managers ended up setting the rules for the "agreed-upon requirements," using traditional criteria and without strong efforts to meet external customer needs. All that was left in the end was the managerial admonition to employees that "Your job is to follow the existing rules." This nicely meshed with the control-oriented large bureaucracies of the 1980s; it was simply more of what managers knew how to do. Ross Perot, a GM board of directors member in the mid-1980s, and an individual whose judgment on business seems more finely honed than his judgments on politics, captured the problem: "In a lot of these big companies, what it takes to be successful has nothing to do with making better products or serving the customer or what I call the rules of the marketplace. It has to do with following procedures" (Detroit Free Press, 1986, 4c). Stressing conformance to requirements, as Crosby did, was in fact not the revolutionary act he claimed it to be. Rather, in the bureaucratic world of many large corporations of the day, it ended up being profoundly conservative, perpetuating the existing rule-oriented thinking. From an employee perspective, it was just another set of arbitrary management rules, and these employees had a wealth of experience in how to subvert them. In short, what was seen by proponents as a program of radical transformation often got translated into profoundly conservative acts.[2]

One last element of Crosby's appeal requires discussion. There is no doubt that in many companies, the application of Crosby's ideas initially did produce quality improvement. If not so, his ideas would not have endured as long as they did. How do we explain this in the light of this discussion? First, one can say that forceful application of the old quality model could produce quality improvement for a while by virtue of concentrating management and employee attention on quality and the need to avoid error. What it could not produce was sustained quality improvement with the customer as the driver. Second, some management teams succeeded with Crosby for a longer time because they were very good managers who knew how to motivate their employees; often they overlaid Crosby with other progressive ideas.

One such example occurred at ARCO, where a strong Crosby-inspired corporatewide initiative in the early 1980s was sustained until the late 1980s only at their Cherrypoint facility. When asked to explain why it was sustained for so long at this facility, an ARCO manager explained that the management at that facility had been "kind of socialistic." By that, he meant that they already had a very strong employee involvement culture with a decentralized approach to problem solving. They were able to use this culture to drive quality improvement. As I noted, employee involvement was a feature all but absent from Crosby's ideas. At Cherrypoint, ARCO also absorbed a variety of quality tools independent of Crosby's program. In short, Crosby's program at Cherrypoint succeeded for a time because it was overlaid with some critical missing ingredients.

A related experience occurred at Signetics which adopted Crosby's program in the early 1980s.[3] In the course of adopting these ideas, leaders modified them in some important ways. Above all, they added the quality performance of a manager's unit as an important element in all their managers' semiannual performance reviews and acted on that information in the distribution of pay increases and promotions. That alone was likely to lead managers to search for effective means of improving quality and to encourage subordinates to do likewise. The firm also became involved with a major customer in a parts per million contract for supplying integrated circuits for automotive engine controls. This experience led to much new learning, including a focus on measuring quality performance as a key element in contractual relationships and pressure to push problem solving back to fundamental design issues. The contract became a flagship program for the rest of the corporation. In other words, companies sometimes made progress while using Crosby's program because they were doing many other things as well, and they remained committed to Crosby for longer than one might have expected. As one can also deduce from these remarks, many companies found it possible to move away from Crosby after their efforts stalled, and to introduce new approaches to quality improvement. Indeed, Easton and Jarrell (1997b) found that many of the companies that had the most advanced deployment of total quality management in the mid-1990s got their start as Crosby customers. Their research, unfortunately, cannot tell us how many efforts foundered after they gave up on Crosby's program. What Crosby did do, above all, was to get firms started, and some were eventually able to build on those initial experiences, however misguided, to create systematic quality improvement.

The Quality Circle Craze

Quality circles first came to the attention of a broad sector of American business through their development at Lockheed Missiles & Space Company. Inspired by a visiting Japanese quality control circle presentation at Lockheed's Missile Systems Division, Wayne Rieker, a manufacturing manager, organized a study trip to Japan in the early 1970s. Rieker was so impressed with the circle concept that he arranged to have the circle training materials of JUSE translated into English. He used them at Lockheed to initiate a circle program in 1974, and by 1977 the company was publicly reporting savings of three million dollars; the ratio of cost saving to the cost of operation was reported to be six to one. Thirty circles were operating at this time. Visitors flocked to the plant for further investigation. Other companies rushed to imitate Lockheed's program. The early quality circle successes at Lockheed and other firms were widely written up in various business journals including the *Wall Street Journal, Time,* and *Across the Board.*

Quality circles are small groups of employees (often in the range of 6–12) at the same workplace organized to identify and solve workplace problems that inhibit quality and productivity improvement. The members are taught elementary but powerful problem-solving techniques; the teams operate on a continuous basis moving from solving one problem to taking up another. They typically meet "off line" during breaks or after work for an hour or so a week to identify, analyze, and propose solutions to problems. Sometimes this time is paid for and sometimes not. Solutions are presented to management for approval and implementation.

There was a fair range of variation in how quality circles operated within U.S. firms and between U.S. and Japanese firms. The very name itself varied. In Japan, they were typically called quality control circles and sometimes zero defect groups; in the United States they were quality circles (the term control was seen as having pejorative connotations). Moreover, many U.S. companies gave them totally different names like "Intel circles" and "employee involvement teams."

During the early 1980s, the quality circle movement gathered steam. A New York Stock Exchange–sponsored national survey of 49,000 U.S. corporations (27% response rate) documents the explosive growth (Freund and Epstein, 1984). Nineteen percent of manufacturing firms reported adopting quality circles by 1982 (though we should not assume that they covered all or most production workers, much less nonproduction employees in these firms). The survey further reported that 44% of all companies with more than 500 employees had QC programs. Nearly three out of four had started after 1980. Lawler and Mohrman (1985: 66) estimate that over 90% of *Fortune* 500 companies had quality circle programs in the 1984 to 1985 period. Okimoto et al. (1984: 58–59) describe the pressures that the quality deficit put on the semiconductor industry and how quality circles were set up in many companies as one of the early responses to address the problem. Industry leaders like Intel and Advanced Micro Devices (AMD) were in the forefront.

There was an enormous bandwagon effect as the quality circle fad took hold; companies adopted them because it was the thing to do, and their domestic competitors were doing it, and the Japanese were doing it, and the media were telling them they were backward if they did not do it (cf., Strang, 1997). Clearly, this environment did not encourage cool, deliberative thought about the firm's strategic choices.

While many might be content to describe the explosive growth of circles exclusively as a fad, there is much more to be said to cast light on the process of managerial decision making. In the auto industry, in particular, managers drawing on the history of their industry could say, "Yes, quality is a problem but it is the result of lazy workers and entrenched union opposition." Indeed, the idea that American workers had lost their work ethic and that unions existed primarily to thwart management's improvement efforts was widely discussed at the time and not only in the auto industry. Given the historical experiences of many unionized manufacturing firms and the specific organizational expertise in labor management relations resulting from this history, it is not surprising that managers initially turned to this explanation as the cause of the problem. Consequently, they sought out tactics designed to get workers to work harder and more diligently through some mix of carrots and sticks. Efforts were made to reach an accommodation with the United Auto Workers (UAW). By 1980, GM had been experimenting for a decade with worker participation including Quality of Worklife Programs (Ouchi, 1981: 150–162).

Given this setting, when Japanese quality control circles burst on the scene in the late 1970s and early 1980s, presented by many as the source of Japanese success in both quality and productivity, quality circles seemed a natural fit for many companies. Because many managers saw lack of worker commitment as the primary source of poor quality, quality circles were seen as providing workers the motivation and opportunity to make a contribution.

There was a strong sense in the early 1980s that the circles could be implemented by "slotting them" into existing structure without much change in other practices or in power relationships. Rather than change other organizational practices or strategic policies, facilitators were hired in many companies to guide the circles and to smooth their interaction with other employees and departments whose cooperation the circles needed. Circles were treated as a "turnkey" technology. They were a safe, clearly defined package that did not require much change and were therefore quite appealing to those who did not fully appreciate the depth of the quality challenge. In short, circles fit my application of Tetlock's model: management, faced with a crisis, initially adopts minimalist tactical changes, dismissing any notion that corporate strategy needed to be changed.

Consultant firms sprung up to install at a fixed price a complete standardized package with training and support materials, including detailed instructions on how to proceed. The standardized package of circle programs being offered also lent itself to the creation of carefully controlled pilot programs in which the numbers of people involved, as well as the size and cost of the program, could be managed. Clearly all this appealed to managers (Lawler and Mohrman, 1985: 66). Many of the materials in use at companies and among consultants were based on the original Rieker-translated JUSE materials with a small twist of Americanization.

While circles fit managers' perceptions of the problem and the circles' seemingly clearly defined and limited character encouraged receptivity, exogenous factors were also at work. Managers were subjected to a media blitz in the business press that presented Japanese quality success as primarily a function of employee involvement through quality circles. In 1980, the NBC documentary, *If Japan Can, Why Can't We?* featured circles and heightened interest.

William Ouchi's book, *Theory Z* (1981), contributed to the hype. Unusual for an academic book, *Theory Z* was on the best sellers list for 22 weeks (Rogers and Larsen, 1984: 211). Ouchi reported that quality control circles were a major contributor to Japanese business success. Readers were told that the Deming Prize was instituted in 1951 to recognize the outstanding achievement of quality control circles in Japan (Ouchi, 1981: 226). Quality circles, in fact, were not begun formally until 1962, and the Deming Application Prize is for outstanding company achievements in quality, not quality circles. But Ouchi's portrayal was typical of the confusion and misinformation that reigned during this period.

Managers were not limited to the media's portrayal, consultants, or the early efforts of Lockheed as their only sources of information. The burgeoning management study tours to Japan in the early 1980s had a major influence, as many American manufacturing firms desperately searched for the secrets to Japanese success. JUSE, the major national organization for promoting quality control circles in Japan, reported that in 1978, 200 foreign groups visited them in Japan to learn about Japanese circles. Some groups were limited to managers at one company, but most represented multiple companies. By 1983, the number had grown to some 1,000 groups (of which American managers were overwhelmingly the largest group), with the number declining rapidly in the mid-1980s to some 200 a year (Lillrank and Kano, 1989: 6).

As part of the agenda for visiting American managers, Japanese manufacturing firms routinely exposed them to a quality control circle meeting or presentation. These were often impressive events with high school graduates presenting their problem-solving experience with great poise and self-confidence. The Japanese were remarkably open in responding to questions about how the circles functioned. This openness partly reflected their sense that to make circles work required a great deal of customizing and enormous effort; therefore, they did not see themselves as sharing proprietary information (Lillrank and Kano, 1989: 7).

From a decision-making point of view, the interesting question is why circles were selected from all that Japanese firms had to offer in the way of approaches for improving quality. Certainly, I have already argued that they provided a solution that addressed what American managers saw as a traditional problem, worker sloth.

More, however, was at work. Quality control circles were exotic and highly visible. Not only were circle-member presentations featured in factory visits in Japan, but circle activities were very visible on shop floor walk-throughs in the special circle meeting rooms set aside right on the shop floor and in the various charts and graphs posted on bulletin boards on walls and partitions describing the progress and contributions of circle activity. Circles also seemed easy to understand and seemed to make sense ("We are not making sufficient use of our human resources"); they appeared transparent. They were also easy to identify and observe. One could easily write reports about them (Lillrank and Kano, 1989: 7). Above all, they seemed easy to package as independent units.

American managers, seeking to make the correct decisions that would lead to effective quality improvement strategies, could not differentiate the unique, distinctive, visible, intuitively understandable and "easily packaged" Japanese practices from other decisive factors explaining Japan's quality success. They simply did not have enough information to draw the correct inferences about causal relations but were under pressure to act. The most immediately available information from quick Japanese factory tours turned out to be unreliable. American managers would have had to dig deeper and longer than most were willing to do to discover the truth.

A Broader Picture

In comparison with quality control circles, many of the more decisive Japanese practices such as policy management and deployment, prevention strategies, and tactics at the design stage such as quality function deployment were not as transparent as one walked through Japanese factories and did not come up in the questions Americans asked on such visits. These were by and large opaque levers of change and quality improvement, at least for American visitors in the first half of the 1980s. Moreover, many of these more decisive, complicated Japanese practices were still evolving in the early 1980s.

Some activities like just-in-time (JIT) were visible through the low levels of in-process inventory on the shop floor, but they were quite complex. Their effective implementation involved great organizational change, including the establishments of new relationships with suppliers. Thus, American firms were slow to adopt them, but did so well before adopting more complex forms like policy management and deployment (Schonberger, 1986). Furthermore, the electronics industry in general was far slower to adopt JIT production methods than the automotive sector (Thurm, 1998). Again, it is hard to be a rational decision maker in the midst of trial-and-error learning, with little applicable experience and no appreciation of the scope of the challenge.

Quality control circles were significant, but they were not the major factor in the Japanese quality equation. Production workers in quality circles worked with the many small problems that contributed to raising quality and productivity. In the aggregate, these were by no means trivial outcomes. Nevertheless, managers and engineers working "upstream" at the prevention stage had far more leverage to reduce impediments to quality and productivity improvement (cf. Lillrank and Kano, 1989: 6).

It was not simply a matter, however, of American managers needing to identify more decisive features contributing to Japanese quality success. Quality control circles in Japanese firms known for their outstanding quality were integrated into an overall quality improvement initiative that included JIT, policy management and policy deployment, continual design improvement, concurrent engineering, and the like. Furthermore, firm-level circle activities were implicated in a broad national quality movement and received nourishment from cross-corporate information-sharing activities and a national organization that helped identify and diffuse best practice, including the recognition of outstanding circles and programs. The Americans, by contrast, ripped quality circles from their moorings and established them as free-standing entities. Without the nourishment of the broader quality improvement initiative, many were bound to fail, as they did.

During the mid-1980s, there was extended discussion in the media about the short life of many of these efforts, and numerous surveys (though none of a national scope) reported high failure rates and diminished management interest in circles. Many quality circle programs seemed to run out of steam. Westinghouse adopted its first circles in 1980, and by 1981 it had 3,500 circles; by 1982 they were already starting to dissolve (Main, 1994: 61). By the mid-1980s HP had 1,000 circles operating, but soon after, a sharp decline set in; before long they had all but disappeared.[4] Just as the three principal managers of the innovative Lockheed circle program were busy setting up their consultant firms, a new manager took over the Missiles System Division in 1978 and proceeded to dissolve circle activities at Lockheed. Over and over, these experiences were repeated.

Apparently, the faddish imitation and adoption had run its course. Edward Lawler and Susan Mohrman wrote an influential article in *Harvard Business Review* in 1985 suggesting that, as a "parallel organizational structure," quality circles were not integrated into daily work routines. Moreover, they argued that quality circles did not move power downward and had limited impact. They described what they saw in firms as a typical short "product life" for quality circles. Rapid expansion of the program led to a growing management resistance and lack of support, and workers started running out of problems to solve. Circles were described as containing the seeds of their own destruction.

Management resistance clearly was a major factor in the decline of circles and reflected the lack of integration of circles into broader quality improvement efforts. Yet it also became increasingly clear that quality circles were not getting the job done. If the primary objective was to close the quality and productivity gap with Japanese competitors, top managers found it increasingly hard to believe that quality circles could accomplish the objective. Many managers came to realize that they needed to move further "upstream" to get better leverage on their quality problems and also that they needed to address the major quality problems at the boundaries between departments and functions (cf. Main, 1994: 61). Circles, by definition, concentrated their activities on the problems faced by local work groups. By the 1990s quality circles had all but disappeared from mention in the business media except as an example of a failed initiative.

A little more than a decade after the circle boom started, Osterman conducted a national survey (1992) of private sector establishments with 50 or more employees (response rate 65.5%). He found that some 46% of manufacturing establishments reported having quality circle–like problem-solving teams, with some 30% reporting a penetration rate of more than 50% of employees (Osterman, 1994: 177). These data are consistent with Lawler, Mohrman, and Ledford's 1990 and 1993 surveys, which report some 65% of *Fortune* 1000 companies used quality circles (1995: 26). For a movement that had been declared dead for at least a decade and came to be the subject of derision, QCs seem to have shown surprising vitality. How can one reconcile this seeming contradiction?

Most of the present-day problem-solving groups are quite different from those QCs established in the early 1980s. Lawler and Mohrman in the 1985 *Harvard Business Review* article suggested that managers should try to convert circle efforts to more ambitious participative directions. They acknowledged, however, that little evidence suggested that many circle programs made the transition to more partic-ipative approaches. The decline of circle activities in the 1980s did seem to coincide with a shift to other approaches such as self-managing teams (Lawler and Mohr-man, 1985: 64–71). At major companies like General Electric, however, they were clearly seen as an alternative to circles, not complementary or supplementary.

Taking a different tack, contemporary versions of problem-solving groups are not bound by the idea that members must be in the same work group. There is a much greater focus on process management in the 1990s, and improving processes often requires improvement team membership that spans work group boundaries. There is also much greater emphasis on forming problem-solving groups for spe-cific improvement projects and then dissolving them. Similarly, the broader quality improvement thrust of the late 1980s and early 1990s bound problem-solving teams into broader organizational change activities. In 1985, Lawler and Mohrman un-derestimated the power and perseverance not of quality circles as constituted in that period (they were right about them). Rather, they underestimated the power and utility of problem-solving group activity whether part of a parallel organiza-tional structure and whether a "higher form of participation" such as self-managing teams. My later chapter on Hewlett-Packard describes this transition.

There is reason to believe that managers learned from their quality circle ex-periences. Present problem-solving groups in the better managed companies appear to be more tightly linked to broader improvement initiatives. This gives them greater credibility in the firm and greater access to resources. They are also tied more tightly into process improvement activities and that gives them broader ap-plication, an opportunity to attack more meaningful problems, and credibility among higher-level managers. Lawler, Mohrman, and Ledford (1995: 51–58) report a range of findings that support these claims. Tom Murrin, the manager who ran the Westinghouse business that started circles in the firm, reflected on the evolution of quality circles into various forms of team activity: "It was a good way to get started and, on balance, a positive phase. As I look back it seems almost trivial, childish. But it had a profound aspect about it. It was the beginning of empowering people" (cited in Main, 1994: 63–64).

This analysis suggests that management learning and fads are not automatically contradictory phenomena. Fads can serve as building blocks for future management activities, but not always in a conscious strategic fashion. Indeed, purposive learning likely occurs at the tail end of a fad, when decision makers realize the limitations of current practices and try to calculate how much of the previous experiences they can salvage and build upon in their new initiatives. Quality circles become building blocks for later team activities in a lengthy process of iterative problem solving.

Nor were quality circles the only example of this phenomenon in the early quality movement. One of the other early quality initiatives in many U.S. manu-facturing industries in the early and mid-1980s was the effort to adopt SPC, the application of statistical techniques for measuring and analyzing the variation in processes. The control process involves a feedback loop through which one measures actual performance, compares it with the standard, and acts on the difference. The use of control charts to measure and analyze the variation in process is one of the standard tools of SPC (see Shainin and Shainin, 1988: 24.1–40; Shewhart, 1931). In the early and mid-1980s, a great faddish wave of interest (quality minifad) in adopting SPC overlapped with and followed the quality circles fad. The effort focused on teaching employees how to construct and use control charts. Schonberger, an active consultant in this area in the early and mid-1980s, observed that by the mid-1980s nearly all of the Fortune 500 manufacturing firms had adopted and were actively using process control charts to identify and address quality problems (Schonberger, 1986: 43). Here, unlike circles, the "technology" was well known to American experts. SPC was also highly visible to the American visitors touring Japanese manufacturing plants in the ubiquitous control charts and other measurements posted next to work stations.

Many of the early American efforts to adopt SPC proved abortive. Hastily trained employees did not know how to apply their new learning to real problems, managers did not know how to supervise the new approaches, statistical experts did not know how to communicate with those in the workplace. Furthermore, there were no process capability studies to determine whether the process was capable of meeting established customer specifications. And the ritualized filling out of control charts without an organizational framework to act on them hardly helped. Supplier firms, under pressure from their OEM customers, often displayed control charts for visitors that had no operational significance and were seldom updated. In short, SPC started out in most American firms as a narrow technical tool that was not well integrated in a framework of process improvement. Many firms took a turnkey approach. Finally, as with circles, SPC represented a downstream approach to quality improvement and thus could add little to solving the bigger upstream-induced failures. These understandings typically did not coalesce until the mid-1980s.

Although many of the early efforts did indeed fail, they were often restarted with more realistic assumptions about what they could accomplish. In the most successful companies, SPC came to be part of the broader process improvement approach that came to dominate in the late 1980s (Buch and Wetzel, 1993: 34–37). Moreover, as part of the expanded employee improvement efforts of the late 1980s, many companies gave front-line production workers more responsibility to devise and take corrective action about the deviation between the actual performance of equipment and the existing standard. This often occurred through collective action using problem-solving groups.

In short, the more successful companies learned how to build each new approach into the next and, in so doing, used each new minifad to cumulate organizational learning. The approach to SPC evolved and merged with the later developing approaches to employee involvement and process management. As with circles, however, this was not a conscious strategy but emerged out of a trial-and-error iterative problem-solving process.

Various survey data suggest that SPC has become a well-institutionalized feature of large American manufacturing plants. In the auto industry, Womack, Jones, and Roos (1991: 159) report that 93% of suppliers used SPC on all their production operations in 1988, up from 19% in 1983. Similarly, in the major survey of semiconductor wafer fabrication facilities, SPC was found to be well institutionalized in almost all the major world producers, including the United States (McMurray, 1996: 133–137). In 1993, Lawler and his associates asked their *Fortune* 500 sample, "How many employees work in units that use statistical control methods carried out by front-line employees?" He found that of his 132 respondents, only 2% reported not using this method, with 67% reporting that they had over 20% of their employees working in units using this form of SPC (Lawler, Mohrman, and Ledford 1995: 48–50).[5] If one keeps in mind the many production arrangements which do not readily lend themselves to SPC applications, this is a quite impressive total.

I have identified and analyzed four of the primary early responses management made to the quality challenge of the early 1980s: quality by exhortation, quality circles, SPC, and the Crosbian program. Some of these initial responses to the Japanese quality challenge proved rather misguided. There were many missteps, and managers made a number of critical decisions that led them down blind, or almost blind, alleys. Sometimes, these paths were associated with positive learning. For analytic purposes, I have isolated these four initiatives, but many firms were tentatively taking other steps as well at this time. Some of these embryonic efforts were later to prove productive.

Okimoto, Sugano, and Weinstein (1984: 58–59) describe the steps taken at AMD in the early 1980s, which started out as a second-source semiconductor chip maker and gradually evolved into an important player in the semiconductor industry. As a marketing strategy, it established a policy of producing all of its chips to Mil Spec 883 (military specifications for semiconductors), even though they sold very little to the Department of Defense. The idea was to give customers the sense that they were producing to a high quality standard (Rogers and Larsen, 1984: 51).

After the 1980 HP Data Systems Division announcement about the large disparity between the reliability of U.S. and Japanese chips, and after the denial stage passed, AMD's leaders realized that their product quality performance was well below world-class standards. They conducted an internal study to assess the quality of their products and how they were perceived by customers; based on these studies they announced a set of quality performance standards for the company. They initiated quality circles, and modified test procedures to incorporate additional sampling. New tests were added prior to shipment to verify the results already compiled and to guarantee that "the quality that had been built was actually there (Okimoto, Sugano, and Weinstein, 1984: 59)." Product flow was modified and new tests were added to prevent subsequent problems. Checks were made to ensure that proper test procedures were followed and that calibration was accurate. AMD also expanded its program for the analysis of rejects and for feeding back that information to the area where the problem had occurred to minimize the probability of repeat errors.

Apart from assessing the status of their quality and the initiation of circles, the bulk of AMD's efforts were appraisal activities. By tightening test and inspection procedures, AMD followed the normal response one would expect under the old quality model. Again, we see the initial response to crisis as more of the same. These responses probably did result in customers receiving fewer defective products and improved quality as measured in field product reliability. However, these solutions added cost (the cost of additional appraisal activities) and, with the exception of the last-mentioned item on the list, did little to move toward prevention, a central theme in the new quality model.

Conclusion

One way to summarize the foregoing is to consider the response I received interviewing participants in a very successful network of key quality executives at the Conference Board. The Conference Board set up its first Quality Council in 1985. Yet many of the Quality Council's early members, like Ford and Xerox, were experiencing severe financial and market share problems in the early 1980s. Moreover, as we have seen, there were plenty of popular media and industry discussions at this time to suggest that part of the problem was quality. So why was an effective network for executives concerned about quality not initiated in 1980 rather than 1985? David Luther, one of the founding members and formerly vice president for Corning, responded to that question as follows:

> At first we looked for the tried and true methods of overcoming our problems. Cost cutting and productivity improvement programs. When they didn't work, we sought out quality as we understood it at the time. We did the easy things, like lots of training, management meetings cascading down in which we stressed to employees the importance of quality and the need to improve it, quality circles, and greater emphasis on conformance to specifications. But the results were meager at best. It was when we realized that we needed serious work and help in figuring out just what was involved with quality improvement and how to do it that the idea of creating a forum for leading quality managers in major firms bubbled to the surface. By the time we put it together, it was 1985.

In short, the market and institutional arrangements for collecting good information did not develop until a variety of seemingly easier routes proved inadequate.

Slowly, management learned that modest tactical changes yielded few positive outcomes and therefore, as we saw in Tetlock's model, were pushed to consider broader changes at the level of strategic policies and practices. In some respects, these initial efforts served as building blocks so that, when other pieces fell into place at a later date, firms could make much greater progress in the late 1980s. The challenge in the next two chapters is to delineate the emergent institutional infrastructure that created the conditions for further progress.

CHAPTER 5

Casting and Harvesting the Nets

Even amid the confusion of earlier efforts to respond to the Japanese challenge, organizational learning was taking place. Managerial leaders came to realize the much larger scope of the quality challenge after their initial denial and early feeble responses proved ineffective and motivational programs based on individual improvement proved insufficient. Quality improvement by management exhortation and directive did not work. Crosby's approach stalled after a few years. Yet all these failures laid the foundation for questioning the strategic policy beliefs, preferences, and ultimately practices that hindered a more thoroughgoing response to the Japanese quality challenge. Gradually, an emergent institutional infrastructure linking managers within and across firms and industries speeded the flow of information about the nature and methodology of quality improvement. The sharing of trial-and-error experiences built up valuable assets that could be applied in different firms and industries.

In this chapter, I focus on two analytic units of analysis for studying this process. The first is the firm and the second is the networks that link firms and connect managers across them (cf. Grabher and Stark, 1997). As the title of this chapter implies, there can be a strategic element to how managers respond. Thus, I am naturally interested in when and how firms and their agents come to use networks and how effectively. I will also look at two different industries, automotive and semiconductors, for the degree of similarity of their responses and the factors behind some apparent differences.

Although firms are important, networks are critical in their own right because they serve as the transmission links that can carry important new information. In this case, this information concerned the relevance of quality as a competitive issue and the modes of responding to this new challenge. A network emphasis shifts attention away from the exclusive descriptions of particular firms and heroic managers celebrated in the business press and focuses equally on the sometimes visible, and sometimes invisible, bonds that link firms, as well as managers within and across industries. To achieve progress in quality improvement, not only a firm's practices but the very networks linking firms needed to be restructured.

As Stinchcombe's ideas discussed in the beginning of Chapter 3 suggest, networks can seek the best, most timely information, conferring competitive benefits on network users. Networks external to the firm become the basis for gaining fast access to knowledge and resources that cannot be secured internally, and, just as importantly, they provide a continuous test of internal expertise and learning capabilities (Powell and Brantley: 1992: 371). Thus, firms learned to locate and tap external networks to (1) correctly evaluate their own standing in quality performance, (2) continually evaluate their progress in quality improvement, and (3) gain the most rapid access to knowledge about the constituent elements of the new quality model. The company without networks is like "a frog in the well, without knowledge of the ocean." I am paraphrasing here an old Japanese proverb that Kaoru Ishikawa, the Japanese quality leader, told me in discussing the important role of JUSE in getting managers out of their firms and participating with others to more fully understand competitive standards, performance, and opportunities and to get them to co-develop new practices.

Speed and the use of external benchmarks to assess internal expertise and standing are not the only considerations. There was an enormous cacophony of information about the significance and method of quality improvement in the early 1980s; indeed, the very meaning of *quality* was unclear and experts argued over its definition. In this environment, it was a matter of some importance for firms to rapidly sort the good and useful information from the bad and trivial. In short, networks served as important screening devices (Burt, 1992: 62) to tell firms what information was useful and help them to identify individuals outside the firm (consultants, managers, trade association officials, academics) who had useful information and skills. Networks brought key agents of the firm into contact with external agents who could provide such information. Clearly, some firms were better than others in negotiating these processes. Successful managers reached out to seek contacts and secure a reliable information flow to and from sites with useful information (Burt, 1992: 63).

Firms needed to acquire good outside information about effective responses and to identify, develop, and spread best practice within, requiring the creation of new networks and the reformation of old ones. I focus particularly on the evolving networks involving suppliers to OEMs,[1] both networks searching out new information on how to organize OEM-supplier relationships and also networks for diffusing the new information throughout the OEM-supplier production chain.

Supplier Networks

I begin discussion with a description of two kinds of networks: the first set is based on dominant centrality ties but loosely coupled and not very cohesive.[2]

Centralized ties means that most ties from one unit to another in the network can occur only through the central actor, the OEM, the key element ("structural hole") in the network that connects most units (Burt, 1992). There is very little choice in this network as to which unit will do the coordination; it must be the OEM. Overall, then, the network itself is characterized by weak ties because few constituent units have direct ties to one another. The ties between the OEM and a particular supplier firm can be strong (the OEM exercises strong power) or weak because of their relatively short duration and the absence of repeated face-to-face, work-related interactions. Low trust is a predictable feature of this kind of network, which characterized OEM-supplier relationships in the U.S. manufacturing sector in the early 1980s as they faced the Japanese challenge. In keeping with the OEMs' primary coordination role, by the mid-1980s they had started strongly pressuring their suppliers to adopt specific quality practices they believed would lead to improvement. This first model is shown in Figure 5.1. Note that this is a "relatively fat OEM" accounting for a high proportion of the value added in the industry (about 50%). One also sees some 44 supplier firms with direct ties to the OEM in the form of contracts specifying the provision of parts, components, and systems. I use GM as the representative firm. Thus, the 44 supplier firms symbolize the some 3,500 direct suppliers to GM reported for 1985; this total excludes material suppliers (Best, 1990: 163; cf. Womack, Jones, and Roos, 1991: 138–168). The overriding impression one gets from looking at Figure 5.1 is the seeming unmanageability of the myriad OEM-supplier relationships.

The second network model, shown in Figure 5.2, shows the broad characteristics of the OEM-supplier relation in the Japanese manufacturing sector in the early 1980s. It is based on an interconnected tight network of small companies organized around larger ones. Figure 5.2 shows a densely coupled cohesive network. I use Toyota as the representative firm. The four lines of suppliers emanating from the OEM box represent the roughly 300 parts, components, and systems suppliers that Toyota directly dealt with at that time. Toyota, in other words, was dealing with roughly 11 times fewer component suppliers than GM. At the industry level, the Japanese automotive pyramidal structure was estimated to contain about 500 first-tier suppliers, 2,000–3,000 second-tier suppliers, and 20,000 tertiary automotive parts suppliers (see Kenney and Florida, 1991: 392). The image conveyed by Figure 5.2 in contrast to Figure 5.1 is one of a highly organized system.

There is a tight hierarchical linkage of first-, second-, and third-tier suppliers. Nishiguchi (1994: 119–123) describes the evolution of this tightly tiered system or what he calls a clustered control structure for the Japanese automotive and electronics industry. The OEM focuses on buying complete assemblies or systems components from a limited number of first-tier suppliers, and the first tier buys specialized parts from a cluster of second-tier subcontractors, who in turn buy discrete parts or labor from third-tier subcontractors.

Where is the action in this second network? The OEM continues to exercise

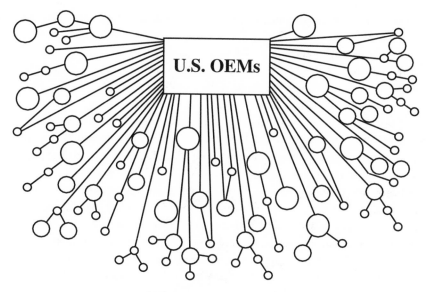

Figure 5.1. Stylized representation of U.S. OEM-supplier relations, 1980.

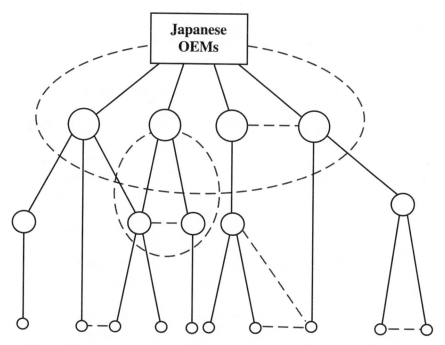

Figure 5.2. Stylized representation of Japanese OEM-supplier relations, 1980.

strong centrality ties, displaying its hierarchical leadership, but it is clearly a slimmed down OEM compared to that in Figure 5.1. Nishiguchi estimates that Japanese OEMs account for only 30% of the value added in the auto industry compared to 50% for the U.S. OEMs (much higher for GM, much lower for Chrysler). To capture this, the size of the Japanese OEM box in Figure 5.2 is three fifths as large as the U.S. OEM box shown in Figure 5.1.

Clearly, the first-tier suppliers absorbed a major coordination role and strong ties developed across selected supplier firms, which were encouraged to share their knowledge with one another and with the OEM. In practice, this arrangement means that the OEM has the time and resources to work with a small number of key large suppliers in upgrading their quality and productivity and then to use them as transmission belts to move information about best practices further down the production chain. It also means that a great deal of quality improvement of the second-tier suppliers is organized by the first-tier suppliers without direct involvement of the OEM. Furthermore, there is considerable horizontal and vertical cooperative activity across suppliers to solve quality and productivity problems. In short, we have a rather decentralized model of continuous improvement but with the OEM maintaining control of the strategic direction.

If I had drawn arrows showing direction, Figure 5.1 would be characterized by downward arrows while Figure 5.2 would display two-headed arrows pointing both up and down. The networks shown in Figure 5.2 thus operate more as a mechanism for mobilizing knowledge and intellectual activities on a collective social basis (Kenney and Florida, 1993: 306). Kenney and Florida further argue that these networks provide a powerful dynamic of innovation, with each firm in the network experiencing economic and social pressures for improvement; the network is continually stressed to produce this outcome.

The supplier associations shown in dotted lines in Figure 5.2 push information about improvement strategies and tactics down into the network in cascading fashion, giving the associations a top-down character. They also operate, however, to encourage cooperative actions among different suppliers. Not only does the OEM organize supplier associations for its first-tier suppliers but the larger first-tier suppliers like Nippon Densō tend to organize them for their second-tier suppliers. Indeed, Nishiguchi (1994: 171–190) documents the process by which Japanese OEMs taught their first-tier suppliers how to monitor second-tier suppliers and how to structure the diffusion of quality control learning. The dotted horizontal and occasionally vertical lines connecting suppliers capture the informal cooperative problem-solving activities among them.

In the early 1980s, these differing characteristics and their significance were by no means clear to U.S. OEM managers. Enough was visible, however, for some firms to take a leadership role in initiating reforms to their supplier chain that would slowly move them toward the Japanese model. Unlike other elements in the new quality model, the alternative arrangements for supplier organization and their relative benefits had a concreteness that many OEM managers could appreciate. I detail the various types of evolving networks that came to constitute the effective institutional infrastructure for diffusing the new quality model and also how firms used these networks.

Elizabeth Haas (1987: 1–2) describes the networking infrastructure between Japanese semiconductor OEMs and their material and equipment suppliers based on study team visits to Italy, Denmark, and Japan. The team reported that the Japanese semiconductor OEMs work with their suppliers continuously to develop and upgrade equipment to suit their requirements. Such efforts help capture the ideas of these suppliers and mold supplier contributions in ways that enhance OEM production outcomes. In particular, this cooperation strongly contributes to superior processing yields. And the resultant higher quality translates directly into reduced costs (see, also, Stowsky, 1987).

The higher proportion of product value accounted for by the supplier chain is notable in the Japanese model. In both the Japanese auto and semiconductor industries, suppliers account for approximately 70% of the final product value (Kenney and Florida, 1993: 241). Even so, Figure 5.2 shows that this greater reliance on suppliers was achieved with a smaller number of suppliers and a smaller number of purchasing staff. Womack, Jones, and Roos (1991: 156) report that Toyota had some 337 employees in its purchasing department, compared to 6,000 in General Motors, in 1987.

These differences had two important implications for quality. First, in keeping with theories of variation, fewer suppliers (with reduced equipment variation, tooling variation, and shipping locations) meant less product variation and therefore fewer quality problems. It also simplified diagnostic activities for just these reasons. Dr. Deming strongly advocated the superiority of these practices, recommending, controversially, that firms needed to limit their number of suppliers for any given part to just one (see Scherkenbach, 1986: 133). This is something even the Japanese have been reluctant to do, except for suppliers of large complex systems involving costly investment (see Womack, Jones, and Roos, 1991: 154). Second, a small number of suppliers meant that smaller OEM purchasing staffs could spend more time working with the first-tier suppliers to upgrade their quality and productivity performance (cf. Nishiguchi, 1994: 178–181). The Japanese OEMs used process capability, rather than product characteristics per se, as a major evaluation criterion in vendor selection and retention.

Consistent with a smaller number of suppliers, the Japanese OEMs developed long-term relationships with the existing supplier base, thereby enabling the OEMs to encourage the philosophy of continuous improvement and joint problem solving among and with suppliers. The improvement activities were expected to focus on both product and process improvement. The Japanese OEMs increased the share of design responsibility assigned to their first-tier suppliers and engaged in more collaborative design and pricing activities with them (Nishiguchi, 1994: 137–138). All this contrasted sharply with the low-trust, arm's-length relationships more prevalent in their American counterparts (see Saxenian, 1994, and Stowsky, 1987, for semiconductors, and Helper, 1991, and Cusumano and Takeishi, 1991, for automotive).

Finally, the quality performance of Japanese suppliers was being accomplished with a very broad product mix and under conditions requiring rapid design changes, quickly changing product variation, and quick and frequent deliveries, all without diminishing quality or imposing prohibitive cost increases (Nishiguchi, 1994: 191–215). These are daunting accomplishments.

Networks and Imitation

In a seminal article in 1983 (repr. 1991), DiMaggio and Powell distinguish between two modes of adoption: competitive and institutional isomorphism. They proposed a stage theory whereby in the early stages of a field or in early stages of adoption, competitive forces will push forward the modeling of one organization upon another, but at later stages isomorphism is more of an institutional nature. That is, it is more a function of a search for legitimacy and a response to uncertainty (mimetic isomorphism), or it may be coerced by other institutional forces (coercive isomorphism).

The path of quality improvement in the U.S. confirms many of DiMaggio and Powell's principles but also presents a much more complicated picture. There is an intermingling of competitive and institutional isomorphism from an early stage and sometimes—in a reversal of the DiMaggio and Powell model—a conscious bet on the part of some players that the coercive mode of institutional isomorphism will turn into competitive isomorphism. Conversely, the process of adoption may began with ritualistic acts and never graduate to more substantive outcomes. In these cases, unless a firm had or could develop unique products or could mobilize political protection, some combination of profits, market share, or organizational survival would be at risk.

Because of the uncertainty about the quality technologies and their implementation in the early and mid-1980s, there was from the beginning a great deal of mimetic isomorphism. Firms responded not directly to Japanese competition but modeled themselves after other American firms that seemed to be developing impressive quality initiatives. Even if they could not establish the linkages between implementing quality programs and quality performance, companies made assumptions that if they adopted similar practices, they would obtain bottom-line benefits. The thinking seemed to be: "after all, the connection seemed to be there for the Japanese." The situation described here is consistent with DiMaggio and Powell's hypothesis that the more uncertain the relationships between means and ends, the greater the extent to which an organization will model itself after organizations it perceives as successful (DiMaggio and Powell, 1991: 75).

Not surprisingly, then, managerial efforts to adopt Japanese practices initially often had a strong ritual aspect. Indeed, DiMaggio and Powell (1991: 69) use the ritualistic adoption of Japanese practices by American firms in the mid-1980s as one of their examples. In these early efforts, high-level managers' evaluation of their firms' quality investment typically focused on how many employees were trained in statistical process control, how many quality circles were operating, how the quality initiative was being "rolled out" (e.g., how many employees had been exposed to the all-day meeting on quality), etc. Peter Kolesar (1995) describes Alcoa's stylized approaches characteristic of many large companies in the early and mid-1980s.

An early 1980s benchmark capturing the starting point for subsequent developments is apparent from a March 12, 1981, article in which the vice president of purchasing at Ford suggested that there was still more room for quality improvement at Ford (a remarkable understatement in 1981) and then proceeded to describe Ford's approach to getting this improvement (Hoeffer, 1981: 51,53). It was by and large a classic old quality model initiative focused on a detect-and-correct approach to defects.

Yet amid the initial responses to the Japanese quality challenge was the recognition by some large original equipment manufacturers like Ford Motor Co., IBM, and Motorola that their supply chain played a vital role in the quality of their final products. They also gradually became aware that their Japanese competitors seemed to have forged different OEM-supplier relationships. They acted aggressively to pressure their suppliers to adopt new practices.

In DiMaggio and Powell (1991) terms, this is a case of coercive isomorphism. The context under which these pressures were exerted is shown in Figure 5.1; it is a network composed of asymmetrical relationships with strong centrality ties between the OEM and a large number of individual suppliers. OEMs, in their strong position as customers with the power to sever contracts, exerted strong pressures on suppliers throughout the 1980s to adopt some version of what came to be called TQM.[3] It became clear to suppliers over a broad range of manufacturing industries that not to do so was to jeopardize their continued business with their customers. Initially the pressure focused on statistical process control but gradually moved upstream to the design area.

Ford Motor Co. was the visible leader in these early efforts, taking steps to convene suppliers in quality improvement workshops, introduce suppliers to specific approaches like SPC, set up supplier quality award programs, institute standards to make clear the more important role that quality would play in future purchasing decisions, move in the direction of long-term contracts with suppliers, strongly encourage and help facilitate fact-finding supplier visits to Japan, recommend resources for helping suppliers with quality improvement, pressure suppliers to work with their own suppliers to bring about quality improvement, and reduce the numer of suppliers with whom it regularly worked.

Ford created its first quality award for suppliers in 1983, the Q101 Quality System Standard Award (Q1, as it is known, which stands for quality first). It rated suppliers with a complex measurement system; a company had to score more than 70 to qualify as a Ford supplier. To be a Q1 supplier, it needed a score over 85 and to be using SPC. In early 1990, Ford raised the required Q1 rating from 85 to 90 and required all new suppliers to have a Q1 rating. Starting in the 1992 model year, all suppliers, as well as all Ford operations, had to have the Q1 rating or they would no longer be allowed to do any business with Ford (Petersen and Hillkirk, 1991: 160).

The Q1 was pathbreaking in its emphasis on a prevention-based approach to quality, use of SPC, quality planning for improvement, and employee participation in the improvement process. It contained many of the elements of the new quality model as applied to OEM-supplier relationships. Ford's adoption of Q1 was quickly followed by GM's adoption of its SPEAR program and Chrysler's Pentastar program (Womack, Jones, and Roos, 1991: 159). Researchers at AT&T reported that Ford's Q1 supplier evaluation system became the model certification program for the industry (AT&T, 1990). In fact, it helped transform procurement practices for a very large number of firms across a broad range of manufacturing industries.[4] The large impact of the Q1 system can be seen in Juran's *Quality Control Handbook* (1988), the leading reference book for quality control specialists; Ford is the only private sector firm's supplier program discussed, appearing under the heading "Models for Supplier Quality Programs" (Gryna, 1989: 15–9). Indeed, Ford's strong influence in shaping the development of American quality practices in the 1980s can be seen in the 11 index entries for it in Juran's *Handbook of Quality Control*, the most references any company receives (IBM is listed 8 times).

Ford had a direct impact in the semiconductor industry since two of their important suppliers for the growing market in automotive electronics were Motorola and Intel. Intel managers report how Ford in the early 1980s sent its quality people into the company to train engineering, manufacturing, quality control, and purchasing personnel in the techniques that Ford required from top suppliers. Intel found itself pressured to rapidly improve quality to remain Ford's "vendor of preference" (Semich and Dowst, 1989: 74). These experiences were repeated many times throughout Ford's supplier chain. Nor was Ford the only driver of these changes. Intel, for example reports being pressed to improve quality in the early 1980s not only by Ford but also by IBM, Kodak, AT&T, and Hewlett-Packard.

Despite these aggressive efforts, Ford found it hard to change its practices, and many of its suppliers were more inclined to follow its mandates in ritualistic fashion. Moreover, overcoming Ford's organizational inertia was not a trivial problem, as can be seen from an account by Ford's vice president for purchasing and supply, L. M. Chicoine, the same vice president cited before for advocating a detect-and-correct approach in 1981. He describes how Ford's CEO issued a mandate to improve relations with and performance of the supply base in 1983. Based on this, Chicoine publicly called for increasing the number of long-term contracts (greater than one year) with Ford. To his surprise six months later, he found there was no change. Because Ford rules called for extensive bureaucratic approval for any contract greater than one year, no supplier was interested in tackling that (Scherkenbach, 1986: 131).

These kinds of roadblocks were common in both OEM and supplier firms even when they sought to make changes, and many firms of course moved far less aggressively than Ford. At GM, it was reported that Roger Smith, the chairman, was reading a summary of Deming's book, *Out of the Crisis*, for the first time in the summer of 1988. It was prepared for him after he continued to argue that the best price was attained by having several suppliers bid against one another, rather than encouraging a long-term relationship with a single supplier (Keller, 1989: 36–37). Keller reports that, to Smith's credit, he finally got the message. Yet his failure to get the message in the previous eight years is more telling.

The new quality model required drastic changes in how suppliers and OEMs managed their businesses and, in particular, their relationships. Typically, the initial supplier response to OEM pressure for quality improvement was often a grumbling acquiescence as suppliers went through the motions of putting in place the systems demanded by their customers. Even if they did not quite understand and believe in the logic of the new mandate, however, some suppliers read the instructions as signaling a long-term effort. They therefore acted aggressively to gain competitive advantage by not only adopting the forms but aiming to deliver the results as well.

On the OEM side as well, most managers saw the problem as changing how suppliers managed quality rather than realizing their great need to change themselves to produce the kind of behavior they claimed they wanted. An Intel official recounted a discussion in the early 1980s with Kyocera, their major supplier and also a supplier to their Japanese competitors. Intel managers believed that their Japanese competitors were getting better service, delivery, and quality from Kyocera than they were. The Japanese managers responded with a riddle to Intel queries: "To Kyocera the customer is always king. But reliable kings have reliable servants." The Intal managers finally figured out that the point of the riddle was that although the customer (Intel) might be king, it nonetheless had to act in certain ways to produce reliable supplier behavior. Above all, that meant no order cancellations, level production, and an overall predictable environment for suppliers (Semich and Dowst, 1989: 74). MacDuffie and Helper (1996) make a similar point in discussing Honda's approach. Stable orders help suppliers achieve an even and stable production flow, which ensures quality improvement and cost control. These were nontrivial changes in how Intel and Ford or any of the typical large U.S. firms operated. Like the suppliers, some OEMs responded to the required change faster than others.

Across manufacturing, various quality certification programs like Ford's Q1 program were set up with the clear understanding that if the supplier company did not receive that certification in the specified time, they would no longer supply the OEM (Bhote, 1989: 6). OEMs began emphasizing quality audits of supplier business processes, assuming that if one got the process right, the proper outcome would follow. The OEM customers were looking typically not only at the adoption of the organizational forms but at results as well. Thus, their certification programs typically looked not only at process measures (such as how many workers were trained in SPC, control charts, the process capability of equipment, etc.) but quality performance as well. Motorola was fairly typical in developing guidelines for detailed quality system reviews for its suppliers (Motorola Corp., 1992). Keki Bhote (1989) provides a good overview of the emergent OEM process and outcome expectations vis-á-vis their suppliers over a broad range of manufacturing firms during the 1980s. The Defense Logistics Agency, which is responsible for 75% of all Department of Defense requisitions, adopted similar activities and standards (Collins, 1988: 19–21).

Despite the stumbling, lack of understanding, and outright resistance on the part of some managers and organizations, gradually progress toward adopting a version of the quality model began to be made in the automotive, semiconductor, and other manufacturing settings. OEM decision-making began to reinforce the rhetoric that dominated the first half of the 1980s. The late 1980s showed rapid implementation as efforts coalesced and reinforced one another. Susan Helper (1991: 15–28) in a 1989 survey of all first-tier auto manufacturing suppliers (response rate 47%) documents these supplier's significant progress on some of the dimensions discussed before. She found that the percentage of suppliers showing their SPC charts to their customers rose from 16% in 1984 to 92% in 1989 (93% of suppliers said they had SPC in all of their plants in 1989, compared to 19% making this claim in 1984). The number of suppliers reporting that they exchanged visits at least every two weeks with customers on matters relating to the product rose from 22% in 1984 to 36% in 1989. Average contract length doubled from 1.2 years in 1984 to 2.3 years in 1989. As a baseline, GM reported in 1984 that 30% of its contracts with outside suppliers were multiyear; Ford reported 70% in 1985 (Helper, 1991: 821). The percentage of suppliers providing customers with a breakdown of the steps of their production process rose from 38% in 1984 to 50% in 1989 and to 80% in 1993. The 1993 U.S. figures roughly paralleled Japanese figures for that same year (Helper and Sako, 1995: 77–84). This kind of information sharing precedes effective OEM guidance for supplier quality and productivity improvement. In customer criteria for supplier selection, quality moved from third position in 1984 (behind delivery and price) to first position in 1989. When asked what would happen if they inadvertently shipped products containing minor defects, in 1989 only 4.4% of suppliers (versus 31.3% five years before) thought their customers would use them.

Comparable developments were occurring in the semiconductor industry. Intel's systems division reduced its supplier base from 1,000 in the mid-1980s to 400 by 1989. By comparison, Ford cut its number of suppliers from 5,000 in 1982 to 2,300 in 1987 (Helper, 1991: 816). As in auto, Intel also moved toward the clustered control system, upgrading 35 firms to key supplier status (Semich and Dowst, 1989: 78). Many of these were equipment suppliers, who in turn bought from component suppliers. Intel also set up its version of Ford's Q1 program in what came to be called in the late 1980s its Supplier Continuous Quality Improvement Program (SCQI). As at Ford, Intel established a Preferred Quality Supplier Award program to recognize outstanding suppliers for performance and services delivered to Intel as well as for "the continuous improvement of their quality management systems."

Despite these kinds of movements, progress toward making semiconductor suppliers fuller partners with the OEMs seemed to occur more slowly on average in the semiconductor industry than in the automotive sector. One close observer of the industry notes that the semiconductor companies did not really address seriously the problem of supplier quality until the late 1980s.[5] Until then, most of the causes producing the Japanese manufacturing advantage were understood to lie in the fabrication area, with the Japanese seen as having a lead in process and manufacturing technology. This is captured in the original focus of SEMATECH, the industry consortium (originally 14 members) with government support set up in 1987 to counter the competitive disadvantages flowing from the fragmented nature of the U.S. industry. Leaders at SEMATECH at first concentrated on those areas where the United States seemed to be losing technical dominance, such as the emergent dominant role of Nikon in lithography. Once they got started and completed systematic comparisons of Japanese and U.S. equipment, however, it became obvious that there was a strong quality dimension. Japanese suppliers had superior, more reliable equipment, as reflected in higher "uptimes," and easier maintenance. Yield differences could be traced to the national origin of semiconductor equipment. Thus, SEMATECH shifted explicitly to improving the quality of equipment supplied by U.S. suppliers and the quality of their relationships with the OEMs.

In 1990, SEMATECH established its Partnering for Total Quality Program aimed at encouraging its OEM members to work with equipment suppliers (often relatively small companies) to upgrade their quality performance. It created a variety of well-attended quality training activities, and its approach was formally recognized by the National Institute of Standards and Technology to be consistent with the Malcolm Baldrige National Quality Award. It created a self-help assessment mode, organizationwide improvement plans that involved customer input and support, and industry-standard tool qualification methodology and programs in the effective use of statistical methods. It created a Standardized Supplier Quality Assessment (SSQA), which synthesized the Baldrige and ISO 9000 as well as specific software quality requirements. In effect, it tailored the dominant ideas about quality improvement to the perceived conditions of the industry. By 1994, it were spending some 3 million dollars a year for quality initiatives.

In response to a GAO assessment of SEMATECH accomplishments, the 12 SEMATECH member companies in 1992 (accounting for the bulk of semiconductor manufacturing in the United States) listed among its five major initiatives: encouraging member companies to establish long-term relationships with their key suppliers through its Partnering for Total Quality Program, improving the yield of semiconductor chips from each wafer, and working with suppliers to improve existing and developing next-generation chips (United States GAO, 1992: 13). Also, SEMATECH set up three regional Total Quality Executive Forums to facilitate member-to-member communication. When SEMATECH's federal funding ended in the mid-1990s, these organs were taken over by the local organizers.

Thus, one of these, the West Coast Quality Forum, (WCQF) is a consortium of some 80 semiconductor-related companies that work together to pursue quality improvement, using SEMTECH-generated training materials increasingly supplemented by curricula based on semiconductor industry circumstances. It focuses primarily on improving quality throughout the supplier chain and in particular works with suppliers in equipment companies like Applied Materials and Electroglas. Major OEMs, especially Intel, play a major role in providing content and themes for meetings and training. It is a way for them to reach the suppliers to their suppliers. At a typical meeting in June 1997, the 65 attendees heard an Intel director describe his views on "synchronizing the PC supply chain," followed by a three-hour workshop on problem solving. Reducing cycle time is another popular theme of the late 1990s. Regular forum meetings are supplemented by monthly user-group sessions at which company representatives hash out how to apply the principles put forward at forum meetings.

Just as Ford had strong incentives for taking the lead in recognizing and responding to the Japanese quality challenge in the automotive industry, there seemed to be special reasons for Motorola performing this same role in the semiconductor industry. As noted earlier, by virtue of their semiconductor division supplying Ford, Motorola had early pressure from Ford to improve quality. The movement to improve quality at Motorola, however, was not led from the semiconductor division. Motorola was facing Japanese competition across a broad range of its telecommunication product lines. It already had been warned by bad experiences in consumer product lines. It had chosen to exit from various consumer product lines such as television rather than compete head-on with the Japanese. In the early 1980s, it reaped a great deal of negative publicity when the sale of the Franklin Park, Illinois, Quasar television facility in 1974 led to its rejuvenation under its new owner, Matsushita. These developments came to the attention of the American public in 1980. Most publicized was the dramatic improvement in quality under the new Japanese owners, despite the same labor force and some of the same management team (Main, 1980: 32). Motorola was determined not to repeat its past mistakes by competing against the Japanese in its most promising product lines such as wireless. Thus, Motorola appears to have been paying closer attention to what was happening in auto and studying the Japanese more closely than its industry peers.

The American Supplier Institute

One reason for the faster response of the auto industry was the earlier development of a network infrastructure to improve supplier quality. A particularly influential role was played by the American Supplier Institute (ASI).[6] American Supplier Institute was created in 1981 as the Ford Supplier Institute, some six years before the establishment of SEMATECH. Dr. Deming provided the original material for supplier training and also served as the first instructor for the institute. The initial activities consisted of supplier training in SPC and manufacturing process capability. From about 1982 through 1985, ASI was running 48 five-day sessions on SPC a year with an average of 50 participants in a class. The enrollment at this time derived almost entirely from Ford Motor Co. and Ford suppliers.

In 1982, ASI began its first annual supplier study missions to Japan, disseminating findings to attendees as well as participants in ASI workshops and seminars. ASI ran these study missions until 1989, with some 250–300 individuals attending over the lifetime of the missions. These efforts, as well as much of its subsequent focus on the product design stage, were aimed to a large extent at analyzing the Toyota group companies' approach to quality technology. Nippon Densō, Toyota Gosei, and Toyota Machine Works were among the regular companies visited. Efforts at ASI represented a pooled approach to learning from Japan that proved remarkably effective, even if it took a little longer to get established than if each company acted on its own. It represented one of the few initiatives in the early 1980s to learn quality improvement sytematically from the Japanese.

Many of the ideas ASI pioneered in the United States, such as Quality Function Deployment (QFD) and Taguchi methods, grew out of the information collected on these trips. One of the developers of QFD was Akashi Fukuhara of the Central Japan Quality Control Association (CQCA), one of the major Japanese partners of ASI. By systematically and continuously gathering data from the various Japanese companies, ASI was able to identify the core characteristics of Japanese quality practices and thereby reduce the noise that companies were experiencing in trying to separate good information from bad. These activities had an impact well beyond Ford Motor Co. and its clients. Based on what he had learned, Larry Sullivan, the president of ASI at the time, wrote a series of influential articles in the 1980s in the major journal of the American Society for Quality Control (ASQC—since 1997, the American Society for Quality [ASQ]) that helped reshape managerial understanding of the new quality model (Sullivan, 1984, 1986a, 1986b, 1987).

In 1984, ASI separated from Ford and was chartered as a nonprofit educational institute. A board of directors was created, which included representatives of the major automotive supplier companies as well as the three OEMs. Even so, the institute continued to be heavily Ford-oriented, with some 70% of the auto industry customers from Ford or its suppliers in the late 1980s. This is somewhat misleading, however, since the majority of Ford suppliers also serviced GM or Chrysler, so these firms benefitted from ASI activities as well.[7] Thus, the multiple production networks in which these suppliers were involved served to diffuse the new approaches and their benefits to the industry at large.

It was not all smooth sailing in the early days. In the first half of the 1980s, most suppliers attended ASI's SPC courses with the full expectation that once they finished their five-day course, they would have the magic pill for eliminating their quality problems. Indeed, some of the ASI staff and those at Ford had similar views. The parallel to the earlier experience with quality circles is striking. Only gradually did both parties come to recognize the broader nature of the challenge, that success required continuous management attention to ensure an integrated application of all the tools at all levels.

Suppliers (not to mention many Ford managers) were especially confused with the alphabet soup that emerged in the menu of ASI courses (SPC, QFD, FMEA, DFA, DFM, ISO 9000, etc.) and how they cohered. In the early and mid-1980s they chafed under the recognition that while Ford was pushing them to get Q1 status and upgrade their capabilities in all these courses, they were often dealing with Ford plants that did not have Q1 status. Moreover, the increasing number of different quality standards, requirements, and audits imposed by the Big Three created a bureaucratic nightmare for those with multiple customers and added cost. Supplier managers and engineers were, in short, not always happy campers when it came to attending and learning from their ASI seminars and workshops.

The institute, itself, was modeled after JUSE and the CQCA, which had its origins in Toyota's effort to train its suppliers in the developing quality methodology and was staffed largely by ex-Toyota officials. In short, ASI made a very conscious effort to replicate not only the content but also the effective diffusion activities produced by these Japanese networking organizations. While ASI's primary audience was the automotive industry toward the latter half of the 1980s, it did encourage firms from other sectors to use its services and in the 1990s a strong aerospace emphasis was added.

Whereas its early activities emphasized SPC, by the mid-1980s ASI was shifting its initiatives upstream to specialize in teaching design of experiments, Taguchi methods, and QFD. QFD provides a formal planning process to understand and stay true to user needs by weaving the identification of these needs through the entire product development process, including downstream manufacturing processes. For all practical purposes, ASI was the initial introducer of QFD and Taguchi methods to American manufacturing audiences; their promotional literature touts their success as the organization that more *Fortune* 500 companies came to for their QFD needs than any other source. Both QFD and Taguchi methods have had a significant impact on American manufacturing practice. The ASI literature talks about its role in "Americanizing" these methods as well. In the case of QFD, it stressed a four-matrix procedure as a more simplified method than the 30 matrices used by Yoji Akai, a key contributor to QFD in Japan. It also presented the materials in readily understandable English, used more graphics, and illuminated the analytic concepts increasingly with American case study material.

By the late 1980s, Keki Bhote (1989: 84) estimated that ASI trained more than 25,000 engineers and executives from more than 150 major companies in extensive seminars and workshops. By 1996, ASI estimated it had trained from 75,000–100,000 employees in over 500 companies. Initially most of the training occurred in large seminars. In 1997 ASI was still conducting some 50 public workshops a year in the various methodologies. Increasingly, however, it has turned toward in-house, case study, problem-solving assistance for evaluating alternative design prac-tices as the chosen intervention method. In the early 1990s, it were doing some 40 case studies a year for Ford (in conjunction with Ford Design Institute) and 10 for automotive suppliers. By 1997, the total had grown to about 80 a year with, however, the automotive sector accounting for only 20% of the total; the rest were being done in diverse industries. For example, it was working with LSI Logic Corporation in the semiconductor industry on robust design and Taguchi methods. These design activities involve staff in intensive "hands-on" problem-solving in-teractions with company personnel. Company officials benefitted not only from solving their particular problems but also in leveraging their new skills to work on other problems. An annual ASI symposium is held to highlight the most successful and illustrative cases and enable companies to share successes and learn from each other's experiences in implementing the various quality methods. Strategic intent at ASI has been to capture the latest world technologies available in quality im-provement and cost-reduction methods while developing applications and imple-mentation strategies. For companies using their offerings, they were often a fast-track method to the implementation and use of these technologies.

At first glance, corporate participants in ASI activities can be seen as loosely tied to ASI. The institute was after all a nonprofit educational organization. More-over, auto firms had other choices. In reality, however, for many firms participating in its activities, ASI was an organization with which they had tight ties and dense networks based on multiple and regular use of its services. This was particularly true of Ford Motor Co. and its suppliers; failure of a supplier to use ASI services would likely be interpreted by Ford as an indication that the supplier was not serious about quality improvement and therefore not serious about remaining a Ford supplier. Indeed, especially in the early 1980s and throughout much of the 1980s and to some extent still today, attendees in seminars from supplier firms say, "I came to ASI because my customer told me too," not because they were motivated by an opportunity to turn ASI knowledge into a competitive advantage. In 1988, for example, Ford told its vendors that to remain on its preferred vendor list, it would be advisable for them to use QFD. In short, a clear signal was sent that few could ignore (Soin, 1992: 137).

This description suggests classic coercive isomorphism of the kind described by DiMaggio and Powell (1991). Nevertheless, firms did often end up learning useful things. Furthermore, those firms and departments that contracted for case study problem-solving activities (which came to provide the bulk of ASI revenues) developed extremely tight ties with ASI staff consultants. Once the contract was let, they needed each other's strong cooperation to succeed on a demanding task, the success of which would be the basis for both their evaluations.

ASI was able to gain entree to conduct its supplier mission in Japan in part because its leader, Larry Sullivan, heard about Taguchi methods during an early visit and was directed to Genichi Taguchi, who in turn suggested he contact the

CQCA to help organize a supplier mission. It did not hurt that some of the key Toyota companies participating in CQCA activities, like Nippon Densō, were major suppliers to Ford as well.

Although the participants on these early supplier missions were overwhelmingly tied to Ford Motor Co., they nevertheless had an open search activity in trying to identify the sources of successful Japanese business performance as it related to customer-supplier relationships. Thus, one sees a situation in which participants are in tightly tied relations with Ford, which served as the central node for almost all of them. And ASI became the link connecting the Ford network with the Toyota network. The success of these efforts was not dependent on the sources of information that the members of the missions were bringing with them (in that sense it did not matter if it was a tight or loose network). Rather, success depended on the ability of Ford and ASI to identify and access locations that had promising sources of information. Generally, members of these missions had almost no previous exposure to Japan and were not in a position to help identify where the search should take place. They were selected by their companies rather for their manufacturing experience and ability to take advantage of what they might encounter.[8] This perspective runs somewhat counter to the network literature with its emphasis on loosely coupled networks as the best mode for searching out new information.

Other Sources of Information

While an early leader, ASI was not the only source of new and appropriate information about the new quality model either for Ford or the industry as a whole. Over time the sources of good information expanded. Joint venture partners played an important role in directly showing the U.S. OEMs how they did things. Mazda was important for Ford, as was Mitsubishi for Chrysler and to a far lesser extent Isuzu for General Motors. The joint venture between Toyota and GM, NUMMI began production in 1984, but as we have seen, it had only marginal impact in its early years. Perhaps its greatest impact was in showing GM that high levels of automation were not the shortcut route to high quality as many in GM believed in the mid- and late 1980s.

In addition, various associations, trade media, and newly created cooperative organs allowed personnel from the Big Three to identify best practice and coordinate actions. ASQ's automotive division held annual meetings in the Detroit area that allowed personnel from the various companies to present best practice cases. Companies could see the direction others were headed as well as pick up tips on useful approaches. The major trade paper, *Automotive News*, regularly reported on new quality initiatives adopted by the Big Three as well as major suppliers. As concern about antitrust faded, the Big Three stepped up cooperative actions, including the formation of the Automotive Industry Action Group (AIAG), designed to work on common industry problems. It worked on matters like developing uniform bar coding; in the early 1990s it began coordinating the quality assessment processes used by OEMs for their suppliers.

The problem was the high costs associated with the Big Three's confusing, overlapping, redundant, and often conflicting quality systems requirements for suppliers. Of course, these were particularly onerous for the many contractors supplying multiple OEMs. Sometimes, some second-tier suppliers were being audited not only by the OEMs but also by the OEMs' first-tier suppliers. Working with AIAG and ASQ, by early 1997 the OEMs were well on the way to implementing uniform reporting methods for vendors to use in verifying that the parts and materials they ship to the OEMs meet each company's requirements for quality. The chosen vehicle, QS 9000 was the realization of an effort to flesh out the International Organization for Standardization's quality standards (ISO 9000 series) so that they were customized to meet the needs of the auto industry. Also, AIAG worked with ASQ in 1991 to develop uniform SPC procedures for suppliers (Kisiel, 1996: 14; Wolak, 1993: 16, 22).

Not all such networking organizations were deemed a success in this period. In 1986, GM, together with the General Physics organization, set up a supplier training activity called Targets for Excellence, aimed at encouraging continuous improvement among its suppliers. It was widely regarded as a bureaucratic effort lacking in practical methods to help suppliers (Bhote, 1989: 85). It was not focused on learning from the Japanese as were Ford's efforts. As late as 1986, GM still had not accepted the importance of assessing a supplier's process capability rather than relying exclusively on the old practice of examining "product" as a measure of the supplier's ability to produce quality.

The Transplants and Their Influence

An additional network that interacted with the OEM-supplier production chain and ASI activities derived from the rapid growth of Japanese transplant operations in the United States. The auto companies were prominent. The major Japanese OEMs (Honda was the first to produce cars in the United States) and over 200 Japanese component suppliers located in the United States by 1990 (Helper, 1991: 821; Nishiguchi, 1994: 193). The bulk of this growth took place between 1985 and 1987, at which time some 140 Japanese automotive suppliers started production in the United States; prior to 1980, there were only 18 Japanese automotive suppliers operating in America (Callahan, 1989: 89).

The number for semiconductor transplants was much lower, with an estimate of 52 in 1990; this included semiconductor materials and equipment (24), printed circuit board (10), and semiconductor production (18) (Kenney and Florida, 1993: 219). Particularly in the auto industry, transplant practices exemplified many of the quality-related practices pioneered by the Japanese. Although there was much debate in the early 1980s, it is now well recognized that the automotive OEM transplants in particular were able to successfully reproduce many of the Japanese management practices that led to high-quality low-cost products (Cusumano and Takeishi, 1991: 563–588; Helper and Sako, 1995: 77–84; Kenney and Florida, 1993). Moreover, these same studies suggest that suppliers to these transplants also absorbed many of these practices. The transfer of practices designed to produce high quality were particularly high on the Japanese automotive OEM agenda, given their fear that they would lose the marketing benefits of their strong quality reputation if the American public thought that they had sacrificed quality by building cars in the United States. While the auto transplant firms represent a case of successful technology transfer, it is also important to remember that the Japanese parent firms chose not to try to reproduce a variety of their "traditional" Japanese practices, including seniority wage systems and enterprise unions.

Kenney and Florida (1993: 149) suggest that by the early 1990s traditional U.S. automotive suppliers were becoming integrated into the transplant supplier complex. They cite data that show roughly 57% of all U.S. automotive suppliers were involved in joint ventures and 85% of these companies had at least one joint venture with a foreign country. One can presume that joint ventures with Japanese companies dominated this category. Furthermore, Kenney and Florida report that 45% of U.S. auto parts companies supply at least one product to the transplants.

Japanese OEM transplants are using an increasing number of U.S. auto parts suppliers in contrast to their original impulse (1985–1990) to simply encourage their traditional Japanese suppliers to set up in the United States. This shift probably reflects both the upgrading of performance on the part of American suppliers and the increasing political pressures to buy from American companies. Results of this shift can be seen in the supplier base of Toyota's Georgetown, Kentucky, plant, one of the last Japanese assembly plants built in the United States, opening in 1989. Seventy-five percent of the 174 domestic suppliers are long-standing U.S. auto parts companies. Similar developments are taking place at other Japanese OEM transplants (for the Mazda case, see Kenney and Florida, 1991: 392).

The Japanese OEM and supplier transplants' approaches to quality, integrated into the U.S. production network, have been a significant factor in spreading these new practices among U.S. companies. In some cases the process has been subtle, as when Japanese suppliers have raised the level of expectations that U.S. OEM customers had for their American suppliers. In effect, the U.S. OEM managers were saying, "If Nippon Densō can supply us with this high quality at this low cost from its U.S. facility, why can't you?" In other words, the Japanese suppliers created new standards of performance in the United States, using U.S. workers, that raised the bar for everyone.

The Japanese transplants give a great deal of direct guidance and training to their own U.S. suppliers, in how to go about improving quality and productivity. Extensive screening takes place in the initial supplier selection to ensure that the firms selected to be suppliers have the capability for producing high-quality products at low cost in volume. In addition to selection, however, there are extensive efforts made to upgrade performance on all competitive dimensions.

Toyota has probably gone the farthest in trying to recreate its Japanese auto parts supplier groups in the United States. It set up a semi-independent organization, the Toyota Supplier Support Center, in the early 1990s to work with U.S.–owned suppliers to upgrade their performance. It also set up regional supplier associations organized around assembly plants to accelerate the diffusion of its practices to improve quality and productivity. Thus, it established the Bluegrass Automotive Manufacturers Association (BAMA) in 1990 for its suppliers to the Georgetown, Kentucky, assembly plant (Kenney and Florida, 1993: 151).

Kenney and Florida (1993: 150) also describe Honda's extensive program in the early 1990s. Honda has gone the farthest of any of the Japanese manufacturers in providing hands-on assistance to suppliers for improving production lines. The vice president of purchasing has two full-time employees whose job is to help suppliers develop employee-involvement programs. Moreover, some 40 engineers in the purchasing department work full-time helping suppliers improve quality and productivity. Another 120 engineers in the quality-control department are responsible for incoming supplier parts. Special teams are set up to help suppliers improve.

Honda set up a minireengineering program (BP Program) in the latter half of the 1980s aimed at strengthening its suppliers. Donnelly Mirrors was one of its first "graduates." A team of Honda employees from different departments was sent to evaluate the production flow and work organization in Donnelly's new Grandhaven plant, built to accommodate new Honda business for exterior mirrors. They examined production control capabilities and opportunities for greater efficiencies and showed how production workers could become more involved. They also worked with Donnelly personally to implement their recommendations (Magnet, 1995: 491–492). It is not unusual for the Honda team of engineers to spend weeks or sometimes even months in their suppliers' plants helping to reorganize them. The objective is to shake the supplier management out of its normal ways of thinking and encourage deep analysis of how to better organize the workshop through root-cause analysis of specific problems (MacDuffie and Helper, 1996). These experiences have been repeated many times over at other U.S. suppliers and to a lesser extent by other Japanese OEMs. In the aggregate these efforts appear to have led to an upgrading of the quality performance of U.S. suppliers to the Japanese transplants (see MacDuffie and Helper, 1996, for case studies of six Honda suppliers).

Many of the Japanese transplant suppliers service U.S. OEMs. Joseph Callahan (1989: 89), an auto industry commentator, reports that of the 232 Japanese supplier plants in the United States in 1989, 85 of them (36%) had contracts with at least one of the Big Three in 1989, and most of the rest were actively seeking such contracts. Because the production volume of their Japanese customers was still relatively small, they actively sought out new business with U.S. OEMs to achieve economies of scale.

One would expect that, since many of these contractors also supply U.S. OEMs, their improvements would spill over to the benefit of U.S. firms as well.

Indeed, Kenney and Florida (1991: 393–394) concluded in 1991 that transplant suppliers were establishing interorganizational links to U.S. producers, leading to the rapid diffusion of Japanese practices among U.S. producers. Of course, there were cases reported in the mid-1980s in which U.S. suppliers set up special production units with higher quality standards for their Japanese customers, achieved mainly through more intensive inspection prior to shipping components (Krafcik, cited in Cusumano and Takeishi, 1991: 582). If these approaches had persisted and become a norm, the higher quality standards of the transplants would not diffuse to other companies. These accounts, however, suggest isolated efforts to "game the system" that were bound to fail as the Japanese OEMs refused to accept the higher costs associated with additional inspection and higher scrap and as their closer and closer scrutiny of supplier production practices exposed weaknesses. Still, there were other more subtle cases in which researchers have documented the failure of Japanese-inspired improvement efforts to spill over to other plants in the very same firm servicing U.S. OEMs (MacDuffie and Helper, 1996). Pride in one's own technology can be a powerful barrier to learning.

Yet there is every reason to think that U.S. suppliers did learn quality improvement practices from their Japanese customers and that much of this spillover improved quality performance for their U.S. customers as well. After all, these U.S. customers were strongly pushing these same suppliers for quality improvement throughout the 1980s and 1990s and increasingly using quality performance as a major factor in awarding contracts. American suppliers to the transplants, looking for more business from the Big Three, had every reason to share the benefits of their improvement with them.

One can put the matter in broader context by comparing the quality improvement performance of the European auto industry with that of the United States. Despite a similar large quality gap with the Japanese throughout the 1980s, the Europeans were much slower to improve, with the bulk of their quality improvement effort taking place in the mid-1990s (see Womack, Jones, and Roos, 1991). This slower response seems linked in part to the relative absence of Japanese transplant operations in Europe and the more modest nature of joint venture operations during the 1980s. Protected markets are another obvious important factor. The Japanese automobile company strategy for internationalization, through the setting up of transplant operations, first targeted the United States in the mid-1980s and only later moved to Europe (initially primarily to England). This delay made it difficult for the Europeans to see firsthand how the Japanese operated their plants to improve quality using European workers and therefore inhibited imitation. There is historical precedence for this kind of thinking. Thus, Guillén (1994: 140) documents how the presence of American multinationals in Germany increased during the 1960s, thereby making it easier for German firms to imitate American organizational patterns.

The case of the Japanese semiconductor transplants in the United States appears to be quite different from the automotive transplants. The evidence to date

(Abo, 1994: 165–177; Kenney and Florida, 1993: 241–259) suggests that the semi-conductor plants stand between the auto firms that have been most inclined to transfer Japanese production and work practices and the consumer electronics firms that have transferred the least. Even so, while the auto transplants sought to replicate their dense supplier networks and have partially succeeded, the semiconductor firms did not develop anything like the dense supplier networks that existed in semiconductor production in Japan.

The semiconductor OEM transplants seemed even more inclined than the transplant auto producers to use American suppliers for the least-valued activities (machined products and general supplies) while procuring 70%–90% of their parts and materials from Japan (Abo, 1994: 170–171). Because of the modest American demand for their products, they have often opted to supply them from Japan and ship to the United States. For similar reasons, many Japanese suppliers have been reluctant to set up operations in the United States. Yield improvement in semiconductor operations is critical and depends in part on close working relationships with suppliers. The OEM transplants have solved this problem in part by opting to work with their traditional Japanese suppliers located in Japan. At the same time they have minimized the problem itself by transferring to the United States low-end highly standardized and routinized production processes (Kenney and Florida, 1993: 258). Such processes do not require the extensive continuous improvement activities for yield and reliability enhancement characteristic of Japanese approaches to quality improvement. Abo (1994: 167) also reports that the semiconductor OEM transplants have mostly set up production lines for downstream processes, in particular for standard memory chip products.

The emphasis in the semiconductor transplants is on "equipment-led" approaches to quality and productivity improvement. The Abo-led research team found that the approach to quality control in the semiconductor transplant firms they studied emphasizes adaptation to local American practices far more than was the case with the auto transplant firms, specifically with approaches to quality control (which was measured primarily in terms of how involved production workers, rather than quality specialists, were in taking responsibility for quality). Similarly, they found that on their measure of procurement method involving assessment of percentage of local content, source of materials, and type of relations with local suppliers, the semiconductor transplant firms scored lower than the auto firms in terms of application of Japanese methods (Abo: 1994: 33, 129, 169).

The upshot is that U.S. suppliers to the transplant operations are not as numerous and important a factor in semiconductors as in auto. As a consequence, they have not provided access to the Japanese approach to quality and have not been an avenue for its further diffusion to U.S. customers. Similarly, the Japanese transplants operations, partially because of their smaller numbers, do not seem to have invested as heavily in bringing over Japanese quality improvement methods (relying more on equipment-led improvements and quality specialists), and they have not been as big a factor in reforming the quality expectations and practices of American customers. To be sure, Japanese semiconductor OEM transplants have been increasing their local U.S. content, turning more to American suppliers, and they have also offered technical assistance and guidance to their local American vendors to bring them up to Japanese quality and productivity standards.

The scale of such activities, however, seems modest relative to the auto experience (see Abo, 1994: 225–226). In summary, the transplants in semiconductor production do not seem to have played as large a role as in auto in influencing quality practices among American firms. Together with the slower development of the kind of network structure, represented by the ASI, that was used to rethink supplier relations in the auto industry, the more modest role of transplants helps to account for the slowness of the semiconductor industry to move more quickly in addressing the need for closer supplier cooperation in raising quality.

There was one additional mode for transmitting the new quality improvement practices to U.S. companies from the experiences of the transplant operations. It draws on a classic method of information transmission, so well developed in the U.S. economy, job mobility. The movement of U.S. managers, who had experienced and learned the new Japanese approaches working for the transplants, to jobs in American firms proved an important network for moving the new information. They served as nodes linking the transplants' experiences with the quality improvement efforts of American firms. Sometimes, this was a conscious strategy, as when GM rotated managers into its joint venture with Toyota, NUMMI, and then slotted them back into its U.S. operations. Other times, these moves simply reflected the entrepreneurial energies of individual managers seeking to improve their situation and apply their knowledge. As noted in the earlier discussion of the relatively poor utilization of the GM managers from NUMMI, the one was not necessarily more effective than the other.

In a related mode, consultants were increasingly influential in the spread of the new quality model. Initially, as I noted in Chapter 4, most of the consultant firms that rapidly sprung up in the wake of the new quality challenge from the Japanese were not all that helpful with their conflicting messages and lack of direct access to Japanese practices. Indeed, in aggregate they probably added to the confusion of the early 1980s. However, over time, the transplants in particular, as well as early U.S. TQM implementers such as Ford, Motorola, HP, Milliken, and Xerox began to build up a wealth of experiences on American soil that could be used as templates for further corporate applications. Increasingly, consultants (as well as other companies) mined these successes. Many principals of the burgeoning consultant industry were former employees of companies that built a reputation for successful quality improvement.

One of the influential consultants was Richard Schonberger, who was a professor of management at the University of Nebraska. He had the good fortune to be able to study on a continuous basis one of the early transplants, Kawasaki U.S.A., a producer of motorcycles, snowblowers, and jet skis in Lincoln, Nebraska. Combining these observations with visits and interviews at other early transplants, Schonberger (1982) published *Japanese Manufacturing Techniques*. It had sales of some 150,000 copies and Schonberger went on to an active consulting career in implementing Japanese manufacturing methods. His major customers in the early 1980s included IBM, HP, General Electric, and Westinghouse.[9]

As more and more corporate experiences accumulated on U.S. soil in the mid- and late 1980s, consultants were able to add more value to implementation efforts. Lawler, Mohrman, and Ledford (1995: 48) found that by 1993, 61% of respondents to their Fortune 1000 survey reported that they had used external consultants for their TQM initiative. Of those, 73 % reported that they had positive or very positive experiences with their consultants. One factor in explaining the initial slow response of American firms toward adopting the new quality model in the early 1980s and then the accelerating pace of adoption in the late 1980s is the differential contribution made by the consultant industry in the two periods. Increasingly, consultants linked the firms experienced in TQM with those late developers seeking to speed up their implementation.

From Coercion to Competitiveness

Throughout the 1980s, the OEMs were betting that their imposition of TQM forms on suppliers would lead to improved quality outcomes. In short, they were betting in a very explicit fashion that the initial coercive isomorphism, would be transformed into a competitive isomorphism to use the language of DiMaggio and Powell. One can cast this bet in terms of learning capability. Can generative learning occur under conditions where institutional pressure to adopt is high? By generative learning, I mean that organizations are developing practices that help them learn how to learn (cf. Argyris, 1992). The OEMs were betting that their suppliers could develop and exploit a learning capability with respect to TQM activities. One detailed study of this issue reported mixed results.

Choi and Wasti (1995) studied six automotive suppliers in the early 1990s to determine the extent to which they adopted Japanese production methods, including quality-related technologies like SPC. They were particularly interested in the ability of these firms to engage in single- and double-loop learning. They defined single loop learning operationally as those situations in which firms responded to external pressures for adoption and adopted practices rather mechanistically, with the methods not being used regularly or to their greatest potential. Double-loop learning was defined as occurring in situations where firms internalized external pressures for adoption, demonstrated a good understanding of how each method tied in with the others, and ensured that employees understood how the success of one method depended on the others.

Of the six firms, the authors found that one demonstrated double-loop learning. This was a firm that converted external customer pressures to adopt Japanese methods to an internally driven motivation to develop world-class competitive practices. Four firms manifested single-loop learning, showing limited success in adopting a particular method to achieve a given end. One firm demonstrated no learning at all. In this case, there was decoupling of the external institutional pressure from the core technical activities of the firm. In short, Choi and Wasti found a full range of outcomes, from the classic institutional situation described by Meyer and Rowan (1991), in which compliance is ritualistic, to one in which managers convert an externally induced pressure into an internal goal and go on to produce substantive changes. In this case, we see successful adoption of new production practices that positively amplify changes in still other areas.

Consistent with this range of outcomes, the 1980s, saw slow but nevertheless striking improvement in the quality of the products manufactured by a broad range of supplier industries serving auto companies, including steel companies and semiconductor companies, as well as other industries. In many cases where there is high dependence on suppliers, improvement in the OEM quality performance is inconceivable without supplier improvement (for auto, see MacDuffie and Pil, 1997; for sheet steel, Leib, 1985: D1,D4; for semiconductors, Finan, 1993; Siegmann, 1993: B3; U.S. GAO, 1992: 10). This is not to say that suppliers captured the full benefits associated with generative learning. Helper identified a number of areas by the late 1980s where not much change had taken place or large gaps existed between the auto OEM rhetoric and practice as seen by suppliers. This included the level of trust suppliers had in OEM decisions, belief that use of SPC led simultaneously to higher quality and lower cost, the efficacy of JIT delivery systems and the amount of assistance suppliers receive from OEMs. Nishiguchi (1994: 207), using John Krafcik's data drawn from J. D. Power and Associates, reports that the Americans were producing .329 automotive component defects per car in 1988 compared to.24 for the Japanese, still a non-trivial gap of 37%. Finally, Cusumano and Takeishi (1991: 574–575) also report a sizable quality gap in the late 1980s between Japanese OEM producers in the United States and American OEMs in defects recorded for received parts and rate of defect reduction.

Notwithstanding these indicators of inertia and slow change, the OEM bets were not misplaced. The overall quality improvement reported here and in Chapter 9 was substantial and could not have been achieved without the active cooperation of supplier firms, which accounted for a significant portion of the total product's value.

Apparently, the unrelenting pressure of the market kept the ritual aspect from dominating supply firm behavior. Nevertheless, these findings are quite consistent with DiMaggio and Powell's hypothesis that the greater the dependence of an organization on another organization, the more similar it will become to that organization in structure, climate, and behavioral focus (1991: 74). In our case, both organizations (U.S. customers and suppliers) were in turn responding to strong external competitive pressures. Rather than a stage theory, these observations suggest a strong tension between competitive and institutional isomorphism from the beginning, with the outcome determined by evolving environmental forces, as well as internal dynamics of the field.

CHAPTER 6

Putting It Together

In the last chapter, I touched on the role of industry-specific organizations such as the ASI and SEMATECH and their role in identifying and diffusing information about best practices. I discussed the activities of customer-supplier networks in spreading and serving as transmission links for the new ideas about quality. Accumulating quality improvement expertise in the 1980s involved not so much adopting a specific approach to quality improvement as creating and participating in an infrastructure for the identification and diffusion of best practices.

This broader institutional network involved users, consultant vendors, and a variety of other nonmarket players. These nonmarket players included professional associations, government interventions, joint government-private initiatives, industry-sponsored organizations, community organizations, regional associations, universities, independent research organizations, and the like. Together, these various players, as well as many others, came to constitute an innovation and diffusion community. This infrastructure aided managers in their search for suitable and effective practices, ones that adapted Japanese approaches to an American environment. It operated to identify and widely diffuse best practices, thereby contributing to the growing success of managers in improving quality.

The constituent organizations in this infrastructure acted to create standards, identify bottlenecks, introduce new methodologies, provide training in these methodologies, disseminate knowledge (including success stories as well as failed directions), focus efforts, evolve forums for networking, and create social locations for learning. By providing overall support to users, the infrastructure eliminated the isolation of managerial decision makers and brought them into regular contact with useful information from fellow practitioners. It is the emergence and flowering of such an infrastructure that distinguishes the last half of the 1980s and 1990s from the early 1980s. Through this infrastructure managers learned about the importance of general principles, such as leveraging their quality improvement through upstream prevention efforts, and developed concrete tactics for implementing and practicing these ideas. In short, it helped them move along the continuum from first absorbing new learning to converting the new learning into effective practice.

This is not the first time the argument has been made that the institutional infrastructure, composed of complex networks, constrains the flow of new technology and affects the rate and amount of diffusion. Particularly relevant to our analysis is the work of Lynn, Reddy, and Aram (1996).[1] They discuss the role of "organizational communities" in diffusing (or inhibiting) the flow of new technologies. They cite a variety of research to document the activities of important constituent elements of these communities including trade associations, professional organizations, and government. Two differences between their account and the one presented here are noteworthy. First, they concentrate on explaining the path by which hard technologies spread; here I am interested in the spread of soft technologies, such as how a firm learns to do quality improvement. The mechanisms appear quite similar. Second, while they examine how existing infrastructural organizations can facilitate technology flows, I am also interested in their emergent properties as the organizations and practices evolve to take on new challenges.

Lynn et al. note that the diffusion of technology can be promoted by organizational communities in a variety of ways. These organizations can influence the emergence of a dominant design for a technology by linking diverse bodies of knowledge, competencies, and techniques, thus facilitating the adoption and integration of interdependent and complementary technologies (Lynn, Reddy, and Aram, 1996: 98–99). The following account provides strong support for these kinds of effects. Each of the major organizations to be described seems to have a specific, though often overlapping, set of competencies, and most perform a specialized role for a distinct audience.

To capture this emergent infrastructure and clarify key elements in the flow of information regarding best practice in quality technologies, I detail the contributions of six major institutional activities that operated at a national level. Together, they represented key elements of the innovation community for large-scale manufacturing firms seeking to understand and implement the new quality paradigm. They are the American Society of Quality, GOAL/QPC, the Conference Board's Quality Councils, the Center for Quality of Management, the Malcolm Baldrige National Quality Award, and ISO 9000. These six performed quite different roles and illustrate a broad range of institutional possibilities for spreading learning about best practice and converting that learning to effective practice. Large manufacturing companies typically participated in multiple networks to obtain new information and knowledge about quality improvement. Furthermore, an interesting set of competitive and cooperative activities link the six institutional modes. To capture the nature of these contributions, I characterize some of their activities as they affected imitation and organizational learning. These six institutional activities represented the tip of the iceberg of what evolved into a dense infrastructure of quality-help organizations and activities. There were other organizations operating at the national level, such as the American Center for Quality and Productivity. This rich and dense network of information helped companies learn what to do and how to do it.

Not all the organizations operated on a national scale. Organizations like the Erie Community Quality Council in Erie, Pennsylvania, was just one of an estimated 200 local community groups that developed initially to use quality improvement to revive and grow local industry. Later, using quality methods, many became involved in attacking a range of communitywide problems, such as improving schools. Often, these community quality councils were a response to the lack of available training in quality methods for organizations not closely tied to large companies or supplier networks. They were built on many different local institutions; the Erie community quality council, for example, was sponsored by the local Chamber of Commerce.[2] The 10,000-member Association for Quality and Participation (AQP) became a clearinghouse organization (taking over from the World Center for Community Excellence in 1996) disseminating literature on how to start and sustain community quality councils and various other best practice information (Association for Quality and Participation, 1996: 3). In a sense, AQP became a supra-infrastructure organization providing support for still other infrastructure organizations.

Community colleges (sometimes serving as the base for community quality councils) and some universities also became involved, seeing a niche for making themselves useful to local industry. The Center for Quality at Eastern Michigan University in Ypsilanti, Michigan, for example, trained some 2,000 mostly auto employees a year in the mid-1990s in various quality methodologies through 53 seminars offered multiple times (1997–1998 schedule) in topics ranging from ISO 9000, to design of experiments, to mistake proofing.

In addition to these various local level organizations, there also arose loosely knit networks such as the Deming Users Groups and Associations. The Deming Cooperative Website listed some 53 such users groups, study groups, work groups, alliances, and associations in the United States in 1998 (*http://www.deming.edu*). Some of these groups have resident experts in Deming's theories guiding their studies each month, while others have visiting teachers. Some groups meet regularly, others more sporadically.

In addition to these local level activities, less visible firm-to-firm cooperative activities also developed, and one cannot discount these more subtle interconnections. Typically based on the promise of reciprocity, a variety of networking and benchmarking activities were established, ranging from short-term to long-term and from dyadic ties to more extended networks. To take just one example I stumbled upon, P&G, an important purchaser of HP products, reached an agreement in 1986 that called for two P&G managers to spend six months studying quality and manufacturing at HP while two HP counterparts took up residence at P&G to study commodity marketing practices. According to Jack Brown of P&G, one of the two managers sent to HP, this exposure greatly stimulated P&G's quality improvement initiatives, especially in the areas of hoshin management, the role of statistics in management, and the need to study the Japanese.[3] These and other kinds of company-to-company exchanges were quite common and effective.

This listing does not exhaust the rich infrastructure that emerged in the late 1980s to support the growing capability of American managers to respond effectively to the Japanese quality challenge. The previous chapter shows how consultant activities become pervasive and this chapter shows how they were interwoven with the activities of the various organizational activities to be discussed. Consultant activities co-evolved with the development of these organizations, both cooperating and competing with them. The focus for the rest of this chapter will be on discrete national-level organizations that arose to facilitate the identification and adoption of new quality practices.

The American Society for Quality

The American Society for Quality (ASQ), formerly the American Society for Quality Control, represents a first approach to infrastructure building.[4] Unlike the other organizations to be discussed, ASQ already existed when the quality challenge became manifest. Many of the new organizations dedicated to quality improvement, like GOAL/QPC, had to consume much energy in seeking resources, support, and legitimacy. However, ASQ, as an existing organization, might have been expected to take advantage quickly of the growing corporate interest in quality.

Historically, however, like many professional associations, ASQ saw its mission as facilitating the career development of its members and raising their professional status rather than upgrading organizational quality per se (Cole, 1989b: 152–179). As late as 1996, 30% of its membership reported that they joined ASQ to become certified. Moreover, in the minds of many top-ranking American managers in the early 1980s, ASQ was part of the problem, if they even knew that the organization existed. For many of those top managers familiar with the organization, ASQ was seen as an association for relatively low-status "techies" associated with failed old methods of quality control. In short, this was not a vibrant organization that rose to meet the new quality challenge. With some 32,000 individual members in 1979, it had an annual budget of about 2 million dollars, which was about half that of comparable professional associations (Cole, 1989b: 157). Furthermore, a financial crisis in 1982–1983 crippled many new initiatives just as they were seeking to take advantage of the new-found national interest in quality.

Yet it gradually regrouped and began to expand its membership, local chapter and divisional activities, conferences, training, and publication programs. Conferences and training activities also become important avenues for networking among members. Its major challenge was to "ramp up" fast enough to revise its offerings and expand it services to meet the explosive demand of an audience hungry for guidance. By 1990 individual membership rose to 71,000, more than double the 1979 figures, and by 1997, it stood at 133,000. This growth of membership meant that the organization had became more attractive as a source of information, training, and certification for quality specialists. Indeed, in a response to a 1997 member satisfaction survey, members agreed most with the statement that ASQ is their source for quality-related information, with a mean score of 8 on a 10-point scale, and 78% reported that ASQ was their primary professional association.[5]

The growth in membership also reflected the growing pool of prospective members associated with the significant rise in employment of dedicated quality specialists at American firms. One of the effects of the quality movement of the 1980s and 1990s was an expansion in the types of employees who could see themselves as quality professionals. Statisticians, customer service representatives, technologists, operations managers, organizational specialists, all could claim to make contributions to quality improvement. In short, ASQ faced a growing market.

Membership in ASQ traditionally represented the "quality troops." The bulk of membership had been accounted for by the following job titles: quality inspector, quality technician, quality coordinator, quality analyst, quality supervisor, quality auditor, quality specialist, quality engineer, and quality manager. Supervisors, engineers, technicians, and inspectors alone accounted for almost 49% of its membership in 1990. This designation conceals, however, the growing shift in ASQ membership from its origins as a manufacturing organization to one marketing its activities to the service sector. The number of members in the manufacturing sector declined from roughly 74% in 1990 to 64% in 1997 as a result of the strong membership growth in the service sector. There has also been an upgrading of the membership so that the percentage of members in the technical/inspector functions fell to just 8% in 1996 compared to 18% in 1990. Similarly, there has been a growth in the number of higher-ranking officers in ASQ, partially attributable to the growth in the number of corporate sustaining memberships, with some 15% of the membership reporting that they were presidents, vice presidents, senior officers, or directors by 1996. In keeping with the transformational theme of the quality movement in recent decades, some 77% of the survey respondents in 1996 considered themselves a "change agent within their organization."

While ASQ moved slowly, by the late 1980s, the training, certification content, divisional and section (chapter) activities, conference content, publications, and educational outreach were all gradually revamped to reflect the new principles of quality management and expanded to meet the enormous new demand. Notable was the shift in content of papers in their annual meeting each year from almost 100% technical in the early 1980s to about half in the mid-1990s devoted to management issues in quality focused around human resource practices, teams, information exchange, and the like.

Membership surveys report that the association's journal *Quality Progress* has been consistently rated the most valuable membership service. By the mid-1980s, the journal began to play a major role in introducing new quality methodologies to the membership, thereby contributing to the series of quality minifads reported in Chapter I. More generally, ASQ is a major provider to its members of publications related to quality; the member satisfaction survey shows this is perceived as a major benefit by members.

Divisional and section activities were particularly important for facilitating a shared in-depth exploration of the new quality practices by employees of the member companies. This, however, was not spread evenly over all divisions and sections. Thus, the automotive division (with 9,460 members in 1997) and sections had regular meetings and conferences (including cosponsoring conferences with sections and with others), all of which allowed managers with quality responsibilities to gain a deeper understanding of the new methodologies. Many case study experiences were presented at these meetings, and each of the stream of new quality methodologies was analyzed and dissected in terms of obstacles and uses. In the heyday of the quality boom in the mid-and late 1980s, it was not unusual for the two big division conferences held annually to draw 400 attendees for each. As we saw in the previous chapter, the automotive division also played an important role in developing industrywide quality-related standards such as QS-9000.

The situation was quite different in the electronics division, which had only 4,336 members in 1997 (peaked at around 6,000 in 1991). These smaller numbers reflect in turn the lower rate of ASQ's penetration into the electronics sector. For many high-tech companies, ASQ reeked of old-fashioned quality control and traditional Midwestern "metal bending" industries. Organizations like the American Electronics Association (AEA) and even more specialized industry trade groups offered services in quality improvement to companies in the electronics industries and thus were quite competitive with ASQ. In the early 1990s AEA developed its activities for smaller companies with the leadership of major electronic companies like HP, Intel, and Motorola; it was led initially by the former corporate quality director at HP. Also, AEA used materials developed and adapted from SEMA-TECH for semiconductor equipment suppliers. It also made available a variety of services to companies attempting to improve quality including a national quality network, "practical" seminars, a large number of publications, and partnerships among member organizations, to share experiences on topics like implementing TQC and ISO 9000 registration. Other organizations devoted to quality improvement in the electronics industry included the Council for Continuous Improvement (especially teams and process improvement) headquartered in San Jose and the Center for Quality of Management (especially hoshin management, voice of the customer, and new product development), which developed a West Coast chapter. A West Coast chapter of the Conference Board's Quality Councils also was set up. Specialized industry groups such as the WCQF were also established.

Despite its relative weakness in the electronics industry, ASQ emerged from its modest origins to become a significant player in the diffusion of new quality improvement methods for the mass of American quality specialists. Alongside the resuscitation of ASQ, a number of competitors emerged for the provision of quality services in specific niche markets. Thus, consultants firms competed with ASQ in running training courses and conferences. Also, ASQ also competed with many of its own consultant members, who number about 8% of its total membership. These consultant members often learn from ASQ activities and then use that knowledge to compete with them in running training courses and conferences and writing books for other publishers. Productivity Press, GOAL/QPC, and the existing commercial publishing houses like McGraw-Hill, riding the quality bandwagon, also became competitors in the production of quality-related publications; many professional business conference holders chose to compete in the quality market and so on. The AQP became an early competitor in the quality circle arena and later more broadly in employee involvement and team improvement activities. Various organizations expanded or were newly created to compete for the attention of quality professionals in the electronics industry. Yet no competitor emerged that encompassed the full range of ASQ offerings for the quality specialist on a national basis, and in particular no serious contender competed for the professional identity of quality professionals. One of the advantages of being a generalist organization is that ASQ could promote any quality technology that developed. When ISO 9000 came along, ASQ could promote it along with its other offerings. Many of the specialist organizations to be described below, however, were by definition wedded to a narrow expertise and experienced a loss of momentum with the rise of the movement for ISO 9000 registration.

GOAL/QPC

GOAL/QPC was originally a local community-based group seeking to revive industry in the Lawrence/Lowell, Massachusetts, area.[6] Its chairperson at the time, Bob King, was inspired by the *If Japan Can, Why Can't We* TV program and met with Deming in 1981. In the early 1980s, its activities focused on gathering information on SPC and teaching it to local industry personnel. Gradually, it became known as a source of translations regarding Japanese quality practices, expanded its scope to TQM, and transformed itself from 1986 to 1987 from a local to a national nonprofit research corporation.

In 1987, GOAL/QPC set about creating an intercorporate research group that would identify best quality practices in Japan, translate key documents, and help interpret them. The organization was particularly prominent in assuming the early leadership in adapting and applying hoshin management in the United States, but it was also active in introducing QFD and total productive maintenance. At a later date, it was among the lead organizations introducing quality ideas to the health care sector. A number of competitors arose to compete with them for market share, particularly for QFD training and conferences. These included specific industry associations such as the ASI, the ASQ, as well as consultant-driven organizations like the QFD Institute. Similarly, the Center for Quality of Management (CQM), a latecomer established in 1989, became a competitor for training and conferences on hoshin management. Sometimes these competitors cooperated on specific projects; at other times they competed with one another.

Thus, GOAL/QPC reports informal cooperation on specific projects with ASQ, the American Productivity and Quality Center (APQC), CQM, and Baldrige-related activities. At the same time, it disseminated its findings to broad audiences. It supplied technical assistance and support to many of the 200 community quality councils and Deming user groups across the country. The prime force behind GOAL/QPC, Bob King, the executive director, had broad aspirations for influencing government and university; King stated to me in our phone interview that he concluded in the late 1980s that the way to achieve its goals was to work with "cutting-edge people" at the major corporations and "let everyone else copy them."

In 1992, GOAL/QPC had 36 sustaining members. The list of companies at that time reads like a "who's who" in American manufacturing (but including some important service companies as well) including GE, HP, P&G, IBM, Ford Motor Co., Xerox, and Intel. These companies were represented largely by middle-management quality specialists. Thus, while ASQ largely represented the quality troops, GOAL/QPC worked with the key technical personnel leading quality improvement implementation. Its goal, however, was to reach the broad mass of employees. Roughly half of its sustaining members in the early 1990s were also sustaining members of ASQ.

In addition, GOAL/QPC conducted a great number of public seminars and conferences on quality subjects. At the height of the quality boom in the early 1990s, its annual conference, begun in 1984, was attracting some 1,000–1,500 participants a year. One major company representative described it to me as a "major learning event." As the organization moved into the mid-and late 1990s, organizational attendance dropped to about 400 a year.

One can see in GOAL/QPC a pattern apparent in the other organizations I will discuss. They move in ladder-like fashion from one quality technology to another as the wave of adoption rose and then fell for each one. Like the others I will discuss, however, GOAL/QPC did not abandon its core expertise in quality, but added on to it and adapted it to new circumstances.

To be perceived as a leader, it needed to be seen as having the ability to identify the next new important approach. As the stock of new product introductions successively drawn from the Japanese quality repertoire weakened in the 1990s, this became more and more of a problem. Moreover, because they did not do consulting, they were not as able to maintain a sense of how American companies were adapting these practices to their needs. As one representative from a major firm put it to me, "They grew too fast and lost touch with how Japanese ideas were playing out in the U.S. environment." A range of competitors emerged depending on the product offered and the nature of the target audience. More company representatives began to complain that they were being put to work on research committees, which only added to their workload. For these and other reasons, the sustaining member system fell apart in the mid-1990s.

The organization commissioned market research on those firms that had been associated with GOAL/QPC as well as other firms, and the results told them that the demand for services in the quality area was still high, but that it was shifting. The scale of activities and organizational revenues continued to grow as it shifted in response to demand from public conferences to producing and selling more publications and instructional modules. In an era of cost cutting, companies were more interested in materials for supporting in-house training activities than sending their employees to outside seminars and conferences. The market research results also suggested that firms adopting the quality technologies they learned about from GOAL/QPC needed in-house guidance on how to optimize these technologies. With this in mind, GOAL/QPC started a coaching service for such firms in 1997. They also expanded into the area of creativity and systematic innovation in 1997.

Actually, GOAL/QPC activities are especially interesting and important because they reveal a collective effort in the late 1980s on the part of important American companies, belatedly to be sure, to be where the news was breaking or in any case where it had broken recently. By acting collectively to retrieve, translate, and interpret key documents, they reduced the costs of learning from the Japanese. By providing a framework for companies to share their implementation experiences, GOAL/QPC facilitated the translation of this learning into effective practice. As one company representative who was critical of many of GOAL/QPC's written materials put it to me, "The virtue of working with GOAL/QPC was the opportunity to make connections with those implementing the same practices at other companies and with some of the key Japanese players." In short, his incentives were pure networking. Of course, GOAL/QPC's activities did not hit full stride until the late 1980s and early 1990s—long after the Japanese quality challenge had become apparent. Nevertheless, they show that some key companies were in effect giving a second look to learning from the source of the new quality model.

The Conference Board's Quality Councils

While company participants in GOAL/QPC tended to be middle-ranking executives with hands-on involvement with quality, the Conference Board's Quality Councils reached a quite different constituency, composed of high-level corporate executives with quality responsibilities.[7] David Luther, vice president for quality at Corning, and Art Nichols, with similar responsibilities at Celanese, were two of the initial key movers. The founding document agreed upon in 1985 by the small group of corporate quality executives and the Conference Board calls for a forum "for the informal exchange of information and experience on the total quality effort among a group of involved corporate executives."[8]

The Conference Board provided a hospitable umbrella for this kind of effort. It had a history of creating councils for high-level executives in functional areas such as marketing and finance, having established their first one in 1926. This experience reduced the start-up costs (in terms of figuring out what organizational practices made sense) for the new quality council. The organizing group for quality, however, believed that the typical Conference Board councils were too large. It agreed to use the Conference Board as its forum under the conditions that the quality council be kept small, since its goal was to develop a closely knit group that could network effectively. It insisted on a qualified membership over which the members, not the Conference Board, had control. It wanted control over membership particularly to ensure that new members were sufficiently advanced in their efforts to be able to contribute to the collective learning effort. It set as conditions of membership that members would be high-ranking executives with quality responsibilities in major corporations, and that no substitutes, consultants, or academics could participate. The exclusion of consultants and academics was based on the premise that members could not air their dirty laundry and were at a greater risk for knowledge, tools, and techniques being pirated if consultants or academics were present (in 1990, the consultant rule was relaxed for one individual who was an experienced corporate executive with both Baldrige and Deming Prize credentials). There was a strong elitist element in member selection; selection was based on people they trusted. Members also had to be Conference Board Associates (entailing a significant annual fee) to join, which effectively limited membership to large corporations.

The first Quality Council meeting took place in 1985. The initial members were Celanese, Corning Glass, First Chicago, Florida Power and Light, Honeywell, IBM, Milliken & Company, Minnesota Mining and Manufacturing Company, Westinghouse Electric Systems, and Xerox Corporation. Over the next few years, the following companies were added: American Express Company, Motorola, Ford Motor Co., and Health Corporation of America. Over an extended period, still more were added. The early members (companies, not necessarily individuals) also showed considerable staying power; of the 17 members of this flagship council in 1997, 13 were among those early members. The founders decided to meet once a quarter for two days. They went on to meet four times a year for the next several years, a frequency greater than for any other board council. In 1997, they were meeting three times a year.

One of the first activities of the council was its participation in helping set national quality policy. Joining with various other groups, its effort culminated in establishing the Malcolm Baldrige National Quality Award. The Conference Board has continued to cooperate with the Baldrige award office, cosponsoring regional Malcolm Baldrige Award Conferences. Of the 18 companies that participated in this quality council, a remarkable 9 of them (or one of their units) won Baldrige Awards (one company was appointed after it won the Baldrige). They also won a variety of state quality awards.

Council members eventually agreed to hold every other meeting at the site of one of the members. This allowed them to vary their focus from general issues to more in-depth pursuit of a particular member's activities. Often the CEO, or other top officers, of the host company addressed the group. Some meetings were show-and-tell sessions as each member talked about new quality methods enacted. Typically one member took the responsibility for leading a session's discussion. It became a very tight group, getting to know each other very well.

Over time, the shared experience of founding the organization and working on common projects like the establishment of the Baldrige award helped build considerable trust among the members. There was minimal turnover among the individuals from the founding companies for the first five years. All this contributed to a positive approach to sharing sensitive information with the expectation that it would not be misused (e.g., passed on to competitors). The council provided for contextual benchmarking of each other's activities since each had ongoing access to others' experiences. Lots of informal interactions took place between meetings. If one was thinking of doing something new and had to see one's chairman at 2:00 pm, one could call the other members in the morning and be able to present to the chairman in the afternoon what each company was doing in this area as a backdrop for what you proposed.

Site visits to member companies, not only on the part of council members but by fellow managers in their companies, were commonplace events. As the era of formal benchmarking and the search for best practices intensified in the early 1990s, such cooperation among the members became routine events. In short, the council made possible quite effective and efficient peer networking. To be sure, there was the predictable posturing, with presentations focusing on corporate accomplishments. Indeed, in one of the meeting minutes from 1987, one member complains, "[T]he one area where I feel we still need improvement is in promoting informal discussion on real problems and issues rather than making speeches to each other about how good we are." Certainly, there is a natural inclination to talk more about successes than failures. Yet public airing of such a complaint suggests that real efforts were made to make these meetings productive. It was not uncommon to hear members say, "My new CEO doesn't have a clue about quality—what can I do?"

There was a very pragmatic emphasis on finding out what works and what does not. As a member from one of the founding companies put it to me, "Our mission was to take something back from these meetings which we could use." He recounted how in his company's case, they first learned the significance of "process management and what it really meant" from the council meetings. Some of the topic areas covered at meetings between 1985 and 1987 included raising supplier quality levels; selecting quality measures; applying quality improvement principles in marketing, sales, and R & D and in support services; giving financial rewards for quality performance; educating customers on corporate quality initiatives; changing the role of quality professionals and upgrading the quality function; pursuing quality improvement in business downturns; involving middle management in the quality improvement process; training strategies; using process management; and keeping the quality improvement process going, including avoiding the establishment of a quality bureaucracy.

One major effort involved sharing strategies for getting top management fully involved in the quality improvement effort; this included having CEOs visit one another. At the site visit to Westinghouse, visitors studied the quality audit system and learned about the practice of measuring how much of the CEO's time was devoted to quality matters. Some applied this to their own companies and got their CEOs to devote more time to quality. The quality council also enabled its members to "network their CEOs." The idea of arranging meetings between one's CEO and a CEO in a pacesetter company to discuss quality improvement was premised on the view that nothing convinces a CEO like another CEO.

Critical to the success of this peer networking was the willingness to share failures, which could happen only as members built up trust with one another. If one said at a meeting, "We are planning on introducing x and we are thinking of doing it this way," others who had tried it would recount their experiences, including approaches they had tried but that had failed. They might say, "Sounds good but let me tell you, don't just do training and expect it to produce results. We tried that and it was a disaster. You need to figure out how to get those employees to apply the training immediately." The success of this kind of peer networking effort depended on the willingness of members to share their mistakes and the things they would do differently.

Implicit here is an emphasis on treating quality methodologies as generic information that could be shared among fellow council members rather than treated as proprietary. The quality of information was enhanced by the long-term relationship among the company representatives participating on the council. This relationship allowed an iterative learning process over time. Sharing among council members was further encouraged by the informal rule allowing an existing member to veto any new member that was a competitor. This principle was operationalized (with some exceptions) through having only one firm per SIC industry code on the flagship council.

At the same time, those receiving documents and participating in discussions were asked to treat the content as confidential. This emphasis on confidentiality, however, was not for the purpose of providing potential competitive advantage to Quality Council members. Rather, members were extremely fearful that a journalist from the business media, especially the *Wall Street Journal*, which, as one member put it, "took an abnormal interest in us," would gain access to information relating to their frank discussions and hold up individual companies to ridicule. Here, we see the clear conflict between media and corporate interests.

For the business media, an article about failure of the hyped-up quality movement would be a juicy story, allowing them to demolish what they saw by then as conventional views on quality. Yet, for the firms to get full benefit from their joint discussions, they needed to talk about failures and paths that turned into dead ends. Such exchanges were critical for real learning to take place among members. This conflict between media and corporate interests has been a continuing problem for those associated with the quality movement, as reflected in the widespread business journalist view through much of its history that quality was a fad.

The first Quality Council was so successful that the Conference Board went on to establish 13 others through 1995. By 1997, some 150 organizations were participating in the councils, with a total of some 200 executives. Those figures have been flat since 1995. The Conference Board's ability to clone the original council met the growing market demand without greatly diluting the original vehicle. The high prestige of the Conference Board made these councils the vehicle of choice for high-level quality executives in major corporations. The requirement that council members be affiliates of the Conference Board limited but did not preclude the participation of small and medium-size firms. Some of the subsequent councils adopted a more relaxed attitude than the original flagship council toward having competitors and academics on the councils. Few competitors could match the cachet of the Conference Board and gain a hold in this particular niche of the quality help market. In an informal survey of current members of he flagship council, I asked if they had alternatives to secure the same level of peer networking. Most reported no organization existed with the same focus. Some organizations mentioned, however, were the Baldrige Winners Networking Group and the Manufacturers Alliance for Productivity Improvement.

The 14 Quality Councils that came to be organized under a TQM Center, are described in a 1995 Conference Board publication as follows:

> The Total Quality Management Center enhances organizations' continuous improvement through shared information, peer networking and learning opportunities. TQMC councils meet several times yearly for informal candid exchanges on topics such as benchmarking, measurement, customer satisfaction, and the role of the CEO in the quality effort. Councils are organized for senior quality practitioners and along functional lines. In addition to shaping the selection of research topics, member companies can participate in the surveys of the Quality Research Panel. Executives of member companies are eligible to attend the twice-yearly TQMC Center Seminar Series. Other activities include special events, such as international and regional joint meetings with other TQMC councils and with The Conference Board's European and Canadian quality councils.

The surveys of the Quality Research Panel were based on identifying and responding to common problems across councils. While some of the councils are concerned broadly with quality improvement, others are based on specific functional areas like the legal quality council or the sales and marketing quality council.

Undoubtedly, the councils developed subsequent to the initial flagship council seldom developed the cohesion and extensive networking achieved by the founders. Indeed, even the flagship council now has fewer long-term participants. Even so, in my informal survey of the flagship council members, they reported that they strongly valued the council and placed equal value on meetings and networking benefits. Indeed, it would appear that the meeting discussions provide signals about what and with whom one should network. It was also reported by staff that the directory listing all council members was much in demand, suggesting that there was extensive informal networking across councils as well.

Composed mostly of large private sector companies, quality council membership again reads like a "who's who" of American industry. Notable also is the overlap with the membership of GOAL/QPC. Thirteen of the 36 sustaining members of GOAL/QPC in the early 1990s, many of them notable for their reputation as pacesetters in quality improvement, were members of one of the Conference Board's Quality Councils in 1996. These overlapping networks would appear to have contributed to reinforcing the growing capabilities of these firms. At the same time, those firms participating in only one of these organizations could draw benefits from the expertise of those involved in broader networks.

The Center for Quality of Management

If ASQ was the carrier of new modes of quality improvement for the troops, and GOAL/QPC for middle-management quality specialists, and the Conference Board's Quality Councils for the senior quality officer, then the CQM emerged as the counterpart organization for senior management, initially in the high-tech area but broadening out over time across industries.[9] It was, however, an institutional solution that arrived late to the party, being founded in 1989 at the height of the TQM boom. The founders, all technology companies, were Analog Devices, Bolt Beranek & Newman, Inc., Bose Corp., Digital Equipment Corp., GE Aircraft Engines, Polaroid Corp., and Teradyne Inc. By 1997, this number had grown to 116 member organizations (of which 30 are affiliates, including some 15 universities); current members include Intel, L. L. Bean, ADAC Laboratories, HP, the Federal Reserve Bank of Boston, and Sun Microsystems. Two thirds of the members are manufacturers and two thirds are firms with more than 500 employees. There are now five chapters including two European ones.

Like the other organizations discussed so far, CQM initially sought to identify and spread to its members the new approaches to quality improvement emanating from Japan. Most interesting, however, is that CQM also sought to model the very structural characteristics of the major organization that spread quality improvement in Japan. The other organizations we have studied that also drew direct inspiration in this fashion were SEMATECH and ASI, whose conception and design were in part influenced by their counterparts in Japan.

The CQM was very much the inspiration of Shoji Shiba, a leading Japanese quality adviser and scholar. He came to the attention of American top management in the late 1980s when he gave a lecture at MIT that several of the CQM founding CEOs attended. Shiba was struck by the seeming fragmentation of the American infrastructure for diffusing quality practices and the often short-sighted actions of consultants. In Japan, the Japan Standards Association (JSA) and JUSE operated as national institutions for validating and spreading information about new approaches to quality improvement.

Shiba, working with Ray Stata, the founder of Analog Devices, and Thomas Lee, a faculty member at MIT, saw CQM as a vehicle to introduce to the United States some of the benefits that flowed from JUSE's structure and activities. These included mutual learning activities, having corporations rather than individuals as members (contrasting with ASQ), attracting participants from all disciplines not just quality specialists, emphasizing education and training, involving academics, including contributors from a broad range of industries, and creating local chapters that would allow for intensive networking.

Through training and education, JUSE seeks to absorb, digest, synthesize, and feed back to members the innovative approaches to quality improvement evolving at the level of individual firms. This societalwide model operates to shorten corporate learning curves. It is a model based on a community of firms moving forward as a community. In effect, JUSE stresses networking and sharing of experiences among member companies, a model that included small "CEO learning communities." Moreover, JUSE evolved a sophisticated model of new product development for creating and introducing best practices (Shiba, Graham, and Walden, 1993: 507–532). JUSE also had a lean staff, limiting itself to being a provider of logistics; the social location of quality knowledge was in the members' firms. This meant using instructors, where possible, from member corporations rather than in-house staff. Thus, CQM sought to borrow and adapt all these features from JUSE. It used top management as an entrée into the corporation, subsequently building on that relationship to enable a more successful diffusion of its methodologies.

For the participant executives to function as a learning community requires a common language and a set of tools; TQM provides that foundation. However, TQM is conceived not as a specific technique or tool but as a framework within which one can place an evolving set of tools. The focus is now on achieving business excellence rather than improving quality per se as in the early 1990s. If one examines the offerings of CQM, one sees both the continuing foundation provided by what has come to be called TQM overlaid with a variety of other evolving technologies that go well beyond conventional TQM. The decision not simply to move to the latest fad technique but to build upon the TQM framework is notable. Thus, an examination of the courses offered in the latter half of 1997 include the predictable TQM topics-TQM for senior executives: planning and implementation (the flagship course taken by over 1,000 executives since its inception); understanding variation: an introduction; voice of the customer method; seven-step problem-solving method; hoshin planning; and practical benchmarking for problem solving (jointly with the APQC). They also include, however, advanced language processing skills for facilitators; concept engineering: theory and practice; conversational competence; mobilizing improvement teams; and introduction to the language-processing method.

Perhaps the distinguishing feature of CQM is that activities are organized to foster mutual learning and joint problem solving on common problems. There is an emphasis on sharing real case experiences and operating explicitly from a weakness orientation, which means openly discussing both the shortcomings of TQM and the weaknesses of each firm's operations. This approach led CQM to conclude that strategic planning was a missing element in TQM and to seek to build in such an emphasis.

Top executives are expected to make major time commitments to implementation activities deriving from their CQM involvement. They make choices as to what problems they want to work on, driven by the business imperatives they experience. Mutual learning is fostered through four sets of activities.

First are the educational programs involving workshops, courses, and seminars. In 1997 CQM was running 19 different courses, most offered several times. Second is networked learning, which takes place through user groups, study groups, and roundtables. By 1997, it was holding some 5–6 seminars and 30–40 roundtables. The seminars were open to the public, involved outside speakers, and typically drew about 75 people. The roundtables are only for members, typically draw about 10–30 individuals per meeting, and are focused on particular topics of interest to members. A survey of topics in 1997 included why some firms doing TQM are successful but others are not, measurement, and personality and job performance. Peer networking acts as a support system for executives implementing specific initiatives. User groups bring together members to implement specific CQM methodologies, and study groups are formed to examine specific topics. Third, in response in part to the growing diversity of member needs, advising and diagnostic services were initiated whereby a team of CQM members visits a colleague's site to evaluate program effectiveness. Of the four, this is probably the weakest area of performance according to the CQM leadership.

Fourth are the research initiatives in which members join together to research promising areas and test findings in the field. The idea is to identify best-in-class methodologies in strategy, operations, and managing change and to integrate them into the TQM framework. Those efforts bearing fruit are then disseminated to members. These R & D activities are seen as critical to keeping the organization responsive to evolving member needs. They are especially important in keeping the most advanced companies motivated and involved with CQM. Thus far, three management methodologies have flowed through this pipeline: Interactive Planning, a blending of Russell Ackoff's work on strategic planning with TQM methodologies, Concept Engineering, a method for dealing with the "fuzzy" front end of product development aimed at assessing customer needs, and Conversation, a methodology aimed at improving the way organizations make and keep commitments with language (Taninecz, 1997: 30–31).

By far, CQM manifests the most sophisticated learning model of any of the infrastructure organizations I have been able to study. To be sure, practice, as always, falls short of the promise. It has had difficulty in achieving its primary mission of keeping CEOs continuously involved; over time the CEO tends to become less involved. Moreover, at the front end, by insisting that the CEO be initially involved, it has lost the opportunity to work with a lot of firms where top management is not prepared to meet that condition. It has also had to struggle with how to grow the TQM concept to keep it relevant. With TQM being out of fashion, it has a strong marketing challenge to convince companies first that they have gone beyond a narrowly conceived TQM but also that it is appropriate to have TQM as their foundation. Finally, with the expansion of the organization from a small group of homogenous technology companies with similar kinds of problems and similar levels of sophistication regarding TQM to a much larger organization with companies from different industries and at different levels, it has become much more difficult to operationalize the principles of mutual learning.

Before and after CQM's creation, those CEOs of large corporations who sought out help in leading the quality improvement initiative typically found it among individual consultants and consultant firms. These were CQM's competitors for the CEO's attention regarding quality improvement. By the mid-1990s, however, the major competition for CQM came from other initiatives that competed for top-management attention, such as business process reengineering, enterprise resources planning, and the growing sense in some corporate suites that ISO 9000 certification could take care of quality improvement needs. All this was taking place in an environment in which managers increasingly came to believe that TQM had been a passing fad or the quality challenge had been met. However, CQM continued to grow and slowly build its reputation, even receiving positive public attention at a time when it was rare for the term TQM to come up in the business media in a positive context (Taninecz, 1997: 28–31).

The Baldrige

Clearly, the most important addition to the national infrastructure for identifying and diffusing best practice in quality came with the establishment in 1987 of the Malcolm Baldrige National Quality Award.[10] This outcome represented a remarkable confluence of separate initiatives pursued by different organizations and interests.[11] The Baldrige, a joint venture between government and business, was a major institutional innovation.[12] The private portion of this venture was formally represented by the Foundation for the Malcolm Baldrige National Quality Award, an organization that draws its membership and funds from many of the leading companies discussed earlier in this chapter. Day-to-day operation of the award program is carried out by the National Institute of Standards and Technology (NIST), with administrative support from the ASQ. Most of the actual work of reviewing, scoring, and judging is carried out by a large number of volunteer examiners from industry. Improving award criteria and processes is led by NIST, with input from the examiners and applicants. As a national award, presented annually by the president of the United States, the Baldrige legitimated and put the national spotlight on the quality improvement effort as no other activity had previously done.

The national ambitions of the program promoters showed a shrewd understanding of what the goals of a successful infrastructure organization should be. The design strategy was to create a national value system for quality, to provide a basis for diagnosis and information transfer, to create a vehicle for cooperation across organizations, and to provide for a dynamic award system that would be continuously improved (Godfrey, 1995:3). By the mid-1990s the Baldrige initiative had made significant progress in these directions.

Godfrey also notes two other uses of the Baldrige: to help raise quality performance standards and expectations in firms and to facilitate communication and sharing, among and within organizations, based upon a common understanding of key quality and operational performance requirements. Undoubtedly, the Baldrige made a major contribution in the late 1980s and early 1990s to creating a common language of quality within large American manufacturing firms and those involved with them in production activities.

The 1980s was an era of competing gurus (Juran versus Crosby versus Deming versus Feigenbaum versus Ishikawa) and dueling consultants. The Baldrige laid these debates largely to rest, providing a road map of the issues companies needed to address for achieving sustained quality improvement. It dramatically reduced uncertainty and confusion for managers seeking to find the most productive path to quality improvement. In so doing, it reshaped power relationships among organizational actors, putting consultants in a somewhat more supportive rather than a leadership role, interpreting for managers what the Baldrige criteria meant and helping them to implement it. This subordinate role, however, lasted only until the emergence of the consultant-led business process reengineering movement of the early 1990s.

Through the active leadership of a remarkable civil servant, Curt Reimann, the first award program director at NIST, the designers, led by NIST, developed the criteria for the award through framework design and development involving interviewing some 75 leaders from different quality communities throughout the country and examining various other award programs. One of the consequences of this effort was that the final criteria operationalized many of the key ideas of the gurus. The original 1988 criteria had seven basic categories (leadership, information and analysis, strategic quality planning, human resource utilization, quality assurance for products and services, quality results from quality assurance of products and services, and customer satisfaction). These in turn built on 44 subcategories and a total of 62 examination items. The heaviest weight was given to customer satisfaction (30%). These criteria did more to create a "dominant design" for how to do quality improvement than any other of the infrastructural activities described in this chapter. It became, for a number of years at least, the driving force of a national movement.

The Baldrige was inspired by the Japanese Deming Prize, but the Baldrige designers were under strong pressure to create a uniquely American version of a national quality award and they did just that. The Baldrige is transparent; the Deming prize is opaque, to be illuminated only under the expert guidance of Deming Prize counselors. The Baldrige provides a generic distilling of central quality principles. It is to the Deming as the SAT is to a unique PhD dissertation. Moreover, there were numerous differences in content between the two awards, including the strong focus on results and outcomes in the Baldrige. The net result was that it was quite easy for American firms to use the Baldrige without being reminded that it was stimulated by the Japanese Deming Prize. Moreover, judging by the spread of Baldrige-like awards around the world, apparently quality leaders in most countries believe that the generic, SAT-like Baldrige is more suitable to volume production and broad involvement than the Deming Prize. The Baldrige office estimates that some 30 countries have or are planning to have a national quality award, with about 90% of them directly modeled on the Baldrige. In 1998, the Japanese were even considering a Baldrige-like award.

More important, the Baldrige protocol proved extraordinarily useful in defining key areas to be addressed for quality improvement over a range of critical areas. The transparency of the Baldrige protocol meant that, unlike with the Deming Prize, firms could do their own self-assessment (though many opted to work with external consultants) to identify opportunities for improvement. The protocol is essentially an assessment framework for telling companies where and in what ways they must demonstrate proficiency to attain superior quality performance.

How was it that the Baldrige protocol proved so useful in defining best practices? First, it was not prescriptive so that those creating the protocol did not engage in trying to micromanage which specific business practices should be adopted. Second, the NIST creators of the protocol actively sought a broad mix of industry and academic views and thus could provide a relatively comprehensive evaluation of what was needed, compared to the parochial consultant views dominant in the mid-1980s. Third, the mechanism of annual review and revision gave examiners and other interested parties the opportunity to modify the protocol to fit changing environmental conditions and to incorporate new learning and understanding.

These annual updates proved especially important, as they allowed the Baldrige to stay current and to build in new developments into its overall framework. Thus, when business process reengineering (BPR) came along in the 1990s, it was marketed by the consultant promoters Hammer and Champy (1993) as totally different from quality improvement. They positioned it as the reengineering of the major business processes of the firm using information technology strategically to produce large-scale improvements. They contrasted this with the incremental improvements wrought by the process improvement activities of the quality movement. Indeed, when BPR burst on the scene, the Baldrige criteria did not explicitly distinguish between incremental and breakthrough improvement; its presentation of process improvement had a decidedly incremental tone (Cole, 1994a).

In response, however, the architects of Baldrige simply used their annual improvement process to distinguish and emphasize both large-scale and small-scale process improvements into the 1992 guidelines (strengthened in 1993). Similar kinds of reconstitution occurred in the mid-1990s in response to the widespread popular interest in creating a balanced scorecard for assessing and driving business performance. This constant reconfiguration of Baldrige criteria allowed its architects not only to stay current but also to always position the criteria and the quality movement as an advocate of best practices.[13] This allows them to keep pace with how competitive companies are responding to more demanding markets. There is much to be said for this strategy.

Nevertheless, there are risks. In moving toward an overall business management model, the designers run the risk of the award becoming so diffuse that it loses its core emphasis on processes and customers. In particular, the rapidly declining number of points devoted to customers, down from 300 of the total 1,000 in 1988 to 80 in 1997, dilutes the very distinguishing feature that made the Baldrige so unique in the first place. While the Baldrige leaders at NIST stress that point totals are not the main message, they ignore the signal that the changing point totals conveys to practitioners.

Over one million copies of the Baldrige protocol were distributed to potential users by the mid-1990s; the peak was 240,000 in 1991. The mechanism for distributing criteria had changed by 1996. In that year, approximately 150,000 copies were distributed by the Baldrige office and 82,000 copies were distributed by state and local programs. Moreover, the Baldrige criteria were put on the web in 1996, and that site received nearly 50,000 hits in that same year; how many downloaded the criteria is not known. Bemowski and Stratton (1995: 43) surveyed those who ordered or purchased single or bulk copies of the criteria between 1992 and 1995 (effective response rate of 28.6%). Eighteen percent of the respondents indicated that neither they nor their companies used the Baldrige protocol, but 22% reported that they had used them at least once a week in the past 12 months. In Figure 6.1, I report their specific use of the Baldrige criteria. Strikingly, only 24% reported using the criteria to apply for the award. Rather, as shown in Figure 6.1, the most common uses involved setting performance standards, improvement, and diagnostic activities. Literature distributed by the Baldrige office promotes both self-assessment and award applications.

In the early 1990s it became quite common for top management in many large companies to use the Baldrige to assess their company to see where they stood and to target weak areas they uncovered for improvement. More recently, a 1996 survey reports that 37% of the Fortune 500 companies responding used the Baldrige criteria for self-evaluation (Lackritz, 1997: 71).[14] There were many variations on this theme. Chevron, for example, a highly decentralized company, developed a "quality fitness review" based on the Baldrige and used it as an improvement

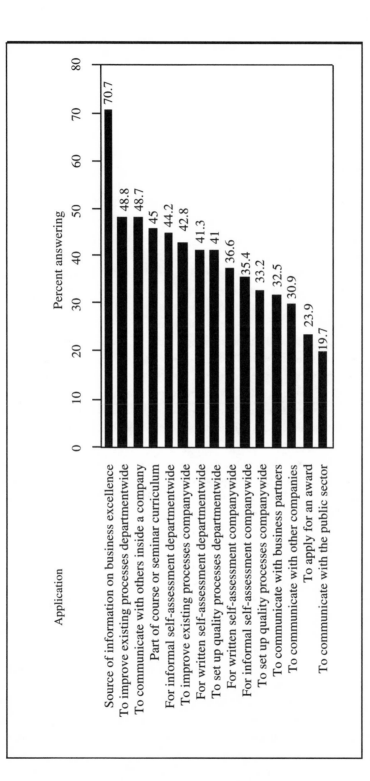

Figure 6.1. Respondents using the Baldridge protocol by type and frequency of use. *Source:* Bemowski and Stratton, 1995: 43.

tool to highlight best practices among the various units (O'Dell and Grayson, 1998). Many firms (e.g., Varian) correlated divisional performance measures with their internally assessed Baldrige scores and rewarded managers for improving Baldrige audit scores. These kinds of activities capture the major significance of the Baldrige award, not how many companies applied for it each year. This distinction escaped *Wall Street Journal* journalists, who in the early 1990s took special relish each year in pointing to the falling number of Baldrige applications.

In terms of building infrastructure, one should also not discount the effects of the training provided the annually appointed crop of examiners. The Baldrige staff have been training some 260 unpaid volunteers a year. The average examiner served a little over two years between 1988 and 1996. Private sector companies, and increasingly schools and hospitals in recent years, have routinely sent their key quality personnel to receive training as Baldrige examiners. Returning to their firm, they brought the added expertise with them. Each year's Baldrige examiner class created important national networks for the diffusion of best practice ideas. Another spinoff involved the obligations of winners of the Baldrige to publicize their quality activities. By 1996, the twenty four winners had given more than 20,000 presentations about what they accomplished and how they achieved their results.

Still another spin-off of the Baldrige was the creation of state and local awards modeled on it. By 1997, there were more than 40 states with quality awards with their own set of examiners and award protocols that were being distributed to wider audiences. Curt Reimann estimated that in the mid-1990s there were some 2,000 additional volunteer evaluators at this level (undoubtedly with some overlap with Baldrige trained examiners). The very growth of the state awards, actively promoted by the national Baldrige organization, partially explains the fall in the number of applications for the national award. While the number of national applicants has fallen steadily from a high of 106 in 1991 to 26 in 1997, the number of state applicants continues to rise, standing at 800 in 1996. Many companies and trade associations also adopted Baldrige-based award systems.

Finally, an army of consultants began to provide diagnostic support for firms that needed hand-holding, thereby multiplying the effects of the Baldrige protocol (e.g., Brown, 1994). Many of these consultants received training as Baldrige examiners; based on my analysis of 1995 data, I estimate that some 29% of all examiners were consultants. Consultants, if successful, almost by definition have broad networks; their economic incentive to become examiners is closely related to their ability to use the acquired expertise over a broad base of clients.

One final word on the sharing activities of companies that won the Baldrige. Certainly, these sharing activities were one of the conditions that firms agreed to in accepting the Baldrige award. Beyond that, however, companies seem to be quite willing to engage in these activities. Executives involved in the quality movement often observe that the quality arena seemed to encourage an unprecedented sharing of information. As one leading Fortune 500 executive responsible for quality said to me, "In all my career as an executive involved in many different functions, I have never seen such an area as quality in the 1980s and early 1990s in which so much information was shared so openly by our company and other companies." The explanation for this phenomenon does not appear to be the dawning of a new day. One important factor behind this sharing was that managers recognized the secret of quality improvement to be in its implementation and execution. This meant one could talk openly and not greatly fear that a competitor could quickly copy one's efforts.

Put more generally, learning broad principles (declarative knowledge) and even practical dos and don'ts was not the same as doing (procedural knowledge). This would explain why the Japanese quality leaders also seemed so open in sharing their experiences with American companies in the 1980s. It also helps explain why it took so long for imitation to take place in a way that began to show modest success. A second factor in explaining this generous sharing of information was that the quality challenge was exogenous, and thus American firms acted to collaborate where possible against a common enemy.

In summary, the Baldrige was the key institutional creation in overcoming the conflicting advice and confusion that dominated the early 1980s. It literally created a dominant design. While it did not prescribe specific action, it nevertheless laid out a clear road map of the terrain that had to be traversed for quality improvement to take hold. Its national prominence legitimated and promoted the quality movement as no other institutional innovation described in this chapter. Using the idea of a competitive award as bait, it led to an extraordinary sharing of information across companies based on a common quality language. Of course, the award has had its critics, who had a field day sniping at its failings, such as the bankruptcy of one of the early winners (Wallace Company) and the decision to give the 1990 award to the Cadillac division of GM (poor judgment because it failed to anticipate the public reaction to an award decision that naively emphasized improvement over time versus the absolute performance relative to Cadillac competitors). None of this diminishes, however, the powerful impact of the Baldrige. Yet, by the mid-1990s, the Baldrige was overshadowed by the rise of the ISO 9000 standard.

ISO 9000 Series

The ISO 9000 series of quality standards burst on the American scene in the early 1990s and increasingly became the initiative of choice in the quality arena, initially for large multinational manufacturing firms but over time increasingly for small and medium firms in a broad range of industries.

Building on prior standards, especially the British Standard Institute's BS 5750 series, the ISO 9000 series was created in 1987 by the ISO in Geneva. The final standards reflected considerable input from experts in America, Canada, and England. They were adopted that same year by the United States as the ANSI/ASQC Q90 standard series. A voluntary professional organization, ASQ assumed responsibility for managing the adoption of the ISO 9000 as American national standards.

It set up a separately incorporated affiliate, the Registrar Accreditation Board (RAB), to accredit the third-party registrars who would carry out registrations. As with the Baldrige, there has been an explosive growth of U.S.–based firms offering consulting services, assessment, and, increasingly, quality system registration as well. One U.S. quality director of a major corporation refers to ISO 9000 as "a full employment act for consultants." The standards were intended to be advisory and were developed primarily for two-party contractual situations or for internal auditing (Kelada, 1996). As is often the case in organizational life, however, intentions and outcomes are two quite different matters.

The ISO 9000 standards are aimed at ensuring consistency in the production of a product or service. The most comprehensive of the standards, ISO 9001 confirms process conformance from the initial product development stage through production, test, installation, and servicing. It is based on a three-tiered system of documents: a quality manual, procedures, and tasks. The quality manual documents the quality policies and objectives to which the supplier commits and specifies the responsibilities of the personnel charged with implementation. Based on the quality manual, the procedures (second tier), are developed for each broad (interdepartmental) system element. The last tier of documents is the departmental step-by-step directions at the task level (Corrigan, 1994: 34–35). Third-party auditors or registration services typically evaluate both the existence of a comprehensive documentation system and the supplier's adherence to that system in practice. Thus, ISO 9000 certification does not measure the quality of a product or service but simply confirms whether a company has fully documented its quality control procedures, whatever they are, and whether they are adhering to them.[15]

These standards might have remained the obscure province of standard experts were it not for the events unfolding in Europe in the early 1990s. The decision to unify the European market by 1992 required removing all barriers to free movement of goods, services, capital, and persons. As part of this effort, the European Community (EC) sought to assure buyers, wherever they were located in the EC, of the quality of goods and services they were purchasing. In this spirit, they proposed replacing national standards of quality management with a common quality assurance system that could be applied through the member states. The EC recommended the use of EN 29000 (European version of the ISO 9000 standard). Based on this, ISO 9000 requirements were built into the quality base in some European directives. Moreover, the EC has specified classes of products designated as regulated or nonregulated. Regulated products are those that have a health, safety, or environmental impact and are required to be manufactured under ISO 9000 conditions. Yet even with regulated products, there are in principle alternative paths to product certification so that ISO 9000 certification remains voluntary.

The complexity of the laws and expense of alternatives, however, led to the growing perception on the part of many American executives that ISO 9000 was mandatory if one wanted to do business in Europe (Mendel, 1996: 12). Formally speaking, this was a "mismessage" according to Jacques McMillan, head of the

Quality Policy, Certification and Conformity Marking Unit of the European Commission (Zuckerman, 1996: 131–132). Whether or not this is Eurospeak for "we think you had better do it," ISO 9000 increasingly became the de facto European standard; foreign firms that sold into Europe, even in nonregulated markets, including the major American-and Japanese-based multinationals, rushed to receive ISO 9000 registration. As David Vogel (1995) observed in his study of environmental regulation, when a major market player sets a new standard, there is a strong tendency for that standard to be adopted by its trading partners and thus become de facto a world standard.

The use of ISO 9000, however, has diffused since then far beyond the originally perceived regulatory requirements. The demand for ISO 9000 registration has come to be primarily, but not exclusively, market-driven and not just for accessing the European market. It is increasingly the large multinational firms requesting that their domestic suppliers be registered and sometimes making ISO 9000 compliance an integral part of their purchase agreements. A 1996 survey of 250 midsize manufacturers with annual sales of 10–500 million dollars, the Seventh Annual Grant Thornton Survey of American Manufacturers Report, found that by the end of 1998, 52% of midsize U.S. manufacturers intend to be certified in the ISO 9000 series (Sebastian, 1996: A1; Quality, 1997: 16,18). Of the 11% registered, 83% cited improved quality as an outcome, but 66% report their motivation was, "to help increase customer satisfaction." The authors of the survey concluded that registration is in reality often a strategy for customer retention in that many multinational companies will now buy only from certified suppliers.

The multinationals, however, are not just the source of pressure for their suppliers; they are also recipients of pressure. The governments in many less developed countries have decided that ISO 9000 registration is a positive step for their country's industry. In their view, having their export-oriented companies become registered will improve their image in the eyes of the world customer and further their country's reputation as a good place to invest. As an example, in Brazil the government worked with shoe manufacturers to gain registration. In 1997, Thailand announced that all manufacturing companies involved in exports should be registered. Malaysia, Singapore, and China have taken similar steps, some overt, others more subtle. The large multinationals that have manufacturing sites in these countries, such as Motorola, have registered their sites, not for market reasons, but rather to cooperate with the government request, to be "good citizens." Unlike in the United States, the registration body in these countries is typically an arm of the government. It is thus often a matter of coercive isomorphism as purchasers and government bodies increasingly put pressure on sellers to receive ISO 9000 certification or lose their preferred business status or the very business itself.

What are the additional motivations of both purchasers and sellers in adopting ISO 9000? Surveys show some suppliers are adopting ISO 9000 as a marketing tool. In the Grant Thornton survey, 45% of respondents said registration enabled them to gain market advantage, and in a more comprehensive survey by Irwin

Publishing and Dun & Bradstreet Information Services, 73% of registered companies cited market advantage as a benefit (Quality, 1997: 16; Litsikas, 1997: 20). Companies are increasingly pointing out their ISO certification in news releases and other promotional material. Hyundai Electronics America is quoted as saying, "We always mention our certification whenever we can" (Sebastian, 1996: A1). Marketing one's registration is a way, particularly for small or new companies whose quality performance is unknown or suspect, to signal to the market that a respected third party has bestowed the mantle of competency upon them. The thinking is that being ISO 9000 registered gives one a competitive advantage. A purchaser, all things being equal, is more likely to award a contract to a registered supplier.

Suppliers also are adopting ISO 9000 as a way to implement quality improvement in their companies. Indeed, the more comprehensive surveys of registered companies, like the Irwin Publishing and Dun & Bradstreet survey, find that "quality benefits" were cited by 77% of registered companies, scoring higher than any other benefit (Litsikas, 1997: 20). The evidence suggests that many companies have shifted from the Baldrige to ISO 9000 as their chosen vehicle for improving quality. The relative falloff of interest in the Baldrige Award is acknowledged by Curt Reimann, former director of quality programs at NIST: "Our participation rate [in Baldrige activities] also has been affected by the fact that many companies are working on ISO-9000 certification. Although it is a fundamentally different instrument from ours, it is unquestionably diverting their resources, particularly in small companies" (cited in Miller, 1995: 615). Reimann goes on elsewhere to note that companies cannot do both ISO 9000 and the Baldrige at once (Ettorre, 1997: 629). Interestingly, the arrival of ISO 9000 in Japan was reported to have had a similar chilling effect on their well-established total quality control activities (*Nikkei Weekly*, 1994: 12).

How different are the activities and outcomes produced by ISO and those envisioned in the new quality model and built into the Baldrige criteria? In fact, ISO 9000 has a much weaker customer focus and does not address the quality of the actual product or service. It also does not focus on continuous improvement, does not emphasize the ongoing evaluation and improvement of quality system elements, nor does it emphasize the support system and processes needed for continuous improvement like strong employee participation (cf. Corrigan, 1994: 36). The ISO 9000 standards are generic; they represent the minimum requirements that a quality system needs to be effective and ensure the product will meet customer requirements (Kelada, 1996: 326). Not surprisingly then, a systematic comparison of the Baldrige criteria and ISO 9000 requirements show not all that much overlap between the two (Reimann and Hertz, 1993: 42–53). Data from the electronics industry suggest that customers are much more inclined to demand that their suppliers adopt ISO 9000 than the Baldrige. Twelve percent of respondents in 1994 said that customers require, or customers will require, the Baldrige award protocol while 100% of respondents said the same for ISO 9000 (Pittiglio Rabin Todd and McGrath, 1995: 48).[16]

This raises an interesting question about the motivation of purchasers for adopting ISO 9000 and pressing their suppliers to do so as well. Certainly, ISO 9000 is intended to ensure the adequacy of a supplier's quality system and to ensure the supplier is adhering to that system. This seems to be, however, of secondary importance relative to having a supplier with a strong customer orientation (both the purchaser and final user) geared to continuous quality improvement, to competitive activity, and to winning market share. The standard response of ISO 9000 adherents is that ISO was not intended for this latter purpose, and they are correct. One might think, however, that companies would be more focused on ways to maximize their competitive edge.

What then are the benefits of ISO 9000 registration as seen by customers? Many customers are making ISO 9000 registration an integral part of their purchase agreements with suppliers. They want consistency and a consequent reduction of in-process inspections (Struebing, 1996: 26). On their side, registered firms report a reduction in the number of customer audits (Schnoll, 1993: 39). The auto industry, as we saw in the previous chapter, has set up its own QS-9000 standards built on the ISO 9000 base. Major suppliers of materials and parts are expected to receive third-party certification and eventually so are their direct and indirect suppliers. In this fashion QS-9000 implementation will progress down through the supply chain. The uniformity across the Big Three is expected to reduce the costs that come from suppliers having to create different quality assurance systems to satisfy their different customers and being subjected to different audit systems. The OEMs will also save on the need for auditors (though indirectly they bear the costs of the auditors for QS-9000 being used by their suppliers). These kinds of outcomes, while less good than the benefits to be achieved from implementing the new quality model, nevertheless are appealing to firms and more easily within reach. These kinds of benefits, if they materialize, are not trivial, but they are also not of the magnitude that one might anticipate would flow from sharply and continuously improving product and service quality based on correctly reading present customer needs and anticipating and creating future ones.

In a similar vein, ISO 9000 registration has become a ubiquitous shorthand for quality compliance, the ISO 9000 check box for screening suppliers and their performance. This is particularly pronounced in the electronics industry. With more and more parts of manufacturing and back-office operations being outsourced, ISO 9000 increasingly serves as a quick first cut in supplier selection (Hunt, 1997: 45).

The fundamental idea of ISO 9000 was to assure buyers of the goods and services they were receiving. Put differently, ISO 9000 is an attempt to minimize an asymmetric information problem in which the seller knows a great deal more about the quality of a product or service than the purchaser. The assumption, not a trivial one, is that by being assured that the seller is using and adhering to consistent process standards, the buyer will be better able to predict the quality of the product or service it is receiving. Yet the buyer may be more interested in the quality of the product or service than its consistency. Quality system registration, in fact, does relatively little to guarantee the former. In short, the correlation between product quality and ISO 9000 is unknown. In the mid-1990s, The United Kingdom accounted for almost half of all worldwide ISO 9000 registrations. Would anyone claim that this was matched by their superior quality performance? If ISO 9000 were even modestly correlated with quality performance, that might help reduce the information asymmetry experienced by purchasers. However, no one knows the extent of that correlation and its determinants in given industries. So we have seemingly rational actors acting boldly in the face of great uncertainty.

Given the weakness of ISO 9000 relative to its own objectives of relieving the asymmetric information problem between buyers and sellers, what then is the appeal of ISO 9000 over implementing some version of the new quality model? To understand the answer to this question, one needs to know how management acts under conditions of uncertainty. By uncertainty, I refer to an inability of actors to estimate future consequences conditional on present actions. Uncertainty is a limitation on understanding and intelligence (March, 1994: 178).

Many firms had been acting for a long period to adopt various elements of the new quality model, usually under the label of TQM. What was the result? At a minimum, they had found the going exceedingly rough, despite heavy investments. Some abandoned the effort. Others made only modest progress with much effort, and only a few claimed outstanding success in both adopting the new quality model and in reaping the rewards associated with that adoption. Interestingly, the most vociferous critics of ISO 9000 and third-party registration have been leading quality officials at those companies, like Motorola and HP, which were most successful in mastering the new quality model.

Although the expected value of success for adopting the new quality model was seen as high, there has been great variance in the probability of success. In short, pursuing the new quality model continues to be seen as risky behavior. Recall that the Baldrige criteria, while laying out a road map, are not prescriptive. Moreover, the criteria's successful application rests very much on the interaction with the peculiar conditions and history of a particular firm. The particular preferences of consultants add to the variation. For small and medium-size firms just starting out, the Baldrige looks both comprehensive and overwhelming. By contrast, ISO 9000 is based on a simple methodology summarized by one manager for me as "document what you do, do what you document, and verify that you are doing it."

When faced with an alternative that is less good but more certain, managers are likely to choose the latter. Managers prefer packaged solutions whose cost and outcome are, if not guaranteed, at least defined and limited. The ISO 9000 is being marketed as a package that is definitely workable within a specific time frame with known costs; firms can be almost guaranteed that if they make a good faith effort, they will be certified, if not on the first attempt, then on the second or third. The Irwin Publishing and Dun and Bradstreet survey found that 85% of the registered companies reported they were successful on their first attempt. Of those not successful, 13% reported that it took them another 4.6 months to attain registration (Litsikas, 1997: 24).[17] This suggests some modest mystery in ISO 9000; while ISO standards tell a company what must be in their quality manual, they do not tell them how to document the quality system or what constitutes adherence to the standards. Nevertheless, there apparently was not all that much mystery given the high initial success rate. Overall, application of ISO 9000 appears much more stable from one company and consultant to the next than does the Baldrige protocol.

In principle, firms should be able to pursue continuous improvement and customer-focused activities aimed at winning market share at the same time as they aim for ISO 9000 registration. Indeed, the typical advice of those experts who are not exclusive adherents of the one or the other approach is exactly that. One should integrate ISO 9000 registration into the TQM effort through building TQM on the foundation of a strong, well-documented quality system is the standard refrain (e.g., Corrigan 1994: 36; Kelada, 1996: 340–341). Certainly, many companies try to do that. Moreover, if one examines QS 9000 being promoted by the Big Three in the auto industry and SSQA being promoted by SEMATECH in the semiconductor industry, one sees that they both involve integrating ISO 9000 and Baldrige ideas.

However, it is widely recognized that the rise of ISO 9000 has led to a concomitant fall of interest in Baldrige self-assessment and improvement activities. Many managers are confused, and the two very different approaches are often depicted as equivalent (Reimann and Hertz, 1993: 52). Under these circumstances, managers find it quite reasonable to select ISO 9000, the easier, more clearly specified approach. It becomes an even easier decision if one's customer is demanding ISO 9000 registration.

Managers have only so much attention and energy to devote to quality. As James March notes, time and capabilities for attention are limited. If managers and their subordinates receive too many signals, they get confused, have trouble prioritizing, and have to take into consideration too many factors to get their job done (1994: 10). Under these circumstances, there are strong incentives to simplify by focusing on one alternative solution to the exclusion of the other even if the official message of top management says we are doing both. Put more colloquially, Georg Lofgren, RAB President, says, "People like to oversimplify things; they look for the silver bullet in quality. They ask: what is the one thing I need to do?" (Hillary, 1996: 35).

What happens once ISO 9000 registration is achieved and before re-registration is required three years later? In principle, it is possible to return to implementing elements of the new quality model in the interim, and indeed that is what many ISO 9000 advocates recommend. Do companies actually do that? To my knowledge, there is no clear-cut survey data on that point. However, the popular wisdom is that many firms seem to act as though they have taken care of the quality problem once ISO 9000 registration is achieved. This fits with a behavioral theory of decision making. Achieving the target of registration contains within it the sense of completion. With quality improvement as with other matters, managers are more likely to satisfice than maximize. Satisficing is a search rule that specifies the conditions under which search is triggered or stopped (March, 1994: 27). Achieving registration is usually interpreted as achievement of the target and thus decreases search behavior.

Data on one industrial sector, electronics, bear on these matters. The data suggest that companies tend to pursue a unitary path to broad objectives like quality improvement. The data are from an annual survey aiming to tap a cross section of high-technology industries, commissioned by the AEA.[18] In 1992, some 10% of responding firms (AEA member firms are mostly small companies) reported using ISO 9000 only, 23% reported using both ISO 9000 and the Baldrige criteria, and 17% reported using only the Baldrige. By 1994, the number reporting using only ISO 9000 rose dramatically to 46%, the percentage reporting using both fell modestly to 18%, and the number using only the Baldrige almost disappeared, falling to 3% (Pittiglio Rabin Todd & McGrath, 1995: 46). In short, over time one sees a striking shift away from Baldrige, with more and more firms relying only on ISO 9000. Interestingly, one does not see the same falloff in firms reporting they are using TQM. That makes sense, since it would be suicidal to approach the market armed only with the kind of consistency induced by ISO 9000 registration. Rather, it is the Baldrige and ISO 9000 that apparently were seen as competitive alternatives to many executives, at least in these firms.

Originally, ISO 9000 was adopted by organizations that saw it as a requirement for doing business in given markets. Implicit in the preceding account is a rapid diffusion in the mid-1990s driven by managers who increasingly view it as a way to manage quality and customer relationships to ensure consistency of performance. With a growing density of adoption, particularly by pattern-setting large firms, the standards became a normative and cognitive model for how professional managers behave (Mendel, 1996). As Mendel notes, these understandings are further reinforced by a professional community of consultants, registrars, and within-firm advocates marketing ISO 9000 as the way to improve quality and a firm's competitive performance by showing the ISO seal of approval. With the spread of ISO 9000 standards, managers were encouraged once again to narrow the meaning of quality to consistency, to delegate it to lower levels, and to detach it from overall competitive performance. It remains to be seen to what extent the nature of competitive activities will provide sufficient incentives for managers to resist these pressures.

Conclusion

This account of the six institutional activities at the national level captures many of the central characteristics of the rich infrastructure that emerged. Notable are the variegated approaches and the different constituencies reached by each organizational initiative. These infrastructure organizations arose to link manufacturing organizations to one another, and in so doing they filled strategic social locations. In a variety of quality technologies, a complex pattern of cooperation and competition developed among the various information and training providers. This emergent infrastructure was critical in facilitating learning and in converting learning to understandings and actions more closely related to effective practice. Thus, these organizational activities reduced knowledge barriers for the potential adopters, thereby speeding up diffusion and implementation (cf. Attewell, 1996: 203–229). The infrastructure also facilitated a kind of organizational isomorphism among the adopters as the content of the various organizational providers merged over time. In so doing, they contributed to the emergence of dominant designs.

Earlier, I noted the contrast between the highly organized model for development, identification, and diffusion of best practices in Japan whereby JUSE monitored developments among firms and brought them back to the center for digesting, synthesizing, and certifying. The most successful practices were then fed back to member companies through various training and education activities.

The model presented of the U.S. infrastructure in this chapter is more chaotic, befitting perhaps the greater suspicion of centrally derived solutions in the United States and the greater geographical dispersion of industry. Although it may not be as efficient as the Japanese approach, it may be just as effective. The highly decentralized structure meant that there were ample opportunities for experimentation in different settings. Yet one sees a remarkable emergent consensus among opinion leaders in different industries and locations over time as to what is important and what is the next step. This becomes particularly pronounced by the late 1980s and reflects perhaps above all the unifying element provided by the Baldrige. While there is a multitude of infrastructure organizations aimed at specific niches of the market, there is also a variety of linkages among the organizations reflected in both competitive and cooperative activities. At the same time, the large manufacturing companies typically participated in multiple networks, building in further cohesion and consistency.

Major manufacturing firms participated in organizations like the Conference Board's Quality Councils, GOAL/QPC, ASQ, CQM, and in designing Baldrige criteria as well as in their respective industry and trade organizations. In doing so, they participated in a process by which influential actors shaped each other's perceptions of what quality improvement was and how they should go about achieving it. Much more than simple imitation is involved here; it was an iterative process of learning, as the major manufacturing corporations, sharing their experiences through participation in infrastructure activities, experimented with implementing a variety of new practices. As they co-evolved the new practices, these major firms, in turn, became models for firms further down the food chain. Major mechanisms for the further diffusion of these best practice ideas for those firms outside the central networks were Baldrige training; diagnostic and award winners' sharing sessions; consultant activity; OEM dictums and training activities for their suppliers;

ASQ's dissemination activities through its journal, annual convention, publication, chapter and divisional activities, training, and certification activities; and company-to-company networking and benchmarking. At the industry level, we also saw how the Baldrige and ISO 9000 became the basis for SEMATECH's offerings to the OEM suppliers, which in turn were used by the offspring of SEMATECH like the WCQF to reach suppliers of SEMATECH members. In trickle-down fashion, many of these suppliers, responding to pressure from their customers, adopted initiatives to improve the quality of products they were receiving from their own even smaller suppliers. In so doing, they further adapted the SEMATECH materials.

The interpretation of the infrastructure for diffusing new quality practices just presented is that these efforts, even when competitive, by and large were additive and complementary. One exception involved the complex role of consultants. Clearly, they often contributed to the spread of new practices and helped to bridge the gap between learning and doing with their hands-on in-house training and mentoring. Yet, with their strong economic incentives to differentiate their products, they often acted against the building block model of development and contributed to faddish adoptions and abandonments. In a similar fashion, the rise to prominence of the ISO 9000 standard engendered a competition among infrastructural organizations and in their targeted business firms, calling into question the emergent dominant design. The ISO 9000 standard led many companies to see certification as an end in itself. In that fashion, it diverted attention from quality improvement per se and weakened the appeal of Baldrige-inspired ideas. Also ISO 9000 gave new ammunition to those opponents of quality improvement initiatives by strengthening the view that quality improvement efforts led to bureaucratization.

None of the previous discussion is intended to suggest that this rich infrastructure, by itself, fully solved the problem of how to convert the declarative knowledge contained in the new quality paradigm to procedural knowledge and effective practice. It was still necessary for firms to try out the ideas on quality improvement and to adjust for the unique setting each firm provided. In short, there is a learning-by-doing aspect of converting learning to effective practice that was essential even once a rich and dense infrastructure was in place. In the following two chapters, I provide a case study of how one firm sought to absorb, adopt, and adapt the new understandings in productive ways.

CHAPTER 7

Modeling the Future for Hewlett-Packard

Much of the discussion in this book has been about the enormous uncertainty that gripped top managers in large U.S. manufacturing firms in the early 1980s as they came to realize that their Japanese competitors had opened up a large quality advantage over them. They did not understand the basis for the Japanese success, and there were many competing explanations as to the cause of the American industry problem and how to eliminate the quality gap. In Chapter 3, I discussed the importance of organizations obtaining the earliest available information to resolve actor uncertainty. The earliest good information that becomes progressively available in distinct social locations shows actors the direction successful competitors have taken.

To be the first to grasp and act successfully on knowledge about the new quality model often meant one could gain advantage over competitors if they were American or quickly eliminate competitive disadvantages if they were Japanese. For this reason I cited Stinchcombe's observation that it is crucial for an organization to be where the news breaks whenever it breaks. Most Japanese manufacturing companies had yet to establish production facilities in the United States at this time and thus were unavailable to model the necessary behavior. Nor had an institutional infrastructure of the type I described in the preceding chapter yet been built. Therefore, the social location at which good information was available on quality improvement in the early 1980s was primarily Japan. This information could be obtained through observing the behavior of large export-oriented manufacturing firms.

Few American companies chose to learn quality improvement directly from the Japanese. Even so, a set of firms was uniquely positioned to learn the new quality model from the Japanese reasonably quickly. These were firms that had either equity shares in Japanese firms, joint ventures with Japanese firms in Japan, or subsidiaries in Japan. If one adds to this total, the large number of American firms with long-standing Japanese suppliers that could have shared information with their customers, one has in fact a very large number of American manufacturing firms with a potential pipeline into Japan. This pipeline, while costly to develop, could have been leveraged to allow these firms to enter into a sustained learning relationship for mastering the new quality model. Yet most of these U.S. firms chose not to be where the news was breaking in a way that engaged them in sustained learning about the new quality model. Few of them even contemplated the possibility. Many made half-hearted efforts that involved the one-or two-week tours by key executives.

Firms that already had ties to Japan were better positioned than others in the early 1980s to draw upon Japanese expertise. Because HP had a long-standing management philosophy of international expansion, they were one of these firms. Potentially, this gave them a systematic learning advantage over those firms without such ties. Not every large Japanese manufacturing corporation, however, was a source of potential learning. If one happened to be tied to one that was not, clearly there was not much to be gained by working with them. Thus, GM had its strongest equity ties in Japan to Isuzu, primarily a truck manufacturer, with no strong expertise in the quality area that could be applied to passenger car production.

Some firms that chose to use their joint ventures for learning about quality were not very successful. I have already noted the experience of the NUMMI joint venture between Toyota and GM (production began in December 1984). Despite GM's very explicit intent to enter into this relationship in order to learn the Toyota production system and to spread it to the rest of the corporation, their progress has been painfully slow. A reading of the literature suggests that this slowness may be attributed to four factors: GM's failure to send the appropriate personnel, their failure to use the personnel rotated into NUMMI effectively, the inherent lack of transparency of many of the target practices, and the lack of receptivity of GM's middle management to NUMMI's example (e.g., Ingrassia and White, 1994: 41–59, 352–353). In short, intent to learn from joint venture arrangements is no guarantee of success (see also Hamel, 1991).

However, a small number of firms noted for their early effective adoption of the new quality model appears to have effectively used Japanese sources to help drive their effort. Notable were FPL with its Kansai Electric ties, Ford Motor Company using its Mazda and Nippon Densō relationships, HP learning from its joint venture Yokogawa Hewlett-Packard (YHP), and Xerox drawing on its joint venture with Fuji, Fuji Xerox. My own reading of the literature, as well as interviews and personal experiences, suggests that of these three cases, Xerox relied far less on its Japanese source than Ford in the middle and HP and FPL at the high end of the continuum. Fuji Xerox officials I interviewed in 1989 claimed that Xerox had "only scratched the surface in their efforts to learn from them." Main (1994: 26) arrives at a similar conclusion, observing that top management at HP was more responsive to the lessons of YHP than was Xerox to Fuji Xerox. Finally, a reading of the account of Xerox's march toward quality by Xerox's former CEO, David Kearns (Kearns and Nadler, 1992), suggests that Fuji Xerox served primarily as a model for Xerox of what could be accomplished rather than as a teacher of how to do it. Xerox relied heavily on Fuji Xerox as a site for the development of its benchmarking capabilities (just as Ford used Mazda). By serving as a model for what could be accomplished, Fuji Xerox helped Xerox managers raise their sights as to what was possible at a critical time. This was a much more limited exchange compared to what occurred between HP and YHP and between FPL and Kansai Electric.

When one talks about one organization learning from another, one thinks of how one organization serves as a model for another; an organization can serve as a model in a variety of different ways. However, management is not about learning per se; management is about creating something of value. This is a point that many academics on the learning organization bandwagon of the 1990s seem to forget. As psychologists learned long ago, learning is not the same as doing. I am interested in how one organization successfully transfers a specific practice or set of practices to another in a way that adds value to the receiving firm. Prior research shows that imitation is often quite difficult (Nelson and Winter, 1982). Therefore, I will pay special attention to those modes of transfer that best close the gap between learning and effective practice. Indeed, my working hypothesis is that organizations that succeed best with technology transfer not only aggressively seek out learning but also best bridge the gap between learning and practice.

This chapter is devoted to describing and analyzing the role that YHP played in the adoption of elements of the new quality model at HP.[1] I hope to show first that learning directly from the Japanese about quality improvement was indeed possible.[2] A second goal is to clarify the process by which this occurred. We also will see the special set of circumstances that enabled this learning process to proceed as well as it did; again, simple intent is insufficient to bring about the desired outcome. My discussion will include the kinds of adaptations that HP managers believed they had to make to Japanese practices in order to get them accepted in an HP culture that was suspicious of centrally directed solutions. Consistent with my observations in the previous chapter, YHP was important to HP because YHP was tightly linked to the most progressive quality community in Japan, JUSE; YHP's top executives, managers, and workers regularly received education/training provided by JUSE. And YHP had regular consulting services from two of the leading quality practitioners in Japan: Dr. Kaoru Ishikawa (1976, 1981) and Dr. Hitoshi Kume (1976–1993). This enabled YHP to enact many of the most innovative practices. Thus, by extension HP was able to tap into the whole Japanese infrastructure for quality improvement.

Senders and Receivers

To assess a process of learning and technology transfer, one needs to know the characteristics of the sender and the receiver at the time of the transfer. These characteristics will also tell us much about the prospects for success. As comedians and "garbage can" theorists often note, timing is everything.

The receiver here is Hewlett-Packard Corporation with headquarters in the United States and facilities around the world. In 1980, HP had sales of 3 billion dollars and 57,000 employees. This was a dramatic increase from sales of 365 million dollars and 16,000 employees in 1970. In the early 1980s, consistent with its tradition of rapid growth and change, HP was undergoing major evolutionary, even revolutionary changes.

The company had prospered with its integrated multidivisional form structure of autonomous product-oriented divisions. This decentralized form allowed the company to grow rapidly, spinning off new divisions as product lines either achieved self-sufficiency or when an existing division got too large. The rough cut point used for creating a new division was more than 1,000 people and/or 100 million dollars in annual revenues. Each division functioned more or less as a stand-alone entity containing all the resources and functional specialties it needed to support its profit-making activities (Beckman, 1996: 159; Kanter: 1983: 170).

These practices came under increasing pressure in the 1980s in the search for a corporationwide response to a variety of challenges. By the late 1970s, HP was going through a major transition from batch production, using highly skilled, high-priced labor (building product by hand basically) in what was largely their instrumentation business (electronic test and measuring) toward high-volume, high-quality production for their emergent computer products businesses. This shift also involved a move from stand-alone instruments to products like computer terminals that had to interact well with whole systems. These new markets required both higher productivity and quality (cf. Main, 1994: 27). Moreover, HP was starting to sell to end users who were not themselves engineers, but rather individuals who expected the product to work immediately. Success in the consumer market required that HP develop new marketing expertise and a means to tap into individual customer expectations. The "next bench method" had been working well at HP, wherein design engineers determined what customers might need by determining what appealed to the HP engineer working at the next bench (Packard, 1995: 97). That worked fine when customers were all engineers, but it was increasingly an inadequate guide as HP's customer base expanded. All this was occurring in an increasingly competitive environment.

Some HP managers believe that the quality of HP products stagnated, if not actually declined, in the 1970s as the company shifted from vacuum tubes to highly integrated circuits and as they entered the computer market. The traditional test and fix, test and fix, test and fix cycle that worked with vacuum tubes and batch production was not suitable for the mass production of highly complex products such as integrated circuits. Moreover, rapid growth of the company, the creation of new divisions, and new employees not steeped in the "HP way," all may have contributed to a stagnation, if not a decline, of quality. Managers were struggling to deal with these problems.

As all these changes and challenges were buffeting HP, the Japanese quality challenge became apparent. The forces driving search behavior and actual changes in manufacturing and market expertise among managers at HP, to a large extent, were endogenous, not exogenous. While the Japanese quality challenge was external, the changes required for an effective response meshed well with the internally evolving pressures to which HP's top managers were beginning to respond. Thus, they were already searching for new approaches to manufacturing, to quality improvement, and for ways to more effectively serve consumer markets. Recall that it was an HP official who shocked the U.S. electronics industry with his public announcement in 1980 that Japanese chip suppliers had vastly superior reliability levels.

One can contrast this situation to that of GM and many other companies where the challenge was truly exogenous; managers saw the changes required for quality improvement to be totally at variance with what they knew, what they believed worked well, and where they believed the company needed to go. Denial, not public acknowledgment, was the operative response. Accustomed to working with a mature technology subject only to incremental changes and working from a position of market strength seemingly secure from new entries, GM was "fat and happy" when the Japanese quality challenge hit. Unlike the situation at HP, and contrary to popular views, there is no objective indication that automotive quality was declining prior to the Japanese challenge of the early 1980s. Nor was there any indication that automotive managers perceived quality as a matter requiring special attention, much less new approaches at this time.

By contrast, HP managers, as we have seen, were already "discontented" and "running hard" to adjust to their changing market circumstances. At the same time many key elements of TQC—focus on the customer, continuous improvement, and workforce participation—seemed very consistent with HP's deeply held core values and experiences (cf. Packard, 1995). This was a company that, in its relatively short history, had been characterized by rapid growth, change, and adaptation. Indeed, many top managers would see a discontent with the status quo as a key element in HP culture. Thus, if opportunities for learning from the Japanese, and YHP in particular, could be presented in the right way at this time, they stood a reasonable chance of meeting a relatively friendly reception. The situation described here is quite consistent with the observation of Ralph Stacey (1996) that organizational creativity occurs when an organization is operating between stability and chaos.

In the late 1970s the corporate quality function was fairly centralized and had considerable clout within the corporation; after all, HP prided itself as being a quality leader. Corporate quality, however, was largely oriented to product quality (typically hardware) narrowly defined. Its emphasis was on quality as an "industrial hygienic" factor; that is, failure to deliver it would lead to customer dissatisfaction, but it was not seen as helpful in delivering positive increases in customer satisfaction and loyalty that would result in higher market share and better business performance. It short, HP did not see quality as a strategic competitive issue.

I turn now to the characteristics of the sender (YHP) as it acted to transfer ideas and practices about quality improvement to the receiver (HP). In 1963 YHP was started as 51% Yokogawa Denki (the leading industrial instrument manufacturer in Japan) and 49% HP. This was the maximum equity share allowed for foreign ownership at the time. Gradually, the product line grew in a way that reflected more of HP's business than Yokogawa's, especially as YHP also moved into computer-related products. Then HP began to complain, arguing that Yokogawa was not putting as much into the joint venture as it was. To keep up its end of the bargain, Yokogawa sent over a new R & D manager in 1973 in response to HP's specific request. In total, Yokogawa sent some 150 employees including many managers to the joint venture. These managers came to constitute the core of the YHP management team in the 1980s and included Kenzo Sasaoka, the aforementioned R & D manager, who was to become president and CEO (in 1975) and Katsu Yoshimoto, who was to become Sasaoka's chief aide for quality matters.

In 1983 HP raised the issue of ownership, given that its part of the business had come to account for the overwhelming majority of the joint venture's activities. It wanted full ownership. As a compromise, however, it settled on 75% HP and 25% Yokogawa. The evolution has been such that the Yokogawa people came to see themselves as full members of HP. This is critical to understanding the strong motivation that developed among YHP's senior executives to transfer what they learned about quality to the parent company. It also helps us to understand the strong proselytizing tone of their efforts that developed over time.

These events constituted a most fortuitous factor for HP. Because Yokogawa was a leading manufacturing company, it could attract top-ranking college graduates to the company. The Yokogawa contribution of high-quality human capital to the joint venture in its early years is an important underlying factor facilitating YHP's ability to develop and apply TQC effectively and to transfer it to HP. One need only think about more recent American subsidiaries set up in Japan where the Americans have been forced to recruit from the leavings of first-rank Japanese companies. High-quality Japanese management employees have preferred the security and opportunity provided by large Japanese companies as opposed to working for allegedly high-risk American subsidiary companies. Consequently, the quality of Japanese managers generally recruited to U.S. companies in Japan tended to be far more problematic than it was for the original management team at YHP.[3]

In the mid-1970s, YHP got involved with TQC. It was part of a second wave of Japanese companies looking for ways to overcome the effects of the first oil shock. Leaders at YHP saw TQC as a particularly effective way to deal with their major business problem. As they saw it, this was a high failure rate of HP products delivered to their Japanese customers within a short time after being installed. They used a broad definition of failure that included late delivery, incorrect documents, wrong options, etc. These products were either designed in the United States and assembled in Japan or designed and produced in the United States and sold through YHP in Japan. Together, they accounted for some 85% of YHP sales. The remaining 15% of sales were of products designed and produced in Japan. The failure of HP products, as well as the failure of those designed and produced by YHP itself, was widely seen by employees as a major impediment to the growth and success of the company. As a consequence, employees were disposed to be receptive to the core ideas of TQC.

Throughout the 1970s YHP complained to HP about the quality of the products being sent to Japan, but was rebuffed for the most part. Again and again HP managers told YHP that those problems only seem to happen in Japan, implying there was something peculiar about the Japanese market. As discussed earlier, feedback from other markets indicated that HP was a quality leader, thereby seemingly contradicting the YHP message. Since YHP accounted for a small proportion of HP sales for most divisions, YHP found it did not have much clout with division and production executives. Managers from R & D would ignore them, saying they would correct that in the next design.

At the suggestion of quality assurance (QA) staff, YHP decided to have the firm reviewed by Deming Prize committee experts in late 1976. The review was done by two well-known experts, Professors Ishikawa and Kume. Although YHP senior managers knew they would not perform that well, they were shocked to see how poor a grade they did receive. In March 1977, Sasaoka and his vice president for sales attended a three-day top-management seminar on TQC sponsored by JUSE. This provided additional inspiration and in April 1977, Sasaoka announced YHP's TQC initiative.

By early 1979, YHP was starting to record dramatic performance improvements, and in 1982 they won the Deming Prize. In a sense it won the Deming Prize at just the right time in terms of having an impact on HP. If it had won it much earlier, no one at HP would have appreciated it (recall that the Deming Prize came to the attention of American managers through the *If Japan Can, Why Can't We* TV documentary in 1980). If it had won it later, it would not have attracted so much attention, since by the late 1980s, U.S. companies were winning both the Baldrige and the Deming Awards. Thus, they timing seems to have been perfect for maximizing the potential impact of YHP's TQC activities on HP itself. In the early 1980s, the Deming Prize was surrounded by a mystical positive aura that seemed to confer almost magical benefits on its recipients.

In the early and mid-1970s, YHP was still a struggling division trying to learn the HP system. It was reporting very modest profits (in the mid-1970s its profit rate was about 25% of the average HP division). All this changed rapidly in the late 1970s and early 1980s when YHP achieved the highest profit rate of all HP divisions from 1981 to 1984 (reporting results from 1980 to 1983). There can be no doubt that this improved performance had a dramatic impact on the marketability of YHP's approach to TQC within HP. Former president Sasaoka has the following recollections on this matter:

> Given our past performance on profitability, I usually sat in the back of the room during the annual corporate general manager meeting at which these figures were announced. Now suddenly our Exec. VP and Chief Operating Officer were publicly commending me, and YHP was recognized within HP as the top performer in front of all the general managers and higher level officials. It gave us great visibility in the corporation and made our emphasis on TQC legitimate and persuasive.

One should not underestimate the importance of these financial results for making YHP a viable model for HP. The perception in the early 1980s that TQC produced these results is what mattered. One sees here an extraordinary confluence of forces in which the sending unit and receiving units developed in ways that favored the transfer of quality improvement practices from the one to the other. In the late 1970s and early 1980s the two entities found themselves for very different reasons moving in directions that facilitated the potential for YHP to act as a model for HP in quality improvement. The prior description is very consistent with the garbage can model of decision making, which stresses the serendipitous combinations of problems and solutions in time and space. Decisions and effective action occur when elements from streams of problems, solutions, participants, and opportunities merge. They did indeed come together in ways that led to effective HP-YHP cooperation in response to HP's quality challenge.

Methods and Accomplishments

The first major breakthrough with TQC for YHP was achieved in lowering the wave solder rate of nonconformity from 4,000 parts per million (ppm) in 1977 to 40 ppm in 1979 and eventually, with the help of quality circles, to 3 ppm in 1982. It was a breakthrough and provided a practical showcase to market TQC throughout YHP. Wave solder equipment at the time was one of HP's most expensive capital investments, and thus improvement in its utilization and performance attracted a great deal of attention. Soldering was a bottleneck in circuit board assembly operations. By eliminating defects, the wave solder improvement contributed to the switch from batch to flow production in these operations. Along with other changes, this led to a dramatic reduction in lead time (from one month to one day) in the number of people required to operate the process (from 22 in 1978 to 12 in 1980) and a large reduction of work in process inventory, which also provided great savings of cash, time, and space.

In short, the wave solder improvement was of major importance from a business point of view and understood as such by employees, not just those from manufacturing but including those from R & D, marketing, and sales. From 1975 to 1982, YHP recorded four times fewer product failures, a fourfold increase in shipments without adding space, a 40% reduction in production costs, a 70% reduction in inventory, a 30% decrease in development cycle time, and market share and profitability levels three times their 1975 level. These remarkable improvements were a part of the reason why the company was awarded the Deming Prize in 1982. Particularly powerful was a slide that was to be shown to many HP personnel. It reported the performance on YHP's proprietary product line (PL 36). As shown in Figure 7.1, it conveyed a clear, simple message with implied causality between falling costs and quality failures and rising profits.

Officials at YHP attributed their success in large part to the operationalization of six principles of TQC (cf. Mozer, 1984: 30–33):

1. A commitment to continuous quality improvement led by top management;
2. The collection of data in analyzing problems (management by fact);
3. Clarification of who was responsible for action in daily work and in problem solving;
4. Systematic gathering of feedback from internal and external customers;
5. Use of Deming cycle (Shewhart's Plan, Do, Check, Act cycle) as generalized problem-solving process to achieve permanent solutions;
6. Use of statistics as a management tool.

To support the implementation of these principles, YHP developed a variety of policies and practices including quality circles, hoshin management, the presidential diagnostic, all R&D engineers trained in and practicing reliability engineering techniques, customer feedback, and problem-solving systems.

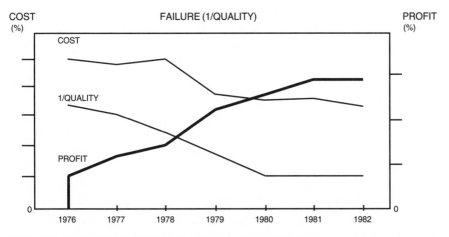

Figure 7.1. YHP product line (36) performance. The expression *1/quality* describes quality as a reciprocal of the annual failure rate of YHP's product line. *Source:* Hewlett-Packard Japan, Ltd.

The Impact on Hewlett-Packard

When one thinks of one organization serving as a model for another, one often thinks in simple terms of how one organization successfully transferred a specific practice or set of practices to the other. Thus, I had one former high-ranking HP executive say to me: "YHP didn't have much influence on what we did. They recommended quality circles and we ended up rejecting them." This statement, as we shall see, is wrong on many levels.

Closer examination reveals that influence from the sending organization can play out in many different ways. One can array the possibilities as follows: a provider of trustworthy information, a provider of information about what is possible and different from what employees in the receiving organization are already thinking or doing (a provider of concrete outcome benchmarks), a provider of a transparent template for concrete processes and practices grounded in actual work practices, and a provider of a broad conceptual template of how an organization should approach major organizational uncertainties. The boundaries among these categories are not always clear or mutually exclusive. My data suggest that YHP's influence on HP operated in all these ways, with the importance of any one factor varying by time period and particular HP division and group.

The importance of trustworthy information in a period of uncertainty cannot be overestimated. Recall that in the early and mid-1980s, U.S. manufacturing managers were very confused about the scope, significance, and very nature of the quality problem and how it should be resolved. There were lots of information and opinions on the matter with little hard evidence. Managers could not distinguish bad from good information. It was the era of competing gurus and consultants seeking to differentiate their products. Under these circumstances, firms that could identify and access social locations that permitted them to better separate good from bad information prospered.

This is what YHP provided—a source of reasonably trustworthy information. In response to those employees responding negatively, based on a pervasive "not invented here" (NIH) mentality, proponents of TQC could respond, "We have a testbed right in our own family." As a division of HP, YHP could be assumed to have no pecuniary or other ulterior motives for its claims. Moreover, the practices it identified as worthy could be made transparent, unlike many other claims being advanced at this time. If HP managers wanted more information about a particular practice or questioned some YHP data, they had only to invite a YHP staff member to their unit or to visit YHP operations in Japan to check it out. However, there was not unmitigated trust, and indeed some suspicion remained about YHP data and the link between quality and YHP's performance. Nevertheless, relative to other U.S. companies that had no internal unit from which they could draw and with which they could compare their results, YHP must be seen as a relatively trustworthy source and therefore a strong corporate asset in HP's efforts to meet the quality challenge.

Katsu Yoshimoto, the YHP quality manager at the time, estimates that between 1979 and 1989 more than 100 of HP managers came to study TQC at YHP. This is quite apart from those HP managers who came for normal business purposes and got exposed in that fashion. And YHP managers visited HP divisions to spread the word as well. Yoshimoto alone, according to his log, spent 600 days at HP outside Japan and mostly in the United States between 1983 and 1990. The CEO Sasaoka made some 30 visits to U.S. HP functions and operations between 1980 and 1985 to make presentations about TQC. The effect of this transparency was to increase the trustworthiness of the information being provided by YHP to HP in the eyes of HP managers.[4] Moreover, the rapid improvement of YHP's business performance in the late 1970s and early 1980s seems to coincide so perfectly with their implementation of TQC that the evidence for the value of YHP practices seemed clear and further increased its credibility.

Testimony to the perceived trustworthiness of the information from YHP was the growing support from top management for adopting TQC as practiced by YHP. The first major visit by HP's top manufacturing managers and QA personnel took place in 1979, led by Ray Demere, the head of manufacturing services at the time; he picked the most promising HP managers worldwide from 10 of the roughly 20 divisions at the time. Demere himself became a student of YHP's activities and strongly promoted TQC at HP.

During this initial visit, in addition to YHP, the team visited leading Japanese manufacturers, most of which were noted for their superior quality. This two-week study visit became the kickoff for TQC at HP. Participants on the tour were "blown away," as one participant expressed it. "The Japanese were routinely doing things that couldn't be done." The visit was followed in December 1979 by what the Swedes call a "hallelujah" meeting of all manufacturing and QA managers at a fancy resort. The meeting featured reports on the trip and TQC received a big send-off. After the meeting Demere developed a two-week course for manufacturing managers based on what they had learned from YHP and other Japanese companies. It is hard to know how much these initial experiences stuck, but in retrospect they can be seen as seed planting. An accumulating set of experiences and observations eventually lent credibility to TQC in the eyes of many HP managers and workers.

Reflecting top management's commitment to TQC, quality became a prominent theme in the annual general managers' meetings in the early and mid-1980s. It is important to understand the significance of these meetings at HP. In this highly decentralized company, general managers are the key players. Each held profit and loss responsibilities for his or her own product-focused division and had considerable autonomy in making business decisions for that division. Very few directives were made from the top of the organization, and divisions sought their own paths in everything from establishing product strategy to process adoptions. The general managers' meeting, then, provided a major channel for communicating a common message across the organization and enabled the formation of corporatewide understandings, evaluations, and objectives. The fact that Sasaoka, YHP's president and CEO, was invited to address HP managers a remarkable four times from 1979 to 1985 suggests that his message was seen as important to senior management and was of interest to the general managers.[5] The meeting and his topics were

1. 1979—Worldwide Manufacturing/QA Managers Meeting. Topic: Quality of Japanese Industries. Number of attendees: 65.
2. 1982—General Managers Meeting. Topic: Observations on the Japanese Competition. Number of attendees: 120.
3. 1983—General Managers Meeting. Topic: Winning the Deming Prize. Number of attendees: 130.
4. 1985—General Managers Meeting. Topic: Report from Japan: Reliability, the Survival Issue. Number of attendees: 140.

The significance of featuring quality and YHP's activities at the annual managers' meetings was captured well by John Young, the HP president during these critical years: "We used the annual general managers' meeting big time. If you budget the most important premium time you have to this [quality], it says a lot about where it sits on your agenda. There's nothing more influential than your peers standing up at a general managers' meeting, getting to tell how they got the job done and getting psychic rewards for it" (cited in Main, 1994: 54). In positioning quality and YHP in this fashion, HP top management not only showed that they regarded YHP as providing trustworthy information but also held up TQC as a broad conceptual template of how the organization should approach and resolve some of the major uncertainties facing it at that time.

Because YHP was "in the fold," when managers questioned YHP's quality performance, as many did, often data could be assembled and analyzed that could overcome the initial skepticism. Few other U.S. companies could easily match this access. For example, many HP managers argued that the higher reliability of YHP products was explainable in term of the simpler nature of its products. It is much easier to achieve higher reliability if one produces much less complex products. In response to that argument, the corporate quality staff working with YHP produced a chart in 1981 that plotted annual failure rates against list price (using list price as a proxy for product complexity) for the various HP, YHP, and Yokogawa Electric product lines. This analysis, in effect, "normalized" product complexity. They found a clear pattern showing the superiority (lower failure rates) of YHP and Yokogawa Electric products across the various price ranges. Publicizing these kind of analyses based on hard data allowed HP's leadership to effectively counter the denials of many HP managers.

None of this emphasis on trustworthiness and access to objective data is meant to suggest, however, that there was unquestioned acceptance of YHP's message. Despite access to a member of the family, throughout the 1980s, some HP managers continued to deny some combination of the following claims: that quality was a serious problem, that it was a major determinant of corporate-and division-level performance, and that the Japanese had found a better way. These positions should not be dismissed as simply manifestations of irrational resistance. In the very same time period of the biggest push for Japanese-style quality in the early 1980s, customer surveys evaluating hardware reliability in a variety of geographical settings and product markets reported HP to be the very best. Thus, many managers, quite understandably, found it hard to swallow the idea that the Japanese were all that good and they were all that bad. Moreover, despite YHP's being in the fold, a few HP managers believed that YHP was exaggerating HP's weaknesses since it was in YHP's interest to magnify quality differences to get the company's attention. Some believed that YHP relied on arbitrary and subjective inspection criteria that produced inflated numbers of defective products. Nor did these suspicions simply weaken over time; when YHP's economic performance began to falter after 1985, reservations about the relation between quality and corporate performance were given new life.

After YHP's winning of the Deming Prize in 1982, CEO John Young, sensing the seemingly good fit between TQC and HP culture, committed to TQC. The Deming Prize gave Young the final evidence he needed. It provided the stamp of approval from Japan Inc. that what YHP was doing was right. In short, the awarding of the Deming Prize legitimated YHP's TQC activities among many of HP's top managers and reduced any lingering doubts that YHP was the source of trustworthy information.

Young publicly symbolized this commitment at a corporatewide HP conference in 1983 held to assess where HP was on quality improvement and to decide what it wanted to do about TQC. Besides 200 quality professionals there were 50 overhead staff and, most important, 50 general managers. It was a three-day "real time" meeting out of which came a corporate definition of TQC, a description of its key elements, and the decision to endorse TQC as a corporate objective. The decision was driven largely by the general managers at the meeting. The ground had been carefully cultivated prior to the meeting to ensure senior management support of this outcome, as reflected in Young's kickoff speech for the meeting. The meeting itself was orchestrated by Craig Walter, the newly appointed corporatewide quality director. Walter's strategy was to drive change in the divisions through his division-level quality managers, whose job had been redefined to reflect new quality principles.

Yet the sources of resistance toward TQC did not then vanish within HP. In keeping with its still quite decentralized structure, there was a lot of variation in division managers' consciousness of quality as a problem and in their recognition of whether new approaches were necessary. Nevertheless, over time, a variety of subsequent developments served to encourage practices associated with the new quality model.

In the early days of the quality initiative, top management did everything to ensure they had early victories and success stories that they could then "merchandise" throughout the corporation. The idea initially was to convince general managers and middle management that lower defect rates paid off in terms of business success (Main, 1994: 54). Not only did they merchandise their own success stories but YHP's as well. The "marketing" of TQC within the company often took the form of using YHP to show what was possible and doing a before-and-after evaluation of YHP efforts (e.g., 1976 versus. 1983), documenting the methods YHP used to achieve improvement. The wave solder improvement story took on almost folk status within many HP divisions. It was still used in some HP training programs when I began my interviews in 1996. The fact that the wave solder improvements had been achieved by a small, insignificant operation in Japan, and achieved on a machine declared surplus (worn out) by the Santa Clara division, amplified its impact.

One of the important lessons HP learned and promoted from these observations was the limits of technology in solving quality problems. Ray Demere, former vice president of manufacturing for HP, introduced President Sasaoka at the worldwide general managers meeting in 1983 with the following observations:

> Let me mention two strategies for improving quality and productivity. One is the automation-driven strategy. . . . The other is the management-driven strategy, which emphasizes the role of people in the context of a well-developed set of management policies, practices, standards, and methods, including statistical tools, aiming at quality. This strategy must precede the automation-driven strategy to achieve significant success. YHP has been most successful implementing a management-driven strategy through the company without extensive automation. Their approach has been to analyze work processes by first measuring and collecting data, using statistical techniques to identify opportunities, taking action to make improvements, and monitoring to control the process. Most improvements have resulted from elegantly simple solutions, scientifically applied to eliminate defects in the process.[6]

These were lessons that GM's top management did not learn until the late 1980s through the experiences of NUMMI and their failure "to leapfrog the competition" through heavy technology investments at Hamtramack and other plants (Keller, 1989: 202–225).

I observed that the sending organization can serve as a model by being a provider of information about what is possible and different from what employees in the receiving organization are already thinking or doing. It is clear that the various examples of YHP success, as exemplified by the wave solder improvement, served just this purpose.

The strongest corporatewide quality initiative launched at HP in the early 1980s was the 10x program. Led by John Young, the CEO, this program, announced in 1983, called for a tenfold improvement in hardware quality (as measured by reliability) over the rest of the decade. It was based on the recognition that orders of magnitude changes were called for within HP to turn quality into a much stronger competitive advantage. While HP still enjoyed a reputation for high quality, it discovered that some 25% of its manufacturing costs were accounted for by the costs of fixing quality problems (Young, 1983: 10). This fact was ignored by those claiming that quality was not a problem for HP. The goal needed to be startling so as to shock employees out of their accustomed belief that HP was a quality leader and to get them to question basic ways of working and improving. At the same time, the program initiators understood that, to be successful, employees must see the initiative as credible and, above all, as achievable.

It is highly probable that YHP's achievements contributed—along with other factors such as customer input—to the setting of the 10x objective itself. By 1979, YHP was already showing great improvements under TQC. The initial results of the wave solder improvement effort were coming in. As noted before, YHP was able to lower rate of nonconformity from 4,000 ppm in 1977 to 40 ppm in 1979; that meant the number of defects in 1979 were 1% (1/100) of what they were in 1977. This improvement was well in excess of the 10x goal that HP set for itself (though the wave solder improvements were at the component rather than product level, and thus the improvement showed up directly in factory yield not field reliability; improvements at the product level were a more challenging task, combining as it does many interacting components). Sasaoka, reflecting back to those days, captured the YHP role as follows:

> We also had a lot of impact on the 10x program. By showing how far behind HP was from the emergent Japanese competition and how much improvement could take place with concerted effort as we did in the wave solder improvement, we contributed to the ambitious goals that John Young chose to set. Furthermore, the application of TQC approaches was one of the important means by which many managers choose to try to meet the 10x goal.

While acknowledging the impressive achievements of YHP, increasingly HP managers visiting YHP came away with the impression that there was no miracle in TQC, just basic blocking and tackling. So it appeared doable. In fact, there was an underlying systems logic behind many of these seemingly unrelated common sense practices that become apparent only through further experience. At the early stages of adoption, however, the belief that it was simply basic blocking and tackling gave managers the confidence to move ahead. In this sense, ignorance (failure to realize the larger scope of changes required) was an aid to organizational transformation.

What were the results of the 10x effort? In 1991 HP declared victory in its internal magazine *Measure* (starting the clock from 1981). Internal observers note that the first few years did not lead to much movement (1979–1982); many employees questioned the seriousness of the goal. Progress accelerated, however, from 1983 and substantial progress was indeed made by 1991. The standard used by HP to measure progress was the number of failures (as measured by warranty costs) per $1,000 of product-selling price. Under a standardized measure, failure rates declined from 1.0 in 1981 to almost .1 in 1991, just short of the 10x goal. Put differently, product failure rates under warranty in 1991 were just 10% (1/10) of what they had been in 1981. Certainly, the rate of improvement varied enormously among divisions, reflecting in part variation in the seriousness with which they embraced the goal and imperfections in the metric (for the former point, see Main, 1994: 165). With regard to the latter point, the nature of the metric was such that organizations subject to declining margins and price erosion (e.g., high-volume consumer business like personal computers and printers), in effect, had to achieve more than 10x improvement because the denominator was getting smaller over time. They argued vehemently for another measure, but they made the target nonetheless.

Warranty costs were reduced by an estimated 800 million dollars, and huge reductions in inventory, lead time, and labor costs were recorded as well. While not directly measurable, one could presume that by reducing customer down time with improved reliability, customer dissatisfaction decreased, customer loyalty increased, and the probability increased that existing customers would recommend HP to others. This improved performance, thus, could be expected in turn to translate into higher sales.

The organizational significance of 10x, however, was that it provided a powerful corporatewide goal within the quite decentralized culture of HP. It became the foundation for all HP improvement programs in the 1980s. Pressure on managers to meet that goal, in turn, led many managers to embrace some version of TQC. The corporate quality department itself moved from a position of weakness to one in which its directives had a certain obligatory weight vis-á-vis the divisions ("Thou shalt do the following"). That is not to say of course that it always got its way. Division managers had elaborate methods of passive and active resistance when they disapproved of particular initiatives (cf. Main, 1994: 165).

In this overall environment, the 10x umbrella contributed to a managerial receptivity to the types of TQC activities being carried out at YHP. As Katsu Yoshimoto, the YHP quality officer put it, "In the early 1980s, HP's division managers were looking for ways to achieve 10x and that made them quite receptive to YHP's ideas on process improvement." In summary, YHP's success had a major impact on HP's goal setting in the quality arena, and YHP's TQC activities provided a set of concrete processes and outcome benchmarks that served as a template for HP action. While not the focus of this research, improvement activities at HP led to further improvements at YHP as well.

The Case of Quality Circles

I turn now to the specific ways in which YHP and other Japanese sources provided concrete processes as well as outcome benchmarks to HP. I deal first with an anomalous case, quality control circles. In Chapter 4, I provided an overview of the major issues in shaping managerial receptivity to Japanese quality control circles as a seemingly prominent feature of the Japanese approach to quality improvement.

I also showed how "quality circles" (as they came to be called in many American companies) seemed to run out of steam in the mid-and late 1980s.

Hewlett-Packard's experience provides a microperspective on this matter. As a company widely cited by the media and scholars as having used quality circles the right way (Kanter, 1983: 249–250), its experience is especially interesting. Did YHP steer HP in the wrong direction on this matter? Was this a case of learning the wrong thing? Certainly it would not be the first time that a firm borrowed information from its model that was ill-adapted to its new environment, thereby resulting in failure. Recall the high-ranking manager who, when asked about YHP's influence at HP in the quality arena, said to me in effect, "We tried quality circles and they didn't work." In fact, the matter is quite complicated, but the short answer is that YHP managers did not actively emphasize the adoption of quality circles at HP. They did, however, play a role, sometimes inadvertent, in legitimating quality circles.

As we have seen, quality control circles are small groups of workers from the same workshop engaged in group problem-solving activities to improve their work practices in ways that lead to improved quality and productivity. They started in North America at HP in 1979 at its Loveland, Colorado, facility and in Palo Alto. Many HP managers and the new corporate quality officer, Craig Walter (served as quality manager at Loveland from 1975 and assumed corporate office in 1983), saw quality control circles as a perfect fit with HP culture. "We thought it was plug compatible," said Walters in one of our interviews and this was certainly the image that Ouchi (1981) and other scholars conveyed. The movement spread rapidly and by the mid-1980s, HP had some 1,000 teams operating in various divisions and geographical locations.

The management impetus to pursue circles began to decline as early as 1983. A task force that studied this decline found that circles continued to be successful under four conditions: where managers "owned" the circles; where the quality circles were integrated into the group's business activities; where teams were well-trained in problem solving, statistics, team building, and process analysis; and last where the circles operated within an organizational and cultural environment that encouraged teamwork (Young, 1985: 30–34). Many managers, however, found circles threatening. There turned out to be many different visions of how to do quality control circles at HP. Some managers tried to tightly control the agenda for problem solving; others left it to the group. Some provided a great deal of training for supervisors on how to introduce and operate circles and build on local practices. Others took a "cookie cutter" approach to circle activity, buying a consultant package. None of these approaches proved durable for much the same reasons as existed in other companies. These problem-solving activities were not effectively tied to important corporate objectives, and thus the circles had an artificial character.

The task force that studied the problem issued its report but had no mandate and no action followed. In the decentralized culture of HP, it was difficult to develop consensus about how to proceed. The name was changed to quality teams in 1983 to try to erase the negative stigma associated with quality control circles, but in vain. By the mid-and late 1980s circle activity sharply declined (but they are still very active in HP's Asian operations), and by the late 1980s and early 1990s many managers were talking about "intact work groups" and introducing self-managing teams, known in HP as "high commitment organizations." In fact, it was a pattern repeated at many companies.

Like many at HP, Craig Walter, the corporate quality manager at the time, clearly was puzzled at the demise of quality circles. As he puts it, "It was quite an education to see how complicated a piece of social engineering this seemingly simple problem-solving activity turned out to be." It was indeed complicated and for two major reasons. First, it takes extraordinary organizational discipline, re-sources, leadership, and commitment to maintain large numbers of problem-solving groups constantly searching for problems and to respond to the solutions proposed by these groups. Such effort easily degenerates into ritualistic behavior and as such will not be cost-effective. Second, quality control circles need to be self-governing, but simultaneously they must be working toward goals established by management (on this second point, see Lillrank, 1995: 979).

In a sense YHP as a firm did indeed contribute to the burst of interest in quality control circles at HP. In fact, YHP had large numbers of quality control circles as part of its approach to TQC, and it was open to discussing how these activities operated in response to visiting managers from HP. The YHP materials on circles were translated into English and the circle stories from their 1982 Deming Prize examination and from subsequent award-winning teams were featured prominently at HP meetings. It was easy to understand how HP managers would see YHP circle activity as a key element in their success. Yet what they did not see until much later was the mechanism that linked broadly dispersed problem-solving activity at YHP to higher-level management goals.

The other side of the story, however, is that there was an explosion of information about quality circles in the United States in the early 1980s. Many of those pushing circle activity at HP offered hardly more than an obligatory bow to the Japanese, if that, as they searched out U.S. sources for guiding their activity. One HP activist in circle activity wrote a book on the subject with just one mention of YHP (Mohr and Mohr, 1983: 249–250).

From a YHP perspective, HP's quality-circle effort was primarily American-driven. Managers at YHP thought it was more important to get top-down TQC institutionalized at HP and they campaigned for that. Circles were a priority for them but by no means the highest. They believed that managers with no experience in TQC had little understanding of how to lead circles and thus were unable to give them proper support. Under these circumstances, it did not make sense to them to push quality circles first. Officials at YHP acknowledge that they were seen as encouraging circles and that they contributed to this perception.[7] One example of inadvertent support arose from the YHP practice of sending over the best YHP quality circles to visit HP and make presentations. However, YHP did this as a way of rewarding these teams rather than as a proselytizing effort. Indeed, this was a common mode of rewarding successful quality control circles for Japanese companies at this time. In any case, very few HP employees came to these presentations, a source of some embarrassment at the time.

Quality circles were not the only quality improvement innovation from Japan that did not take firm hold in the corporation. Quality function deployment—widely touted at many American companies as one of the more effective quality management tools—had its day at HP but did not sink deep roots in most parts of the corporation. When the corporate quality office decided to no longer support it in the early 1990s, its popularity in the divisions declined, though it is still being used in some parts of the corporation and experienced somewhat of a resurgence in the mid-1990s. In accounting for the weak institutionalization of QFD, quality leaders suggest that members of product development teams tend to attribute their success to their own team and its creativity, not to the tools they used. It was thus not unusual for a team that had successfully used QFD on one project to not use it on its very next project. Apparently, many HP managers believe that the returns are modest relative to the heavy time and people resources associated with preparing the requisite QFD tables.

Modes of Influence

Although QFD did not sink deep roots into the company and although HP, along with many other American companies, was unable to avoid the painful failures associated with adopting quality circles, it did absorb many of the principles and practices associated with TQC. If YHP was not pushing HP to adopt quality circles, what were they encouraging and through what routes did they do it?

We can think of the diffusion of TQC from YHP to HP as having proceeded along two tracks. The first track was its diffusion in the course of solving ordinary business problems faced by YHP. A second track involved YHP in efforts to consciously spread TQC throughout HP.

The first track was narrow and deep. It did not reach all divisions because it aimed at only those units of HP with which YHP had business relations. While it was not as broad as the second track, it can be evaluated in many ways as more effective in that YHP modeled the new business practices in its dealing with other HP units. As such, the learning and technology transfer that took place was embedded in normal business problem-solving activities and routines. As such, it is the closest to learning by doing of any mode used in the transfer process between HP and YHP and thus was, by far, the most effective in bridging the gap between learning and practice.

Back-and-forth visits by HP personnel to YHP in Japan and vice versa to solve specific problems characterized this mode. The practical character of these exchanges and the clear business purpose of the new practices made the technology transfer less threatening, more transparent, more understandable, and therefore easier to carry out. As part of this effort, Yoshimoto, the YHP quality manager, estimated that he did some 200 informal problem-solving diagnostics for HP units from 1983 to 1990. Most of these were done to help YHP solve its business problems by getting HP divisions to do a better job satisfying its Japanese customers. In effect, YHP focused in the 1980s on improving customer feedback and getting HP personnel to listen to the voice of the customer. Managers at YHP believe that this focus on responding to customer complaints contributed to HP's 1982 decision to polish up and reinvigorate its traditional corporate objective of customer focus.

YHP targeted what they called the "rainbow divisions"—the seven worst divisions in terms of product quality delivered to them—in what later came to be known as the "DOA (dead on arrival) problem." One cannot help but be aware of the cultural differences here; American managers in a similar situation would have undoubtedly chosen a more aggressive label like "the dirty seven." Yoshimoto, the quality officer, made quarterly visits to the United States to meet with those divisions and to work with those most needing to improve the quality of their products. He typically met with group general managers and functional managers. Yoshimoto and other YHP personnel conducted joint improvement projects with HP personnel in areas like DOA products and product design and manufacturing capability improvement.

Product reliability was also a major continuing focus for YHP, and it often organized joint improvement activities with HP managers. In 1982, for example, YHP formed a joint improvement group with the Desktop Computer Division (DCD) located in Fort Collins, Colorado, to deal with problems they were having with products manufactured in both locations. The DCD team members visited Japan in 1982 and a YHP engineer spent six months in Fort Collins. The improvements made by this team led to a 60% reduction in warranty failure rate as well as lowered manufacturing costs (Mohr and Mohr, 1982: 249–250). Through these kinds of hands on improvement activities, much of YHP's quality improvement expertise was transferred to HP.

Earlier I noted that YHP's initial complaints were often ignored by HP personnel. With the rising reputation of YHP within HP, however, YHP was in a position to have its complaints taken more seriously. Who would want to be the division or group manager or engineer resisting YHP's overtures when top management was touting its accomplishments at companywide meetings? And YHP learned how to escalate pressure for change. If an engineer in charge was not responsive, YHP would move up to the division manager, and if he was not responsive, YHP would involve President Sasaoka in putting pressure at the group level. Of course, matters did not always come out according to their script, and actual outcomes were the result of a complex of interacting factors.

At the same time, to make HP more aware of customer complaints in a way that would produce action, YHP managers realized that they had to develop more effective feedback to HP. To maximize the probability of a positive HP response, they concentrated on sending the right information to the right person at the right level in the right format. Gradually the quality of their feedback began to improve. They taught their personnel to analyze a problem to see if it should be the subject of a "hot site action" (having a high-level manager meet with irate customers to assure them that everything was being done to solve their problem) or if it should be sent to a quality team or one of the functional units for their disposition and if the latter, which one, at what level.

Managers at YHP mapped the feedback approach to be taken and trained their personnel in the appropriate response. Using TQC, they trained YHP personnel to no longer just complain to HP or rely on emotional appeals. Instead, the YHP feedback became increasingly characterized by a clear description of the problem and analysis of its causes. When possible, YHP recommended a fix (temporary or permanent). It found the "QC story" format (a series of steps mimicking the actual problem-solving process), with its clear problem statements and data analysis, was most useful for facilitating international communication to resolve specific problems. Basically, YHP was providing HP with data on end customer complaints. Increasingly, YHP was passing on the customers' voice in a clear strong fashion. It saw this as critical to getting HP managers to listen. It used real business problems to spread TQC ideas to selected HP units through their normal business behavior. With this modus vivendi, learning and effective practice seemed to merge.

Success stories grew up around these activities and were marketed through the company. Thus, the Disk Memory Division in Boise became a model of improvement as part of their effort to better satisfy Japanese customers. In 1984, HP hard disk products were at a competitive disadvantage vis-à-vis their Japanese competitors. The HP products operated with a mean time between failure (MTBF) of 8,000 hours compared to Japanese top products, which operated with 30,000 MTBF. Cooperating with YHP, the Boise operation was able to set the industry standard by increasing its MTBF to 300,000 hours by 1992 and 800,000 hours in 1995. However, HP closed this business in 1996. Thus, we have a reminder that models of corporate success often have a short life as new events quickly outdate past successes.

Predictably in this loosely integrated company, some HP units were more resistant to the TQC message than others. Some managers were skilled at giving lip service to TQC but did little to change their practices. Often units were reluctant to make a permanent fix to a problem because of the high cost of design change. One YHP manager recalled:

> During my visit to HP units, I could see managers struggling between the need to show short-term profits and their support of long-term business strategies, which included integration of TQC into their practices. Depending on their business background, and the signals they were getting from their general manager and the overall profitability of their operations, they tended to emphasize the one or the other.

Yokogawe Hewlett-Packard was the first HP unit to conduct and publicize DOA studies of HP products arriving to be sold in Japan. As managers began to study the reasons why installed products were failing at customer sites, they came to realize that many were arriving DOA in Japan. Up to then, this had been somewhat of a taboo subject in the corporation. They found in their first 1980 study that a remarkably high 10% of HP products were arriving in Japan DOA (a figure that some HP managers considered inflated due to what they saw as the arbitrary inclusion of cosmetic and other minor defects). Partially through YHP's strong efforts to publicize the problem, and the resources they devoted to working with HP on the problem, by 1990 the DOAs detected in Japan fell to 1%. Also YHP contributed to the development of the more differentiated approach to DOA through adding the category of DEFOA (defective on arrival for reasons including late delivery, and missing accessories, kits, and documents). This new category helped eliminate confusion by creating greater agreement on the separate criteria to be used for DOA and DEFOA. Overall, YHP's DOA activities came to serve as an HP performance benchmark in the late 1980s and early 1990s. As one veteran HP employee told me, YHP came to be the source for "warranty failure rate" data; the DOA rates for products shipped to YHP were considered the most rigorous measure of outgoing quality.

This DOA campaign by YHP was one of the seeds for the development of HP's global order fulfillment reengineering project in the early 1990s. Earlier, HP had been weak on the delivery of complex systems products (often with components produced in different locations) leading to delayed delivery and DOA problems (cf. Main, 1994: 166–167). Initially, HP managers had been resistant to YHP's negative interpretations of the DOA studies. The HP European quality manager took the lead in championing the YHP position and used DOA data as an initial base for creating the global order fulfillment process. Thus, YHP actions provided the inspiration, and its DOA data the launching pad, for the ensuing development of the corporation wide effort to improve the fulfillment of orders requiring global coordination of HP units. In so doing, it also helped link the HP reengineering movement of the 1990s to the quality initiative in a way that built continuity between the two.

In addition, YHP's influence was felt in the sales organization. In 1980, YHP appointed what may well have been the first quality manager for sales in any American or Japanese manufacturing company. The idea was that the principles of TQC could be applied to sales by treating sales activity as a process and acting to structure that process better (see Soin, 1992: 187–198). Around 1984, the idea caught fire at HP and it began putting quality managers into sales organizations. This decision helped legitimate the important message that quality was not just a matter of product quality to be determined in manufacturing. In the late 1980s, the sales organization in HP's United Kingdom operation was experiencing dismal financial performance. Managers implemented TQC principles and achieved a strong turnaround in performance. Although this was not the whole explanation, the experience was publicized within HP as a success story in applying quality principles to sales and helped further legitimate the initial direction forged by YHP. By the mid-1990s it was quite normal for sales organizations to have quality managers, especially in test and measurement, medical, and printer operations. Even those units that did not make this decision often added customer assurance managers, who served much the same purpose; some HP managers were simply more comfortable not using the Q word.

After YHP won the Deming Prize in 1982, YHP developed a second track through which it more consciously sought to spread TQC throughout HP. This track had the opposite characteristics of the first track in that it was broad but not very deep. It was more a stage-setting phenomenon involving policy advice, exhortation, and the provision of a broad conceptual template. It spread declarative knowledge (knowledge of facts and propostions) and was effective only when followed by specific training and action at the operational level. Nevertheless, by proceeding along both tracks, YHP's TQC activities had a significant influence on developments at HP.

The second track was encouraged by HP's top management and took many forms, including President Sasaoka's presentations to all company general managers noted before. It also operated through Yoshimoto's participation in developing corporate quality policy. Yoshimoto was appointed to membership of the corporate quality council in 1983 and attended quarterly council meetings. The council was composed largely of group quality managers (of both product and geographical groups) and key corporate quality staff. In those days, the council was quite influential in setting corporate directions. It operated as a learning organization, picking topics to study such as hoshin management. The council engaged in top-down agenda setting, aiming to use quality managers at the division level as its transmission belt for actualizing the new learnings.

Of course, this was by no means a smooth or complete process. The quality managers, armed with their new quality mandate, often ran smack into division-level managers who had their own strong ideas about ingredients for business success. The extent of melding and dovetailing of the two depended on the proclivities and receptivity of division-level management; the cleverness, flexibility, and social skills of the quality managers in packaging the new ideas; the nature of the specific quality practice being advocated; how well the business was doing; and the kinds of pressures the division mangers were getting from their own bosses.

Further, YHP provided support for developing the Quality Maturity System (QMS), a corporatewide diagnostic activity and for implementing hoshin management (policy planning and policy deployment). These are my subjects for the next chapter. One needs to understand how the process of adoption interacted with adaptive innovations to bring about the successful institutionalization of these practices.

CHAPTER 8

Adoption, Adaptation, and Reaction at Hewlett-Packard

This chapter deals with three major quality initiatives at HP, how they came to be adopted, in what form, and how they further evolved to fit HP culture and its preexisting practices. The first two, QMS and hoshin management were Japan-and YHP-inspired, and the third, the "Quality 1 on 1" initiative, built on both the accomplishments of these earlier efforts, as well as their perceived limitations.

In the mid-1980s, HP had begun to use the services of a well-known quality counselor in Japan, Professor Noriaki Kano. He had worked with many Deming Prize companies, was a disciple of the dean of quality management in Japan, Kaoru Ishikawa, and had sufficient command of English to be effective in an American environment. Thus, not only did HP go to where the news was breaking in Japan, but it brought the news directly into its own environment. Kano had worked with some success for Malaysia HP and then Singapore HP, helping them implement TQC; a corporate HP manager who became acquainted with his work there recommended him to HP's group general manager at the components group in 1984. Professor Kano began working for HP in 1985 and continued to come periodically for the next seven years—typically making two visits a year of three to four days each. His typical work mode was to carry out diagnostic activities, asking key managers in a group setting about various aspects of their business practices and problem-solving activities, then making recommendations based on that information. He practiced a Socratic style as he pushed managers to reveal their underlying assumptions and practices and to show them their limitations. Overall, he worked with about 20 divisions, sometimes just once, but in a small number of cases he worked regularly with divisions (e.g., divisions within the components group). Professor Kano was particularly struck by the weak corporate function at HP in comparison to the Japanese companies with which he had worked. This weakness meant that even if one fully solved a quality problem in one division, under the same conditions at other divisions, the same problem would repeatedly appear. At this time, there were few mechanisms for diffusing new directions and best practices within the company. This was one of the costs of HP's decentralized structure of autonomous product-oriented divisions.

Professor Kano sometimes embarrassed HP managers who did not always understand the purposes of his questions. He would often ask executives, "What is your management system?" They would answer, "We use MBO [management by objective] to set our annual individual objectives." When he asked to see their annual objectives, however, top managers not infrequently had none or they were an aggregation of lower-level management goals. For those below top managers, the list of annual objectives was often just a pro forma document carried over from the previous year to show superiors, but it had no operational significance. Rather than a top-down process of goal setting, it seemed to Professor Kano that HP had a bottom-up process. Moreover, when front-line managers were asked how they set their target, they answered in effect that it was more or less by "gut feel." One should be careful not to dismiss tacit knowledge in goal setting, a role highlighted by Japanese scholars, among others (Nonaka and Takeuchi, 1995). Moreover, at the highest level in the divisions, there was certainly product planning and new technology planning in those days. Yet the company lacked a method of coordinating and aligning different parts of the company (horizontal and vertical) and giving it strategic direction, and divisions often lacked planning activities that focused directly on customers.

Craig Walter, the corporate quality director at the time, was trying to use Professor Kano to further the spread of TQC, but he was only one person, his time was limited, and HP was a big company. The challenge was to find a way to capture Kano's expertise and insights. Action proceeded along two lines: the first led to QMS and the second contributed to hoshin management.

The Quality Maturity System

The impetus to establish QMS at HP came from Chairman John Young in the mid-1980s as a result of his insistence that HP needed to know "if the quality initiative had stuck." Craig Walter, responded by initiating a one-time survey to evaluate the level of implementation of TQC. He created a small design team that included Katsu Yoshimoto of YHP and Sarv Singh Soin from the Singapore subsidiary. Soin played the major role in designing what was to become the major quality diagnostic tool at HP, the QMS (Soin, 1992: 241–279).

Soin was familiar with Professor Kano's diagnostic activities. In his preparation of the original survey document, he tried to capture Kano's Socratic method of asking questions, using a discovery interview model instead of the traditional audit procedure of relying on people filling out forms. The survey Soin developed, in effect, was an expert system modeled on Kano's diagnostic activities with an added dose of the Deming Prize. Professor Kano reacted to the written drafts of the QMS protocol written by Soin and pointed out items that were missing or needed to be revised.

The decision to develop this expert system was a creative adaptation of Japanese practices by HP management. Japanese companies practicing TQC typically conduct a presidential diagnostic in which the president periodically visits units to assess their progress in meeting annual goals. However, as we have seen, HP did not have a strong top corporate function that could drive quality assessment through the large number of HP divisions.

Professor Kano's recommendation for solving this problem was to strengthen the role of HP's top corporate officers so that they could drive the quality initiative more strongly. The corporate quality staff, however, understood that this would not work at HP and pushed for a standardized version of QMS that could be conducted by a large number of ordinary managers who would be trained to conduct such activities. Kano came to believe that this was a more robust approach than in Japan because it institutionalizes the review process, whereas in Japan, a shift to a new president can often lead to the quality improvement emphasis running out of steam. Even though QMS may be more robust and flexible, it is typically not as strong, focused, and prescriptive as a successful Japanese TQC initiative. In the Japanese version, a strong president (the president is typically comparable to the American CEO) in a highly centralized company can drive the improvement initiative in a focused fashion.

The QMS involved a two-day review by two evaluators, who would meet with division management and ask a set of questions designed to tap the level of maturity of their quality system. Based on that evaluation, they would make recommendations for improvement. Yoshimoto, as a member of the design committee, worked with Soin. Also, YHP sent over Yoshimoto out of its own budget to do some of the initial reviews and to teach others how to do them. The original reviewers were corporate quality staff members, though general managers were recruited later to do the reviews as well.

The initial QMS reviews were done in 1988. Twenty divisions were evaluated and the results showed high variability. Results were scored on a scale of 0–5 in the initial year with the average score for factories being 2.2 and for field organizations 1.8. However tough the scoring, this exercise made clear HP had a long way to go before TQC was fully institutionalized. As a result of this first experience, in 1989 HP set a goal of an average score of 3.5, which it believed corresponded to a capability of challenging for the Baldrige Prize (later reduced to 3.0).

The experience with the initial survey was so revealing and constructive that HP decided to carry out the QMS as a regular diagnostic review. It took some time to fine-tune that effort and it was not until 1990 that it was ready to move from experimental to volume production (capable of churning out a large number of QMS reviews a year). The QMS measured a unit's quality maturity on five dimensions: customer focus, planning process, process management, improvement cycle, and total participation.

Why did HP choose to use a more Japanese-based vehicle than the Baldrige for this purpose, particularly since John Young was chair of the Baldrige Foundation Committee while HP was creating its QMS review? The explanation is that HP was already committed to QMS when the Baldrige came along in 1987. No doubt, some "not invented here" (NIH) sentiment was involved as well; HP owned the QMS and knew it could continue to tailor it to HP culture.

In addition to changing the level of person doing the review, HP found that it needed to make other revisions to the typical Japanese diagnostic approach. This occurred in three stages, first during the design of the original survey, second during the fine-tuning to turn it into an instrument for mass reviews, and third in a major revision in 1992 (rolled out in 1993) to meet a variety of criticisms. These revisions demonstrate that the successful transfer of Japanese quality practices to American firms often involved major adaptations of the original ideas and practices.

One of the first changes involved introducing a scoring system. While lower-level HP managers did not want a scoring system, top management did and still does. In the second version of the QMS, HP adopted the Baldrige categorization, distinguishing among approach, deployment, and results. Generally speaking, these adaptations made the original Japanese ideas more transparent, practical, and simple. In that connection, President Sasaoka observed that such characteristics are lacking in the Deming Prize because it was produced by academics.

Initially, units were required to undergo a QMS review, though some managers did not like it and found ways to avoid it. As HP began to move into broad usage, resistance peaked in 1991. A number of vocal divisional managers doubted its effectiveness. The thrust of their objections was that QMS "allows me to know if I am doing better in TQC but doesn't tell me if it is making my business better." The corporate quality office convened a conference of several general managers who most actively opposed QMS. Responding to their views, the corporate quality office decided to make QMS more educational, more business-focused, to let businesses own it by making reviews optional and to put more pull into it. The latter point involved creating more of an incentive for managers to want to do reviews. To this end, a Presidential Quality Award was created, and a 3.0 QMS score was made one of the conditions for winning it. These are the changes that drove the creation of QMS2, which became effective in 1992.

We can see QMS1 as basically a mode of checking whether units had incorporated Japanese-style TQC as characterized by YHP's activities. The QMS2 represents a major adaptation of these principles to the U.S. business environment with a sharper focus on strategic directions and business outcomes. In many ways, it paralleled and reflected the shift to TQM occurring in the United States in the early 1990s. The quality improvement initiative became more tightly integrated into overall management activities. This evolved the quality improvement initiative in a number of new directions that were vital for the survival of the quality initiative at HP. It is highly unlikely that Japanese ideas about quality improvement represented by YHP practices would have survived long in HP without undergoing the kind of adaptation represented by the shift from QMS1 to QMS2.

In HP presentations on quality to customers, employees often refer to QMS2 as a TQM review, but that language is less widely used within the company (with a few exceptions, like the Medical Products Group, it is not widely used in their U.S. operations); few U.S.–based HP employees outside of the quality department would see either QMS or hoshin management as part of TQM. Indeed, the QMS reviewers seldom use the term quality, in deference to the resistance to the Q word that developed at HP. This seemingly trivial adjustment in language must be seen, in fact, as still another of the important adaptations of Japanese practices to the American environment. As discussed in an earlier chapter, the public drumbeat, the bandwagon effect, and the often extravagant claims made on behalf of quality led many American managers (and academics) to dismiss quality as a serious issue. Not to adjust the language under these conditions might well have endangered the prospects for HP's quality initiatives.

Figure 8.1 captures the transformation from QMS1 to QMS2. First, one sees a shift in language from customer to strategic focus. The intent here is to encourage units to give more attention to strategic directions and the business environment and to better coordinate the emphasis on customers with the traditional managerial focus on markets and competitive analysis. The second shift is from emphasizing the short-range hoshin planning process in QMS1 to full business planning in QMS2. Business planning includes long-term as well as short-term planning with a particular emphasis on aiming for selected breakthrough initiatives (via hoshin management) and on meeting ordinary business objectives (called business fundamentals at HP).

The third category retains the same language of process management in both QMS1 and QMS2 but the reviews in QMS2 now assess the mastery of business management tools that facilitate improvement of major cross-functional processes (e.g., planning, product development, order fulfillment process, channel sales, etc.). Under the approach to process improvement embodied in the TQC activities of QMS1, each work team acted to improve its individual process with the assumption (on faith) that this would lead to optimization in the aggregate. The QMS2 emphasis on cross-functional activities showed teams how from the start to think about the whole process. This latter perspective was not explicitly featured in YHP practices. Support for this interpretation comes from Noriaki Kano, who acknowledges that the Japanese quality leaders weakly marketed the whole process approach. They were focused on getting employees to understand TQC and so aimed to get people in specific sites to use it to improve their own business processes. He further observes that engineers developed TQC in Japan and were interested in techniques, concepts, and narrowly defined systems but not in organizationwide thinking.

The improvement cycle emphasis in QMS1 becomes operationalized in QMS2 as improvement projects. Whereas the old emphasis was on using the PDCA (Plan, Do, Check, Act) cycle for improvement, the new emphasis shifts to the process for managing improvement projects and its coordination with key strategic objec-

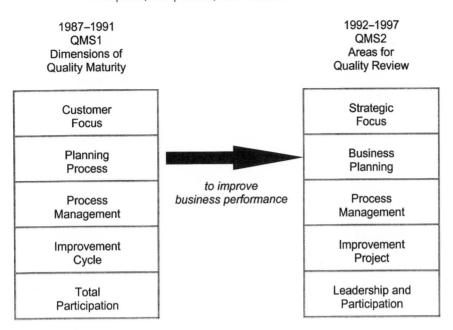

1987–1991 QMS1 Dimensions of Quality Maturity	1992–1997 QMS2 Areas for Quality Review
Customer Focus	Strategic Focus
Planning Process	Business Planning
Process Management	Process Management
Improvement Cycle	Improvement Project
Total Participation	Leadership and Participation

to improve business performance

Figure 8.1. Evolution of QMS at Hewlett-Packard. *Source:* Hewlett-Packard Company.

tives. There is a stronger emphasis on the criteria for choosing an improvement project, especially the importance of the project. This moved the balance from small to large improvement projects. Finally, total participation in QMS1 becomes leadership and participation in QMS2. Total participation was associated narrowly with quality circles at HP. Leadership and participation are more broadly about general managers harnessing the combined intelligence of the workforce and using it to serve business objectives. The stress is on opening a dialogue with the work team about leadership and empowerment and teamwork and getting managers to listen better. Regular employee surveys are typically a part of this effort.

Running through all these changes in the QMS is the shift in thinking about teams. A composite set of HP manager observations captures this shift:

> With quality circles it is clear we didn't understand the guiding principles and how they fit in. Management was told to be supportive but didn't know how. The circles worked on low-level improvement projects. We blanketed the organization with them whether individual units needed them or not and kept them alive whether they were making a contribution or not. By contrast QMS2 encourages problem-solving team activity to be linked to critical business issues, especially the improvement projects pushed by business teams. We create these teams on a local workplace or cross-functional basis as we need them, and we disband them when they have made their contribution or keep them alive for long periods if there is a continuing problem needing

their attention. We are doing small-group activities today the way we should have been doing them in the early 1980s.

However, preliminary research results by George Easton and Sherry Jarrell indicate that HP had not achieved complete success in managing teams. They found that the improvement teams in one HP division were using only traditional brainstorming techniques and had virtually dropped TQC problem-solving methodologies (Easton and Jarrell, 1997b).

The described changes helped revitalize the QMS. By 1996, 70% of the divisions were using it and the corporation as a whole was carrying out 50–60 reviews a year. This represents a small decline from when the QMS was "obligatory," but the reviews are now based largely on the wishes of those who experience them. Still there is corporate pressure to do them. In January 1993, soon after taking office, Lew Platt, John Young's successor as CEO, publicly stated his support for the QMS, endorsing the recommendation of the Corporate Planning and Quality Committee that all business be trained to lead QMS reviews. In 1997, 51 of the 102 QMS evaluators were division managers or group managers (the rest were quality managers); however, many of the division and group managers do only a few reviews a year. By the beginning of 1997, over 400 formal QMS reviews had been done at various levels and entities (e.g., divisions and business units, geographic regions, sales offices) since that first survey. In addition, more than twice as many informal reviews have been completed.

Of course, there is still some criticism of the QMS. Some charge that those administering it are into forms management. Some units being reviewed treat it as a "dog and pony show." With the emphasis on a dialogue format and the growing number of experienced reviewers, however, this is much less likely to happen. A successful review is composed of open and honest discussions, positive attitude toward learning and sharing, presentation of actual work, minimal preparation time for the evaluation, and short presentations by those being reviewed, with lots of dialogue between evaluators and reviewers. In principle, that sounds good, but in practice there is a tension between stressing what one has done versus showing one is open to learning and improvement. By emphasizing the latter, the unit being reviewed risks getting a lower score. There are also some features of QMS2 that do not work as well as had been hoped, such as the efforts to document best practice and have the "referenced unit" conducting that practice share its experiences with other units. The review process itself does contribute to the identification and diffusion of best practices both through new recognitions by the reviewed unit and through line managers who serve as reviewers carrying back good practices to their own units.

One can examine trends in the scores of those units that have had multiple reviews over time. The scoring is on a scale of 1–5, with a score of 5 recording the strongest quality performance. An examination of these trends shows that the average score rises from 2.4 on the first review to 2.6 on the second review stays flat at 2.6 for the third review, and rises to 3.2 on the fourth review (under 10 units have been reviewed four times by late 1996; thus, the small sample makes generalization risky). Some of the increases, of course, could be the result of increased experience in "test taking." Also, HP has data on the average QMS scores achieved annually, which do show a modest rise overall (the review content has changed over time, so it is difficult to draw conclusions). However, HP has not been able to demonstrate a clear statistical relation between a unit's QMS performance and its business results. This may reflect the inability to control statistically for the complexity of interactions or it may reflect the lack of relationship between the two. Whatever the case, it provided a basis for criticizing the activities of the corporate quality department in the late 1980s and served as an engine for rethinking approaches to quality in the 1990s.

What started out as a one-time survey closely modeled on Japanese practices as embodied in Dr. Kano's expertise was modified and became institutionalized within HP. The QMS had its origins in John Young's insistence that HP needed to know just how successful it was in instituting TQC. It led to the adoption and adaptation of a Japanese quality practice, the quality diagnostic (Ishikawa, 1987:39–41). The QMS became the primary instrument through which HP routinely evaluates the quality system of many of its organizational units. In short, it came to provide an operational definition of quality that was consistent throughout the firm and provided opportunities for both coaching general managers on modes of improvement and self-assessing organizational capability.

Although units are encouraged to explore the utility of ISO 9000 quality audits (many must do them for business reasons), the ISO 9000 series of quality standards has not displaced the QMS. The QMS remains the preferred instrument for diagnostic/audit activities because it is tailored to HP managerial concerns, and it has a much sharper focus on customer needs, strategic issues, and competitive performance. In short, QMS came to perform many of the same functions as the Baldrige did for many other U.S. companies. The face-to-face dialogue built into the QMS between reviewers and the unit being evaluated, however, arguably provides a more dynamic and effective mode for coaching and improvement.

Hoshin Management

Another quality theme pursued by HP that had a strong Japanese flavor is policy management (*hoshin kanri*). Hoshin management was a set of practices developed by companies like Toyota, Komatsu, and Bridgestone Tire Company that crystallized in Japan in the early 1970s and came to constitute one of the core elements of Japanese TQC. Like many American companies, HP chose to keep the Japanese term. The management system is known in HP as hoshin planning, as opposed to the management by policy (or policy management), the direct translation favored by the Japanese.

Following Shiba, Graham, and Walden (1993: 412), one can describe hoshin management as a planning and implementation approach that seeks to align all organizational layers and employees toward key company goals with a sense of urgency. By focusing and coordinating employee efforts and resources on key company goals whose achievement can make a competitive difference, the firm seeks to create breakthroughs. Careful selection of such objectives is expected to quickly and effectively bring a company's goals and activities in alignment with the firm's changing environment. It provides a systems approach to the management of change in critical business processes and involves negotiated dialogues both vertically and horizontally through the organization in the selection and coordination of the means to achieve them (Watson, 1991: xxii–xxxiv). The Japanese refer to this back and forth dialogue as *kyatchi boru* (catch ball).

Although hoshin management crystallized in the early 1970s as a key element in Japanese TQC practices, it came to the attention of American managers much later. Involving planning activities as it did, it was one of those invisible elements of the new quality model that eluded most American companies in the early and mid-1980s, including HP. In the early 1980s, the thinking of YHP leaders on how to approach quality improvement at HP was to first get HP managers to understand elementary TQC. That would serve as the building block that would allow YHP to proceed to then introduce them to hoshin management. However, YHP's initial overtures to HP general managers on hoshin management were not warmly received, for HP managers were committed to their ongoing use of MBO, involving individual managerial goal setting and measurement, and did not see hoshin's advantages over MBO.

In 1985 Craig Walter, head of corporate quality, heard from YHP that it had documented hoshin management. At the same time, YHP was campaigning for HP's adoption of hoshin management as the next most important step in its TQC initiative. Walter saw it as basically an approach to strategic planning. Also YHP stressed that it would be an effective mode for stepping up achievement of HP's 10x goal (King, 1989: ii). It had the YHP documents translated, and Katsu Yoshimoto came over to help explain hoshin management. Independently, Kano had begun working at HP and his activities over the next few years strongly reinforced the idea that hoshin management was important; he helped HP understand its proper role and how to eliminate some of their problems in implementing it. In particular, he stressed the importance of "catch ball," that objectives could stretch over more than one year, and the importance of the PDCA cycle in reaching breakthrough objectives.

In the mid-1980s HP was struggling. Profits were going down and divisions were still operating under decentralized controls. This difficult situation fueled the movement for greater coordination and consolidation among divisions (Beckman, 1996). Thus, there was growing interest in finding some better mechanism for coordinating the different parts of the company and giving the company strategic direction. The de facto bottoms-up planning process resulting from the use of

MBO was of little help. Hoshin management, however, seemed to fit the bill and came along at just the right time. Again, we find evidence for the garbage can model of decision making.

Nor was hoshin the only solution to give the company more strategic direction. Not long after hoshin planning began, a 3–5 year 10-step planning process was also successfully championed by Central Engineering and Consulting Services. This planning process came to be used by the divisions together with hoshin planning; it is based on 14 characteristics of a good plan (e.g., strategic direction, competition, customer satisfaction).

The corporate quality office took the lead in getting some managers to use hoshin management. That group of managers met regularly to discuss problems they encountered. A forum to showcase what 4–5 groups had achieved after using hoshin for 1–2 years was held for an audience of other general managers and interested parties. The chief operating officer at the time, Dean Morton, became involved and began practicing it himself. This gave a major boost to efforts and helped legitimate hoshin management. General managers responded well and seemed to like it—it helped them run their business and focus energies and resources. They liked its clarity and the sense of control it appeared to gave them. Over time, they came to see it as a kind of a more mature MBO using the PDCA cycle to increase the power of traditional MBO. Traditional MBO was entirely results-oriented, but the overlaying of it with the hoshin management system sought to balance that focus with an emphasis on process. Rather than arguing for the superiority of hoshin over MBO, it was marketed within the company as a "turbo MBO."

Hoshin planning became a widely used annual planning tool and became expected (not mandated) for all divisions around 1989. Upper management was attracted as it gave structure, coherence and common language to the company's strategic direction, thereby providing greater coordination among the divisions and groups. John Young has played down the significance of hoshin planning (Main, 1994: 166). Yet Young was never fully involved and often delegated his hoshin responsibilities.

Young's successor, Lew Platt, however, has been a strong supporter and user, even leading the periodic review process when business units are evaluated to see if they are on target to meet their objectives and to detect any shortfalls. As a user, Platt modeled for other managers what he expected. When Platt took over in late 1992, at his first meeting with the general managers he started out saying in effect that he supported and intended to use it to run the company. It was a clear message of support for hoshin management and implicit advice for others to get on board.

Yet the path was not so straight and easily traversed. Managers at HP struggled mightily and still struggle with getting hoshin management to meet their needs. At first, HP managers had a tendency to set too many objectives each year, a problem Kano calls "chasing too many rabbits;" it took time to learn that they needed to concentrate on a very small number of breakthrough objectives. Managers found it, and still find it, difficult, to keep these breakthrough objectives separate from their obligation to meet their ordinary business fundamentals (e.g., the usual financial objectives). Many managers had trouble letting go of their traditional MBO practices and went through the motions of "doing hoshins" but never measured their own progress and would create new hoshins each year without any reflection on the previous year's accomplishments or lack thereof. Some managers misused hoshin management planning by treating it as a control tool (not using the "catch ball" function). They simply worked out the hoshin themselves and then announced a fait accompli to subordinates. Still others turned it into a bureaucratic enterprise or ignored their periodic performance reviews.

In preliminary results from a study of hoshin planning at one HP division, George Easton and Sherry Jarrell (1997b) report the following problems. There is a failure to fully resolve the relationship between the 10-step planning process and hoshin planning. Process facilitators, typically selected from key staff personnel for top division management, often play such a large role that senior managers in effect delegate their hoshin responsibilities. This raises the question of whether hoshin is operating as effectively as it might and whether the failure of top division management to model the desired behavior will have long-term negative consequences. Finally, Easton and Jarrell question the importance of hoshin planning relative to how the business is run. The salience of the issues they raised varies widely across divisions, given the autonomy of the divisional general managers.

By and large, many U.S. companies, including HP, were better at hoshin planning (upfront setting of breakthrough objectives) than deployment and the monitoring of that deployment (implementation and regular reviews).[1] In this sense, the use of the term hoshin planning at HP is not a misnomer in that it reflects the weaker emphasis on implementation and review (though planning is required for implementation as well). This strong tendency has some interesting parallels in the American scholarly literature on strategic planning. Dean and Bowen's survey of the literature finds that strategy theorists generally have emphasized strategic content over strategic process and strategy formulation process over strategy implementation (1994: 404).

The review process at HP was much less formal than that of the typical Japanese practitioner of hoshin management. The Japanese tend to methodically look for deviations from the plan. But HP does not freeze a plan because a variety of contingent events come into play once the plan has been adopted. They believe these contingencies require a more dynamic approach. The attitude is that spending time and resources documenting in detail differences from the original plan and committing to countermeasures is not a good use of resources. Hoshin is a success at HP, says Richard LeVitt, the corporate quality director, because "it helps us to understand who we are as a business and where we are going. It is the act of planning, itself, that builds consensus and brings about alignment. The process of creating alignment around common breakthrough objectives is what matters most."

An emphasis on the methodical Japanese and the more flexible informal Americans, carried to the logical extreme, feeds into the stereotype of the ritualistic and bureaucratic Japanese versus the dynamic, innovative Americans. Yet, according to Noriaki Kano, the most effective Japanese companies are also quite willing to do midcourse corrections to adjust their plan to new circumstances. As many at YHP see it, moreover, a weak review process means managers will not likely formulate an effective recovery plan if they are falling short or undergo root cause analysis of their problems. As a result, managers have a more difficult time understanding what process actually led to the results they produce. Is it a defective process that led to the plan not being met, or was it the introduction of some changes in the environment? Without a careful review process, managers do not know and will not learn from their experience. Thus, they may easily choose the same ineffective methods in the future. Put differently, by not practicing the PDCA cycle, they lose important knowledge. In short, from a Japanese perspective, there is incomplete use of the hoshin methodology.

Furthermore, HP modified still other Japanese hoshin practices. Befitting their greater emphasis on implementation, YHP typically expected four layers of management to construct their own implementation plan consistent with their responsibilities (division managers, functional managers, department managers, and section managers). At HP, however, managers at all levels (especially middle management) have been reluctant to create their own implementation tables. Leaders at HP believed they had to simplify hoshin management in order to get it accepted. The YHP approach was seen by many HP employees as overly bureaucratic and ritualistic. As one senior corporate HP manager, reflecting on the potential receptivity by middle managers, bluntly put it, "If we don't simplify it, the dogs won't eat it."

By and large, top management and general managers came to believe that hoshin management evolved in a way that served the company well. The revitalization of the United Kingdom sales region was a major business success story attributed to the use of customer satisfaction as a breakthrough objective. Yet hoshin at HP operated at less than optimum fashion from a variety of perspectives, including the relatively weak application of the PDCA cycle to reviewing the progress of implementation. Even more to the point, some very successful divisions, like the InkJet division, ignore hoshin management, and their very business success allows them to argue successfully that their own planning activities seem to work well without hoshin. Perhaps these adaptations and allowances were the price of getting hoshin management accepted at HP.

A More Recent Initiative

The adaptation of YHP-inspired initiatives continued into the 1990s. The sharpest changes occurred with the appointment of Richard LeVitt to the position of director of HP quality at the end of 1992. He got his job to a large extent as the most visible critic of HP's mode of application of Japanese-style TQC practices.

LeVitt was influenced particularly by the findings of French cultural anthropologist Clotaire Rapaille, his experience at HP, and the results of a major benchmarking activity he initiated. He concluded that there are deep cultural differences about what quality means to employees and to customers. He believed that Japanese culture strongly predisposed Japanese managers and employees to emphasize perfection and this often led them to a ritualistic approach to quality improvement (see Hammond and Morrison, 1996: 79, 310–312). He did not see this as fitting well with the dynamic and innovative culture that HP needed to cultivate to survive in the future.

LeVitt wanted to loosen up the obligatory nature of many of HP's quality practices; he thought there was too much emphasis on the use of rigid, prescribed tools and not enough allowance for flexibility in approaches and modes of implementation, too much emphasis on methods and not enough on results, particularly as they related to the needs and priorities of customers.

These concerns developed at a time at HP when the interest on satisfying and working with customers continued to escalate. Ideas about customer-centered solutions that would then drive design and production became increasingly prominent in many of HP's businesses. Similarly, the popularization of the ideas of mass customization for many of HP's mature technologies was also taking place. Generally speaking, managers perceived that they faced rising and rapidly changing customer expectations for more flexible, speedier, and higher levels of service. Increasing dependence on suppliers, partners, and third-party channels also heightened concerns about maintaining HP's franchise with its customers and the ways it could be jeopardized by these other parties. Actually, the shift away from reliance on the firm's own direct sales force to reliance on retail distributors and resellers for volume distribution of products began in earnest with the introduction of LaserJet printers in 1984 (Beckman and Mowery, 1996: 13).

In 1994, HP corporate quality initiated a worldwide benchmarking study of quality with 12 leading companies in comparable businesses. The quality tools, ideas, and methodologies were much the same as those in place at HP. While the results showed HP was as good as anyone else, the results also meant that the most competitive companies had caught up with HP and that they all seemed stuck in about the same place. To once again wield quality as a competitive advantage, HP would need to develop new approaches. In this environment, the idea that customers should be the focus of quality activities received new emphasis.

It seemed that the traditional quality emphasis on planning, testing, data analysis, and incremental improvement alone would not be able to keep pace. Moreover, while other HP technologies were in rapid flux, why did quality technology (tools and ideas) seem stagnant? Many of the quality management ideas discovered in the early 1980s had failed to change very much. Maybe HP could not demonstrate business payoffs for improved QMS scores because they had gotten too focused on the vehicles and forgotten the customer. Directly aiming to improve customer experiences was more likely to lead to positive business results. This was the way Richard LeVitt argued the matter to his colleagues.

With these concerns in mind, HP's Planning and Quality Committee (composed of high-level group managers), sponsored the creation of a full-time R & D team to rethink the role of quality managers and to evaluate the value contributed by the quality function. In pursuing that theme, the team soon realized the need to address the broader issue of what quality should mean at HP; they concluded it should mean a commitment to customers and not to tools per se. The team spent much of 1995 conducting action research with customers, seeing what other companies were doing, and looking outside the quality tradition for new ideas. Based on a variety of other inputs, including various experimental activities in the divisions, a companywide conference was held in November 1995 to roll out the new Quality 1 on 1 initiative. It was attended by 390 HP managers, including 60 general managers. Although the audience was responsive to the vision, they wanted more direction as to the specific behaviors and practices that would help them reach the new objectives specified in Quality 1 on 1.

The new initiative stresses seeing the product or service from a customer point of view, moving from being producer-centered to also being customer-centered, and creating one-on-one relationships between employees and customers where possible. The terminology of 1 on 1 was chosen to personalize quality. Quality 1 on 1 means that HP employees should know quality as a customer does and systematically act "across the value chain" on that knowledge to grow their businesses (LeVitt, 1996). Employees document the various links and the motivation for participation of the various actors across the whole design, production, distribution, and use chain to identify and shore up weak links and bolster customer satisfaction and loyalty. The new initiatives led to an expansion of HP training activities that encourage employees to think in terms of a "customer value delivery framework." The new initiative stresses working directly with customers in creative ways rather than relying on customer satisfaction surveys to assess their needs. Over time, experience showed that employees resonated most with the concept of customer centered and value delivery systems so they gradually discontinued use of the Quality 1 on 1 phrase. This had the added effect of removing any negative historical baggage associated with the Q word.

Whereas corporate-initiated training is helpful in making clear the new directions, it hardly suffices to operationalize the new emphases. Central to this development effort is a pattern observed earlier. The corporate quality office seeks out division managers with sufficient interest in the new ideas to begin experimental efforts to operationalize them. The quality office supports these efforts as needed, sometimes conducting a joint research effort. Each of these units starts from a different place and brings different perspectives to the matter.

The divisionalized approach encourages multiple experimental activities. The corporate quality office acted to identify individuals and organizations predisposed to be pioneers and then targeted these potential early adopters. Thinking of the divisions as potential customers (since they were no longer in a position to mandate adoption), they used Geoffrey Moore's categorization of a continuum of customers to distinguish between technology enthusiasts, visionaries, pragmatists, conservatives, and skeptics (1995: 19). They then attached names of individuals and organizations to the categories and targeted the technology enthusiasts and visionaries with whom they would co-develop the new conception of quality. They also sought out "heavyweight" divisions that made strong contributions to HP profits and therefore could serve as role models if successful.

Four units have played a particularly important role in the evolving conception and practice of Quality 1 on 1: the InkJet group in the Vancouver, Washington, Division, the Business and Personal LaserJet Divisions, the Medical Products Group, and YHP. The Inkjet group had a big initial impact on the form that Quality 1 on 1 would take. They pioneered developing new ways to do customer research, including using teams trained in human factor analysis to visit customers and observe how they use products in different kinds of environments and what they were trying to accomplish. The teams come back to HP and share these observations of customer behavior and the team's interpretation of them with relevant HP groups. Thus, HP personnel achieve a much richer interpretation of what customers do. Greater awareness of customer intentions and actions opens up a broadened set of opportunities for HP designers and manufacturing personnel. The InkJet internal consultant leading this effort was later hired by corporate quality to develop these and other new approaches to customer research for wider use within the company.

The InkJet group was also active in developing metrics to correlate the impact of business decisions on customer satisfaction. It learned to package customer value information in an integrated, accessible, and relevant format that demonstrated the link between customer value and business results. It acted to persuade the division to value and pursue customer loyalty and not just market share. Overall, this example had a strong impact on positioning Quality 1 on 1 as a strategy for growing a business.

The Medical Products Group was a leader in developing the management of customer knowledge. It modified the existing global customer database to make it accessible to all employees who want to use it. This database gives insights for new product generation and for correcting problems with existing products, and it is of value to sales and other groups by showing a customer's recent history with HP. Corporate quality took that tool to other businesses to emulate.

The Business and Personal LaserJet Divisions redefined the role of the quality function to be more customer-centered. They piloted corporate quality's initiative to revise the job description of quality managers to emphasize their contributions and accountability. They also piloted what became the core element in the customer-centered approach of Quality 1 on 1: assessing performance across the entire value delivery system, including suppliers and distribution sales channels, in terms of impact on customers. They showed that the process could be managed, and that they could drive improvements from their understanding of the role of each player in the value delivery system.

The involvement of YHP is quite interesting in view of its past influence on developments at HP. Very little of the current inspiration for Quality 1 on 1 comes from Japan; indeed, in some ways, it is a reaction to earlier Japanese influences. Yet YHP has been active trying to reconcile the new ideas with traditional TQC practices. This may turn out to be an extremely important contribution that encourages continuity between past and present approaches.

The corporate quality organization also adopted the company's Work Innovation Network (WIN), a methodology that involved identifying and assembling people from throughout HP who were interested in and experimenting with new work innovation. The methodology was pioneered in the early 1990s by the change management team within HP's product processes organization, an organization that also houses the corporate quality organization. The quality organization, seeing this methodology work for other innovations, introduced it for customer-centered quality in 1995 by hiring a consultant from the change management team to develop and manage the new network. The idea was to identify and bring together leading practitioners of customer-centered quality. The first meeting was held in late 1995, a second in 1996, and a third in 1997. On average, some 120–180 individuals attended each of the meetings, with perhaps one third being quality department personnel from the groups and divisions. The purpose was to share experiences with the new practices but also to give emotional support to those isolated individuals experimenting on their own who were not getting much local support. Most important, the meetings serve to connect individuals sharing common interests and thus enable them to build and pursue networks with similarly interested individuals.

In so doing, the corporate quality office performed a brokering role within the corporation, acting to increase its visibility and power in the organization through providing useful benefits to innovators. In a large, highly divisionalized corporation such as HP, it is not always easy to find out who is doing what and with what effectiveness. Corporate quality seeks to fill the "structural hole" by providing a framework and venue for finding this out (Burt, 1992: 72–73). By acting as an entrepreneurial third party, it potentially can provide important information benefits to its constituencies.

Corporate quality leaders at HP envision a co-invention process whereby they sponsor, absorb, digest, and synthesize the field experiences of the various experimenting units as well as the reactions to these field experiences by relevant HP employees. These activities often involve jointly sponsored "action research" at business unit sites. This process tends to build trust. It contrasts with the trust-destroying consequences more likely to emanate from the top-down cascade model with its effort to force diffusion of best practices.

Corporate quality leaders engage in a large-scale marketing effort within the corporation to feed back an integrated set of practices to potential adopters; the marketing features heroic accomplishments of these pioneering divisions. Storytelling about customer experiences at HP is seen as a device to engage employees to make things happen (Hammond and Morrison, 1996: 281). The "roll out" of the new initiative is a major occasion for these events to take place. The CEO Lou Platt has been a featured speaker at a number of events to cement the view that this is a corporate initiative rather than one being driven by the corporate quality department. The marketing effort was already well under way with Quality 1 on 1 in 1997; indeed, it was occurring parallel with the evolution of the identification of best practices. It is an iterative process, with the definition of best practices constantly evolving as more experience is gained at the divisional level.

To see this process as simply a brokering function performed by the quality department for the network of actors within HP, however, is to miss the important role the quality department can play in terms of coordinating and synthesizing what it learns from both within and outside the organization. Divisions will often arrive at overlapping, redundant, or even contradictory solutions to the same problem (e.g., developing a global database for customers). The quality department tries to identify a set of best practices in each area. This is not a simple task because it takes discernment to understand which pieces of local knowledge are worth extracting (Brown and Duguid, 1997: 11–12). Furthermore, the corporate quality department seeks to integrate the essential local knowledge with input from outside the firm from other companies, consultants, industry groups, academic and nonacademic researchers, and quality technology developers (from inside and outside the quality field). Still further efforts are required to successfully embed this integrated knowledge in other divisions. The self-conscious nature of this process is notable. Clearly, this template is familiar to the HP organization; it has been used before and HP managers know how to apply it. This does not guarantee its success. It is used enough to suggest it is one of a number of patterned approaches to change at HP.

Traditionally at HP, the only highly centralized functions have been finance and personnel. Outside of these, it has been hard to get coordinated action from groups and divisions, especially in situations where there is uncertainty and incomplete knowledge. In these situations, there is a real incentive to encourage divisions to experiment and to cooperate to identify best practices. Corporate quality is under pressure to make the best business case it can for each proposed initiative and then to provide help as needed for the division to try out the new ideas. The head of the quality organization captured his need to work with the divisions to develop best practices in a variety of expressions: "I didn't have any choice," "Nothing was available off the shelf," and "It seemed like the natural thing to do." What comes through here is the very taken-for-granted institutional character of his behavior that flowed from the structural situation in which he found himself. That situation stemmed from a shift in the early 1990s from funding the corporate quality function fully through a corporate surcharge on business units to having a significant part of the budget for this roughly 45-member group (in 1997) come directly from those business units they partnered on specific projects.

One of the consequences of engaging in "co-invention" with the divisions is that corporate quality, of necessity, has to give up control since it cannot completely predict what will happen. Division experimentation can develop in directions not anticipated by corporate quality. This can result in fruitful local modifications. "It will morph on you," as one manager expressed it to me. Thus, the test and measurement organization hired a businesswide customer satisfaction manager with a marketing background who proceeded to create a hybrid out of Quality 1 on 1 and the marketing initiatives in "relationship marketing." These efforts in test and measurement may in turn influence other business units, particularly if highlighted by corporate quality as best practice. This example suggests that the co-invention process sometimes develops in a quite nonlinear fashion. The benefits to corporate quality giving up control, however, are not trivial; the corporate group gets to work with energized, committed individuals, willing to try out new ideas. In this seedbed, the best ideas are tested and strengthened through real-world experience.

The situation with Quality 1 on 1 is somewhat different from what occurred in the absorption of TQC in the mid-and late 1980s. In the case of TQC, there was seemingly a relatively clearly defined package of practices that evolved in Japan and provided a template of what needed to be done. Thus, the early experimentation of divisions, such as in the case of hoshin management, was more on the order of selected divisions giving public testimony that they had tried these practices and indeed they seem to work in their HP environment. With Quality 1 on 1, however, there was a co-evolution of problems and solutions along the path of developing and operationalizing the new ideas.

One might argue that this model leaves too much to chance under conditions in which the top corporate leaders have identified important new strategic directions that they believe the corporation needs to pursue. After all, a weak corporate quality department without any levers of control over the divisions depends on the willingness of those divisions to experiment with its new ideas. Indeed, it would appear that HP top management was concerned about this issue. Thus, to understand the current process of change at HP in the quality arena, one also needs to examine a set of top-down imposed incentives that encourage divisional management to experiment with new initiatives like Quality 1 on 1. One sees here a subtle interaction between the decentralized model of innovation so enshrined in HP culture and top-down influences.

How this works brings us back to hoshin management. Each year the CEO, Lew Platt, issues a few selected breakthrough objectives (hoshins) for the corporation (typically two to three). One of these has always been customer-focused. It is submitted to him by the planning and quality committee referred to previously, and the corporate quality director plays the major role in the drafting. Thus, the series of annual hoshins from 1994 to 1997 stressed achieving and sustaining leadership in the following areas: order fulfillment process (1994); customer satisfaction (1995); customer satisfaction and customer loyalty (1996); and customer loyalty, attraction, retention, and referrals (1997).

As can be seen, these annual objectives intentionally build on one another. What is the mechanism by which these objectives become more than words? The 1997 customer hoshin calls for each business to set specific and measurable customer satisfaction goals to achieve competitive leadership in customer loyalty.

The CEO holds quarterly review meetings for roughly 10 major groups (another 9 or so groups are subsumed under these 10). The group managers are held accountable for these and other business objectives at these meetings and have their results publicly displayed at the meeting. To have one's deficient results displayed publicly to one's peers is an embarrassment and likely at a minimum to lead to the CEO's explicit expression of concern. This puts strong pressure on the group managers to hold their divisional managers responsible for meeting these objectives.

At HP, befitting its decentralized tradition, it is understood that the groups and divisions are in control of the specific metrics and goals set to meet the broad hoshins, as well as other business objectives (though they are encouraged to work with corporate staff in developing their plans). Although there is undoubtedly a dilution of the accountability pressures as one goes down the ladder, these breakthrough objectives are nevertheless likely to be a significant motivator for divisional managers to evolve new approaches to meeting customer needs. These corporate pressures were not the only incentives for divisional managers to experiment. They had their own ideas about how to grow their business and for some that meant better satisfying the needs of present and potential customers. In the end, what is most fascinating and ironic here is that in the name of moving away from the prescribed Japanese-style TQC, the initiators of the new Quality 1 on 1 effort consciously and pragmatically drew on one of its core elements—hoshin management—to provide incentives to divisional managers to experiment with new approaches.

A final link in the chain was forged with the development of a new version of the QMS, rolled out in fall 1997. Recall that top management has strongly encouraged the use of the QMS. The QMS3 is intended in part to measure an organization's fit with Quality 1 on 1, just as QMS1 mapped TQC and QMS2 mapped TQM. The QMS3 assesses how a business unit's work affects end customers and how the organization manages the links in the whole value delivery system for meeting customer needs. It stresses the importance of scanning the environment. The intent is to encourage the divisions to benchmark against a Quality 1 on 1 standard, identifying those areas needing improvement and then providing them with help toward that end.

Figure 8.2 displays the full model for the development of Quality 1 on 1 as described in the preceding pages. It appears to be a quite robust model for multidivisional corporations in situations of high uncertainty and incomplete information. Moreover, it is likely to be superior to the approach typically taken by highly centralized companies in these situations. In the latter case, top management often identifies a new approach and the associated operational practices that they deem promising and engage in a top-down cascade process, one with strong overtones of forced diffusion. While they may succeed in imposing innovations through this process, they often meet severe resistance, both active and passive, from those who have had no part in developing the ideas, lack the means to achieve them, and meet situations

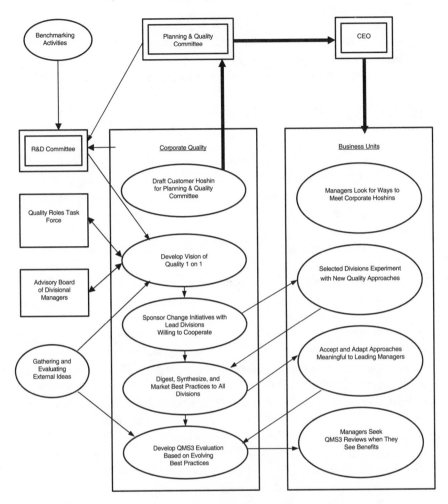

Figure 8.2. Creating the Quality 1 on 1 change process using hoshin management incentives. Rectangles denote committees or offices. Ovals denote activities.

in which these prescribed new approaches do not appear to fit. With little sense of ownership on the part of the implementers, the fate of such efforts is uncertain at best. This top-down approach was a common way in which many highly centralized American companies responded to the Japanese quality challenge, some with good, but others with disastrous, results. Alternatively, some firms responded with a bottom-up approach to quality improvement (Wilson, 1995). They, however, typically underestimated the difficulty of spreading best practice across units in the absence of top management support and a common language.

The approach to Quality 1 on 1 at HP represents a much more subtle combination of top-down incentives, corporate-divisional linkages, and bottom-up initiatives. As a result, when managers adopt new practices, they are more likely to have a sense of ownership in them even if they have been developed elsewhere in the corporation.

One should be careful not to carry this argument too far. Even going through this elaborately orchestrated process of creating and spreading best practices, HP has, in fact, great difficulty spreading best practices to all units. The expression popularized in the corporation by Lew Platt captures the lost opportunities: "If only HP knew what HP knows, they would be three times as profitable." If divisions have strong business results, they can often avoid adopting business practices being pushed by the corporate organization. Implicit here is the old view that "if it ain't broken, don't fix it." In the case of the QMS, for example, we saw that it had only 70% market share despite being pushed by the CEO. Moreover, if one adjusts for percentage of HP profits added by divisions, the penetration of QMS is even lower.

Barriers to the acceptance of Quality 1 on 1 initiatives pioneered in one division by other divisions include lack of senior level sponsorship in potential adopting divisions, the perception on the part of these potential adopters that they are already customer centered, a lack of know-how and tools, and pressure from current work demands that stretch resources, systems, and processes. HP's strategy has been to employ the quality managers in the divisions as change agents, using them to try to forge a partnership with the general managers running the divisions. The aim is to get the general managers to serve as sponsors and champions of the new initiatives. A major problem is that there is enormous variability in the competencies and leadership skills of the quality managers in the divisions. Some two-thirds of quality managers have been in their jobs less than three years. This high turnover suggests that the quality manager position is seen as a way station until something better comes along, rather than a promising career opportunity in its own right. All this makes it less likely that quality managers will be capable of providing the necessary leadership in their dealings with the general managers running the divisions. Speed of adoption is not a strength of this design. By the end of 1998, there were still large numbers of HP managers who had never heard of the Quality 1 on 1 initiative.

However clever the design of the Quality 1 on 1 initiative, as displayed in Figure 8.2 to enlist the division in creating and spreading the new practices, it still will bring about, at best, only partial convergence of HP practices across divisions. The failure of other divisions to adopt seeming best practices and, even more important, the failure of the nonimplementing divisions to systematically share their successes suggests considerable suboptimization. Nor is this a simple problem to solve. As Lew Platt has observed, knowledge transfer is a sufficiently complex problem to yield not to one clever initiative, but to 10 different initiatives (Stewart, 1997: 160). More generally, this situation reflects the trade-off one must accept for achieving the benefits associated with giving the divisions the autonomy to grow their businesses. It is extraordinarily difficult to find the right balance between fostering autonomous behavior on the part of the divisions and the need to build a coherent overall corporate strategy through directed action (Brown and Duguid, 1997: 17). Moreover, my analysis suggests that the right balance shifts over time in response to the changing environmental challenges faced by the firm.

One additional problem brings us back to the efforts of YHP previously described. The initiators of Quality 1 on 1 were careful to position the new emphasis as building on past quality practices. Indeed, it is testimony to the institutionalization of many of these past practices that the new leadership had to move slowly and reassure the many employees who believed that their existing quality improvement practices worked. For example, in one of the first messages from the corporate quality organization to the business managers on the new Quality 1 on 1 approach in January 1995, the new leadership described the situation as follows:

> Clearly, the traditional view of quality does not address the most significant demands facing businesses today. The issues we struggled with in the 1980s, such as improving reliability and managing core processes are still important. But with HP participating in new markets, particularly consumer markets, things have radically changed.
>
> HP has learned a lot over the years and the company has earned a fine reputation for quality. . . . Following YHP's lead, quality organizations played an important role by making hoshin planning and process improvement a part of our culture.[2]

One sees here the subtle interaction between the case for change and the recognition of the utility of existing practices. Analytically, one can see quality improvement as composed of three pieces: capturing the customers' ideas and experiences, reflecting these ideas and experiences in product or service design characteristics and specifications, and staying true to these characteristics as the organization produces and delivers the product or service. To pursue the new emphasis on customers risks compromising the third key element in the quality equation.

The customer focus potentially draws energy, legitimacy, and resources away from the discipline required to maintain and improve organizational processing to secure higher customer satisfaction levels. In principle, this should not be the case since employees are expected to focus on whatever matters most to the customer. In practice, customers do not always articulate a clear emphasis on process control; they may take it for granted. Moreover, for all the management emphasis on figuring what the world looks like to the customer, in practice, it is an imprecise art; what poses as the science of understanding customer needs among popular management gurus is often scientism (e.g., Gale, 1994). Finally, managers cannot put in place a system that ensures, once and for all time, process problems do not result in defective products. The dynamic nature of the workplace and the tendency for regression makes organizational processing that stays true to design criteria a problem that must be continually addressed. Traditional TQC contains a successful set of methods for dealing with these continuing problems, especially its emphasis on statistical process control.

Thus, using each new quality initiative as a building block—rather than acting in ways that encourage employees to see them as separate initiatives, one replacing the next—makes sense not just as an abstract principle but as a practical matter. Nevertheless, this effort to develop a balanced approach emphasizing all three building blocks contains a delicate motivational issue, one which I have referenced earlier. One risks demotivating those whose career development and skills came to be associated with the traditional TQC methodology. As Richard LeVitt, the architect of the new approach, noted, HP's quality leaders need to build on where HP has been, but these leaders also need to build the case for profound change. He is aware of the paradox and looking for ways to resolve it. One example of such an effort is to ensure the development of measurement systems that provide balanced data, addressing both producer-centered and consumer-centered issues. This, however, speaks to only part of the problem.

Institutionally, HP has a significant advantage in balancing the old with the new. Precisely because of HP's past success with quality, there is an internal constituency for building Quality 1 on 1 on past practices. However much current quality leaders might want to embrace Quality 1 on 1, there is a significant core of quality managers and other divisional managers around the installed base of existing quality approaches. They operate as a political constituency that requires, for example, the careful negotiation of the content of QMS3 to reflect their interests and concerns. The effort to create QMS3 disturbed the extant political truce among competing factions and required the renegotiation of existing arrangements (Nelson and Winter, 1982: 107–112). In this way, the change process is being managed to accommodate the defenders of the existing quality practices while introducing major changes.

In this spirit, a quality roles task force (see Figure 8.2) was set up in 1994 and 1995. With roughly 12 members, it was organized to represent a cross section of the quality community, including both the old guard and the innovators, and to provide for broad geographical representation (a YHP representative participated). The task force provided a sounding board for the Quality 1 on 1 designers, evaluating strategies and tactics for redefining the role of quality managers.

The second body shown in Figure 8.2, which helped position the new initiative as building on the past, was the planning and quality committee, a standing council of senior managers whose concerns launched the reinventing quality initiative and whose sponsorship as an internal board of directors was essential in the public roll out. Finally, an advisory board of general managers was also created in this same period. They were the immediate customers for the new Quality 1 on 1 initiative and their involvement kept program designers focused on meeting the everyday business needs of managers. The advisory board had to review and sign off on new materials; at the same time because of their high status and position in the corporation, their association with this effort added legitimacy to the final product.

They helped the corporate quality office anticipate and accommodate many issues that would subsequently be raised. Through these committees and the embracing of the past in the packaging of Quality 1 on 1, the creators of the new initiative created "backward compatibility." They tied the past and present to the future in building-block fashion and acted to accommodate resistance and minimize opposition in the process.

Yet, change is endemic, and dissatisfaction with current organizational instruments is an ongoing process at HP. Concern about the effectiveness of the corporatewide hoshins grew in the late 1990s. Managers questioned the value of a common corporatewide plan, given the increasing diversity of HP business. In particular, many thought that the customer hoshins did not appear to be driving sufficiently different behavior than the business otherwise would have adopted. As a result in 1998, the enterprise-wide hoshins were dropped along with the requirement that the hoshin process be used by businesses for their planning. At the same time, the Planning and Quality Committee, whose job among other things was to generate the corporate plan, and the group managers' meeting for the quarterly review of progress was also discontinued.

In their place, the CEO introduced a change initiative under the banner "Power of One, Best of Many," which was supported by three strategies. One of these strategies, called "Customer Intensity," was introduced to drive the same customer-centered behavior sought by the old customer hoshin. To ensure that this change initiative was taken seriously, top management, with Corporate Quality's help, developed a set of standardized matrics for which group managers would be accountable. In addition to various financial measures, these included a customer loylity index that had been used successfully by several divisions. The customer loyalty index (and equivalents in use by a few organizations) would now serve as the visible measure of progress toward customer intensity. The goal was for each business to achieve the leadership positions in customer loyalty in comparison with its toughest competitors. In so doing, the Quality 1 on 1 initiative would be effectively implemented.

The Quality 1 on 1 movement is as much an indicator of the past success of YHP-inspired initiatives and the changing competitive environment as it is a further adaptation of Japanese-inspired practices to American business culture. The risk HP faces is that in pursuing the new directions, it does not lose the anchor of TQC practices for ensuring effective organizational processing of customer needs. What is the potential for the Quality 1 on 1 initiative to produce significant organizational change? The company is providing managerial incentives and is investing in an institutional infrastructure (QMS3) to facilitate the change process. Yet the outcome is far from clear. Anticipating and meeting customer needs is not a science but an art, notwithstanding the best efforts of marketing gurus and consultants. Nor will the fiercely autonomous HP divisions yield easily, nor should they.

Spreading the Word

The significance of the HP case goes far beyond HP. Just like Florida Power and Light, HP served as a key link for other companies in a two-step learning process. As we have seen, many American companies chose to wait and learn from the seemingly successful American adopters of the new quality model rather than learn directly from the Japanese. Frequently benchmarked,[3] HP was seen as one of those pacesetters. Prominent areas in which its quality initiative has been benchmarked include planning (especially hoshin management), people practices, process management, and reengineering. It has worked closely with Motorola and Xerox, seeing Xerox as the company most like it in terms of its approach to quality. But HP is not eager to cooperate in benchmarking without a reciprocal return in benefits. Those with whom HP initiates benchmarking activities will also want a return. Thus, HP provided a report to all 12 participating companies detailing results of its aforementioned 1994 world benchmarking study.

Customers are very active in making benchmarking requests; if they are big and important, they get priority. Customer supplier networks of this nature are an underappreciated source of diffusion of best practice. We saw in Chapter 6 how an extended exchange of quality information took place between HP and one of its good customers, P&G.

Eventually, HP emerged as one of the early U.S. leaders in implementing hoshin management (along with Xerox and FPL) and its approach was made available to many other American manufacturing companies (see Watson, 1991). As discussed in Chapter 6, the organization that took the early leadership in adapting and applying hoshin management in the United States was GOAL/QPC, and HP cooperated in their efforts. Indeed, even YHP's CEO, Sasaoka, participated in one of GOAL/QPC's public conferences.

Another organization that came to promote hoshin management beginning in the early 1990s was CQM. CQM member companies contribute staff and training in their areas of expertise to other member companies. HP often contributed instructors to provide training in hoshin management.

In addition to GOAL/QPC and CQM, HP cooperates in the quality area with a broad range of other organizations, including ASQ, the Council for Continuous Improvement, the American Productivity and Quality Center (in which it was a founding member), the AEA, Manufacturers' Alliance, various consultant-initiated groups like the Customer Value Council, and the Conference Board's Quality Councils. The Conference Board experience was helpful in getting HP to realize in the early 1990s that many companies, not particularly noted for their quality, were doing innovative things and closing the quality gap. This spurred HP's efforts to search for new approaches that would create sustainable advantages.

The HP quality office is also active in a number of semi-institutionalized company-based networks. Among the more interesting ones is the Informal Learning Group (ILG), a network with some 25 major international corporations begun in 1994. The focus of their meeting is process improvement aimed at business results. With a few exceptions (P&G, and Lever Bros.) most members are not direct competitors in their major markets; as we have seen previously, this facilitates the exchange process. Still another such network focusing on process improvement began in 1996 as a breakaway from the American Productivity and Quality Center's (APQC) International Benchmarking Clearinghouse. With the rapid expansion of the APQC's membership, these larger firms came to believe that they were giving more than receiving as their interests were sacrificed to the large influx of newer, typically less advanced, members (in terms of benchmarking capabilities), so they set up their own exchange.

One gets a further sense here of the rich infrastructure for diffusing quality-related practices that gradually grew in the decade of the 1980s and 1990s. In summary, the pipeline from YHP to HP had an amplified effect with HP serving as a secondary transmission belt for diffusing quality improvement practices (now modified to fit HP's corporate culture) to other companies and organizations. These organizations, such as GOAL/QPC and ASQ, extended the two-step learning process to a three-step learning process by diffusing quality improvement ideas to still wider audiences.

Conclusion

From about 1979 to 1986, YHP's role in diffusing ideas about quality to HP was played out in a relatively short time frame. Just as HP's interest in YHP's quality practices rose dramatically with the profitability of YHP, it fell rapidly once YHP's profitability sank. In 1985 the Plaza Accord took effect with a resultant rapid rise in the value of the yen. The business results of YHP started to decline. Over the next few years, this downward turn was reinforced by a variety of micro and macro factors including internal HP accounting changes that raised transfer prices for YHP's sales organization (thereby raising the prices of imported products to be sold in Japan), the bursting of the bubble associated with Japan's hyperspeculation, the high expenses YHP incurred moving into new facilities, and their very high investment to get into the integrated circuit tester market.

In 1992, the YHP manufacturing division actually reported a loss.[4] This was the low point. Not until 1995 did it restore a high profit rate again, especially in the test and measurement sector, where it once again achieved the number-one position at HP. From a practical point of view, one can argue that this brief window of acceptability from 1979 to 1986 was all that was needed. The "bloom was off the rose" by 1986, but as one YHP manager put it, "We had already pretty much transferred most of what we had to offer as regards TQC." The negative results of YHP were offset for awhile by the continuing popularity in American companies of absorbing things Japanese until the early 1990s. At that time, the impact of the bursting of the Japanese bubble started to be felt, and those presenting Japan as a model to be emulated disappeared rapidly from the popular dialogue.

These events raise a more general point. In the introduction and chapter 3, in particular, I discussed managerial decision making in response to the Japanese quality challenge and argued that in the early 1980s managers seemed to be making systematic errors in their assessments. For this discussion, one can ask what the basis is by which managers decide that a given company, or a unit within a company, is, or is not, a model. There is no doubt that success in the marketplace is a powerful predictor of which companies and units come to serve as models. Yet, one can ask, was the astounding success of YHP in the early 1980s clearly a function of TQC? Not necessarily. In the early 1980s, Japanese companies (not all of which were doing TQC) faced an increasingly favorable business climate, and in that environment, TQC proved extremely effective, but so were some other practices. While certainly a good case can be made for the independent contributions of TQC to YHP's success, the causal linkages are in fact not all that clear. We are dealing with complex systems. Yet HP took YHP's financial success as a clear indicator of TQC's effectiveness.

Similarly, HP managers (and even some YHP managers) increasingly questioned the relevance of YHP quality practices as soon as YHP's profit position dissipated in the mid-1980s; YHP clearly lost its attraction as a magnet for other HP managers after the mid-1980s. Yet were YHP's TQC activities any less effective from 1987 to 1992 than they were in the early 1980s in terms of their contribution to manufacturing efficiencies, to HP's quality performance and reputation, and indeed to the bottom line itself? Probably not. On logical grounds alone (assuming that their TQC activities had stabilized by the mid-1980s), constants cannot explain a variable. Instead of being a negative factor, one can just as strongly argue, as Kenzo Sasaoka does in his reflections on this matter, that by staying true to TQC practices during the downturn, YHP's business decline was not as steep as it would otherwise have been. Similarly, YHP's rapid recovery from the 1992 low point can be seen as a reflection of its adherence to TQC improvement activities while gradually installing a new, improved business strategy (Sasaoka, 1996: 19–23).

The point here is not that Sasaoka is right or wrong, but rather that managers observing this kind of situation often do not know which position is right or wrong. They do not know the cause and effect linkages. Yet, faced with this kind of situation, they invariably assume that a decline in corporate success must mean the practice(s) being considered for borrowing are not working. Managers tends to equate the efficacy of their management systems with their financial performance.

In this case, what are the underlying conditions that increase the probability of this outcome? Under conditions in which the innovative practice challenges conventional wisdom and not much hard evidence supports its positive or negative effects, a kind of negative halo effect flows from declining corporate performance. This leads managers to conclude that what they want to adopt from their prospective model may not affect the model's most important measure of all, corporate performance. The burden of proof is on those supporting the innovative practice.

Under the two conditions described, and the fact that many other changes are occurring simultaneously, managers will tend to conclude that it is better to err on the side of caution and to drop learning from that model. They will try to find something else that can turn around corporate performance more quickly. In this context, it is hard to stand up in management meetings and argue the positive case for the innovation. Yet acting on very little evidence creates a big component of uncertainty and a large chance of being wrong. Quality advocates undoubtedly contributed to these management decisions by exaggerating the benefits of quality initiatives and presuming a very high correlation between quality performance and short-term corporate financial performance. When that correlation could not be shown, the advocates were defenseless.

What can be learned from these two chapters about organizational design for learning? Clearly many serendipitous factors contributed to YHP serving as a model for HP's new approaches to quality improvement starting in the early 1980s. As the garbage can model of decision making suggests, YHP was in the right place at the right time with the right solutions for the right kind of company. This does not mean that going to Japan to learn how to do quality improvement would work only under these circumstances. Nevertheless, not that many American companies could have duplicated all the propitious conditions in the HP-YHP relationship in the early 1980s. This suggests that strategic intent to learn and ability to consciously design the learning process are more limited than scholars and consultants writing on this subject might have us believe. Major constraints conditioning a successful technology transfer process are often outside the control of those engaged in organizational engineering.

The benefits to HP of the YHP relationship were enormous. First and foremost, YHP served as a source of trustworthy and transparent information. It raised the sights among HP managers for what was possible in the quality arena, including the provisions of outcome benchmarks and provided a paradigm of a new approach to resolve major organizational uncertainties, as well as a template for specific processes and practices. These were no small contributions. Further, YHP offered both objectives and means to reach those objectives. Thus, HP grabbed a huge head start over many other U.S. companies and distinctively marked its approach to quality improvement in ways that are still quite visible. Furthermore, the ways in which the Japanese quality diagnostic metamorphosed into QMS2 at HP and the adaptations made to hoshin management clearly facilitated HP's transition from learning how YHP "did it" to effective practice. Managers at HP actively managed the conversion of learning into effective practice.

Learning, however, takes on a very special meaning in a highly decentralized company. At HP, typically some divisions would take the lead experimenting with innovative practices such as quality circles, activity-based accounting, JIT manufacturing, hoshin management, and QFD. They would really think through the meaning and purpose of these activities and what needed to change to make them work. They would then make the necessary changes. If they were successful, managers from other divisions would visit and "cherry pick" specific practices aiming for the same results but without the deep system thinking that led to initial success.

A mutation process evolved over time more consistent with dilution than with the development of best practice. In a highly decentralized company like HP, no one at the corporate level forces divisional managers to identify and "stay true" to best practice.[5] At best, as we have seen, executives can only encourage such activities. One can distinguish the 1980s from the early 1990s. Throughout much of the 1980s, the corporate role of quality increased, aligned as it was with top-management efforts to meet the Japanese challenge. Not surprisingly, top management saw the need for a strong coordinated response on the part of the whole organization. But with demonstrated success in meeting that challenge, there was increasing resistance at the division level to this corporate imposition.

Responding to this resistance, corporate quality officers adopted a market-driven approach in which they had to "sell" their services to the groups and divisions. This greatly reduced their ability to impose their own vision of quality improvement and the priority of specific approaches. At the same time, however, when they could make common cause with their customers (groups and divisions), they were in a position to create a much more spontaneous cooperative activity. Certainly, the company did not return to a totally decentralized model; top management's use of hoshin management built incentives for experimentation and subtly reinforced the new Quality 1 on 1 initiative developed by corporate quality.

These changes in the position of quality as a competitive issue and the role of the corporate quality group paralleled some broader changes in the corporation. In the early 1990s David Packard led a movement to reverse many of the centralizing practices and coordinating committees that had developed over the decade (Packard, 1995: 149–150). He and others believed that the company had become too bureaucratic, too slow to respond to changing market conditions, especially in the computer business. Quality was a bit player in that reversal, but as we just saw, a set of conditions specific to quality favored this reversal as well.

One sees these patterns played out in the fates of four practices discussed in the last two chapters: quality circles, the QMS, hoshin management, and Quality 1 on 1. Quality circles were initiated in the early 1980s with little corporate direction and control. Very little effort was put into ensuring the identification and diffusion of best practice; the central quality office lacked the authority to ensure these outcomes, and top management was not all that committed to circle activities. Under these circumstances, the practice of quality circles mutated as they extended into new work environments, diluted over time, and dissipated. The history of quality circles throughout HP's Asian operations is quite different, and they still show great vitality there.

The QMS was initiated somewhat later as a major corporate thrust at a time when corporate direction over how the divisions should respond to the Japanese quality challenge increased. Intended as a central diagnostic/audit function, its very aim was to identify and support best quality practices. Thus, QMS evolved in a controlled and strategic fashion as managers adapted it to HP's changing circumstances and understandings. Even after it became voluntary for divisions to request QMS audits, the rate of participation among divisions remained high.

Hoshin management represents a middle case. It began in the era when top management saw great benefits to developing common planning processes among the divisions. Having been developed in Japan, like the rest of TQC, it appeared to be an "off the shelf" product. There was strong pressure for divisions to adopt hoshin management, and corporate quality provided a template for how to do it. Nevertheless, over time, its importance to specific divisions has varied.

Finally, Quality 1 on 1 arrived on the scene in the mid-1990s, a time in which corporate quality's ability to impose its will on the divisions was much lower, top management's support was more indirect, and it drew its budget partially from its ability to work with business units. Thus, corporate quality took the natural path of forming alliances with divisions that were willing to experiment with new quality approaches and develop the technology associated with it. As that technology develops, they seek to integrate the various new practices developed at the divisional level both with each other and with other understandings gathered from external sources (e.g., external consultants, publications, benchmarking activities, etc.) and to market the newly synthesized package across the corporation.

In the introduction, I cited the observations of Sidney Winter (1994: 101–102), who noted that the diffusion of soft organizational innovations suffer from a substantial ambiguity of definition and therefore mutate in different environments. His focus was on the puzzling trail of definitional issues this posed for the analyst. What I add to that understanding here is that within organizations, this ambiguity can be amplified by specific organizational structures, including the degree of centralization and the role of centralized functions.

One should be careful not to overemphasize YHP's contribution to HP's quality practices and performance; many other influences were important. Thus, to take just one significant decision, in 1984 HP added to its 10 criteria for performance appraisal an evaluation item for quality applicable to all levels of employees. This decision had no connection to YHP but was one that a number of innovative American quality leaders such as Ford Motor Co. started making. It was a way of aligning incentives with the new quality emphasis and signaling to management employees that career success required attention to the quality issue. As more and more experience accumulated in American companies, and the institutional influence of the Baldrige was established, YHP's role as a model for HP declined. Without discussion of these other influences, YHP looks like the decisive factor. The intent in this chapter is to show only that access to YHP gave HP a huge head start over many other U.S. companies and visibly shaped current practices.

Some HP personnel will be surprised by this account since the sources of ideas, practices, models, and templates are not always clear. Retrospective history writing tends to diminish the source and play up the implementers (Kanter: 1983:

282–289). This is especially the case when the company is backing away from borrowing from that source, as was the case with HP vis-à-vis YHP in the late 1980s. Also key HP managers as early as the mid-1970s started pressuring for quality improvement and laid the groundwork for some of the responses I have recorded.

Quality was never the umbrella theme at HP that it was in some other famous quality leaders, such as Milliken and Motorola. In the decentralized culture of HP, it is easy to lose sight of the broader picture. As one HP manager put it to me, "New practices spread in HP in osmotic style. So many employees, who are somewhat removed from the original source, don't recognize the origin of many new ideas." Some of YHP's influences are more apparent to those down in the divisions (diffusion of TQC process improvement practices) than to staff serving at headquarters. Still others are more visible to headquarters personnel. For those at the very top of the corporation, however, the nature of YHP's contributions was quite clear, as evidenced in a formal resolution of appreciation by the Executive Committee of the Board of Directors of HP upon the retirement of Kenzo Sasaoka in 1996. The resolution included the following statement:

> Mr. Sasaoka championed the improvement of quality at YHP resulting in the company's winning the Deming Prize in 1982; he served as an inspiration to the rest of Hewlett-Packard ultimately leading to the pervasive implementation of quality improvement methodologies and significant breakthroughs in quality and cost effectiveness in Hewlett-Packard's worldwide operations.

The phenomenal success of HP through the first half of the 1990s as it continued to grow at a very rapid pace has many sources. Although I cannot demonstrate quality's role statistically, the company has nurtured throughout this period a strong quality reputation which cannot help but have been a major business asset. The American Customer Satisfaction Survey reports results from the personal computer and computer printer industry from 1995 to 1997. While the overall score for the industry declined over these years, in each of the three years, HP achieved the highest quality score of any of the major firms surveyed. For 1997, the mean score of the industry, adjusted for market share, was 70 while HP's score stood at 75 (http://acsi.asq.org). Many other independent surveys rank HP first in customer satisfaction in a variety of product lines. Most recently, it ranked first in customer satisfaction surveys in the following areas: consulting and systems integration, technical features of systems integration, business benefits of system integration, network and systems-management software systems, notebook and desktop personal computers, and technical support for desktop computers, network servers, and desktop printers. It also ranked highest in reliability for notebooks, desktop personal computers, and servers (Hewlett Packard Corporation, 1997: 4–5). Underlying their strong quality reputation has been the demonstrable improvements in product reliability and availability (as measured in mean time between failures and mean time to repair). The 10x initiative symbolized these improvements in the 1980s. Even in the recalcitrant area of software, HP reported a sixfold reduction in software defect density from 1989 to 1994 (Ristelhueber, 1994: 41).

Participating in product lines characterized by recurrent periods of explosive growth (e.g., ink jet and laser printers) as a result of short product cycles and dramatic new advances in technology, HP has assumed a leadership role in quality improvement practices that has been an enormous asset. In such industries, the ability to rapidly ramp up production for the mass market with a minimum of quality glitches and with high yields is critical to success; HP has excelled in exactly this area (Moore, 1995: 81). Moreover, YHP's contribution to these achievements has not been trivial, but its contributions have continually been modified and adapted to fit new competitive circumstances and different cultural conditions. Truly, HP found a way to be where the news was breaking and to turn that to competitive advantage.

None of these past successes, however, guarantees HP's future. Some HP initiatives raise concerns. In line with HP's vision of becoming a premier design and technology company, it began in the late 1980s to subcontract various "non-core" functions including manufacturing expertise. The idea was to concentrate one's core manufacturing capabilities and to free up resources for other investments. Vertical disintegration began with the least critical manufacturing activities (e.g., sheet metal and machining) and rapidly expanded downstream to include product final assembly and testing (Beckman and Mowery, 1996: 21).

An alternative scenario, however, sees the interaction between manufacturing expertise and design and technology competence as critical to developing design and technology excellence, as well as maintaining quality excellence. One needs to control the learning that arises from an iterative feedback process between manufacturing and design personnel to hone one's technological capabilities. Furthermore, if HP is increasingly contracting out certain functions, such as design or manufacturing, to the same best contractors as its competitors, it is hard to see where the quality advantage will come from.

In short, HP's vertical disintegration may well threaten its quality success, not to speak of its technology excellence. The HP benchmarking study mentioned before showed clear signs of eroding quality advantage. Yet HP's activities along these lines have yet to demonstrate serious impairment of its quality capabilities. Moreover, as the Japanese experience demonstrates, a situation of modest vertical integration combined with closely coordinated relationships with contractors can be a recipe for quality success (though the Japanese model presumes more dedicated suppliers with less leakage of proprietary information to competitors).

Finally, one finds strong evidence that pacesetters like HP played a major role in diffusing a version of TQC more adapted to its corporate culture, if not an American environment. It cooperated in a variety of networking activities with other firms and institutions that led to the diffusion of its approaches to quality improvement. I have discussed a number of HP's quality results. In the next chapter, we paint quality outcomes on a broader canvas.

CHAPTER 9

Quality Outcomes

In the early and mid-1980s, American manufacturing managers in internationally competitive markets such as auto and semiconductors/electronics were wringing their hands, despairing of competing with the Japanese. The overall attitude among executives was that quality was a Japanese possession that would be hard, if not impossible, for Americans to acquire. What a difference a decade and a half makes! The Japanese quality advantage has disappeared from the front and even back pages of the business media. Indeed, quality as an internationally competitive issue has greatly receded from public discussion. When it is mentioned in the business media, the focus is likely on how long it takes or how much it costs firms to acquire ISO 9000 certification.

The quality models held up for admiration today are American firms like Motorola, HP, and Federal Express. American managers appear confident when it comes to quality. They have seen their firms achieve substantial, sustained improvement in quality. The quality gap, even when not eliminated, has been greatly diminished in many industries. The gap has diminished so much that the advantage no longer necessarily lies with the Japanese. Nowhere is that more apparent than in the automotive and electronics/semiconductor sectors.

The Automotive Industry

In Chapter 2, I reported that in the early 1980s Ford's internal studies found that the ratio of trouble frequency for Ford vehicles to Japanese vehicles was a remarkable 6 to 1.[1] Industry data suggest that in 1980 the Big Three domestic car companies averaged between six and eight defects per car with the Japanese averaging about two defects per car (Ealey and Troyano-Bermúdez, 1996; Industrial Bank of Japan, 1996: 9).[2] There was wide variation not only in the reliability performance of the Big Three vis-á-vis the Japanese but also in contrast to one another and among the different models of the same car company. On top of this, the U.S. manufacturers had severe competitive problems resulting from an absence of fuel efficient cars and much higher costs than the Japanese.

By the mid-1990s, the situation had changed dramatically. There has been a remarkable convergence in quality performance as measured by reliability. Improving from an average seven defects per car, the U.S. domestic industry now is averaging around one defect per vehicle. While the Japanese have continued to improve, the gap between the American and Japanese has shrunk dramatically. When the first Initial Quality Survey (IQS) was done in 1987, there was a gap of 340 defects per 100 cars between the industry-leading model, the Toyota Cressida (69 defects per 100 vehicles) and the worst-performing model, the Alfa Romeo Milano (409 defects per 100 vehicles). In 1997 the gap between the worst-performing Pontiac Firebird and the best-performing Lexus LS 400 (38 defects per 100 vehicles) was down to 140 defects per 100 cars (Rechtin, 1997a: 3, 28). The change over the 11-year period from 1987 to 1997 represents a 59% reduction in the range of variability between the worst and the best performers. Light trucks on average have a higher number of defects per vehicle, but the trend toward reduction in the range of variability has paralleled that of passenger cars.

Moreover, over the course of the last decade and a half, the Japanese have shifted more of their production and car content to the United States. By 1996, imports accounted only for one third of total Japanese auto sales in the United States (Chappell, 1996: 3). Thus, what increasingly matters most for customer experiences is not Japanese cars made in Japan but Japanese cars made in North America. Japanese cars produced in the United States have a somewhat higher number of defects than those produced in Japan. Thus, if one compares U.S. cars manufactured in North America with Japanese cars manufactured in North America, the quality gap shrinks even further. Adjusted to reflect only assembly plant–related problems, in 1995, the U.S. firms' North American plants scored 61 defects per 100 vehicles (82 in 1989) versus 56 (65 in 1989) for the Japanese assembly plants in North America (Womack, Jones, and Roos, 1991: 92; MacDuffie and Pil, 1997: 26). One sees from this data not only the modest gap between the North American plants of the American producers and the Japanese but also how the gap has closed since 1989.

For the curious, Japanese assembly plants in Japan recorded 45 defects per 100 vehicles (60 in 1989) in this same time period. These data should not be overinterpreted because the Japanese have tended to keep the production of their high-end products like Lexus and Infinity in Japan, and predictably more attention is paid to squeezing out any defects from high-priced luxury vehicles. These data also conceal a number of smaller stories. For example, MacDuffie and colleagues found increasing variation in quality performance among Japanese manufacturers in the early 1990s, with Toyota and Honda getting stronger and some of the weaker firms suffering deterioration.

Overall, one sees an extraordinary convergence among the industry producers with a reduction of variance not only between the Japanese and the Americans (and the Europeans for that matter) but also among the domestic producers themselves and across models of any given producer. Additional convergence has occurred on a variety of performance features (another dimension of quality performance) such as fuel economy, safety, acceleration, braking, and cornering. Many of these developments have been driven by the introduction of new technologies such as fuel injection, multivalve engines, radial tires, and semi-metallic brake pads (Ealey and Troyano-Bermúdez, 1996: 65).

Moreover, one can define quality more broadly to include the ability of manufacturers to delight and surprise customers through novel features, styling, performance, and creature comforts. These issues often involve aesthetics and perceived quality. When one uses these broader definitions, the American producers perform even better than the Japanese in many categories on surveys carried out by leading firms such as Strategic Vision and on J. D. Powers APPEAL survey (e.g., Rechtin, 1997b: 51, see note 2, this chapter, for a definition of APPEAL). These surveys are structured to measure both customer enthusiasm for a vehicle and dissatisfaction over defect problems and allows for the former to outweigh the latter.

Consider Chrysler Corp., notorious for its reliability problems during much of the 1990s. Until 1998, no Chrysler division has ever finished above the industry average in the Initial Quality Survey since the study was begun in 1987 (Stoffer, 1997: 8). Its warranty costs have also been reported to be above average for the industry (Henderson and Suris, 1995: A3). In recognition of its problems, the firm adopted the Chrysler Operating System in 1997, based on the Toyota model with the guiding mantra that workers, through their work teams, take responsibility for evaluating and fixing problems as they occur (Kisiel, 1997: 24–25). Notwithstanding its quality problems, Chrysler developed an exciting reputation for styling, market leadership (minivans, sports utility), and innovative engineering (e.g., cab-forward design). By contrast, the Japanese were quite slow in responding to the shift to light trucks (minivans, pickup trucks, and sports utility vehicles). This sector rose steadily to account for a record 43.7% of all new vehicles sold in the United States in 1996. Thus, if quality is fundamentally about anticipating and responding to customer needs, as I have argued it is, then the Japanese clearly fell behind. Certainly, they had some added handicaps in the light truck market induced by differential tariff treatments from passenger cars, but these were known handicaps to which they could have adjusted.

Despite the convergence in quality and performance characteristics, the Japanese producers show continuing competitive strength, as evidenced in market share. Thus, the Japanese share of the American auto market rose from 18.2% in 1985 to a high of 25.7% in 1991, fell in subsequent years and rose recently to 23.5% in 1997. These data conceal the fact that their share of passenger cars stood at 31.1% in 1997; what dragged their total share down was their weakness in the light truck sector, 14.3% in 1997, which, as mentioned, grew dramatically over the previous decade (Automotive News, 1998: 46). Yet, because the Japanese producers spent much of the 1990s reducing costs to cope with the strong yen, after the yen began to weaken after 1995, they once again have been gaining market share.

What is remarkable is that the overall Japanese automotive share did not fall more than it did during the first half of the 1990s, given not only the convergence in quality but, most important, the rapid rise in the value of the yen, which peaked in 1995 at 80 yen to the dollar. Under the currency pressures, the Japanese were forced to significantly raise their prices. Two explanations seem relevant for the continuing Japanese market strength under these circumstances. The first is the tendency of the American producers to emphasize profit over market share and thus not take full advantage of their pricing flexibility. The second is that quality reputations are hard to lose, but once lost, they are very hard to gain back. Thus, many American consumers refused to believe the Japanese were producing superior cars in the early 1980s, and the American producers thus benefited from their long-standing quality reputations (i.e., they did not lose as much market share in the 1980s as they deserved to). Conversely, in the 1990s, many Americans, particularly those over 35 who could remember bad quality experiences with American cars, refuse to believe that the American producers have improved. Thus, the Japanese producers continued to benefit from their now less deserved reputation as producers of superior quality vehicles.

The Electronics/Semiconductor Industries

As in the automotive industry, a huge concern emerged in the electronics industries in the early 1980s publicly triggered, as shown in Chapter 2, by the HP announcement that its best-performing U.S. suppliers of 16K DRAMs had defect rates six times higher than those of their best-performing Japanese suppliers. Studies also showed significantly lower yield on the part of American producers (as reported in Chapter 2, the difference in probe yield approached 20% in 1987 according to a GAO study). As memory chips moved quickly from one generation to another, the overall yield became a major determinant of commercial success. With their great production expertise resting on the excellently managed handoff from R & D and close working relationships with equipment suppliers, all continuously refined through feedback from in-house users, the Japanese achieved high yields and previously unseen levels of high quality and productivity in mass-produced chips (cf. Ziegler, 1991: 161; Florida and Kenny, 1990; Angel, 1994). They used this to rapidly increase their share of global markets.

By the mid-1980s, many U.S. merchant firms left the memory chip business and shifted to microprocessors and other more specialized devices. This proved to be a wise decision because logic chips are more difficult to design, cannot easily be copied as they can be protected by patents, and allow the producer to create "lock in" with customers further down the production chain because the product is designed around a particular chip. In the end, however, given the rapid diffusion of knowledge in a global economy, they only bought enough time to solve their quality and productivity problems.

The Japanese share of the worldwide memory chip market peaked at 71% in 1988 and of the overall worldwide semiconductor market at 51% in 1988. The new challenge in memory chips came from the Koreans and more recently from the Taiwanese. A further challenge came from the Americans with the growing importance of microprocessors, driven by the growth of the computer industry.

Semiconductors are of course only part of the broader electronics industry, which includes many sectors of economic activity. The AEA includes firms from such sectors as aerospace and defense, computers, computer peripherals, electronic components, instruments and systems, medical equipment, production equipment, semiconductors, software, telecom equipment, as well as others. Moreover, unlike in the automotive sector with its finite number of products purchased by consumers, electronic industry output is an intermediate product imbedded in almost the full range of manufacturing products including automobiles.

Given this diversity, selecting one or two indicators to show the trajectory of quality in the electronics industry over the last decade and a half is impossible. Nonetheless, clearly the quality (as measured in internal defect rates and reliability) of electronic components has improved dramatically over the course of the 1980s and early 1990s. Component quality is now typically measured in ppm defectives rather than percent defective, the common measure in the early 1980s. Metal film resistors, multilayer capacitors, semiprecision resistors, and integrated circuits, to name just a few common electronic components, have registered orders of magnitude improvement as measured in ppm defectives (Godfrey and Kerwin, 1988: 29.2–4). Indeed, it is fortunate that these improvements occurred because as the complexity of products and systems increases, the negative consequences of unreliable components grows ever larger.

Other suggestive evidence comes from HP's research. Engaged in a broad range of activities in the electronics industry, HP achieved dramatic improvements in its quality performance across many sectors of activity and generally ranks very high on customer satisfaction surveys, including markets in which HP competes against Japanese firms. It is recognized as one of the U.S. firms that had a strong tradition of emphasizing quality, absorbed many of the Japanese lessons in quality in the 1980s, and became a pacesetter in quality performance.

I reported in Chapter 8 that in 1994 HP undertook a large-scale benchmarking effort with other high-technology companies. This effort looked at four business segments: computer products, computer systems, component products, and instrument products. Seven of the 11 firms HP benchmarked against were American and two of the four non-American firms were Japanese. While HP did not directly measure quality performance levels, all the firms selected were recognized leaders in quality. The designers of the study identified the major drivers of high quality performance according to their understandings. These included a prevention focus, the extent of resources devoted to quality improvement, extent of top-management activities on behalf of quality improvement, extent of external focus on customers, and so on.

The study found that the firms and divisions benchmarked against were using much the same ideas, tools, and methods that they were. By and large, though there was variation in implementation strategy and resource allocation, there was very little difference in the fundamental approach to quality among the bench-marked companies. None had a clear lead. The conclusion that HP had lost its commanding lead sent HP off on its Quality 1 on 1 journey, described in the previous chapter. For my purposes, here, the critical point is HP's sense that all the major firms they benchmarked against had arrived in the same place by the mid-1990s. As a reflection of the changing times, the report contains nothing to suggest that Japanese firms, either individually or collectively, had a commanding lead, or for that matter any lead at all. Just as in the automotive area, there is a seeming convergence of quality performance.

Before one jumps too hastily to that conclusion, it is useful to examine in depth one major area of electronics that offers detailed comparative data: the sem-iconductor industry. If one could choose only one electronics sector to examine, this seems a most appropriate choice, for it was, after all, the disparity in chip-makers' performance that led to the initial public awareness of a quality gap in electronics. Of course, there are reports from major firms of major improvements in quality performance. For example, Intel's yield of usable silicon has more than doubled since the 1980s. Similarly, the reliability of chips, as experienced by end users, improved dramatically (cf., Main, 1994: 183, 185).

Industry officials claimed that, by 1988, they had reached parity with their Japanese competitors in product quality. They reported reducing their defect rates to about one part in 20,000, a 40-fold improvement from 1980. The very firm that first went public with claims of U.S. quality weakness among its chip suppliers, HP, publicly proclaimed tremendous improvement in the product quality of U.S. producers. The director of HP's corporate procurement office, Ken Newton, an-nounced in 1993 that HP no longer saw any national differences in quality of product sent from suppliers (Siegmann, 1993: B3).

Yet one would prefer more detailed data to substantiate such claims. Industry officials, whether in auto or electronics, have a tendency—based on strong incen-tives—to exaggerate their improvements. Moreover, one can say one is not ship-ping inferior products, but it is quite different to say that one is not producing them. If one solves a quality problem by rigorous inspection and not shipping defective product, one has, in the quality professional's jargon, a high cost of quality. This cost directly undercuts a firm's bottom line and weakens its compet-itiveness. The high costs derive not so much from scrap but from the opportunity costs associated with lost production of good product; given the escalating costs of fabrication facilities (fabs), it is critical to amortize costs over as large a pro-duction total as possible.

We do get some indication of quality's growing importance as seen by managers in a National Institute of Standards and Technology study published in 1990 (Quick, Finan and Associates, 1990: 16). The authors found that in the late 1980s roughly 20–35% of the total budget of U.S. semiconductor companies was devoted to achieving quality improvement. In absolute terms, total quality-related outlays in the semiconductor industry increased fourfold from 1980 to 1990—an annual rate of increase averaging 15%. These data are certainly quite suggestive, but we can't confuse inputs with outputs. How has quality performance actually changed?

Fortunately, the University of California, Berkeley, Competitive Semiconductor Manufacturing (CSM) Program provides data that allow some key comparisons between Japanese and American semiconductor producers over time and specifically addresses some of these issues.[3] The data are for eight wafer fabs in the United States and three in Japan. They represent eight and three companies, respectively. All are major companies in the semiconductor industry with sales of over 500 million dollars a year. The three companies in Japan have reputations for high quality and productivity. There is somewhat more variability in the reputations of the American companies, but if it can be shown that these American firms have closed the gap with top Japanese performers, then the results would be all the more impressive. All the fabs included in the sample to be discussed are submicron Complementary metal Oxide Semiconductor (CMOS) fabs built in the late 1980s or early 1990s and producing CMOS logic chips. It makes sense to look at CMOS logic products because both the United States and the Japanese are producing them, as opposed to DRAMS where few American players are left.

The quality metric to be reported is for integrated yield in 1.0–1.25 logic chips. Integrated yield is the product of line yield (average fraction of wafers started that emerge from the fab process flow as completed wafers) and die yield (fraction of the total die on a wafer that passes the wafer probe test). Line yield loss and die yield loss generally result from different causes, in line yield, gross misprocessing or wafer breakage, and in die yield, minor misprocessing and particulate damage.[4]

Figure 9.1 reports the integrated yield for 1.0–1.25 micron CMOS logic process flows. The data are for the aggregated performance of sampled fabs by region (United States and Japan) from October 1990 to October 1993 based on self-reports of monthly measures. One sees that the gap in October 1990 was considerable, with the U.S. fabs scoring on average 42.40 as their integrated yield and the Japanese producers averaging 78.48. As shown in Figure 9.1, scores oscillate greatly over time for both sets of national fabs; the sudden drops reflect primarily the disturbances that result from the introduction of different families of logic products at the respective companies. But the American fabs showed sustained improvement so that by October 1993, their integrated line yield rose to 79.70, while the Japanese stood at 80.78, close to where they started. Researchers in the CSM program also examined the integrated yield performance in Japanese and U.S. fabs for 0.7–0.9

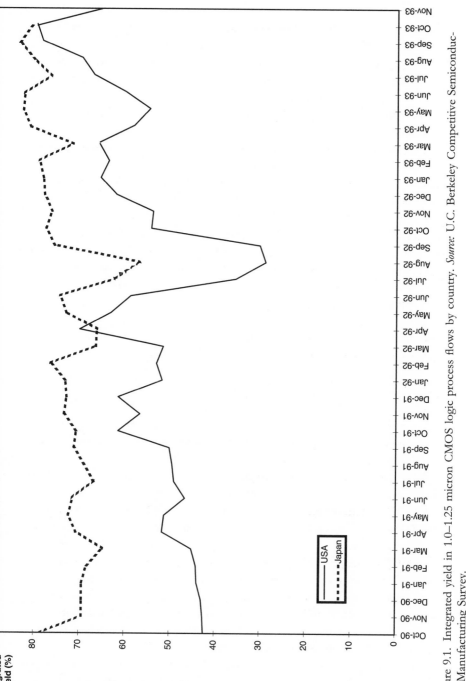

Figure 9.1. Integrated yield in 1.0–1.25 micron CMOS logic process flows by country. *Source:* U.C. Berkeley Competitive Semiconductor Manufacturing Survey.

micron CMOS memory process flows and 0.7–0.9 micron CMOS logic process flows. The results were similar to those just described; the Japanese started with a large advantage in 1990, but the Americans sharply reduced the gap by 1993.

These data overall suggest that the American spokesman may have been right about having parity with the Japanese in the late 1980s, but it was in field reliability, achieved, by and large, through improved process control and utilization of more intensive internal testing processes to screen out defective devices, thereby ensuring that customers did not receive them. This approach required, however, that firms, and eventually their customers, absorb the costs that went with this defect detection approach. In effect, they had turned a quality problem into a cost problem. To be sure, the American producers did make progress in improving their yield, especially the leading firms, during the late 1980s (United States GAO, 1992: 10; Finan, 1990). Not until the 1990s, however, were the Americans able to substantially eliminate the Japanese advantage in integrated yield, thereby ensuring a more level playing field in costs as well. Improvement in the U.S. producers' integrated yield suggests their ability to implement a more proactive prevention approach. Rigorous inspection and other appraisal activities did not totally disappear with these newer approaches, but they were more likely to be used to trigger in-line and other forms of problem solving to improve manufacturing performance rather than used simply to keep defective product out of the hands of customers.

Explaining the Results

What explains these improvements in quality performance? Although many readers may want to frame the question simply in terms of whether TQM produced these changes, it is the wrong question. But a four-layer multicausal set of explanations is more illuminating: tactics, infrastructural support, strategic policy preferences and beliefs, and fundamental management assumptions.[5]

At the outermost layer are the specific quality improvement methodologies, hoshin management, QFD, SPC, six sigma, Taguchi methods, systematic benchmarking, the seven tools, and so on typically associated with TQM. They are some of the tactics devised to improve quality. There is considerable variance across industries and firms as to the extent of adoption. SPC eventually came to be seen as de rigeur in semiconductor fabs where improved process control was critical to yield improvement. It diffused even more rapidly in the automotive industry, but it was adopted somewhat more variably in other sectors (for semiconductors, see Finan, 1990: 72–73, 80–81; Leachman, 1996: 135).

Even when the application of a given quality technique appears to yield quality improvement, however, many firms have only partially adopted and deployed it. And then, mutations have been the norm. Even in, or perhaps especially in, a sophisticated firm like HP, the characteristic quality technologies have been intentionally reconfigured to make them more acceptable and productive.

There is, in fact, widespread ambiguity about what makes up the quality toolkit. Broader descriptions of the quality toolkit in the United States will include business process reengineering, cross-functional problem-solving teams, concurrent engineering, JIT manufacturing, design for manufacturing, computer integrated manufacturing, supplier process audits, OEM improvement teams working with suppliers to improve quality, a variety of approaches to enhance customer input into product development, and so on.

Indeed, as time has gone on, quality improvement promoters have intentionally sought to broaden the toolkit to bring under the umbrella other tools currently being defined as best practice and fundamentally consistent with quality improvement.

At the next outermost layer are the infrastructural organizations discussed in Chapter 6. Most were established in the 1980s and early 1990s to support and diffuse ideas and the very practices of quality improvement. They were critical to providing information not only about broad directions, including the transmission of strategic policy preferences and beliefs to firms, but also about specific paths to be taken and ones to be avoided. They removed knowledge barriers. They brought isolated managers into a complex and mostly decentralized structure of information networks tailored to specific industries, firm size, and employee constituencies. The unifying element in that structure was the Baldrige award network and protocol that played a major role in the late 1980s and early 1990s in defining the basic paths to be traveled. Industry-specific organizations, such as SEMATECH and its offspring, were important, however, in providing guidance on the importance of working with suppliers.

Closer to the center are the strategic policy preferences and beliefs adopted by those firms that successfully improved quality performance:

1. Top managers setting quality improvement as an important corporate priority and authorizing the creation of systems for measuring, publicizing, and rewarding quality performance;

2. Firms aiming for a closer integration of product design and manufacturing work (or in more science-based industries like semiconductors a closer integration of R & D and manufacturing) with the understanding that such approaches would reduce the quality problems arising from "sloppy handoffs" associated with traditional models of product development;

3. Firms aiming to reduce the number of suppliers even as firms also came to believe in the benefits of increased outsourcing. This reduction enabled manufacturers to work more closely with each of their major suppliers to ensure quality improvement. This included improvement at the most elementary level of making it easier to isolate the source of its quality problems.

4. Firms aiming to build customer expectations and needs into both research activities and product development as well as creating feedback mechanisms for assessing and reacting to customer experiences with products in the field;

5. Firms aiming to better control and improve their business processes; this involved the novel idea of using continuous improvement as a central driver for improvement throughout the firm.

At the innermost layer are the parallel fundamental assumptions of management. Thus, a rethinking of assumptions was required for quality improvement to take place. These changes involved, above all, developing a top-management understanding that quality performance was important to business success. This emphasis on changing cognition is consistent with how Kaoru Ishikawa, the leading quality promoter in postwar Japan, described TQC. He saw TQC fundamentally as requiring a "thought revolution in management" (Ishikawa, 1985). His vision displays a sophisticated understanding of what is involved in changing management behavior.

This thought revolution involved a recognition that successful innovation required not just effective R & D or product design but also involved a close collaboration of R & D or product design personnel with manufacturing personnel. Implicit in this thinking was that an upstream prevention strategy was more effective than downstream efforts to control quality. Top management also had to learn that reducing the number of suppliers and collaborating more closely with those remaining made economic sense. This was a major cognitive hurdle for many managers, who had grown up on the idea of treating supplier management more as a spot market playing off one supplier against another. There also had to be increased recognition that quality improvement involved getting closer to current and potential customers in designing, manufacturing, and order fulfillment. This meant working to anticipate the needs of final users and intermediate customers. Last, the idea that the firm was made up of work processes and that their continual improvement could be a major contributor to business success had to take hold. Better control over business processes was one part of that effort.

It appears that substantial progress was made toward adopting these fundamental assumptions, although only partial and not so well institutionalized that it cannot be reversed by a subsequent generation of managers. Nonetheless, these understandings were probably most critical to generating the kind of quality improvements I reported.

Managers acted on these assumptions in many ways, not all of which are captured in the specific tactics of TQM at the outermost layer. All of the strategic areas and changes in management assumptions mentioned before fit squarely in the new quality model (with upstream prevention and cooperation between design and R & D, on the one hand, and, on the other, with manufacturing, supplier cooperation, customer as driver, and process improvement focus). In the light of this discussion, efforts to measure the impact of TQM on either quality improvement or business outcomes, in terms of the use of a small set of characteristic tools and methodologies, seem problematic. The difficulty of the task reflects the diversity and diffuseness of the tactics chosen. To compound the measurement problem, it is entirely plausible that even modest incorporation of the principles of the new quality model yielded very large benefits.

The Legacy of Quality

The legacy of the quality movement has been its focus on much stronger cooperation between product designers and manufacturing, the continual improvement of organizational processes (based in part on systematic benchmarking), and customers as a basis of corporate improvement efforts. The quality movement did not invent these foci, but it did make significant contributions to them. Here, one must understand the launching of the quality initiative in the early 1980s as part of the broad currents sweeping American industry; these currents, many of them flowing from Japan, led to major shifts in management belief systems about successful business performance in global markets.

Today top managers in our major corporations accept that strong cooperation between product designers and manufacturing, a continuous improvement of business processes, and a customer focus are sources of competitive strength that need to be cultivated. Yet each of these understandings evolved slowly over time and arose from multiple sources.

The Japanese approach to the cooperative relationship between product design and manufacturing had a strong influence on the thinking of American managers. It was well developed in the Japanese automobile industry but owed relatively little to the quality movement per se, yet it contributed greatly to quality improvement. These approaches were popularized in the United States especially through the work of Clark and Fujimoto (1991), who showed the benefits of such cooperation. In the case of semiconductors as well, the need for an integrated approach to R & D and manufacturing came to be recognized as central to improving productivity and quality (Angel, 1994: 108–114). The Japanese achieved this integration in part through having the R & D personnel, involved in developing the new generation of products, follow the development process into the manufacturing plants. Intel developed a new model of the integrated development facility ("copy exactly") in which the R & D personnel were located on the future production site and the manufacturing personnel were moved in to replace them as the production volume was ramped up. In short, while the Japanese may have provided the model of cooperation across these key functions, American companies such as Intel found new ways to do it.

Process improvement was a well-established tradition in American industrial engineering but seldom caught the attention of managers and thus lay relatively dormant in most business firms during the post–World War II period. The quality movement, as personified in Japanese practices, had a profound effect on legitimizing and popularizing this avenue of improvement. Moreover, the quality movement gave it the added twist of continuous improvement of business processes, arguably the most innovative element of the quality movement as seen through American eyes (Weick, 1997).

The customer focus was an evolving theme that came to be emphasized by popular business gurus like Tom Peters and others in the early 1980s. It was fed by growing international competition across a range of industries and the deregulation of markets. The quality movement fed into and strengthened these ideas and provided concrete methodologies for improvement such as QFD. The penetration of some of these methodologies—like QFD—was less persuasive than many of its proponents would claim. Yet the ideas survive in more diffuse ways. Major manufacturing companies today are far more likely to make serious efforts to incorporate assessment of customer needs into their product development activities than was the case a decade ago. While marketing departments might have been perceived as having the customer as their natural domain, much of their efforts prior to the quality movement were focused narrowly on how to gain market share, with customers seen as objects to be manipulated by marketing efforts. In many of the leading companies, the quality movement helped broaden these perspectives.

All of these legacies of the quality movement, augmented by other streams of development, can be found in the earlier history of American companies and industries. Anyone who has read the history of Ford's River Rouge facility will recognize some of them. Many, however, had been allowed to atrophy. What made the 1980s and early 1990s special was the resurgence and coalescence of these themes, sometimes in very original forms, as a response to deregulation and, above all to a concerted competitive challenge from a somewhat mysterious challenger from the East. This view of organizational paradigms and management practice is consistent with the position advocated by Mauro Guillén (1994: 288). The history of organizational development is not a march to greater and greater managerial sophistication as some business historians, consultants, popular writers, and managers seem to think but rather an oscillation among fundamental principles, sometimes combined in novel ways in response to particular environmental circumstances.

Scholars, cynics that we are, often react disdainfully to popular management movements and almost gleefully report their demise and superficiality. We share this behavior with consultants, who are always looking for the next wave and for a way to differentiate their current product with their last one. Part of the evidence for the demise of a particular fad arises from an often narrow interpretation and lazy use of the positivist research tradition. Thus, in the case of quality, it leads researchers to see only evidence of the quality movement's contribution if we can show the application, deployment, and contributions to organizational success of specific well-formed quality methodologies.

Thus, scholars will look for evidence of the use of specific quality methodologies in a prescribed fashion (e.g., the use of the seven tools as rational problem-solving methods, hoshin management) and when they do not find it, they point to the gap between TQM rhetoric and reality and analyze the causes of that gap. The existence of the gap is used typically to suggest that TQM as practiced is only faintly related either to the rhetoric used (Zbaracki, 1994) or to perceived robust Japanese practice (Easton and Jarrell, 1997c). In either case, TQM is thought to be ineffectual. The association of TQM with specific quality methodologies accounts for many scholars' belief that quality movement has disappeared without a trace. After all, its not highlighted in the business media anymore and managers are not talking about it the way they once did. The scholarly view contrasts strikingly with managers' views that they have met the quality challenge and have incorporated the important ideas and improved quality.

The gap in thinking between the two audiences would be a lot smaller if scholars thought about institutionalization more broadly. Some management movements (not all by any means) leave important legacies at the more general level of significantly modifying or changing managers' or workers' fundamental assumptions and preferences. Changed beliefs and values translate into new behavior. Researchers can track such outcomes, but they require a much more sophisticated and subtle research model than is typically used. As often noted, measuring only what is easily measured leads to significant distortions in the reality one is trying to capture.

Under the banner of the twin emphases of continuous improvement of processes and customer focus, a great variety of new improvement initiatives have been developed in the 1990s that one does not necessarily even associate with quality improvement: business process reengineering, concurrent engineering, modes of organizing and operating improvement teams, and a whole array of soft technologies associated with tapping into the voice of the customer and building that into the firm.

Business process reengineering is particularly interesting because it was marketed by its consultant popularizers as totally different from quality improvement (Hammer and Champy, 1993). It was the classic case of market differentiation for a new product. Yet, at its base, it was fundamentally about process improvement. Indeed, one can hardly imagine how the business process reengineering movement could have arisen in the early 1990s if it had not been preceded by the quality movement. By the late 1990s we learned from the media that the reengineering movement was now also dead (along with quality). Yet the idea that process improvement activities should not only seek to optimize "small processes" internal to specific work groups but also focus on major business processes in their entirety, such as order fulfillment, appears now to be reasonably well institutionalized in the thinking of many business executives.

One of the legacies of the quality movement has been an enhanced definition of the kinds of people interested and involved in quality. As we saw in Chapter 6, quality is no longer the province of low-level, narrowly engaged technical types involved in inspection and other such detection tasks. Indeed, top-ranking quality officials today, by and large, have more commanding positions in our leading manufacturing firms than was the case in the early 1980s.

Consider the case of a major corporation like HP. With domestic employment of roughly 60,000 employees in 1997, it had effectively some 1,100–1,200 employees conducting quality-related activities, two thirds of whom are in new product development. That is approximately 2% of their domestic labor force and similar to what existed in the mid-1980s.[6] However, the total would be significantly higher than it was in the mid-1980s if it included those doing incoming inspection and factory in-process inspection. These tasks were merged with manufacturing work in the late 1980s and thus no longer report to quality functions.

Lest the 2% figure seem high, HP's 1995 benchmarking study of the 11 global high technology firms, found that the average percentage of quality personnel to total employees to be 3.3%.[7] This number varied widely by business. Thus, high-volume businesses seemed to require more quality personnel, with the percentage going to 5%. Naturally, electronics companies may have higher demands for quality personnel than other sectors of the economy, but the findings nevertheless indicate the situation in high-growth sectors of the economy. In short, the legacy of the 1980s quality movement is the much larger number of higher-status individuals covering a broader range of tasks, who are now part of an institutionalized quality infrastructure.

The building and survival of a strong national infrastructure for diffusion of quality improvement initiatives also shows durability. The organizations described in Chapter 6 have been the key players in the quality movement throughout, and they have survived by continuing to teach many of the fundamentals of quality improvement, developing new approaches and methodologies, and sometimes applying them to new areas (the service sector industries in particular). Much of the behavior cultivated in the social movement phase of development has now been institutionalized and taken for granted as everyday behavior. Such behavior is seldom the subject of media coverage; thus, the absence of such discussion is assumed by many to mean that quality, or TQM, was a passing fad.

Yet declaring the war won does involve some risks. There are signs in many of the leading U.S. companies that the attention devoted to quality has greatly diminished. The rate of quality improvement progress, after its spurt upward in the late 1980s and early 1990s, seems to have declined. The American Customer Satisfaction Index, based on a national survey of consumers' actual experiences with goods and services, showed three straight years of decline since 1994, a decline many attribute to the cumulative effects of often mindless downsizing, reengineering, cost cutting, and short-sighted staffing decisions. The overall index fell from 74.5 in 1994 to 70.7 in 1997 (American Customer Satisfaction Index, 1994, 1995, 1996, 1997).

The quality community itself moved toward broadening its focus to emphasize business performance outcomes and the balanced scorecard, thereby integrating it more deeply with other business objectives. Although a natural response to the single-minded pursuit of quality in the early days of the movement, if pushed too far, this strategy risks losing the distinctive features of the quality movement. Furthermore, much quality improvement comes not from technology per se, but from employees' heightened awareness and attention to quality and their focus on continuous process improvement. This dependency on motivation means that if one is not going forward, then one is likely moving backward. To the extent that "taken for granted" can mean one loses focus and discipline, quality performance is likely to decline. As top management starts talking less and less about quality and reverts to its traditional cost-cutting mentality, middle management quickly picks up on the new messages and, with limited time and other resources, quality considerations fall to the side. Without awareness and focus, the process capable of delivering high and continuously improving quality tends to degrade over time. Such outcomes are by no means inevitable; all it takes is a few aggressive quality competitors to keep the other firms honest. It is, nevertheless, a concern that makes many thoughtful managers nervous.

In the course of responding to the Japanese quality challenge, a social movement developed, filled with zealots, nonbelievers, inspirational leaders, opportunists, and institution builders. As success was achieved in eliminating the quality gap as a major competitive disadvantage for American producers, quality improvement has become more a part of normal management. The organizational routines for doing it have become more institutionalized and taken for granted. Much of the mystery is gone. It took less organizational change to achieve more modest outcomes than many quality leaders had led top management to believe. Gone were many of the grandiose notions of a new era of management based on decisions by fact and a vision of quality as fundamentally about elevating the quality of management. Many quality leaders have come to miss the the good old days when they were the center of attention and their issue entitled them entry into corporate suites. Such is the nature of normalization.

What do the outcomes reported in this chapter mean for tensions typically reported between institutional and market explanations of managerial behavior? Institutional analysis served as the guiding framework for much of this book, and it has proved a valuable tool. Initially, researchers in this tradition aimed to show that, despite managerial rhetoric framed in the language of rational action to meet specific goals and invoking progress, managers actions belied their terminology. Their language is often merely a label to bestow legitimacy on management; managers will appear rational to their constituencies if they appear to use certain management techniques (Abrahamson, 1996: 261). In a similar vein, homogenization of corporate responses to new challenges results not just from competitive factors but institutional ones as well, especially as a response to uncertainty, coercion, and professional norms (DiMaggio and Powell, 1991). Scholars doing institutional research win plaudits from their colleagues by demonstrating these processes at work; the ability to show a disjuncture between discourse and intention, on the one hand, and practice, on the other, makes for a lively story. Similarly, the failure of managers to make decisions based on rational technical criteria challenges conventional wisdom and begs for explanation. While capturing an element of reality, these formulations give the impression that all social movements are incapable of producing enduring substantive change because they are incapable of moving beyond discourse.

Fortunately, in recent years a number of institutionalists have adopted a more complex and subtle view (Fligstein, 1990). This new perspective stresses that institutional structures provide the frameworks within which rational action takes place, defining the actors, the interests, and the legitimate ways of acting (Powell, 1991: 183–203; Scott, 1995: 136, 152). Thus, markets and the institutionalization process are not alternatives.

Various practices of the quality movement are often used to illustrate the early institutional perspective, which juxtaposed institutional factors and rational action in opposition. Indeed, discourse and action taken in the name of quality improvement but without apparent results presents a target for many institutional researchers. In this journey through the quality movement, I described a number of ways and areas in which these principles seem to have manifested themselves, especially in the early days of the movement when goals and means were very ambiguous. I also showed how adoption of similar responses to the quality challenge across firms flowed from coercion as OEMs imposed solutions on their suppliers as well as from firms adopting ritualized responses to uncertainty. Even in recent years, the rush to adopt ISO 9000 demonstrates many of the discussed characteristics. I also pointed out a number of key decisions that seemed to defy expectations of rational action, such as the reluctance to learn directly and systematically from the Japanese during the early 1980s and the problematic criterion that firms (HP was the example) use to start and stop emulating a particular model.

At the same time, my presentation is in keeping with the new model of institutionalism, which sees rational action played out in the context of institutional behavior. In that vein, I traced how the existing institutional framework of action at firms in the early 1980s locked actors into existing priorities, routines, and goals and made it difficult for them to respond quickly and intelligently to the Japanese quality challenge. Conversely, it took a great deal of time to build the new extra-firm institutional networks that were to play a critical role in firms responding to an exogenous quality challenge by helping them reorder their routines, priorities, and goals and convert learning into practice. By observing this total process, one can better understand why it took so long for the Americans to respond to the quality challenge.

In the end, despite numerous stumbles, retreats, and posturing, the product quality of the automotive and electronics/semiconductor sectors did demonstrably improve over the nearly two decades I have analyzed. Performance gaps were closed. No doubt, improvement did not always take place for the reasons managers proffered. But quality as measured on a variety of dimensions did improve, and the improvement was roughly tied to at least partial adoption of the ideas embodied in the new quality model. And that adoption in turn was tied to the emergence of a large quality infrastructure at the national, industry, and local levels. The competitive nature of these industries simply did not allow free-floating posturing to survive indefinitely. The point is not that competitive factors eventually triumphed over institutional factors but rather that the result entails both.

CHAPTER 10

On Organizational Learning

After this long journey through the history of the modern American quality movement, what knowledge have we gained about how organizations learn? To clarify an answer is my charge for this final chapter. First, however, I need to clarify that ubiquitous term, organizational learning. Karl Weick and Frances Westley, with tongue firmly in cheek, have suggested it is an oxymoron. After all, to learn is to disorganize and increase variety, the very antithesis of organization (Weick and Westley, 1996: 440). Yet they go on to discuss the conditions under which our images of organizations can be consistent with learning.

I use the definition of organizational learning offered by Levitt and March (1988: 319). They believe that organizations learn by encoding inferences from history (either theirs or others) into routines that guide behavior. Organizational learning is routine-based, history-dependent, and target-oriented. Cohen and Bacdayan (1996: x, 409) supplement this understanding with the notion that organizational learning builds into individuals both declarative and procedural knowledge. The former is knowledge of facts and propositions; the latter the knowledge of well-practiced skills, both motor and cognitive.

Organizational learning has enjoyed a certain vogue in the business world in recent years. Indeed, by the mid-1990s it was already being eclipsed by its cousin, knowledge management. Consultant firms have been busily trying to figure out if there are real products to market to companies in these areas, products "with legs." In the popular literature, organizational learning is almost universally portrayed as good; those who do not do it have a "learning disability" (Senge, 1990). It is seen as bringing flexibility, adaptiveness, and speedy response to organizations. Moreover, as the concept worked its way down to the level of action, it often mutated to the point that many high level managers believed all that mattered was to maximize the amount of training employees received.

The Competency Trap

Reflecting on the analysis presented here, one can see that from the early 1980s to the mid-1990s, American firms did indeed learn a great deal about quality improvement and how to do it. However, from a rational actor perspective, the path to that learning was relatively slow and circuitous, with many blind alleys and high costs (lost jobs and market share). Management did not optimize the search or implementation process. It is almost a cliché to say that prior organizational success often throws up obstacles to effective adaptive responses to new challenges. Past career success in traditional functional specialities often created blinders that inhibited managers from effectively responding to the initial Japanese quality challenge.

Because one can attribute past success at the individual and organizational level to effective learning, a well-known paradox arises: individual and organizational learning can deepen expertise in existing technologies and routines while deadening the impulse to explore new ones. In the case of quality, it was not so much that our major manufacturers were busy refining traditional quality control but that they saw it as a low-level function with no strategic implications. As a consequence, they busily applied their expertise to areas that they thought mattered. In the words of Jim March:

> Refinements and improvements in competence associated with improving standard paradigms, conventional knowledge, and established methods provide local gains that are compelling. As they develop greater and greater competence in using existing technologies, knowledge, routines, forms or strategies, however, decision makers become less and less willing or able to change to newer ones that offer long-run superiority. They become better and better at an inferior practice. In this sense at least, adaptation is self-destructive. (1994: 239–240)

By proceeding in this ostrich-like fashion, top management left organizations vulnerable to blindsiding through challenges from new directions. They were ill prepared to respond to Japanese quality superiority. The trap of exploitation March notes flows not from stupidity but from learning. Moreover, the trade-offs of pursuing either exploitation of expertise or discovery are not easy to specify, nor is it a simple matter to specify the appropriate balance. In the late 1970s, the automotive firms were concentrating on increasing market share in the mid-size market, which accounted for the bulk of their profits, and on incrementally improving existing technology. In semiconductors, the focus was on being quick to market with the next generation of chips. In the late 1970s when yields reached about 50%, they redesigned for the next generation, and yields dropped dramatically. Withdrawing resources from these key sources of competitive advantage to explore the newly emergent bases of competition around quality seemed pointless to top management.

Fads as Building Blocks

Throughout this book, I observed that the quality movement evolved as a series of minifads spread over time. I have described two scenarios. The first is one in which each successive minifad was an occasion to discard the previous one and refocus organizational energies around a new initiative. In many companies, for example, business process reengineering had this effect on total quality initiatives. Similarly, I showed how the drive toward ISO 9000 registration dampened interest in the Baldrige. Often these new initiatives were presented as striking off in entirely new directions, unencumbered by the past. In these cases little organizational learning occurs, and employees are more likely to describe the new quality initiative with the pejorative term, "flavor of the month." In these scenarios, managers often allow themselves to be manipulated by consultant firms with strong economic incentives to differentiate their products and to move quickly from the current to a new generation of products. Here, the process most closely resembles that described by Abrahamson (1996: 254) in which management fads take on the characteristic of cultural commodities, marketed to users as rational methods aimed at putting practitioners on the cutting edge of progress.

In the second scenario, the more sophisticated companies seemed to use prior initiatives as foundations on which to build new quality initiatives. Sometimes, this was done consciously, as in HP's efforts to launch the Quality 1 on 1 initiative from the foundation of the existing quality infrastructure. This involved a very subtle process whereby organizational designers had to build the case for profound change while reassuring those wedded to existing quality improvement practices. That core of quality managers and others committed to TQC practices operated as a political constituency on various committees and task forces, ensuring that their interests would be represented in the adoption of Quality 1 on 1. They restrained the designers of Quality 1 on 1 from moving away from existing TQC moorings too quickly. By building backward compatibility, however, they tied the past and present to the future, minimized political opposition, and created a logical progression from the old to the new.

At other times, the building on past initiatives is more unconscious. Quality circles are an interesting example, widely described in the popular literature as failures. Yet a strong case can be made that they laid the foundation for the team-based activities of the 1990s. Indeed, we noted how quality circles merged with evolving SPC activities which, in turn, evolved and merged with the developing employee involvement and process management initiatives. The demise of quality circles reminds us that a building-block vision of organizational learning and change does not always have to include the survival of each and every initiative as long as some pieces of those prior initiatives (belief systems, preferences, or behavior) are embodied in its successors.

Still another variation is represented by the increasing number of companies that downplayed the use of the terms TQM and quality. Those that aimed to improve quality, nevertheless, engaged in efforts which had a "just do it" character to them. This probably made it easier to adopt a building-block approach. With less fanfare, they simply added new skills and routines to the organization. The downside of this approach is that it relinquishes the benefits flowing from the creation of a common language of quality improvement throughout the firm.

Whether through conscious or unconscious efforts, the building-block approach to quality improvement seems more likely to produce organizational learning than more disjointed, less consistent efforts. Even though this statement has face validity, it is worthwhile to dig a little deeper to understand why. A relevant research tradition that builds on the early work of the English psychologist Frederic Bartlett (1932) can help with the excavation. This research holds this premise: the way we come to understand our physical and social world and act on our understandings is by connecting the new with something we already know. In other words, we do not learn something until we can use it by connecting it to something we already truly understand and use. Much learning by adults can probably be thought of as occurring through the potentially time-consuming navigation of two issues. The first is that new knowledge must be properly integrated within the memory structures of previously acquired knowledge; the second is that there must be a suitable set of background knowledge and memory structures before any particular new knowledge is sufficiently incorporated so that it can be productively used (Lindsay and Norman, 1977: 532–534). To the extent that these conditions are absent, the probability of successfully using new learning is reduced.

Indeed, building on the work of Piaget among others, Robbie Case (1985) traces this same principle in the cognitive development of children. He argues that all complex cognitive structures in adulthood result from a building process across the childhood years, in which building takes place by putting lower-order units together recursively. That is, children are learning different things at different stages of their lives, but these are related and build on each other. To speak his or her first words, a child requires the coordination of a variety of other previously learned skills. As Piaget argued, children do not acquire certain types of understandings and capabilities until prior understandings and structures have been constructed (Case, 1985: 23, 146–147). This is the major way that productive novelty is achieved in cognitive development, almost never by just striking out in some new direction and abandoning what already exists. For our purposes, the significance of this perspective is: if each management initiative is presented as a clean sheet and the past is stigmatized, then its potential users are likely to lack a context for understanding and applying the ideas and prescribed actions.

Of course, the counter view argues that business firms need to foster dramatic revolutionary transformations that will occur only if employees are freed from their prior constraints. Managers are constantly urged to think "out of the box." Some consider continuous small improvements anchored to the past as antithetical to American culture (Hammond and Morrison, 1996: 79–80). Business process reengineering advocates, for example, played on this theme, even though when actually applied to organizational improvement, BPR was characteristically incremental (Stoddard, Javenpaa, and LittleJohn, 1996: 57–76).

The small-win strategy anchored in existing practices, moreover, is often underestimated for reasons that Weick and Westley (1996: 455) outline. First, small wins in large systems can occur in parallel as well as serial form, resulting, in the aggregate, in large change. Second, a series of small wins often precedes and paves the way for large changes. By providing momentum and basic learning, small wins make large-scale change possible. Third, when many seemingly revolutionary changes are scrutinized, they are found to be based on a series of small wins. Finally, by being anchored in current practices, small wins allow for learning rooted in daily work routines. This is exactly the kind of learning likely to be transformed into effective practice. Students of the quality movement will recognize, of course, the emphasis on continuous improvement in this account. Continuous improvement has been a persistent theme of the quality movement and undoubtedly has contributed to the building-block approach to organizational improvement.

Because national infrastructures for the diffusion of quality played a major role in helping firms make sense of the different initiatives and order them in some logical way, they increased the likelihood of a building-block approach. Japan provides a striking example: JUSE actively digested and synthesized the field experience of companies, using it to systematically generate new quality technologies. Moreover, JUSE rolled out improvement technologies every few years starting in the late 1960s though the 1980s, at which time the pipeline seemed to go dry. Each initiative was nestled within the broader coherent structure for quality improvement.

The more decentralized national infrastructure that emerged in the United States was incapable of imposing such order on managerial understanding. Nevertheless, in the late 1980s and early 1990s, the Baldrige performed many of these same functions; each year the Baldrige protocol was revised to capture new trends and initiatives. The value of creating a national sense of coherence and logical development, and an agreed-upon process of how quality improvement could and should unfold, needs to be acknowledged. This framework helped managers within individual firms make sense of the events and information swirling around them. Common understandings greatly facilitated cooperation and learning across firms and made it more likely that individual managers and workers would be engaged in common undertakings, thereby reinforcing one another's learnings.

By promoting something labeled TQM, the various infrastructure organizations helped managers and employees make sense out of their changing everyday environment. Even if managers decided not to use the term TQM in their firm, they become multilingual, translating the external TQM messages into their company-specific languages. These infrastructure organizations helped organizational members not only understand what was happening to them but provided an explanation and a set of behavioral prescriptions on how to respond. In short, they served as a cognitive tool to frame problems and to enable managers and employees to draw compelling explanations from the swirling mass of their ambiguous daily experiences (cf. Guillén, 1994: 282).

Learning and Doing

As I have pointed out many times in these explorations, learning and doing are not the same thing. Yet one often reads about individuals or firms having learned something, the implicit assumption being that once something has been learned, the party is able to productively use it. Nelson and Winter (1982: 123–124) have pointed out that imitation is often difficult. On closer examination, seemingly similar conditions between the original adopter and the imitator often differ in quite subtle ways. A great deal of tacit knowledge unavailable to the would-be borrower may be involved in optimizing the target practice. These were some of the problems faced by Americans trying to emulate Japanese quality practices. This helps explain why, from a rational model perspective, it seemed to take so long between learning the principles of the new quality model and even partially applying them so they begin to show significant improvements.

I told two stories about the gap between learning and practice, pointing out effective ways of bridging the two. The first story comes from the experiences of HP and its ability to draw on the experiences and practices of YHP, its subsidiary. The second story emerges from the evolution of a national infrastructure for identifying and diffusing best practices in quality improvement.

The HP case is interesting precisely because it was exceptional. Few American companies had the opportunity to do what HP did with YHP; others that did have similar potential partners chose not to use them. The HP-YHP relationship proved to be a very effective mode of transferring knowledge from one organization to another, allowing the receiving firm to productively use the source knowledge. It also illustrates the trite, but nevertheless important observation that effective imitation turns out not to be imitation at all, but a process of creative borrowing and adaptation. Analysis over too short a time frame makes it appear that imitation has occurred; using a longer time frame reveals innovation and adaptation.

The importance of HP's learning from YHP directs our attention to the networks along which knowledge about experiences, routines, strategies, and technologies travels (Levitt and March, 1988: 329). Fortunately, HP got more than timely access to quality improvement methodologies through its links to YHP, for YHP, through its strong involvement with JUSE and JUSE counselors, participated in Japan's national infrastructure of quality. As such, YHP's TQC practices incorporated what it had been able to absorb and productively use from this broader network. In effect, this meant that HP, using YHP as a conduit, was able to tap into the entire Japanese national network for quality improvement instead of waiting, as many American companies did, for such an infrastructure to develop in the United States.

In principle, one might think that HP's borrowing from its subsidiary was ideal. After all, YHP stood to lose nothing from having HP learn from it; indeed, its managers stood to enhance their reputations within the corporation. As a result, HP also had ready access to many of the tacit features of YHP practices, or could obtain them to the extent that YHP personnel could articulate them. All this differs markedly from normal business situations wherein, as noted, access to tacit knowledge enveloping the target practice is difficult to obtain. Firms often resist having others copy from them because copying may lead to loss of technical secrets and competitive advantage (Levitt and March, 1989: 331). Yet, despite the seemingly ideal environment for sharing knowledge between HP and YHP, there were formidable barriers to successfully adopting YHP practices and outcomes resting on a perceived lack of fit with the specific work practices of HP divisions. This perceived discrepancy was based on both concrete business differences and distinctive cultural facets of American organizational life, which often combined with resistance to new ideas, vested interest in established routines, and incredulity on the part of American managers.

Notwithstanding these difficulties, HP did make progress in both learning about quality and in converting that learning into practice. My analysis described several characteristics of the YHP-HP relation that facilitated the transfer of key elements of the new quality model to HP. In essence, YHP provided a template for concrete routines, grounded in actual work processes; it raised the sights among HP managers as to what kinds and amounts of quality improvement were possible; it provided outcome benchmarks; it served as a source of trustworthy transparent information; and, most broadly, it provided a paradigm for resolving some major organizational uncertainties facing HP managers in the 1980s.

The aid from YHP helped model the future of quality improvement for HP and enabled HP to upgrade quality relatively rapidly compared to its competitors. In short, learning from others often involves a complex system of elements that must work harmoniously in order to maximize the speed and effectiveness of the borrowing process.

Although many elements are involved in facilitating the learning process and turning it into practice, the most effective mode was YHP modeling the new business practices through collaborative problem solving in everyday work relationships with selected HP divisions. In this fashion, the tacit knowledge necessary to optimize business processes was made visible and explicit. As such, learning and technology transfer became embedded in normal business problem-solving activities. By proceeding in this fashion, HP took advantage of the benefits that flow from tightly linking work, learning, and innovation (Brown and Duguid, 1991). With the corporate spotlight on YHP's quality improvement activities and its strong economic performance, divisions with whom it had a working relationship were highly motivated to cooperate.

As effective as this linkage was, it was by definition limited to divisions with which YHP worked. To be sure, successful projects developed through these relationships were then publicly featured by corporate staff and packaged for broadcast throughout the divisions. Still, this secondary mode of transmission was undoubtedly less effective than the primary mode. Also YHP served HP as a whole through the other modes of facilitation described before (providing trustworthy information, etc.). Such activities helped diffuse the quality improvement methods by spreading declarative knowledge, but again in a less powerful fashion than the direct modeling through solving everyday business problems, which spreads procedural knowledge.

In many situations, of course, the adopting firm lacks the opportunities to engage in the kinds of joint problem solving available to HP and YHP. Consequently, in such circumstances, successful imitation that involve tacit knowledge and soft organizational technology are likely to be very difficult. There are, however, a variety of situations—for example between customers and suppliers—in which such direct modeling of the desired behavior is possible and from which organizations would benefit.

The second story I told about bridging the gap between learning and doing concerned the evolution of an infrastructure for identifying and diffusing the new quality model. The emergent institutional infrastructure was composed of both new and reinvented organizations, which filled different but sometimes overlapping market niches, and both competed and cooperated with one another. These organizations operated at the national, industry, and local levels. Many large manufacturing firms participated in multiple networks creating overlapping organizational communities, which facilitated the flow of the new quality improvement methodologies among the various levels. The six organizations examined here represented a broad range of institutional possibilities for sharing learning about quality improvement applications.

The organizations composing this infrastructure created best practice standards, identified bottlenecks, introduced new methodologies, provided training, disseminated knowledge about both successes and failures, and evolved forums for networking firm-level personnel. Overall, they created social locations for learning that helped eliminate the isolation of individual managerial decision makers by bringing them into local, industry, and national learning communities. Gradually, a growing consensus evolved around a dominant design for quality improvement. This was furthered most powerfully by the Baldrige road map. This consensus grew out of influential actors shaping each other's perceptions of quality improvement and its methods. The infrastructure provided a location for an iterative process of learning among major players as they exchanged ideas about all manner of issues relating to quality improvement. With the introduction of the ISO 9000 standards in the 1990s, however, this emergent consensus was diluted.

Although much of this discussion has focused on the formal infrastructure, there is good evidence to suggest that extensive learning geared to practice took place through informal exchanges among companies. These informal networks became increasingly popular, particularly with the growth in the formal benchmarking movement, which grew out of the quality movement at Xerox (Camp, 1989).

The developing national infrastructure moved practitioners along the continuum from first exposing them to the new ideas about quality improvement as abstract concepts, then helping them to absorb and convert these learnings into effective practice. In the end, as one saw with HP, practitioners still needed to engage in trial and error at the firm level to see what specific mix of practices produced quality improvement. Nevertheless, the new infrastructure greatly facilitated their efforts as they grappled with what to try and how to do it. The lesson of this analysis is that researchers need to explore more deeply the intermediary role played by institutional infrastructures to determine how organizations learn from one another.

One additional feature of sharing information and practice among companies deserves to be explored. In several places I noted something seemingly unusual: corporations sharing information about how to do quality improvement. This willingness to share helped lubricate the institutional infrastructure and made it more effective. Benchmarking was particularly valuable. It taught companies that, by benchmarking generic processes such as order processing, they could learn from firms in other industries, which were not their competitors. This meant, of course, that there was a higher probability that sharing between companies could take place without a loss of competitive advantage.

A second element encouraging sharing among major multinational firms in the 1980s was their sense of being under attack by a common enemy. Many managers saw Japan as the threat to America's economic sovereignty, which led to a national collective effort to share information and other resources to overcome this enemy. Sharing knowledge is quite rational economic action under the following circumstances: when one set of cooperating competitors (large U.S. manufacturing companies competing in international markets) builds up the total capital in quality improvement technology available to each company in that set and thereby eliminates the existing competitive advantage held by another set of competitors (large export-oriented Japanese manufacturing companies). In view of the diminishing gap in quality performance between the Japanese and the Americans in key industries such as semiconductors and autos, this strategy, in fact, appears to have been quite successful. The movement to rationalize supplier chains is analogous. Driven by international competition, major U.S. manufacturing firms pushed their suppliers to collaborate with one another and with the OEMs themselves to upgrade quality and productivity in ways theretofore unseen. This perforce involved abundant sharing of information and knowledge across firms.

The explanations for the increased sharing of information presented thus far show how proprietary concerns of individual firms were modified by circumstances. Still, the explanations presented do not seem to fully explain the extent to which information about quality improvement was shared. Given the extent of sharing, even among competitors, this question remains: why would companies be willing to share when those receiving the information might be able to use it to reduce the competitive advantage of the company doing the sharing? The benefits that sharing might eventually achieve—leveling the playing field with the Japanese—were distant and uncertain, but the costs of a local competitor successfully copying an important business process could be felt immediately.

Certainly, there were safeguards; thus, firms could and did strip detailed knowledge from the information being made public, aiming to share only on a generic level. This action appears to be based on the presumption that the organizational capability to optimize the practice is critical, and that, in turn, is based on extensive tacit knowledge embedded in communities of practice built up over time. So, information stripped of detailed knowledge would be less valuable to others, especially since it takes the receiving firm time to fill in the blanks during which the sharing firm will presumably move on to further evolve its organizational capabilities. In short, the secret of quality improvement was seen to reside in the act of doing it; therefore, sharing explicit information appears not to pose a great threat. Put more formally, the conversion of learning to practice involves moving from explicit, declarative knowledge to procedural knowledge that often has a strong tacit component. One could share explicit knowledge without fear that competitors could immediately optimize practice.

There are two problems with this line of thought. The first is that while it helps minimize risk, the strategy of sharing just generic information contains much uncertainty. After all, it is hard to judge just how much one can share without helping one's competitors. In some cases, all they need is a little clue that points them in the right direction (Nelson and Winter, 1982: 123–124). A second problem lurks in the assumption that each firm participating in these infrastructural networks seems to bring to the exchange. By participating, they are in effect saying that they believe that they can somehow extract more value (i.e, figure out the underlying elements producing the organizational capability) from them than the other firms participating in these networks. The obvious weakness of this logic is that they can't all be right. Each firm is, in effect, betting that it can do better than the average firm. In the case of quality improvement where so many causal agents are involved, it is often impossible for firms to know when they were right and when they were wrong. Perhaps that is why they could make these assumptions and have them go unchallenged.

Models of Knowledge Transfer

Thus far in this chapter, I have focused primarily on how organizations learn from one another, sometimes with the organizations composing the institutional infrastructure serving as intermediaries. An additional theme of the organizational learning literature, and especially the knowledge management literature, is how one part of an organization learns from another. This question is often posed: how do managers learn to identify best practices and diffuse them across an organization? Survey data suggest the answer is, not very well (Ruggles, 1998: 82).

One of the issues involved in answering such a question concerns the role of central units and how they deal with business units. The HP experience with quality is extremely revealing in this regard; it sharply contrasts with the cascading-down model of diffusion so often favored by top management. This model was particularly visible in the efforts of major manufacturing firms to spread the new quality model during the 1980s. One saw the role of the corporate quality function at HP grow increasingly significant in the first half of the 1980s as the corporation mobilized to meet the Japanese challenge. Corporate quality, under the mantle of top management's authority, worked with divisions to figure out what was immediately usable from YHP and what needed to be adapted to fit HP culture and practices. For all its growing legitimacy and power at this time, corporate quality was still a staff function that had to convince divisional managers to cooperate and adopt specific approaches to quality improvement. In the early 1990s, as the quality challenge was gradually met, many business unit mangers reacted strongly against the directives of a more centralized quality department. Responding to this resistance the corporation acted to reduce the directive role of corporate quality (even at its peak it was not nearly as strong as in other major companies). Viewed from two decades of adjustment, the organization adapted its structure by centralizing somewhat to meet a major corporatewide challenge and then returned to its more decentralized roots when the challenge was met—a quite predictable response.

Florida Power and Light, discussed in Chapter 3, shows some of the implications of the use of the cascading-down model of change in comparison with HP's approach.[1] HP is a highly decentralized company in which many of the individual businesses are in highly dynamic environments with rapidly changing technologies. In the period under investigation, the company moved from an instrument company to a broad-based electronics firm. By contrast, FPL was a highly centralized company. Even though it had distinct business units like generation, distribution, and transmission, most employees saw themselves as being in the same business of providing electricity and equally subject to the decisions of corporate management. In this context FPL initially adopted the Japanese quality system almost intact. While there were some long-term changes on the horizon regarding deregulation, the firm was not in what would be considered a dynamic industry. Employees at FPL were accustomed to a strong top-down managerial hierarchy, and their approach to quality improvement was consistent with that pattern. In this highly centralized environment, management strongly pushed implementation of a fixed set of practices down the hierarchy to all units. The weakness of the FPL approach, however, was that it lacked a method for calibrating these new practices to its new U.S. business environment, and it was also susceptible to changes in top management.

In 1990, not long after FPL won the Deming Prize, just such a management change took place. The new management team, headed by James Broadhead ran into a minefield of employee dissatisfaction and realized that many employees felt stifled by the quality initiative's large bureaucracy. There was a widespread feeling among employees that the quality program had become mechanical and inflexible, creating a paper-based bureaucracy that in some cases actually put up roadblocks to continuous improvement. Because Broadhead believed that power was a commodity, he saw the real challenge for the company as how to adapt to the increasing threat posed by the coming deregulation of the industry. In this context, it did not pay to make quality the overriding management concern. Instead, he instituted a major downsizing initiative to cut costs, drastically reducing the quality department and many documentation requirements. It was a traumatic time for those associated with the quality initiative, and many left the company.

Nonetheless, a streamlined quality initiative survived at FPL, and Broadhead continued to provide support for quality improvement, aiming especially to integrate it with overall business objectives. In the 1990s, the company made a number of changes in the quality initiative, consistent with what other major companies did at this time. These changes included the introduction of extensive benchmarking, an emphasis on self-managing teams, a greater stress on accountability, adoption of BPR, and more opportunities for employee creativity and flexibility (Broadhead, 1996: 13). A variety of key measures showed continued quality improvement that surpassed FPL's performance at the time it won the Deming Prize (e.g., further reduction in number of unplanned outages and dramatic improvement in quality performance at the Turkey Point nuclear plant). Nevertheless, data from the 1998 American Customer Satisfaction Index show a very low ranking for FPL. Correspondence with a company official confirms recent slippage. In summary, one sees at FPL a rather discontinuous process of implementation and adaptation that flowed, in part, from a centralized management system's lack of responsiveness to employee implementation experiences. It took a new CEO to redirect the effort, but in so doing, considerable disruption took place.

The contrast with HP is instructive. Its decentralized structure ensured a much more continuous process of adaptation: managers and employees tried out various practices, used what seemed to work, adapted them as necessary, and discarded the rest. Those driving the HP corporate quality initiative instinctively modified and simplified the often complicated and resource-intensive Japanese procedures in order to gain acceptance of the division managers and their subordinates. The closest HP came to a discontinuous process was with the changes introduced by the new corporate quality director, Richard LeVitt, in the early 1990s, but these changes were mild compared to the disruption at FPL, symbolized by the drastic slashing of the quality department and related documentation requirements, and the departure of key quality personnel. All in all, the decentralized model at HP led to a more robust and flexible approach to quality improvement, but it was not necessarily focused enough to respond quickly to specific problems. Yet, although the process was different, both FPL and HP essentially moved in the same direction of integrating an initially stand-alone quality improvement initiative with overall business objectives. Indeed, this was the path taken by many American manufacturing companies in the 1990s.

The mode of operation described for HP stands in sharp contrast to the mode the company used to develop and spread the Quality 1 on 1 initiative. Quality 1 on 1 arrived on the scene in the mid-1990s, when corporate quality's power to impose its will on the divisions was much weaker, and top management less focused on quality improvement. In keeping with its new status, corporate quality now drew its budget partially from its ability to work with business units. Thus, corporate quality took the natural path of forming alliances with divisions willing to experiment with new quality approaches and develop the technology associated with it.

Moreover, Quality 1 on 1 did not arrive as a relatively well-formed external package like TQC; rather, it was a set of new ideas that needed to be developed and shown to work. This emergent aspect of Quality 1 on 1 brings into even sharper relief the difference between how it was developed and deployed and the standard cascade-down model of development and diffusion, so commonly used to deploy new initiatives in U.S. corporations.

I described a process through which top management, by applying corporate-wide hoshin objectives, created subtle incentives for divisional managers to adopt new approaches to quality. At the same time, the corporate quality office worked with leading divisions to co-invent these new approaches, with the bulk of the innovation falling to the divisions. The strength of this approach is its ability to foster great variety in the innovative activities, developing Quality 1 on 1 based on the large number of divisions experimenting with it. Corporate quality's role was to support such efforts as needed, sometimes cooperating in jointly sponsored action research at business unit sites. More broadly, its task was to sponsor, absorb, digest, and synthesize the field experience of the various experimenting units. Corporate quality then engaged in a large-scale marketing effort within the corporation to offer these best practices to potential adopters. It was able to celebrate the successes of leading divisions, the high-status members of the HP family. Furthermore, with innovation rooted in the routine work of divisions, the new initiatives more likely would become grounded in everyday work, reflecting a building-block model of change. The corporatewide Quality Maturity System assessment is periodically revised to incorporate new understandings and best practices; most divisions routinely undergo a diagnostic so that they can assess where they stand in relation to these practices and what actions are necessary to bring them into compliance.

By and large, this approach to knowledge generation and diffusion appears to be a quite robust model for a multidivisional company, particularly in situations of high uncertainty and incomplete information. It is precisely under such circumstances that one needs to maximize variety to ensure the development of best practices. At the same time, large firms need a centralized function to identify, synthesize, and diffuse best practices; otherwise, the mutation process will lead to dilution and degeneration.

All things being equal, the HP experience with Quality 1 on 1 represents an effective model of how to create certain kinds of new knowledge and diffuse it across a multidivisional corporation. Under conditions of uncertainty and incomplete information, it is likely to be superior to the cascading down model so often used by our major organizations. In the latter, top management identifies a new approach and the associated operational practices that it deems promising; then it engages in a top-down cascade process, one with strong overtones of forced adoption. Because successful examples of the new initiative often come from other firms, they may be rejected by middle managers, who claim, "That would never work at our company." Hatched by top managers and subject to the latest business vogues and acronyms, these new initiatives are unlikely to be rooted in the existing work routines of employees, and therefore they are less likely to fit into a building-block model of organizational learning. While top management may succeed in imposing innovations through this process, they often meet severe resistance, both active and passive, from those who have had no part in developing the ideas or the means to achieve them, and who are faced with everyday work situations in which these newly prescribed approaches do not appear to fit. One saw this outcome at FPL. This top-down approach was a common response of many American companies to the Japanese quality challenge; some results of this approach were good, others were disastrous. The HP approach represents a much more subtle combination of top-down incentives and bottom-up initiatives, with the result that managers adopting new practices, are more likely to have a sense of ownership and the designated best practices are likely to be more meaningful in the context of everyday work.

No model of work organization is without its limitations and weaknesses, if only because maximizing some outcomes, of necessity, minimizes others. The weakness of this co-invention model lies primarily in the time it takes to implement and the incompleteness of its acceptance, a result of the need to leave most of the initiative in the hands of autonomous divisional managers.

There is a remarkable parallelism among two major themes in this book, which I have treated separately. First, I spent a great deal of effort characterizing the process by which the organizations composing the national infrastructure acted to create and spread the new quality model among individual firms. The evolution of the Baldrige protocol played a pivotal role in that story. Second, I described a model by which the corporate center at a multidivisional company like HP acted to generate and diffuse new quality practices through a process of co-invention.

In both cases, one can see the problem of creating and spreading knowledge as a center-periphery relationship. How does the center mobilize the periphery to take innovative action? In one model, the center is omniscient and seeks to prescribe what those in the periphery should be doing. For a complicated social technology like quality improvement, which requires strong linkages to existing work routines and a strong sense of ownership among those carrying out these initiatives, this solution is not very effective.

I have posited, however, an alternative model that, while not without blemishes, appears more productive for a decentralized set of actors. In this model the center sets overall directions but then treads softly and learns from the field experiences of those at the periphery. It absorbs, digests, synthesizes, and then feeds back information about best practices to those at the periphery. Of course, in this model, the periphery is anything but peripheral; it is, rather, the heart of creative action. The QMS assessment/diagnostic at HP worked for the divisions, just as the Baldrige protocol, developed nationally, worked for individual companies. In both cases, people at the center identified current best practices and compared it to operational performance among those at the periphery. By so doing, those at the center sought to call attention to areas needing improvement, contain "drift" among the operating units, and set the stage for remedial action, which would bring the operating unit's performance in line with the best practices.

In the end, however interesting the recent history of the quality movement might be, its deeper significance lies in what it tells us about the ability of organizations and their leaders to respond to exogenous competitive challenges and the role of organizational learning in that response. From one perspective, the response was slow. I have shown, however, that the response took place at a pace quite consistent both with overcoming existing institutional barriers and building new institutional arrangements to accommodate the new organizational routines necessary to improve quality. Product quality did indeed improve across the automotive and semiconductor industries and across a broad range of other manufacturing industries. It required less of an organizational transformation than was envisioned by the quality visionaries but more than the naysayers anticipated. It left in its wake a greatly expanded infrastructure, a partial adoption of a variety of quality methodologies, and a renewed focus on how to serve customers better and how to use business processes to improve competitive performance.

Notes

Introduction

1. A 1991 Gallup survey of American, Japanese, and German consumers based on a representative sample asked consumers how much more they were willing to pay to get a better-than-average quality product (American Society for Quality Control, 1991: 14–15). The specific products sampled were shoes, washing machines, TVs and automobiles. American consumers were willing to pay significantly more for quality increments than were their Japanese or German counterparts. For example, they were willing to pay 52 percent more for a better-than-average washing machine and 29 percent more for a better-than-average auto. This compares to 21 percent and 15 percent over the baseline price in Japan and 32 percent and 9 percent, respectively, for West German consumers. One might infer that the Americans were less accustomed to receiving quality products or believed that real quality requires higher costs and therefore higher prices.

2. It is noteworthy that the Japanese media played almost no role in the formative stages of the Japanese quality movement, and thus practitioners could take a long-term perspective without worrying about mass media commentary or stock market analysts questioning their use of corporate resources (cf. Kano, 1995: 233).

Chapter 1

1. The number of respondents requesting such clarification, is unknown but even without requesting clarification, some, or many respondents, may think of TQM in this way.

2. The 1988 survey had 176 firms responding whereas the 1994 survey had 485 participants representing a cross section of high technology industries. In the 1994 survey, the largest number of respondents was accounted for by telecommunication equipment (73), instruments and systems (57), software (54), electronic components (50), aerospace and defense (52), and computer peripherals (37), semiconductors (31), and production equipment (31). The unit of analysis was the whole company (68%), divisions or subsidiaries (25%), plant or production facilities (3%), or other (3%). Re-

spondents were high-level executives. Twenty-two of the respondent firms had a sales volume over $500 million in the 12 months preceding the survey.

3. This section on the new quality model draws heavily from my earlier treatment of the subject (Cole, 1994: 72–79).

4. For an account of the overall principles, see Shiba, Graham, and Walden, 1993: 411–460, and Soin, 1992: 49–91.

5. Conference Board staff searched their database for companies they knew had active quality activities, and many companies were called to identify the appropriate quality executive. The response was notably higher for firms able to identify the leading quality executive. Due to "lack of evidence of a quality process," 152 firms were eliminated from the sample. All respondents were asked if they had a "process or program in place to manage quality throughout their firm (often referred to as Total Quality Management)." Of the manufacturing respondents, 146 answered yes, 6 answered that they intended to begin such an effort shortly, and only 3 responded no. These 3 were not included in the data analysis and reports.

6. According to William Golomski, a former president of the American Society for Quality Control, the term quality assurance arose in the 1960s as the result of a search to designate corporate and division quality functions with a term having broader implications than quality control. Mr. Golomski also pointed out that the actual form a quality control career took varied by manufacturing sector. Personal communication, Feb. 28, 1996.

7. Respondents were allowed multiple responses.

8. Interview with Craig Walter, May 31, 1996, Palo Alto, California. Corroborating data on this matter were also collected from Michael Ward, member of the corporate quality staff at an interview on May 29, 1996, at HP headquarters.

9. I am very much indebted to Michael McGregor, who conducted the laborious task of searching the quantitative databases, carrying out various follow-up tasks as well as organizing the data for presentation. My thanks also to Lincoln Moses, statistical consultant to the Center for Advanced Studies in the Behavioral Sciences, for advice on how to analyze and present the data.

The companies included in this study are members of *Fortune Magazine*'s Industrial 500 in 1980, 1987, and 1994. Each year, the *Fortune* 500 includes the 500 largest American manufacturing companies based on annual revenues of the previous year. Executives identified on this list have positions of vice president, whether classified as senior, executive, corporate, staff, group or other, on the corporate level only with titles containing one of the following responsibilities: quality (including quality control, quality assurance, total quality, and quality management), product integrity, continuous improvement, corporate effectiveness, customer satisfaction, and customer service. Executives were identified from annual reports to stockholders issued at any time during the year; that is, annual reports were used for each year regardless of the quarter the company uses as the end of its account cycle. In 1987 and 1994, annual reports to stockholders were reviewed in electronic form on Nexis/Lexis. Actual annual reports of companies in the 1980 *Fortune* 500 were reviewed. First, all executives at corporate or divisional levels whose title contained any derivative of the above responsibilities were identified. Second, executives with titles below vice president (e.g., director, manager, or executives) and executives at divisions were called to verify that there was not a vice president at the corporate level. Twelve such executives were called. They did not nominate vice presidents for inclusion in this list, and thus their entries were removed.

To verify that this list was inclusive, press releases were searched using Nexis/Lexis for announcements of appointments of the executives defined above. Five announcements were discovered; each was consistent with our list. As a further check, my research assistant, Michael McGregor, looked at the Standard and Poors 1995 Register of Directors and Executives and selected firms that had vice presidents with "quality" and "customer" in their title. This yielded 67 companies. I then eliminated non-*Fortune* 500 companies and eight companies were left. My research assistant contacted these eight companies by phone; this led to three new listings for 1994 and some changes in the names of those holding the position at a few other companies.

Chosen randomly, 20 1994 *Fortune* 500 companies where executives were not identified, were called to verify that no relevant executive post existed. Additionally, 10 1994 *Fortune* 500 companies where executives were identified were called to verify that the 1980 and 1987 executive lists reflect when the post was established. Finally, the Conference Board shared their data from a 1992–1993 survey of the highest ranking quality executives in the *Fortune* 1000 companies. These further inquiries revealed 27 possible discrepancies with my results. All 27 companies were called and in the end 12 new positions were added, and 4 listings were expanded to include additional years during which the position was held.

Although further inquiries no doubt would yield still more revisions, I believe that I have sufficiently valid data to identify the central tendencies in corporate practices.

10. Technically speaking, mining (SIC code: 10) is not part of manufacturing, and I included it only because it is included in the *Fortune* 500 listing.

11. The discrepancy between number of companies and number of vice presidents flows from two sources. Some companies had the same vice president for quality in multiple years. This worked to reduce the total number of names. At the same time, some companies had more than one vice president with "customer" or quality in the title, and if I could not identify the appropriate one, I left all names in. Thirteen companies fell into this category. This worked to increased the total number of names. The net result was 174 names, two less than the number of companies we identified.

12. The American Society of Quality Control, founded in 1946, changed its name to the American Society for Quality in 1997. The name change was intended to eliminate the negative connotations many associated with the term "control" and to make the organization more attractive to those outside the traditional manufacturing base.

13. I am indebted to Brad Stratton, former editor of *Quality Progress*, the flagship publication of ASQ, for arranging ASQ's cooperation on this matter and to Kim Vogt for matching the Fortune 500 names with ASQ membership records.

14. Eva Chen, director of business processes, ABB Power T&D, pointed this out to me.

Chapter 2

1. It is noteworthy that in all three of Alfred Chandler's classic works on American business history, "quality" does not appear once in the indexes.

2. Materials for this section drawn from Millstein, 1983: 2106–2141; Magaziner and Reich, 1982; and conversations with Michael Borrus, University of California, Berkeley, Nov. 16, 1995.

3. Interview with David Hodges, former dean, College of Engineering, University of California, Berkeley, Dec. 9, 1993.

4. Telephone conversation with Wes Monty, president of Films Inc., Feb. 27, 1996.

Chapter 3

1. This section also draws on a lecture by Amos Tversky on framing at the Stanford Law School, Feb. 12, 1996.

2. Management practices, however, were interwoven with differential responses to government regulations.

3. If TQM became the defining term for American efforts to adopt the new quality model, TQC was the equivalent term for the early postwar Japanese quality movement.

4. I am indebted to Kent Sterett of Fidelity Investments and formerly head of the quality improvement department at FPL in the mid-1980s, whom I interviewed extensively on this subject, San Francisco, Jan. 7, 1995. Vicki Amon, formerly supervisor, Deming Prize Support Group at FPL, also shared her observations. "Bear" Baila, coordinator of external interfaces at FPL and later to become vice president of Qualtec (1988), was also kind enough to provide detailed information on the visitor's program at FPL and companies working with Qualtec, Feb. 28, 1996. J. Michael Adams, manager of quality services at FPL, provided important insights into recent developments. See also Hudiburg, 1991: 17–19.

5. The observations on Ford are based in part on a presentation made by Edward Baker, a key figure in the Ford quality improvement efforts in the 1980s. The presentation was to my class on organizational quality at the University of Michigan in spring 1987.

6. Whirlpool, an industry leader, did not begin its strong quality initiative until the last 1980s.

7. Parenthetically, I observe that perhaps because of Japanese managements' almost continual experience with borrowing from abroad, Japanese managers display little need to jettison the American origins of their organizational practices. If one asks Toyota Motor Co. executives how they developed their suggestion system, they immediately point to its origins in Ford Motor Co.

8. The idea that high quality and low costs went together was not a foreign concept to a number of American experts. Armand Feigenbaum and Joseph Juran had long preached this message. These principles grew out of prewar and early postwar thinking in industrial engineering that if one concentrated on basic work elements and tasks, one could reduce costs by identifying the tasks to be reduced or eliminated if things were done right the first time. While such conceptualizations were part of the thinking of selected American scholars and practitioners, the advocates' voices were clearly whispers in the wind that few companies heard. A partial exception was in industries like semiconductors where yield is one of the traditional quality measures. The connection between high yield and low cost is readily apparent to managers.

9. Interview with Mr. Akiba, June 13, 1990.

Chapter 4

1. I am indebted to my eminent colleague at the Center for Advanced Study in the Behavioral Sciences in 1996, Pascal Boyer, an anthropologist at the Centre National de la Recherche Scientifique in Lyons, France, for his insights on this matter. Dr. Boyer worked for the Paris office of Philip Crosby Associates in the mid-1980s. The firm prides itself on teaching its materials in exactly the same way so that everyone learns exactly the same thing, no matter where they are learning it (Byrne, 1991: 38).

2. These observations are not intended as a statement on the current activities of Philip Crosby Associates. Their approach evolved over time. By the 1990s, they were teaching business process reengineering, applied statistical quality control, etc. My analysis here is intended only to capture the dynamics of the early 1980s. Philip Crosby sold the firm to Proudfoot PLC in 1989 and repurchased it in 1997.

3. Interview with Charles Harwood, who was the CEO at Signetics at this time, Palo Alto, California, July 15, 1996.

4. Interview with Craig Walter, former director of corporate quality at Hewlett-Packard, Jan. 22, 1996.

5. The data are reported for the *Fortune* 1000, including service firms. Professor Lawler was kind enough to break out the manufacturing data from the total and report it to me separately. Personal communication, June 4, 1996.

Chapter 5

1. OEM is usually used to refer to producers of systems rather than components. I extend the usage to apply it to the large semiconductor companies or divisions of such companies like Intel, Texas Instruments, and Motorola. However, the semiconductor producers, unlike the automotive companies, are not typically producing final products but rather systems built into final products by other companies.

2. I am indebted to David Stark, a colleague at the Center for Advanced Studies in the Behavioral Sciences, 1995–1996, for taking the time over a number of lunches to explain the various fine points in the network literature. If I did not quite get it, it was not due to his lack of effort or knowledge.

3. There are always some cases in which given suppliers, because of their dominant market position, are in a stronger position than their customers, and thus customers have a great deal of difficulty pressuring them to change their behavior. The relation between Intel, the supplier, and Packard-Bell, the customer, would be one such example.

4. George Easton, in his joint survey with Sherry Jarrell of 44 firms with advanced quality activities, comes to a similar conclusion. Their sample was selected initially from firms reporting active TQM programs in their annual reports and is composed primarily of manufacturing firms. Personal communication, George Easton, June 6, 1996.

5. Communication from Michael Borrus, University of California, Berkeley, May 29, 1996. The following discussion draws heavily from his observations.

6. For much of this information, I am indebted to Larry Sullivan, who was the head of the Ford Supplier Institute and later president of ASI and to Peggy Jennings, a long-term employee and current vice president, telephone interviews in April 1994 and May 1996. In the 1980s, I had occasion to meet with a number ASI personnel and talk with managers who used their services.

7. Unpublished data from a study of U.S. automotive suppliers in the mid-1980s I conducted with Michael Flynn showed that roughly 11% of the suppliers serviced only Chrysler, 17% only Ford, and 33% only GM. These figures are included to suggest direction and orders of magnitude rather than precision.

8. This was of course not always true. For those suppliers going through the motions to satisfy their important customer, Ford, sometimes study mission members were selected for reasons other than their ability to learn and to apply that learning.

9. Telephone interview with Richard Schonberger, June 10, 1996.

Chapter 6

1. See also Cole (1989b); Reddy, Aram, and Lynn (1991: 295–304); and Shiba, Graham, and Walden (1993: 507–532).

2. I am indebted for many of these observations to Paul Hess, a PhD. candidate at Brandeis, who has been studying these organizations.

3. Interview with Jack Brown, Nov. 8, 1996.

4. My thanks to Richard Sandretti and Brad Stratton of ASQ and David Luther, former president of ASQ, for their generous sharing of information and knowledge about ASQ.

5. Data are from their 1996 and 1997 member satisfaction survey. The response rates are 42% and 22%, respectively. Subsequent discussion of the data draw from these and other members surveys. I am indebted to ASQ for making this data available to me.

6. My thanks to Bob King, executive director of GOAL/QPC, for his cooperation in providing materials and in discussing GOAL/QPC activities.

7. I am indebted to Larry Schein of the Conference Board, and to David Luther and Kent Sterett, two of the early founders of the first Quality Council, for their accounts of the organization and its activities. In addition, I had the good fortune to make a presentation to the flagship quality council in June 1997 and explored with current members how they used the council.

8. These and other materials were made available to me by David Luther, the Conference Board's Quality Council, Purpose and Processes, Oct. 3, 1985.

9. Thomas Lee, president of CQM, was most helpful and forthright in providing information on the organization.

10. Barry Diamondstone, deputy director of quality programs at the National Institute of Standards and Technology, was especially helpful in providing materials and offering clarifying suggestions for revision of an early draft. I also received input from Curt Reimann, the former director of quality programs at NIST, and the current Director, Harry Hertz.

11. For a summary history of these activities, see Neil de Carlo and W. Kent Sterett (1990: 21–25).

12. In this era of "the government can do nothing right," it is worthwhile noting another direct government intervention in the quality area, SEMATECH. Set up to help American firms address the competitive advantage the Japanese developed in the 1980s in the semiconductor industry, SEMATECH created a major initiative in quality and established a significant infrastructure for supporting quality improvement among semiconductor suppliers. The suppliers themselves organized an adjunct organization,

SEMI/SEMATECH, to serve as a communications link between its members and SEMATECH. Since the initiation of SEMATECH's "partnering for total quality" program, there has been substantial improvement in the business performance of U.S. equipment suppliers. To be sure, there are many possible explanations for that, but an early study suggested the quality improvement program was making a significant contribution (U.S. GAO, 1992: 13–14).

13. I am indebted to my colleague David Levine for this observation.

14. The survey responses do not tell us how much of the corporation uses this diagnostic tool. Moreover, the response rate for the survey was only 19%, so these figures can be used only as a rough guide.

15. Traditionally a third party certifies a product (giving written assurance that a product conforms to specified requirements) and registers a system, but the distinction has become blurred in discussions of ISO 9000. I use the terms interchangeably here, but with the understanding that when use the term certification I am referring to the certification of a quality system (see Kelada, 1996: 329).

16. Respondents were allowed to respond to both categories, so there is some double counting involved.

17. These data of course do not tell us how many companies failed to achieve registration on their first try and eventually gave up trying to get certified.

18. See Chapter 1 for more detail on the survey.

Chapter 7

1. Yokogawa Hewlett-Packard became Hewlett-Packard Japan in 1996. Since it was called Yokogawa Hewlett-Packard during most of the time covered by this analysis, I use that name.

2. I am particularly indebted to the following individuals who gave generously of their time and provided many relevant corporate documents to make this analysis possible: Craig Walter, former corporate quality director at Hewlett-Packard; Richard LeVitt, current corporate quality director; Kenzo Sasaoka, former CEO Yokogawa Hewlett-Packard; Katsu Yoshimoto, former country quality manager for YHP in the 1980s; T. Michael Ward, TQM manager HP quality; Bill Mohr, quality consultant, Finance and Remarketing Division, Hewlett-Packard; Sara Beckman, former director, Change Management Team; Richard Moss, reliability engineering manager; and Professor Noriaki Kano, quality counselor for HP from 1985 to 1992.

3. In fact, subsequent hiring of management employees by YHP faced the same problems as experienced by other American subsidiaries and joint ventures, and they were forced to recruit at B rather than A schools.

4. While Hamel (1991: 83–103) discusses the importance of transparency in interpartner learning within international strategic alliances, he does not explicitly link it to trustworthy information.

5. I am indebted to my colleague Sara Beckman, a former HP manager, for clarifying the significance of these meetings.

6. Text from notes provided by Kenzo Sasaoka, July 1996.

7. A few HP managers believe that quality circles were very much on the proselytizing agenda of YHP and that YHP's denial at this time is a retrospective effort to distance themselves from a failure.

Chapter 8

1. These observations benefited from conversations with Bob King, executive director, GOAL/QPC, Oct. 6, 1996.

2. Hewlett-Packard Corporation, Corporate Quality Department, "Reinventing Quality at HP," Internal Company Document (1995: 3).

3. Benchmarking is a formal process of comparative analysis designed to identify and surpass industry best practice in a specific area of performance. Pioneered by Xerox in the early 1980s and developed in part through its analysis of copiers produced by Fuji-Xerox, it became a widely used U.S. management tool in the mid-and late 1980s (Camp, 1989).

4. As a company YHP is actually composed of a manufacturing division and a sales division, and the financial results of the company are a combination of both. The influence of YHP's financial performance on HP has been based primarily on the results of its manufacturing division.

5. This section benefited from conversations with my colleague Sara Beckman.

Chapter 9

1. I am indebted to David Cole, Michael Flynn, and John Paul Macduffie for their thoughtful comments on this chapter.

2. In the automotive industry, the commonly used measures of quality by both the popular media (*Consumer Reports*) and the industry (J. D. Power and Associates) have been reliability measures. Typically the data are for the number of reported problems of surveyed owners within a fixed period of ownership of a new car. The J. D. Power and Associates survey (Initial Quality Survey), used since 1987, is based on the number of problems reported in the first 90 days of ownership. It includes not only operational problems but also dissatisfaction with gaps in trim, etc., so it is not exclusively a reliability measure. J. D. Power and Associates has also expanded its measures in recent years to include customer experiences with dealers (CSI), customer satisfaction after five years of ownership, and in 1997 a "things gone right" survey (APPEAL).

3. I am indebted to Robert Leachman, the director of the study, for his very generous cooperation in both sharing data from the study to make possible the comparisons to be reported as well as providing input regarding the interpretation of the findings and their causes. I also want to thank Chien Leachman, researcher for the CSM, for creating the graphs of semiconductor quality metrics by region. The UC Berkeley Competitive Semiconductor Manufacturing Program is funded by the Sloan Foundation.

4. Line yield is normalized for number of mask layers (20 mask layers) and die yield is normalized for size of the chip area (.05 sq. cm die). See Benson, Cunningham, and Leachman, 1995: 203–205.

5. For the fourfold framework used here, I have adapted a model developed by Phillip Tetlock (1991: 28–32).

6. These figures should be considered as a rough estimate only since there are numerous part-time quality contributors and they do not always self-identify as members of the quality community.

7. Again, the measurement problems are severe since in addition to the part-time problem, some firms exclude some activities that others include in their quality function because they are located in other departments (e.g., reliability engineering or metrology). Thus, the figures provided should be seen as providing orders of magnitude understanding rather than being precise measures.

Chapter 10

1. Noriaki Kano, the Japanese quality advisor, provides an interesting common element in the two cases. In addition to his work at HP described in earlier chapters, he visited FPL on several occasions and presented his ideas, especially on policy deployment. These presentations and discussions were not only with senior management but also with regional/line personnel. I benefited from his insights on similarities and differences in the two cases.

References

Abernathy, William. 1982. *The Competitive Status of the U.S. Auto Industry*. Washington, D.C.: National Academy Press.

Abo, Tetsuo. 1994. *Hybrid Factory: The Japanese Production System in the United States*. New York: Oxford University Press.

Abrahamson, Eric. 1996. "Management Fashion." *Academy of Management Review* 21 (January): 254–285.

American Customer Satisfaction Index. 1994, 1995, 1996, 1997. American Customer Satisfaction Index Results Summary. Ann Arbor: University of Michigan.

American Iron and Steel Institute. 1985. "Domestic Steel Producers Respond to Automakers' Demand: 'Quality or Else.'" *Quality Progress* 18: 57–59.

American Society for Quality Control. 1988. *'88 Gallup Survey: Consumers' Perceptions Concerning the Quality of American Products and Services*, Milwaukee: ASQC.

———. 1991. *An International Survey of Consumer's Perceptions of Product and Service Quality*. Milwaukee: ASQC.

American Telephone and Telegraph. 1990. *Leading the Quality Initiative*. Berkeley Heights, N.J.: AT&T Quality Steering Committee, AT&T Bell Laboratories.

Angel, David. 1994. *Restructuring for Innovation: The Remaking of the U.S. Semiconductor Industry*. New York: Guilford Press.

Aoki, Masahiko. 1988. *Information, Incentives, and Bargaining in the Japanese Economy*. Cambridge: Cambridge University Press.

Argyris, Chris. 1992. *On Organizational Learning*. Oxford: Blackwell Publishers.

Association for Quality and Participation. 1996. "AQP and World Center for Community Excellence Team Up." *AQP Report* (February/March): 1–3.

Attewell, Paul. 1996. "Technology Diffusion and Organizational Learning: The Case of Business Computing." *Organizational Learning*. Thousand Oaks, Calif.: Sage Publications.

"Automotive News." 1998. *1998 Market Data Book*. Detroit: Crain Publications.

Barley, Stephen, et al. 1988. "Cultures of Culture: Academics, Practitioners and the Pragmatics of Normative Control." *Administrative Science Quarterly*. 33: 24–60.

Bartlett, Frederic. 1932. *Remembering: A Study in Experimental and Social Psychology.* New York: Macmillan.

Beauchamp, Jaime. 1994. "Return on Quality." *Business Week* 3384 (August 8): 54–59.

Beckman, Sara. 1996. "Evolution of Management Roles in a Networked Organization." In Paul Osterman (ed.), *Broken Ladders: Managerial Careers in the New Economy.* New York: Oxford University Press.

Beckman, Sara, and David Mowery. 1996. "Corporate Change and Competitiveness: The Hewlett-Packard Company." Presented at the Conference for Corporate Strategy, Organization, Innovation, and Performance in Large Electronics Companies," London School of Economics, Sept. 23–25.

Bemowski, Karen. 1996. "Something Old, Something New." *Quality Progress* 29 (October): 27–34.

Bemowski, Karen, and Brad Stratton. 1995. "How Do People Actually Use the Baldrige Award Criteria?" *Quality Progress* 28 (May): 43–47.

Benson, Robert, Sean Cunningham, and Robert Leachman. 1995. "Benchmarking, Manufacturing Performance in the Semiconductor Industry." *Production and Operations Management* 4 (Summer): 201–216.

Berwick, Donald, A. Godfrey, and Jane Roessner. 1990. *Curing Health Care.* San Francisco: Jossey Bass.

Best, Michael. 1990. *The New Competition.* Cambridge, Mass.: Harvard University Press.

Bhote, Keki. 1989. *Strategic Supply Management.* New York: American Management Association.

Bleakley, Fred. 1993. "Many Companies Try Management Fads, Only to See Them Flop." *Wall Street Journal* (July 6): A1, A6.

Bourdieu, Pierre. 1981. "Men and Machines." In K. Knorr-Cetina and Aaron Cicourel (eds.), *Advances in Social Theory and Methodology.* Boston: Routledge and Kegan: 304–318.

Bowles, Jerry, and Joshua Hammond. 1991. *Beyond Quality.* New York: Berkeley Books.

Brecka, Jon, and Laura Rubach. 1995. "Corporate Quality Training Facilities." *Quality Progress* 28 (January): 27–30.

Broadhead, James. 1996. *The Evolution of Quality at FPL.* International Conference on Quality, Oct. 15–18. Yokohama: Japanese Union of Scientists and Engineers: 11–17.

Brown, John Seely, and Paul Duguid. 1991. "Organizational Learning and Communities-of-Practice: Toward a Unified View of Working, Learning, and Innovation." *Organization Science* 2 (February): 40–57.

———. 1997. "Organizing Knowledge." Draft paper. Palo Alto, Calif.

Brown, Mark. 1994. *Baldrige Award Winning Quality,* White Plains, N.Y.: Quality Resources.

Buch, Kim, and Dave Wetzel. 1993. "The Evolution of SPC in Manufacturing." *The Journal of Quality and Participation* 16 (October/November): 34–37.

Burgelman, Robert, and Andrew Grove. 1996. "Strategic Dissonance." *California Management Review* 38 (Winter): 8–28.

Burt, Ronald. 1992. "The Social Structure of Competition." In Nitrin Nohria and Robert Eccles (eds.), *Networks and Organizations.* Cambridge, Mass.: Harvard Business School Press: 57–91.

Business Week. 1983. "Chipwars: The Japanese Threat." *Business Week* (May 23): 80–90.

Bylinsky, Gene. 1981a. "The Japanese Chip Challenge." *Fortune* (March 23): 115–122.

———. 1981b. "Japan's Ominous Chip Victory." *Fortune* (December 14): 52–57.

Byrne, John. 1986. "Business Fads: What's In and What's Out." *Business Week* 20: 40–47.

———. 1991. "Managing for Quality: High Priests and Hucksters." *Business Week* Special Issue (Oct. 25): 52–57.

Callahan, Joseph. 1989. "Tora, Tora, Tora." *Automotive Industries* 169 (February): 89–112.

Camp, Robert. 1989. *Benchmarking*. Milwaukee: ASQC Quality Press.

Carroll, Glenn, and J. Richard Harrison. 1994. "On the Historical Efficiency of Competition Between Organizational Populations." *American Journal of Sociology* 100 (November): 720–749.

Case, Robbie. 1985. *Intellectual Development: Birth to Adulthood*. Orlando, Fl.: Academic Press.

Chandler, Alfred, Jr. 1962. *Strategy and Structure*. Cambridge, Mass.: MIT Press.

———. 1990. *Scale and Scope*. Cambridge, Mass.: Belknap.

Chappell, Lindsay. 1996. "Japan's Plan: Build (a Lot) More in U.S." *Automotive News* (October 28): 3, 44.

Choi, Thomas, and S. Nazli Wasti. 1995. "Institutional Pressures and Organizational Learning: The Case of American-Owned Automotive Parts Suppliers and Japanese Shop-floor Production Methods." In Jeffrey Liker, John Ettlie, and John Campbell (eds.), *Engineered in Japan: Japanese Technology Practices*. New York: Oxford University Press.

Clark, Kim, and Takahiro Fujimoto. 1991. *Product Development Performance*. Cambridge, Mass.: Harvard Business School Press.

Clark, Tom, Larry Walz, George Turner, and Bish Miszuk. 1994. "Intel's Circuitous Route to Implementing Total Quality." In James Cortada and John Woods (eds.), *The Quality Yearbook*. New York: McGraw-Hill.

Cohen, Michael, and Paul Bacdayan. 1996. "Organizational Routines are Stored as Procedural Memory: Evidence from a Laboratory Study." In Michael Cohen and Lee Sproull (eds.), *Organizational Learning*. Thousand Oaks, Calif.: Sage Publications: 403–429.

Cohen, Stephen, and John Zysman. 1987. *Manufacturing Matters*. New York: Basic Books.

Cole, David. 1981. "Analysis of U.S. and Japanese Automotive Technology." In Robert E. Cole (ed.), *The Japanese Automobile Industry: Model and Challenge for the Future*," Ann Arbor: Michigan Papers in Japanese Studies, No. 3: 99–122.

Cole, Robert E. 1979. *Work, Mobility and Participation*. Berkeley: University of California Press.

———. 1981. "The Japanese Lesson in Quality." *Technology Review* 83: 29–32, 36, 38, 40.

———. 1987. "What Was Deming's Real Influence." *Across the Board* 24, (February): 49–51.

———. 1989a. "Large-Scale Change and the Quality Revolution." In Allan Mohrman, Jr. et al. *Large-Scale Organizational Change*. San Francisco: Jossey-Bass.

———. 1989b. *Strategies for Learning*. Berkeley: University of California Press.

———. 1990. "U.S. Quality Improvement in the Auto Industry: Close but No Cigar." *California Management Review* 32 (Summer 1990): 71–85.

———. 1994a. "Different Quality Paradigms and Their Implications for Organizational

Learning." In Masahiko Aoki and Ronald Dore (eds.), *The Japanese Firm: Sources of Competitive Strength*. New York: Oxford University Press.

———. 1994b. "Reengineering the Corporation: A Review Essay." *Quality Management Journal* 1 (July): 77–85.

Collins Jr., F. C. 1988. "Department of Defense Renews Emphasis on Quality." *Quality Progress* 21 (March): 19–21.

The Conference Board. 1994. *A Profile of the U.S. Senior Quality Executive*. New York: The Conference Board.

Cook, James. 1983. "You Mean We've Been Speaking Prose All These Years?" *Forbes* (April 11): 142–149.

Corrigan, James. 1994. "Is ISO 9000 the Path to TQM." *Quality Progress* 27 (May): 33–36.

Crosby, Philip. 1979. *Quality Is Free*. New York: McGraw-Hill.

Cusumano, Michael, and Richard Selby. 1995. *Microsoft Secrets*. New York: Free Press.

Cusumano, Michael, and Akira Takeishi. 1991. "Supplier Relations and Management: A Survey of Japanese, Japanese-Transplant, and U.S. Auto Plants." *Strategic Management Journal* 12: 563–588.

Dean, James Jr., and David Bowen. 1994. "Management Theory and Total Quality: Improving Research and Practice Through Theory Development." *Academy of Management Review* 19 (July): 392–418.

DeCarlo, Neil, and Kent Sterett. 1990. "History of the Malcolm Baldrige National Quality Award." *Quality Progress* 23 (March): 21–27.

Dertouzos, Michael, Richard Lester, and Robert Solow. 1989. *Made in America*. Cambridge, Mass.: MIT Press.

Detroit Free Press. 1986. "Ross Perot: The Man Who Speaks His Mind on GM." *Detroit Free Press* 156 (Nov. 25): 4c.

Diehl, E., and J. D. Sterman. 1995. "Effects of Feedback Complexity on Dynamic Decision Making." *Organization Behavior and Human Decision Processes* 62: 198–215.

DiMaggio, Paul, and Walter Powell. 1991. "The Iron Cage Revisited: Institutional Isomorphism and Collective Rationality in Organizational Fields." In Walter Powell and Paul DiMaggio (eds.), *The New Institutionalism in Organizational Analysis*. Chicago: University of Chicago Press.

Dobyns, Lloyd, and Clare Crawford-Mason. 1991. *Quality or Else*. Boston: Houghton Mifflin.

Dore, Ronald, et al. 1989. "Review of Flexibility in Japanese Labor Markets." *Working Paper, Manpower and Social Affairs Committee, OECD*. Paris: OECD.

Ealey, Lance, and Luis Troyano-Bermúdez. 1996. "Are Automobiles the Next Commodity?" *McKinsey Quarterly* 4: 63–75.

Easterbrook, Gregg. 1992. "Driving Quality at Ford." In Rosabeth Kanter, Barry Stein, and Todd Jick (eds.), *The Challenge of Organizational Change*. New York: Free Press.

Easton, George, and Sherry Jarrell. 1997a. "The Emerging Academic Research on the Link Between Total Quality Management and Corporate Financial Management." Chapter 2 in M. J. Stahl (ed.), *Topics on Total Quality* (forthcoming). London: Blackwell Publishers.

———. 1997b. *Patterns in the Deployment of Total Quality Management: A Preliminary Analysis of Interviews with Twenty-five Leading Companies*. Paper presented at the Workshop on

Integrating Social Science Theory and Research in Quality Improvement, Washington D.C., National Science Foundation.

———. 1997c. "Strategic Quality Planning: An Analysis of Factors Deriving Effectiveness." Presented at the NSF Design and Manufacturing Grantees Conference, Seattle, Jan. 8.

———. 1998. "The Effects of Total Quality Management on Corporate Performance: An Empirical Investigation." *Journal of Business.* 71 (April): 253–307.

The Economist. 1992. "The Cracks in Quality." *The Economist* 323 (April 18): 167–168.

Ettorre, Barbara. 1997. "Is the Baldrige Still Meaningful?" in James Cortada and John Woods (eds.), *The Quality Yearbook, 1997 Edition.* New York: McGraw-Hill.

Finan, William. 1990. *A Comparison of Japanese and American Approaches to Quality in the Semiconductor Industry.* Chapel Hill, N.C.: Semiconductor Research Corporation: 1–90.

———. 1993. *Matching Japan in Quality: How the Leading U.S. Semiconductor Firms Caught Up With the Best in Japan.* MITJP 93–01. Cambridge, Mass.: Center for Industrial Studies, MIT.

Finan, William, and Annette LaMond. 1985. "Sustaining U.S. Competitiveness in Microelectronics: The Challenge to U.S. policy." In Bruce Scott and George Lodge (eds.), *U.S. Competitiveness in the World Economy.* Boston: Harvard Business School Press.

Fine, Charles. 1986. "Quality Improvement and Learning in Productive Systems." *Management Science* 32 (October): 1301–1315.

Fligstein, Neil. 1990. *The Transformation of Corporate Control.* Cambridge, Mass.: Harvard University Press.

———. 1991. "The Structural Transformation of American Industry: An Institutional Account of the Causes of Diversification in the Largest Firms, 1919–1979." In Walter Powell and Paul DiMaggio (eds.), *The New Institutionalism in Organizational Analysis.* Chicago: University of Chicago Press.

———. 1996. "A Political-Cultural Approach to Market Institutions." *American Sociological Review* 61 (August): 656–673.

Fligstein, Neil, and Kenneth Dauber. 1989. "Structural Changes in Corporate Organization." *Annual Review of Sociology* 15. Palo Alto: Annual Reviews Inc.

Florida, Richard, and Martin Kenney. 1990. *The Breakthrough Illusion.* New York: Basic Books.

———. 1991. "Transplanted Organizations: The Transfer of Japanese Industrial Organization to the U.S." *American Sociological Review* 56 (June): 381–398.

Florida Power and Light. 1989. *FPL 1989 Deming Prize Examination: Examiner Opinions.* Miami: FPL.

Flynn, Michael, and David Andrea. 1994. *Corporate Learning From Japan: The Automotive Industry.* Ann Arbor: Office for the Study of Automotive Transportation, University of Michigan, Report Number 94–14.

Freund, William, and Eugene Epstein. 1984. *People and Productivity.* Homewood, Il.: Dow Jones-Irwin.

Fruin, W. Mark. 1992. *The Japanese Enterprise System.* New York: Oxford University Press.

Fuchsberg, Gilbert. 1992. "Total Quality Is Termed Only Partial Success." *Wall Street Journal* (October 1): B1, B8.

Gale, Bradley. 1994. *Managing Customer Value.* New York: Free Press.

Garvin, David. 1983. "Quality on the Line." *Harvard Business Review* (September-October): 64–75.

———. 1988. *Managing Quality*. New York: Free Press.

Gellner, Ernest. 1979. *Spectacles and Predicaments*. Cambridge: Cambridge University Press.

Godfrey, A. Blanton. 1995. "The Malcolm Baldrige National Quality Award: Seven Years of Progress, Seven Thousand Lessons Learned." In John Hromi (ed.), *The Best of Quality* 5. Milwaukee: ASQC Quality Press.

Godfrey, A. Blanton, and Robert Kerwin. 1988. "Electronic Components Industries." In J. M. Juran and Frank Gryna (eds.), *Juran's Quality Control Handbook*. 4th edition. New York: McGraw-Hill.

Grabher, Gernot, and David Stark (eds.). 1997. *Restructuring Networks in Post-Socialism: Legacies, Linkages and Localities*. New York: Oxford University Press.

Groocock, John. 1986. *The Chain of Quality*. New York: Wiley.

Gryna, Frank. 1988. "Supplier Relations." In Joseph Juran and Frank Gryna (eds.), *Juran's Quality Control Handbook*. 4th edition. New York: McGraw Hill.

Guillén, Mauro. 1994. *Models of Management*. Chicago: University of Chicago.

Gunter, Berton. 1987. "A Perspective on the Taguchi Methods." *Quality Progress* (June): 44–52.

Haas, Elizabeth. 1987. "Applying the Lessons: Networking Semiconductor Companies." *Entrepreneurial Economy* 6 (July/August): 40–41. Washington D.C.: Corporation for Enterprise Development.

Hamel, Gary. 1991. "Competition for Competence and Inter-partner Learning Within International Strategic Alliances." *Strategic Management Journal* 12: 83–103.

Hamel, Gary, and C. K. Prahalad. 1994. *Competing for the Future*. Cambridge, Mass.: Harvard Business School Press.

Hammer, Michael, and James Champy. 1993. *Reengineering the Corporation*. New York: HarperBusiness.

Hammond, Josh, and James Morrison. 1996. *The Stuff Americans Are Made Of*. New York: Macmillan.

Hayes, Robert, Steven Wheelwright, and Kim Clark. 1988. *Dynamic Manufacturing*. New York: Free Press.

Heil, Jennifer. 1994. "Companies Seek Automakers' Secrets of Success." *Automotive News* (May 23): 19.

Helper, Susan. 1991. "How Much Has Really Changed Between U.S. Automakers and Their Suppliers?" *Sloan Management Review* 32: 15–28.

Helper, Susan, and Mari Sako. 1995. "Supplier Relations in Japan and the United States: Are They Converging?" *Sloan Management Review* 36 (Spring): 77–84.

Henderson, Angelo, and Oscar Suris. 1995. "Chrysler Documents Show Sharp Rise in Costs for Warranty-Covered Repairs." *Wall Street Journal* (October 23): A3, A8.

Henkoff, Ronald. 1989. "What Motorola Learns from Japan," *Fortune* 119 (April 24): 157, 160, 164, 168.

Hewlett-Packard Corporation, Corporate Quality Department. 1995. "Reinventing Quality at HP." Internal Company Document, Hewlett-Packard Corporation: 1–4.

Hewlett-Packard Corporation. 1997. *Company Facts*. Http://www.hp.com/abouthp/CorporateOverview.html#CorporateFacts. 4–5.

Hillary, Rachel. 1996. "Behind the Stars and Stripes: Quality in the USA." *Quality Progress* 29 (January): 31–35.

Hoeffer, El. 1981. "How Ford Makes Quality Happen." *Purchasing* 90 (March 12): 51, 53.

Huczynski, Andrej. 1993. *Management Gurus.* London: Routledge Press.

Hudiburg, John. 1991. *Winning with Quality.* White Plains, N.Y.: Quality Resources.

Hunt, Jim. 1997. "ISO 9000 Registration or Compliance." *Quality* 36 (January): 42, 44–45.

Industrial Bank of Japan. 1996. "Japanese Automakers' Operations in Europe: Present Condition and Problems." *Japanese Finance and Industry* 3: 1–23.

Ingrassia, Paul, and Joseph White. 1994. *Comeback.* New York: Simon & Schuster.

Ishikawa, Kaoru. 1985. *What is Total Quality Control.* New York: Prentice Hall.

———. 1987. "The Quality Control Audit." *Quality Progress* 20 (January): 39–41.

———. 1990. *Introduction to Quality Control.* Tokyo: 3A Corporation.

Joint Commission on Accreditation of Health Care Organizations. 1994. *Accreditation Manual for Hospitals 1994.* Chicago: Joint Commission on Accreditation of Hospitals.

Juran, Joseph. 1966. "Quality Problems, Remedies and Nostrums." *Industrial Quality Control* 22 (June): 647–653.

———. 1978. "Japanese and Western Quality: A Contrast." *Quality Progress* (December): 10–18.

———. 1985. "Catching Up: How is the West Doing." *Quality Progress* 18 (November): 18–22.

———. 1988. *Juran's Quality Control Handbook.* With Frank Gryna (assoc. ed.). 4th edition. New York: McGraw Hill.

———. 1989. *Juran on Leadership For Quality.* New York: Free Press.

——— (editor-in-chief). 1995. *A History of Managing for Quality.* Milwaukee: ASQC Quality Press.

Kano, Noriaki. 1995. "A Perspective on Quality Activities in American Firms." In Robert E. Cole (ed.), *The Death and Life of the American Quality Movement.* New York: Oxford University Press.

Kanter, Rosabeth Moss. 1983. *The Changemasters.* New York: Simon and Shuster.

Kearns, David, and David Nadler. 1992. *Prophets in the Dark.* New York: Harper Business.

Kelada, Joseph. 1996. *Integrating Reengineering With Total Quality.* Milwaukee: ASQC Quality Press.

Keller, Maryann. 1989. *Rude Awakening.* New York: Harper Perennial.

Kenney, Martin, and Richard Florida. 1993. *Beyond Mass Production.* New York: Oxford University Press.

Kikuchi, Makoto. 1983. *Japanese Electronics.* Tokyo: Simul Press.

King, Bob. 1989. *Hoshin Planning: the Developmental Approach.* Metheun, Mass.: GOAL/QPC.

Kisiel, Ralph. 1996. "QS-9000 Total Could Hit 1,000 by End of Year." *Automotive News* (December 23): 14.

———. 1997. "With Toyota as Guide Chrysler and UAW Renew Long Journey to Improve Quality, Reduce Fat." *Automotive News* (September 29): 24–25.

Kodama, Fumio. August 3, 1991. "Japan Success: New Paradigm or Just Adaptation?" *The Nikkei Weekly*: 23.

Kofman, Fred et al. 1993. *The Organization of Product Development*. Cambridge, Mass.: MIT IPC Working Paper 93–008WP.

Kolesar, Peter. 1994. "What Deming Told the Japanese in 1950." *Quality Management Journal* 2 (Fall) : 9–24.

———. 1995. "Vision, Values, Milestones: Paul O'Neill Starts Total Quality." In Robert E. Cole (ed.), *The Death and Life of the American Quality Movement*. New York: Oxford University Press.

Kondo, Yoshio. 1979. "Ningensei to QC (II)" [Humanity and QC(II)]. *Hinshitsu* 9: 5–10.

———. 1990. "Creativity in Daily Work." *Human Systems Management* 9: 7–13.

Lackritz, John. 1997. "TQM Within Fortune 500 Corporations." *Quality Progress* 30 (February): 69–72.

Lawler, Edward, and Susan Mohrman. 1985. "Quality Circles After the Fad." *Harvard Business Review* 63 (January–February): 64–71.

Lawler, Edward II, Susan Mohrman, and Gerald Ledford, Jr. 1992. *Employee Involvement and Total Quality Management: Practices and Results in Fortune 1000 Companies*. San Francisco: Jossey Bass.

———. 1995. *Creating High Performance Organizations: Practices and Results of Employee Involvement and Total Quality Management in Fortune 1000 Companies*. San Francisco: Jossey Bass.

Lazarsfeld, Paul, et al. 1944. *The People's Choice: How the Voter Makes Up His Mind*. New York: Duell, Sloan, and Pearce.

Leachman, Robert. 1996. *Third Report on the Results of the Main Phase, Competitive Semiconductor Manufacturing Survey*, CSM-31. Berkeley: University of California, Berkeley.

Leib, Jeffrey. 1985. "Steelmakers Listen to Detroit." *The New York Times* D1, D4.

Levin, Dorin. 1995. *Behind the Wheels at Chrysler*. New York: Harcourt, Brace and Co.

Levitt, Barbara, and James March. 1988. "Organizational Learning," In W. Richard Scott and J. Blake (eds.), *Annual Review of Sociology*. Palo Alto, Calif.: Annual Reviews Inc.

LeVitt, Richard. 1996. "Quality 1 on 1: Becoming Customer-Centered." *Proceedings from Sixth Renault Symposium* Vol. 2. Paris: Institut Renault: 1099–1120.

Lillrank, Paul. 1995. "The Transfer of Management Innovations from Japan." *Organization Studies* 16: 971–989.

Lillrank, Paul, and Noriaki Kano. 1989. *Continuous Improvement: Quality Control Circles in Japanese Industry*. Ann Arbor: Center for Japanese Studies.

Lincoln, James, and Yoshifumi Nakata. 1997. "The Transformation of the Japanese Employment System: Nature, Depth and Origins." *Work and Occupations* 24 (February): 33–55.

Lindsay, Peter, and Donald Norman. 1977. *Human Information Processing: An Introduction to Psychology*. 2nd edition. New York: Academic Press.

Litsikas, Mary. 1997. "Companies Choose ISO Certification for Internal Benefits." *Quality* 36 (January): 20, 22, 24, 26.

Lynn Leonard, N. Reddy, and John Aram. (1996). "Linking Technology and Institutions: The Innovation Community Framework." *Research Policy* 25 : 91–106.

MacDuffie, John Paul, and Frits Pil. 1997. "Quality and Productivity Performance in the World Auto Industry, 1989–1994: Contingency vs. 'One Best Way' Perspective." Paper presented at the National Science Foundation Workshop: Integrating

Social Science Theory and Research in Quality Improvement, Haas School of Business, Berkeley, Calif., May 16–17.

MacDuffie, John Paul, and Susan Helper. 1996. "Creating Lean Suppliers: Diffusing Lean Production Through the Supply Chain." In Paul Adler, Jeff Liker, and Mark Fruin (eds.), *Remade in America* (forthcoming). New York: Oxford University Press.

Magaziner, Ira, and Robert Reich. 1982. *Minding America's Business.* New York: Random House.

Magnet, Myron. 1995. "The New Golden Rule of Business." In James Cortada and John Woods (eds.), *The Quality Handbook.* New York: McGraw-Hill.

Main, Jeremy. 1980. "The Battle for Quality Begins." *Fortune* 102 (December 29): 28–33.

———. 1994. *Quality Wars.* New York: Free Press.

March, James. 1978. "Bounded Rationality, Ambiguity, and the Engineering of Choice." *Bell Journal of Economics* 9 (Autumn): 587–608.

———. 1991. "Exploration and Exploitation in Organizational Learning." *Organization Science* 2 (February): 71–87.

———. 1994. *A Primer on Decision Making.* New York: Free Press.

March, James G., and Johan P. Olsen. 1976. *Ambiguity and Choice in Organizations.* Bergen: Universitetsforlaget.

Mathews, Jay. 1992. "The Cost of Quality." *Newsweek* (September 7): 48–49.

McMurray, George. 1996. "Process Control." In Robert Leachman (ed.), *Competitive Semiconductor Manufacturing Survey, Third Report on the Results of the Main Phase.* CSM-31. Berkeley: University of California, Berkeley: 133–138.

Mendel, Peter. 1996. "The Institutional Development of Global Production: The Case of ISO 9000 International Management Standards." Paper presented at the Third Annual European Academy for Standardization Conference, *Standards and Society*, Stockholm, Sweden, May 3–5: 1–29.

Merton, Robert. 1968. *Social Theory and Social Structure.* New York: Free Press.

Meyer, John, and Brian Rowan. 1991. "Institutionalized Organizations: Formal Structure as Myth and Ceremony." In Walter Powell and Paul DiMaggio (eds.), *The New Institutionalism in Organizational Analysis.* Chicago: University of Chicago Press.

Micklethwait, John, and Adrian Wooldridge. 1996. *The Witch Doctors.* New York: Random House.

Miller, William. 1995. "Success Isn't Enough." In James Cortada and John Woods (eds.), *The Quality Yearbook.* New York: McGraw-Hill.

Millstein, James. 1983. "Decline in an Expanding Industry: Japanese Competition in Color Television." In John Zysman and Laura Tyson (eds.), *American Industry in International Competition.* Ithaca, N.Y.: Cornell University Press.

Mizuno, Shigeru. 1988. *Company-Wide Total Quality Control.* Tokyo: Asian Productivity Organization.

Mohr, William, and Harriet Mohr. 1983. *Quality Circles.* Reading, Mass.: Addison-Wesley.

Moore, Geoffrey. 1995. *Inside the Tornado.* New York: HarperBusiness.

Motorola Corp. 1992. *Motorola Corporate Quality System Review.* Schaumberg, Il.: Motorola.

Mowery, David. 1990. "Technology and Organizations: An Economic/ Institutional Analysis." In Paul S. Goodman, Lee Sproull, and Associates (eds.), *Technology and Organizations.* San Francisco: Jossey-Bass.

Mozer, Clark. 1984. "Total Quality Control: A Route to the Deming Prize." *Quality Progress* 17 (September): 30–33.

Musashi, Miyamoto. 1982. *A Book of Five Rings*. Woodstock, N.Y.: Overlook Press.

Nadler, David, et al. 1992. *Organizational Architecture*. San Francisco: Jossey Bass.

Naj, Amal. 1992. "Some Manufacturers Drop Efforts to Adopt Japanese Techniques." *Wall Street Journal* May 7: A1, A6.

National Center on the Educational Quality of the Workforce. 1995. *The EQW National Employer Survey: First Findings*. Philadelphia: University of Pennsylvania, The Wharton School.

Nelson, Richard. 1994. "Evolutionary Theorizing About Economic Change." In Neil Smelser and Richard Swedborg (eds.), *The Handbook of Economic Sociology*. Princeton, N.J.: Princeton University Press.

Nelson, Richard, and Sidney Winter. 1982. *An Evolutionary Theory of Economic Change*. Cambridge: Belknap Press.

New York Stock Exchange. 1984. *U.S. International Competitiveness: Perception and Reality*. New York: NYSE.

Nikkei Weekly. 1994. "Japan Looks Abroad for Quality Standard." *Nikkei Weekly* 32 (May 16): 12.

Nishiguchi, Toshihiro. 1994. *Strategic Industrial Sourcing*. New York: Oxford University Press.

Nohria, Nitrin. 1992. "Introduction: Is a Network Perspective a Useful Way of Studying Organizations?" In Nitrin Nohria and Robert Eccles (eds.), *Networks and Organizations*. Cambridge, Mass.: Harvard Business School Press.

Nonaka, Ikujiro, and Hirotaka Takeuchi. 1995. *The Knowledge-Creating Company*. New York: Oxford University Press.

Nonaka, Izumi. 1995. "Recent History of Managing for Quality in Japan." In J. M. Juran (editor-in-chief), *A History of Managing for Quality*. Milwaukee: ASQC Quality Press.

Oberle, Joseph. 1990. "Quality Gurus: The Men and Their Message." *Training* (January): 47–52.

O'Dell, Carla, and C. Jackson Grayson. 1998. "If We Only Knew What We Know: Identification and Transfer of Internal Best Practices." *California Management Review* 40 (spring): 154–174.

Okimoto, Daniel, Takuo Sugano, and Franklin Weinstein. 1984. *Competitive Edge: The Semiconductor Industry in the U.S. and Japan*. Stanford: Stanford University Press.

Osterman, Paul. 1994. "How Common is Workplace transformation and Who Adopts it?" *Industrial and Labor Relations Review* 47 (January): 173–188.

Ouchi, William. 1981. *Theory Z*. New York: Addison-Wesley.

Packard, David. 1995. *The HP Way*. New York: HarperBusiness.

Pascale, Richard. 1990. *Managing on the Edge*. New York: Touchstone.

Petersen, Donald, and John Hillkirk. 1991. *A Better Idea*. Boston: Houghton Mifflin.

Pittiglio Rabin Todd & McGrath. 1995. *1994 Survey of Quality and Productivity Programs*. Mountain View, Calif.: KPMG Peat Marwick LLP, Pittiglio Rabin Todd & McGrath, American Electronics Association.

Porter, Michael. 1990. *The Competitive Advantage of Nations*. New York: Free Press.

Powell, Walter. 1991. "Expanding the Scope of Institutional Analysis." In Walter Powell and Paul DiMaggio (eds.), *The New Institutionalism in Organizational Analysis*. Chicago: University of Chicago Press.

Powell, Walter, and Peter Brantley. 1992. "Competitive Cooperation in Biotechnology: Learning Through Networks." In Nitrin Nohria and Robert Eccles (eds.), *Networks and Organizations*. Cambridge, Mass: Harvard Business School Press.

Powell, Walter, and Paul DiMaggio. 1991. *The New Institutionalism in Organizational Analysis*. Chicago: University of Chicago Press.

Price, Michael, and Eva Chen. 1995. "Total Quality Management in a Small, High Technology Company." In Robert E. Cole (ed.), *The Death and Life of the American Quality Movement*. New York: Oxford University Press.

Quality. 1997. "Improved Products Instrumental in Export Confidence." *Quality* 36 (January): 16, 18.

Quick, Finan, and Associates. 1990. *Report on U.S. Investment Strategies for Quality Assurance*. Washington, D.C.: U.S. Department of Commerce, National Institute of Standards and Technology.

Rechtin, Mark. 1994. "Lexus Sets a New Norm in Initial Quality Study." *Automotive News* (May 30): 8, 52.

———. 1997a. "As Quality Gap Narrows, Power Rethinks the IQS." *Automotive News* (May 12): 3, 28.

———. 1997b. "Japanese Take Back Seat to GM in Customer Excitement Survey." *Automotive News* (September 1): 51.

Reddy, N., J. Aram, and Leonard Lynn. 1991. "The Institutional Domain of Technology Diffusion." *The Journal of Product Innovation Management* (December): 295–304.

Reid, Peter. 1990. *Well Made in America*. New York: McGraw-Hill.

Reimann, Curt, and Harry Hertz. 1993. "The Malcolm Baldrige Quality Award and ISO 9000 Registration: Understanding Their Many Important Differences." *ASTM Standardization News* (November): 42–53.

Ristelhueber, Robert. 1994. "HP-America's New Best Managed Company." *Electronic Business Buyer* 20 (June): 36–41.

Robinson, Arthur. 1980. "Perilous Times for U.S. Microcircuit Makers." *Science* 208 (May): 582–584.

Rogers, Everett. 1995. *Diffusion of Innovations*. 4th edition. New York: Free Press.

Rogers, Everett, and Judith Larsen. 1984. *Silicon Valley Fever*. New York: Basic Books.

Ross, Lee. 1977. "The Intuitive Psychologist and His Shortcomings: Distortions in the Attribution Process." In L. Berkowitz (ed.), *Advances in Experimental Social Psychology* 10. New York: Academic Press.

Ross, Lee, and Mark Lepper. 1980. "The Perseverance of Beliefs: Empirical and Normative Considerations." In Richard Shweder (ed.), *Fallible Judgment in Behavioral Research*. San Francisco: Jossey-Bass.

Ruggles, Rudy. 1998. "The State of the Notion: Knowledge Management in Practice." *California Management Review* 40 (Spring): 80–89.

Rummler, Geary, and Alan Brache. 1990. *Improving Performance*. San Francisco: Jossey-Bass.

Sasaoka, Kenzo. 1996. "Sangyōkai kara mita hinshitsu kanri shikō" (Personal thoughts about how industry sees quality control). Presented at the 1996 Meeting of the Japanese Society for Quality Control, Tokyo, Nihon Hinshitsu Kanri Gakkai.

Saxenian, Annalee. 1994. *Regional Advantage: Culture; and Competition in Silicon Valley and Route 128.* Cambridge, Mass: Harvard University Press.

Scherkenbach, William. 1986. *The Deming Route to Quality and Productivity.* Washington D.C.: CEE Press.

Schneiderman, Arthur. 1986. "Optimum Quality Costs and Zero Defects: Are They Contradictory Concepts?" *Quality Progress* 19 (November): 28–31.

Schnoll, Les. 1993. "One World, One Standard." *Quality Progress* 26 (April): 35–39.

Schonberger, Richard. 1982. *Japanese Manufacturing Techniques.* New York: Free Press.

———. 1986. *World Class Manufacturing.* New York: Free Press.

Scott, W. Richard. 1995. *Institutions and Organizations.* Thousand Oaks, Calif.: Sage Publications.

Sebastian, Pamela. 1996. "International Standards Took Root With Manufacturers That Export." *Wall Street Journal* (November 14): A1.

Semich, J. William, and Somerby Dowst. 1989. "How to Push Your Everyday Supplier Into World Class Status." *Purchasing* 107 (August 17): 74–78.

Senge, Peter. 1990. *The Fifth Discipline.* New York: Doubleday Currency.

Sethi, S. Prakash, Nobuaki Namiki, and Carl Swanson. 1984. *The False Promise of the Japanese Miracle.* Boston: Pitman.

Shainin, Dorian, and Peter Shainin. 1988. "Statistical Process Control." In J. M. Juran (ed.), *Juran's Quality Control Handbook.* 4th edition. New York: McGraw-Hill: 24.1–40.

Shewhart, Walter. 1931. *The Economic Control of Quality of Manufactured Product.* New York: D. Van Nostrand.

Shiba, Shoji, Alan Graham, and David Walden. 1993. *A New American TQM.* Portland: Productivity Press.

Siegmann, Ken. Dec. 20, 1993. "An American Tale of Semi-success." *San Francisco Chronicle* B1, B3.

Sloan, Alfred. 1964. *My Years With General Motors.* Garden City, N.Y.: Doubleday.

Soin, Sarv Singh. 1992. *Total Quality Control Essentials.* New York: McGraw-Hill.

Stacey, Ralph. 1996. *Complexity and Creativity in Organizations.* San Francisco: Berrett-Koehler.

Stalk, George, Jr., and Thomas Hout. 1990. *Competing Against Time.* New York: Free Press.

Starbuck, William, and F. J. Milliken. 1988. "Executives Perceptual Filters: What They Notice and How They Make Sense." In D. C. Hambrick (ed.), *The Executive Effect: Concepts and Methods for Studying Top Managers.* Greenwich, Conn.: JAI Press: 35–65.

Stewart, James. 1997. "Why Dumb Things Happen to Smart Companies." *Fortune* 135 (June 23): 159–160.

Stinchcombe, Arthur. 1990. *Information and Organizations.* Berkeley: University of California Press.

Stoddard, Donna, S. Jarvenpaa, and M. Littlejohn. 1996. "The Reality of Business Reengineering: Pacific Bell's Centrex Provisioning Process." *California Management Review* 38 (Spring): 57–76.

Stoffer, Harry. 1997. "Chrysler Recalls 876,200 Vehicles." *Automotive News* (July 7): 8.

Stowsky, Jay. 1987. "The Weakest Link: Semiconductor Equipment Linkages and the Limits to International Trade." Working Paper No. 27. Berkeley Roundtable on the International Economy, University of California at Berkeley: 1–77.

Strang, David. 1997. "Cheap Talk: Managerial Discourse on Quality Circles as an Organizational Innovation." Ithaca, N.Y.: Department of Sociology, Technical Report 97-1, Cornell University.

Strang, David, and John Meyer. 1993. "Institutional Conditions for Diffusion." *Theory and Society* 22 (August): 487–511.

Stratton, Brad. 1993. "U.S. Energy Secretary Leads Department's Quality Initiative." *Quality Progress* 26: 12.

Struebing, Laura. 1996. "9000 Standards?" *Quality Progress* 29 (January): 23–28.

Sullivan, Larry. 1984. "Reducing Variability: A New Approach to Quality." *Quality Progress* 18 (July): 15–21.

———. 1986a. "Quality Function Deployment." *Quality Progress* 19 (June): 39–50.

———. 1986b. "The Seven Stages in Company-wide Quality Control." *Quality Progress* 19 (May): 77–83.

———. 1987. "The Power of the Taguchi Methods." *Quality Progress* 20 (June): 76–79.

Taninecz, George. 1997. "Mutual Learning." *Industry Week* 246 (July 7): 28–31.

Tetlock, Phillip. 1991. "Learning in U.S. and Soviet Foreign Policy: In Search of an Elusive Concept." In George Breslauer and Phillip Tetlock (eds.), *Learning in U.S. and Soviet Foreign Policy*. Boulder, Co.: Westview Press.

Thurm, Scott. 1998. "Unstock the Shelves." *San Jose Mercury News* (February 22): E1, E5.

Tsuru, Shigeto. 1993. *Japan's Capitalism: Creative Defeat and Beyond.* Cambridge: Cambridge University Press.

Tsutsui, William. 1996. "W. Edwards Deming and the Origins of Quality Control in Japan." *The Journal of Japanese Studies* 22 (Summer): 295–325.

Turner, Christena. 1995. "Structuring Culture for Change: Strategy and Participation in a Japanese Factory." Unpublished manuscript. Univ. of California, San Diego, La Jolla, Calif.

Tushman, Michael, and Philip Anderson. 1986. "Technological Discontinuities and Organizational Environments." *Administrative Sciences Quarterly* 31: 439–465.

Tversky, Amos, and Daniel Kahneman. 1990. "Rational Choice and the Framing of Decisions." In Karen Schweers Cook and Margaret Levi (eds.), *The Limits of Rationality*. Chicago: University of Chicago Press.

United States General Accounting Office. 1992. *SEMATECH's Technological Progress and Proposed R&D Program.* Washington, D.C.: GAO/RCED-92–223BR (July): 1–44.

Vogel, David. 1995. *Trading Up: Consumer and Environmental Regulation in a Global Economy.* Cambridge, Mass.: Harvard University Press.

Walton, Mary. 1986. *The Deming Management Method.* New York: Perigee Books.

Watson, Greg. 1991. "Understanding Hoshin Kanri." In Yoji Akao (ed.), *Hoshin Kanri: Policy Deployment for Successful TQM.* Cambridge, Mass.: Productivity Press.

Weick, Karl. 1976. "Educational Organizations as Loosely Coupled Systems." *Administrative Science Quarterly* 21: 1–19.

———. 1995. *Sensemaking in Organizations.* Thousand Oaks, Calif.: Sage Publications.

Weick, Karl, and Frances Westley. 1996. "Organizational Learning: Affirming an Oxymoron." In Stewart Clegg, C. Hardy, and W. Nord (eds.), *Handbook of Organization Studies.* London: Sage Publications.

———. 1997. "Total Quality Management: A Sensemaking Perspective." Presented at

National Science Foundation Workshop, *Integrating Social Science Theory and Research in Quality Improvement*. Berkeley, Calif.: Haas School of Business, May 16–17.

Westney, Eleanor. 1987. *Imitation and Innovation*. Cambridge, Mass.: Harvard University Press.

———. 1997 "Organization Theory Perspective and International Business." In Brian Toyne and Douglas Nigh (eds.), *Perspectives on International Business*. Columbia: University of South Carolina Press.

Westrum, R. 1982. "Social Intelligence About Hidden Events." *Knowledge* 3(3): 381–400.

Wheelwright, Steve, and Kim Clark. 1992. *Revolutionizing Product Development*. New York: Free Press.

Williamson, Oliver. *The Economic Institutions of Capitalism*. New York: The Free Press.

Wilson, Phillip. 1995. " 'Working on the Work' to Make Enterprisewide Quality Improvement." In Robert E. Cole (ed.), *The Death and Life of the American Quality Movement*. New York: Oxford University Press: 139–155.

Winter, Sidney. 1994. "Organizing for Continuous Improvement: Evolutionary Theory Meets the Quality Revolution." In Joel Baum and Jitendra Singh (eds.), *Evolutionary Dynamics of Organizations*. New York: Oxford University Press.

Wolak, Jerry. 1993. "Auto Industry Quality—What Are They Doing?" *Quality* 32 (January): 16–22

Womack, James, Daniel Jones, and Daniel Roos. 1991. *The Machine That Changed the World*. New York: HarperPerennial.

Yates, Brock. 1983. *The Decline and Fall of the American Automobile Industry*. New York: Empire Books.

Young, John. 1983. "One Company's Quest for Improved Quality." *Wall Street Journal* (July 25): 10.

Young, John. 1985. "Teamwork Is More Easily Praised Than Practiced." *Quality Progress* 18 (August): 30–34.

Zbaracki, Mark J. 1994. *The Rhetoric and Reality of Total Quality Management*. Doctoral Dissertation, Industrial Engineering, Stanford University, Palo Alto, Calif.

Ziegler, J. Nicholas. 1991. "Semiconductors." *Daedalus* 120 (Fall): 155–181.

Zucker, Lynn. 1983. "Organizations as Institutions." *Research in the Sociology of Organizations* 2: 1–47.

Zuckerman, Amy. 1996. "European Standards Officials Push Reform of ISO 9000 and QS-9000 Registration." *Quality Progress* 29 (September): 131–134.

Index

273

EQW. *See* National Center on the
Educational Quality of the
Workforce
Erie Community Quality Council, 131
European Community (EC), 152–153
Executives. *See* Quality executives

Fads
as building blocks, 99, 235–238
chronology of quality minifads, 18–
20
definition of, 14–15
demise of particular fads, 228
discarding of previous fad at
appearance of new fad, 235
"Fallacy of centrality," 54
Federal Express, 216
Federal Reserve Bank of Boston, 142
Feedback and learning, 7–8, 180–182
Feigenbaum, Armand V., 73, 83, 86,
252n8
Fine, Charles, 78
First Chicago, 138
Fligstein, Neil, 13, 84–85
Florida, Richard, 108, 122, 123, 124
Florida Power and Light (FPL), 15, 66–
71, 138, 162, 163, 208, 243–244,
246, 252n4, 257n1
Flynn, Michael, 80, 254n7
Ford Motor Co.
and American Supplier Institute (ASI),
72, 116–120
beginnings of quality improvements at,
56–57, 71–72, 74, 252n5
in Conference Board's Quality
Council, 102, 138
consultants for, 56, 74
as GOAL/QPC member, 136
improvements at generally, 82
and Mazda, 71, 120, 162
old quality model at, 25, 27
Q1 (Quality First) Award at, 57, 112
and quality gap, 53, 54, 216
and quality improvement in suppliers,
111–114
as quality leader, 6, 18, 213
River Rouge facility of, 228
suggestion system of, adapted by
Toyota, 252n7

suppliers of, 114, 254nn7–8
as TQM implementer, 126
Ford Supplier Institute, 253n6
FPL. *See* Florida Power and Light
Fujimoto, Takahiro, 227
Fuji Xerox Co. Ltd., 77, 162–163, 256n3
Fukuhara, Akashi, 117

GAO. *See* General Accounting Office
Garvin, David, 25, 33, 34, 35, 79
GE Aircraft Engines, 142
Gellner, Ernest, 89
General Accounting Office (GAO), 80,
115
General Dynamics, 68
General Electric (GE), 25, 99, 127, 136
General Motors (GM)
Baldrige Award to Cadillac division of,
151
beginnings of quality initiative at, 61,
113
corporate strategies in 1980s, 59–60
and criticisms of U.S. auto industry,
53, 55
and Crosby training program, 88–89
employees in purchasing department
of, 109
and Isuzu, 120, 162
and Japanese quality challenge, 165
and NUMMI, 60, 64, 71, 120, 126,
162, 174
old quality model at, 25, 27
profitability of, 71
quality executives at, 40
and quality gap, 80
and Quality of Worklife Programs, 95
SPEAR program of, 112
suppliers of, 106, 108, 113, 114, 117,
254n7
and Targets for Excellence, 121
and Toyota, 120
General Physics, 121
Generative learning, 127
Germany, 65, 124, 249n1
Gerstner, Louis, Jr., 61
GM. *See* General Motors
GOAL/QPC, 130, 132, 135–137, 142,
159, 208–209
Godfrey, A. Blanton, 146